DEREK BAILEY
AND
THE STORY OF
FREE IMPROVISATION

BEN WATSON is a writer on music and culture. He is the author of numerous books, including *Adorno for Revolutionaries*, *Honesty Is Explosive!*, *Frank Zappa: The Negative Dialectics of Poodle Play* and *Art, Class and Cleavage: A Quantulumcunque Concerning Materialist Esthetix*.

DEREK BAILEY
AND
THE STORY
OF FREE
IMPROVISATION

BEN WATSON

VERSO

London • New York

This paperback edition first published by Verso 2013
First published by Verso 2004
© Ben Watson 2004, 2013

1 3 5 7 9 10 8 6 4 2

Verso
UK: 6 Meard Street, London W1F 0EG
US: 20 Jay Street, Suite 1010, Brooklyn, NY 11201
www.versobooks.com

Verso is the imprint of New Left Books

ISBN-13: 978-1-78168-105-3

British Library Cataloguing in Publication Data
A catalogue record for this book is available from the British Library

Library of Congress Has Cataloged the Hardcover Edition as Follows
Watson, Ben, 1956–
Derek Bailey and the story of free improvisation / Ben Watson.
p. cm.
Includes bibliographical references and index.
Discography: p.
ISBN 1-84467-003-1 (hardcover : alk. paper)
1. Bailey, Derek, 1932– 2. Guitarists–England–Biography. I. Title.
ML419.B13W38 2004
787.87_092–dc22

2004003582

Typeset in Sabon by MJ & N Gavan, Truro, Cornwall
Printed in the US by Maple Vail

CONTENTS

THANKS: I should like to thank Harry Gilonis for his highly informed read-through and fact-check; Matthew 'The Quickener' Hughes, Patrick 'Dallas Boner' Atkinson and Tim Fletcher for keeping the critical discussion informed and flying; Peter Riley, Peter Stubley and Andrew Shone for essential data; Tony Oxley, Gavin Bryars and Steve Lacy for granting me interviews; Marco and Christiano of Lendormin; André Cholmondeley of Project/Object; Gavin Everall from Verso for saving me from a quadruple nightmare; Esther as always.

SPECIAL THANKS: Derek Bailey and Karen Brookman for the cups of tea and making this book possible.

THIS COMPACT DISC FOR YOUR CEREBRUM IS DEDICATED TO STU 'N' MARIE AND WHATEVER (WHOEVER) THEY PRODUCE (HELLO DUNYA)

PREFACE TO THE
PAPERBACK EDITION

When this book was first published, Derek Bailey was still alive. It was a joy to present him with a pile of copies for his record label to sell (payment for the interviews), and he was most complimentary. The writing process was an intimate collaboration, with me transcribing his spoken word from countless interviews held at his house in Clapton, Hackney, and he being allowed to edit out anything he disliked (mainly unfinished sentences and swear words). He'd correct errors of fact, but never sought to interfere with my opinions or judgments. He'd relocated to Barcelona by the time the book was published, drawn there by a combination of the warm, dry climate (good to old bones) and performance opportunities – he posted me a cassette to play at the launch, which was at Ray's Jazz in Foyles bookshop overlooking Charing Cross Road. And then motor neurone disease took over. What was originally thought to be a hand injury, sustained when taking baggage off a moving belt at an airport, turned out to be fatal. Carpal Tunnel Syndrome meant he could no longer hold a plectrum, but he taught himself to play using thumb and fingers, a process he documented in a release on John Zorn's Tzadik label, *Carpal Tunnel*. He died on Christmas Day 2005.

How I miss Derek and his wry, Sheffield-jazzer's take on the metropolitan avant-garde! Distracted by an intense few years of babyminding, I didn't register his death fully until the summer of 2012 when, children at nursery and school, I stumbled upon Robin Ramsay's excellent little book *Conspiracy Theories* in the Oxfam Shop on Goodge Street. I liked it so much I got in touch with the author. Turns out that in the late 60s, Ramsay used to improvise on trumpet with drummer Jamie Muir, a collaborator Derek recalled with particular affection. Ramsay's brave exposure of Peter Wright and the MI5 smear campaign against Harold Wilson's Labour Government took on a new lustre: Free Improvisation, with its complete disdain for the spectacle of the music industry, its honesty and directness, its hatred of management, its proletarian pride, is the *natural ally* of Ramsay's anti-bourgeois, whistle-blowing politics. I found myself walking to the phone. I had to tell Derek about Robin Ramsay, his political understanding of conspiracy theory and his past as an improvisor ... Death. It's a hard one.

Still, it's exciting to be asked for a preface to this paperback edition. Commenting on 'the current state of Free Improvisation' is a temptation, but that would entail a tirade which would distract from the matter in hand, which is to get the measure of Derek's legacy. Punters flooding out of the Vortex, a London jazz venue, are confronted with a street sign reading 'Bailey Place'. I imagine it being the occasion for comments and jokes about Improv and its vexed relationship to jazz, with few people knowing that the street *was* actually named in his honour in December 2007. (Apparently the London Fire Brigade doesn't like complicated street names, so 'Derek' was deleted.) In the years since 2004, Derek has become a legend, his name dropped in every issue of *The Wire*. But rather than any grand pronouncements about his legacy, I thought it'd be more appropriate to talk to someone who played with Derek at the very end, someone with a very particular take on music and life. So I conducted a brief phone interview with Stu Calton, a Manchester call-centre worker who's known as T. H. F. Drenching when he's improvising on Dictaphone (or releasing his stream of computer-music CDs).

I wanted to know how Calton, a Derek devotee – and back then a young and almost totally unknown musician – got to play with the Grand Old Man of Improv. The idea, he told me, came from Marie-Angelique Bueler, improvisor on bricks (as Sonic Pleasure) and mother of Calton's two children. The pair were indignant that Incus had stooped to releasing avantesque ironies by Jim O'Rourke, so in 2000 they declared themselves 'Improvers' rather than simply Improvisors. Marie suggested Stu mail Derek a brick-and-Dictaphone improvisation they'd recorded in a Liverpool Airport disabled toilet at four in the morning (you need to be in charge of a baby – or be a junkie – to know just what a *wonderful place* a disabled toilet can be). They wanted to show Derek that his original duets with Han Bennink were still inducing sparks. Their plan worked.

Derek was particularly impressed by the packaging, encrusted with collage and doodles and slogans by Calton, and he made comments about it to me at the time. (I was very pleased, since I knew Stu from his days in Pence Eleven, but I kept quiet, because Derek hated it when I recommended musicians to him; he sabotaged a gig in Rome with Lendormin's Cristiano Luciani because I waxed too enthusiastic about his drumming; Derek found his musicians *himself*, thank you very much.) Derek replied with a postcard – 'I didn't know people were still doing this!' – and included his home phone number. The power and originality of their duo playing – an unwitting reinvention of the power and unpredictability of Tony Oxley's drums – and their address in Levenshulme, Manchester doubtless confirmed an old piece of Derek wisdom: improv is better in the provinces. Calton dialled the number on the postcard: 'Call back in six months, I'm busy now ...' Six months later, Calton called and needed to remind Derek what instrument he played. 'Ah! You're the one who plays Dictaphone ... with a woman!' So they came down to Derek's home in Clapton for a play, and there 'in the midst of all the tea cosies and other old-Sheffield-guy stuff' was 'this person with a large amount of fluffy ginger hair looking very awkward called Alex Ward.' The four of them played together (Derek made a recording of this initial try-out; it can be heard on the Incus CD-R release *Visitors' Book*). With the addition of Tim Bevan on bass saxophone, they became Limescale.

When Derek put Limescale together, he was acting as a composer, a composer of people. He could hear how these musicians thought and was eager to get them playing together. Calton was impressed. He couldn't believe how good it was to play with Alex Ward. In the playing, all awkwardness vanished. 'Every single place I put my foot, Ward was already there; and everywhere Ward placed his foot, I was able to catch him up!' Derek was wary of 'bands', deeming them excuses to standardise the music and preferring ad-hoc encounters, but Limescale was a group he created and believed in. His move to Barcelona and his fatal illness cut the project short, but listen to Incus CD56: this really is the dawning of a New Music, the bric-à-brac of anti-power suddenly gone fluid, filthy and all-encompassing. 'Derek was very gentle with us, I thought, he wasn't particularly oppositional. He did his best to make us feel comfortable, doing some sort of bizarre accompaniment.'

Tony Bevan brought in what Calton calls a 'more rockist, abusive edge' (this is praise in Calton's lexicon). Limescale's first gig was in Northampton – to practically no audience at all. This tallies with my personal experience of jazz and improv in Leeds: great music as the inverse of commercial success. When the crowds flood in (John Scofield, Jan Garbarek), expect to be bored. Rows of empty seats, in contrast, promise delirious musical excitement. Limescale hammered out its music as a quintet. They didn't play solos, duos and trios Company-style. 'We stuck to it, we didn't fuck about ... And afterwards we gathered at the bar. Derek had a half a pint of Guinness in his hand, and said: We should go into the studio with this.' Calton describes Derek as pleased as punch to 'hide' in the ensemble, be subsumed in a collective entity. In Calton's opinion, 'solo' Derek was a product of economics, not aesthetics: 'a way of practising in public rather than really creating something'.

At the launch of the Incus CD *Limescale* aboard Sybil Madrigal's floating venue on the Thames (Boat-Ting), I heard some punters complain at the back: 'Where's Derek? I came to see Derek Bailey and I can't see or hear him!' It was difficult to explain that, with Limescale, Derek had found the nirvana he stumbled on in drummer John Stevens's Spontaneous Music Ensemble: the extinction of the ego in a musical collective. Limescale was built on the foundation of the Bueler–Calton rhythm section as surely as the SME was founded on Stevens (or the Joseph Holbrooke Trio on Oxley), and Derek loved it. So right near the end, he rediscovered the *collectivity* which he'd enjoyed when he first played free music in London.

Derek tried again and again to interest promoters in the quintet, but again and again tripped across the consequence of personal fame: *he* was the draw, so why should a promoter shell out five times the airfare/hotel costs/fee when it wouldn't bring in any extra punters? 'Here comes success, here comes the zoo ...' as Iggy Pop put it in 1977 (*Lust for Life*). Derek Bailey's fame as 'avant icon', something that has increased exponentially since his death, didn't serve his real intent, which was the music. The neglect of Limescale by critics and promoters (Derek's place could easily have been taken by John Russell or Joe Morris or Stefan Jaworzyn or Eugene Chadbourne or Jef Lee Johnson or ... Hugh Metcalfe?) shows once again how the star system strangles music rather than promoting it. Of course, I'm dealing with a paradox here: you're probably reading this because you're curious about Derek Bailey, not out of commitment to something as nebulous as Free Improvisation. But let's not forget that Derek Bailey is a name to conjure with *precisely because he derided fashion and opposed the promotion of music for the purposes of profit.* The Stu Caltons of this world remind you that Free Improvisation is not simply about consummate music-making. It's about attitude: the edge and prickle and indignation which made every note Derek Bailey played (and every word he said) so piercing and interrogative.

Ben Watson
Somers Town
11 January 2013

INTRODUCTION: ON FREEDOM

Derek Bailey is a guitarist, a guitarist's guitarist, a guitar fetishist's *ultimate* guitarist, a player whose playing proceeds from his instrument in a way that hasn't been done with such unswerving devotion since Hendrix amazed London by sleeping with his instrument. As the record industry desperately seeks to manufacture 'personalities' who can hold consumers' attention for the time required to make a purchase, Derek Bailey remains there, just as John Lee Hooker remained there: one man hunched over his guitar, more important and more spine-tingling than a thousand processed and packaged stars – or a thousand books of post-rock theory telling you that sampled and remixed old records are the dawning of a new era. A sinister alliance between the corporate drive to sell hi-tech equipment and the 'anti-elitism' of radical cultural theory declares that instrumental skill is irrelevant to the production of music. Bailey, on the other hand, makes everything hang on split-second decisions about fingers and strings. Although Bailey has evolved a personal language beyond the parameters of any known technique, his playing is all about what dexterity and imagination can achieve – without software and hardware props. Yet what he plays is more consistently surprising than anything constructed on a computer: it happens in real time. Those who model cultural life on private property relations will decry Bailey's 'difficult' art as elitist, the preserve of the supermusical; those who understand culture as interaction, provocation, and consciousness expansion hail Bailey as the best stimulant going. Here's stuff you can learn volumes from (and his gigs are some of the cheapest in town).

If you're serious about the guitar, you'll get to Derek Bailey eventually, and what you will learn will shatter your world picture, and cause you to reconsider every fact about twentieth-century music – and artistic meaning, and politics, and class society, and the concept of the 'good album' – you ever thought you knew. Bailey places the guitar at the centre of his aesthetic. In fact, he places it above aesthetics! He said the following to his biographer, but he could have said these words to anyone who expressed an interest in his music.

I would think one of the problems you might have with what I do is that I would claim to be a guitar player, that's what I do. I'm not an artist. The art market has never appealed to me. Playing an instrument creatively – improvising – will include art, I suppose, but it goes well beyond the boundaries of art in many ways. And, in particular, the guitar is such a universal instrument. It's found in almost all areas of music. Most instruments are tied to one or two musics. The outstanding example is the saxophone, of course. Though sax players have struggled valiantly in recent years [*laughs*] to shed – or at least not to be associated with – jazz, it's always reclaimed them. The guitar is *the* universal instrument, it seems to me – the only instrument which comes anywhere near it is the drum. [8–ix–97]

Derek Bailey is a guitarist, but he's also an avant-garde extremist, a theorist, an *enragé* and a cunning *saboteur* of overground values. When Charles Saatchi's 'Sensation' was exported to Berlin, a concert by Bailey was included in the programme as if he were an integral element of glossy, TV-friendly, 'shocking' late-nineties Brit Art. The publicists who wrote the brochure cannot have known that Derek Bailey's art is too hard and jagged and underground for the limelight-hogging Brit Art celebrities. In terms of commitment, involvement, experience and thought, his art simply asks too much. And, unlike the seventies 'experimental composers' (sometime followers of Cornelius Cardew's revolutionary critique) who now adopt the role – and lucrative commissions – of the bourgeois composer, Derek Bailey has adumbrated a genuine counter-theory: Improvisation.

Nothing, Bailey argues, is quite as interesting as improvisation, and nothing is quite as dull and boring and dead as knowing precisely what is going to happen – whether that is listening to computerised electronica, watching a rock group thunder through their set, or hearing a symphony orchestra saw through some genius's *opus*. Musicians who specialise in creating something new in real time cut through manipulation and the star system – all the bullshit produced by arts administrators and the music industry – and speak to an audience of peers. If free improvisors are dissed by the general public, by the businesses that service that general public's alienation and inertia, by journalists with stakes in the star system, this merely proves how right they are.

Jazz and rock fans sit around and dream about righteous beboppers at Minton's Playhouse on 118th Street, or seeing the John Coltrane Quartet in the flesh, or standing with Andy Warhol to watch the Velvet Underground at Café Bizarre in 1965, or of pogoing to the Sex Pistols at the Roxy – but they're just victims of the corporate labels that buy up and market the archive. Real life happens now, in the teeth of public disapprobation. You can find it if you've got the guts to forget celebrity fixation and spectacular daydreams and confront with sober senses the actual reality and the aural possibilities of your own miserable life. It's a movement! It's an ethos. Unlike rock and punk and drum'n'bass, it can't be bought and sold by capitalism, it can't be ripped off by A&R sharks or managed by managers. It doesn't deal in the coin of wishes and images. It's *music*. It's called Free Improvisation.

Derek's arguments can certainly be upsetting. Your own precious 'radicalism' is under permanent attack. On occasions, the debate has nearly reduced me to tears when trying to defend the things I love – Thelonious Monk or Frank Zappa, for example – against his strictures, his insistence that composition always limps behind the creative musician. But even an organ as devoted to the recorded commodity as *Record Collector* couldn't deny that Bailey's commitment to improvisation keeps allowing the man to cut record after record of provocative, challenging, high-grade, densely packed, infinitely rewarding, always-happening *music*: the most eventful back catalogue since Charlie Parker, and the most arresting, icepick-in-the-forehead guitar notes since Johnny 'Guitar' Watson. Bailey professes disinterest in records and incomprehension of record listening as a pastime, but his name on a CD is one of the most dependable indications of a worthwhile purchase. For people who've taught themselves music by acquiring records, that is one hell of a tip for hallowed status.

A sane person – or anyone with a regard for the canon of music outside Bailey's active orbit – cannot credit his polemic completely (quite), but you can't deny that it works for him. And the insistence on freedom, the challenge to live in the here and now – instead of relying on treasure hoards of certified culture (whether that's a shelf of Beethoven scores, or of 12-inch white-labels) – throws the hapless fan into the whorls of difficult philosophy. Freedom, time, contingency, necessity, action, mind, matter, ego, id . . . all one's concepts are busted on the rim of Bailey's musical event horizon, the insistence that musicians can collect together and attempt to play the never-before-heard, and that this step into Nothing is better than 'having a good time'. Free Improvisation is the unalloyed humming dynamo of creativity, the essence of the Hip everyone's looking for, the Holy Grail MacGuffin Poodle Duende Absolute. It's the ineffable spice of life capitalism turns into something you have to buy. No mystery, folks: it's human labour, human activity – maybe it could actually be *us*!

For those too young to have experienced the cultural tumult of the sixties, Free Improvisation is a thread of gold spun from the happenings and situations that rocked that period. It's the one art practice that has managed to preserve that revolt as activity and experience rather than image. It lacks the tedious 'irony' that collusion with art-gallery and music-industry alienation inevitably entails. Of course, if a record or a performance concentrates an entire philosophy of opposition to today's society into a running time of forty minutes or an hour, it's hardly going to be easy to assimilate. As much as it changes music, revolutionary art expects *you* to change. People who are happy with the way things circulate in this society – those at the top of the heap – aren't going to welcome an experience that tilts assumptions about what constitutes communication and cultural value. Radical? Free Improvisation will give you radical!

Free Improvisation demands that the listener acknowledge all the possibilities of modern music denied by a hierarchical, commodity-based, fool-the-punter system. People who run that system – those employed by record labels and distributors, radio DJs, pop pundits, pop academics, newspaper critics – will decry what they hear as charlatanry and put-on. That's because the procedures of Free Improvisation threaten their livelihoods and demand a completely different way of doing things. In his obituary of bassist Motoharu Yoshizawa, Bailey pointed out that anyone who has experienced the music business from the musician's point of view is bound to be cynical 'about music and often, in fact, about everything. To talk about any musical activity and not be cynical is usually to open the door to bullshit.' However, Bailey's particular cynicism is closer to the barking-mad 'Who's-impressed-with-kings?' of Diogenes than it is to the smug and facile cynicism of those who operate the mass media.

In 1937, in order to denounce the evils of Modern Art, the Nazis staged an exhibition in Munich called 'Entartete Kunst' (Degenerate Art). As a prime example of modernism's Jewish–Bolshevik degeneracy, they displayed a critic's appreciation of dadaist Kurt Schwitters on a panel on the wall:

Merz drawings by Kurt Schwitters? Merz poems by Kurt Schwitters? Both meaningless. Printed words in lines of different lengths, and those are supposed to be poems. Words stamped all over the notepaper and childish drawings of coffee grinders, houses, and wheels, and those are supposed to be drawings. Damned if I can make head or tail of them. One goes like this:

> Umdumm.
> So hear glands scream tormented Morea
> Wawall squeal unlarned you self sing
> Shrill blazing glands equalk being
> Like axletrees screaming scream
> Blaze toremented bodyhot unlarned gleam
> Oh Hear! Eh unlarned tormented torment
> Hey you Sibaylie splats the moon
> Oh see oh sing along
> The dragonfly golds Gloyteyah
> But toorment dream chokes off my sing.

Now if anyone asks me what all this is supposed to mean I can only laugh in his face, along with the poet and painter himself. Art is not there to be 'understood', Merz poems are not for professors of philology. Dada – yes, Dada – is there for joining in, for laughing at yourself and the world at large, for being a happy dope. If you don't feel it, you won't ever get it. To think that someone has the courage to kid around in art! A slap in the face to meaning and gravity! To Kurt Schwitters – many thanks. [Paul F. Schmidt, review exhibited at 'Entartete Kunst', 1937]

'Hey you S*ibaylie* splats the moon'!! With this line, Kurt Schwitters prophesied how Bailey would one day kill the bourgeois moonlight and retune all its sentimental sonatas.

The Nazis' *do-not-do-this* 'Degenerate Art' exhibition was staged alongside their *this-is-how-it-should-be-done* 'Great German Art' exhibition, replete with winsome female nudes and muscular heroes rendered in the kitsch pseudo-classical style favoured by Hitler (as usual, the *Verboten* proved more enticing than the Improving: two million people attended the former exhibition, a mere four hundred thousand the latter). The Nazis were so confident in their case for artistic seriousness, they assumed everyone would tut at Paul Schmidt's levity – or at least be too intimidated to protest (the atmosphere at the 'Degenerate Art' show was one of pious horror – there were very few objections, and those that occurred led immediately to arrests). As we have seen in the wake of 9–11, the banning of humour is one of the great weapons of authoritarian oppression. In this sense, Derek Bailey's art – perpetually breaking the spell of grandeur cast by so much music – is anti-Nazi music *par excellence*. It also hasn't much time for art pretentiousness – or religion.

When I interviewed Derek Bailey for *The Wire* in 1996, he described watching TV evangelist Jimmy Swaggart at work in Alabama. In particular, he objected to the musical manipulation of the congregation. Bailey's dislike of musical sententiousness runs deep.

Great music often is funny, don't you find? One of the strange things is that there seem to be vast swathes of music where the sense of absurdity has completely disappeared. I was watching a television programme where this guy was playing Bach on a keyboard with his head inside a brain scanner! At the same time, the guy who's introducing the programme is standing there in a doctor's white coat! Imagine what Morecambe and Wise could have made out of this. There was nobody cracking a laugh or anything, but this was fucking hilarious! And this happens so often in music, this posturing – you get it from rock guitar players through to fat tenors. The audience just never buckles down and pisses themselves at these characters. Sometimes it's obvious the performer thinks it's funny, I was watching a clip of a young Elvis Presley – to me he obviously thinks he's being funny . . . apart from everything else, he *is* funny – but these huge swathes of music that get launched at us, there's a complete absence of any sense of absurdity. It's strange stuff, music, a lot of it is highly suspect, I should say. [29–v–1996]

Yet despite such statements by its foremost theorist, the image of Free Improvisation one gleans from newspapers and listings magazines is of deadly earnestness and high-minded austerity. 'Hair-shirt improv' is one memorable phrase. Why such misrepresentation? Because journalistic commonsense is so disciplined by class society that it can't imagine that non-commercial or critical art might be hilarious: fun is light-headed froth manufactured for the masses, heavy-duty culture is a serious, neo-religious experience for the middle-class elite. Despite the best efforts of postmodernism, no one seems to believe that anything amusing could be historically or psychically progressive. This separation of different aspects of our potential experience into warring camps (high versus low, laughter versus learning) has diminished our capacity to understand and feel. Class society divides us, and culture itself is distorted and sectioned. Reacting against the *Sturm und Drang* movement of his youth, Goethe insisted that 'cheerfulness' was an essential component of progressive culture: that is the approach that connects Kurt Schwitters to Frank Zappa, and Frank Zappa to Derek Bailey.

How to map this fragmented and warring culture? The overview from the Olympus of academia is about as useful as a tourist's snapshot from an aeroplane. It simply doesn't deal with how it feels down here, or what the real tensions and conflicts are. Boosting particular genres or bands or artists – the language of the press release – doesn't work either. Not only do such efforts reduce everything to competition (the only effective social dynamic recognised by capitalism), they make assumptions about genre that technical musical developments have already wrecked. A fragmented culture requires *triangulation*, a staking out from points of perception grounded in the culture's actualities. I propose three propositions to explain why playing one genre off against another doesn't work:

1. No one can say anything perceptive about 'jazz' who hasn't understood the assaults on schooled musicianship represented by blues, punk, DJ scratching and computer techno.
2. Cyber Theory hypes digital technology, but if DJs have no idea about the reverberation of their instruments – record decks and DATs, samplers and laptops, amplifiers and speakers – in acoustic (analogue) space, that is, the space *between people* and the space *inside your ears*, they remain trapped in the paradigms of their software, and can't make anything *happen*.
3. Supporters of Free Improvisation who believe that 'pure' music replaces the need for politics spout craven fund-me drivel.

This book attempts to speak about Free Improvisation whilst holding these three propositions in mind. It attempts to cut loose from both promotional falafel and the jargon of genius, and talk directly about aesthetic value, about the success and failure of the music *as music*. This won't make the author popular amongst improvising musicians, but that is not the intent. Audiences and their thoughts and post-gig discussions need to be addressed: that's the culture this book seeks to contribute to.

To abandon the covert authoritarianism of categories like 'good musicianship' and 'fine playing' is risky. Judgements become concrete, partisan, ideological. You're attacked for 'bringing politics into music'. Accounts of gigs that seek to uncover motivations, inspirations and animosities invite the put-down 'you don't know what you're fucking talking about, you weren't playing'. Of course, that's true – but if that really is the attitude, why do musicians bother to play in public at all? We leave critics who make sure they can never be proved wrong to their tight-fisted righteousness. If no one'll say what they *think* is happening at these rare points of heat in a lukewarm culture, then we may as well all pack up and go home, certain that no one can communicate with anyone else in the modern world (because that's what capitalist business-as-usual would rather we did).

Derek Bailey's philosophy of Free Improvisation is fully in line with that of Heraclitus – you can't step into the same river twice. The water changes, you change, everything changes. The first take is the best because it's unique, and all imitations are ghastly. The real world is concrete, ever-changing and specific, irreducible to fixed concepts and eternal laws. For Bailey, music is a tissue of concrete utterances, irreducible to scores and systems: Free Improvisation is thus militantly dialectical. It confounds bourgeois assumptions about music being a matter of scores and records, fixities derived from the world of property relations and promising profits to those with capital to invest. In a commercial music-world aswim with talk of 'crossing boundaries', Free Improvisation is the real thing: when an ensemble plays the music properly, the individual musicians can't even tell who played what. Improvisation challenges all proprietary limits. In short, anyone who talks about music today and ignores Free Improvisation is drivelling over a corpse.

To get a grip on Free Improvisation, music criticism needs a science of the sign, a revolutionary theory. Anything tainted by existentialism, structuralism or post-structuralism will not suffice. All that Parisian nonsense was a product of the failure of 1968: neo-Kantian despair, pseudo-radical Nietzschean sentimentality. We need the theory that emerged in Russia in the 1920s.

> The old bourgeois linguistics, commanding an already-established object of investigation – the Indo-European languages of the historical epochs – and taking its departure, moreover, almost exclusively from the petrified forms of written languages (dead languages foremost among them) can't say *anything* about speech in general, its origins or purpose. The greatest obstacle in our way is not the difficulty of research nor the lack of solid data, but our scientific thinking, which is locked into the traditional outlook of philology or 'cultural history', and has not been nurtured by analysis of *living speech* in its limitlessly free and creative ebb and flow. [Valentin Voloshinov, *Marxism and the Philosophy of Language*, p. 72]

If critics and musicologists put Free Improvisation into focus, what they say about music in general – including that heard via records and the radio – might start to make sense!

However, though I believe that Bailey's position is ultimately compatible with my own Musical Marxism (a confluence of punk, Zappa and Adorno), I don't expect to hear him say so. Theory and abstraction are immediately suspicious to Bailey: they freeze the moment, generalise the instant, abuse the actuality, bully the musician. Thus far, it does seem that theory hasn't helped improvising musicians much. The literature is littered with statements and papers which in retrospect merely seem to echo the intellectual fads of the day. Of course, I believe this book is of a different calibre. Refusing to pitch my drift towards the seminars of academia, I imagine the scorn of the creative musician burn into the back of my neck as I type each sentence. This tension makes this book an unstable composite of opposites.

Introductions are written to forestall criticism, or at least the more gruesomely predictable examples, so let it be stated upfront that *Derek Bailey and the Story of Free Improvisation* is DESIGNED to be contradictory, argumentative and unfinished – in short, improvised and dialectical. Author and subject haven't reached agreement about anything, especially about Free Improvisation – either as method, scene, or all-embracing philosophy (a point made repeatedly in the text, though this will of course not deter the stupid from pointing it out). Bailey is a *musician*, interested in opportunities for playing which engage and challenge him. As he put it to me in an interview for *The Wire*, criticism is anathema to him ('I'm not here to slag off people who might give me a gig or something like that'). Watson is a *listener*, seeking to understand what repels and attracts him, to relate musical experience to philosophical and political tenets and issues. Hence *criticism* – news of who's worth paying to see and who is not – is crucial. Bailey plays gigs and makes records. Watson writes about them. Indeed, in opposition to the cosy collusion of the conventional biography, this glowering gap between author and subject is here proposed as a field of play for the imaginative and thoughtful reader (those who'd prefer to read Bailey's uncontaminated opinions should turn to his excellent book *Improvisation: Its Nature and Practice in Music*, published in 1980, and reissued with new material in 1993).

If I've made mistakes in assessing gigs or CDs, I hope those involved will inform me – publicly – so we can bring the light of reason and the sweetness of truth to bear on these fascinatingly complex, ambiguous, inspiring events that happen under the name of Free Improvisation. The process is not going to be easy, but Derek Bailey deserves no less.

Out To Lunch
Somers Town
1 April 2004

A TEXTUAL NOTE

Derek Bailey's spoken word – derived from my taped interviews with him – is indented, and is followed by the date of the interview in square brackets. Other people's words are also indented, followed either by a book or magazine reference, or – in the case of interviews I've conducted myself – the speaker's initials and the date of interview, also in square brackets. My own questions and jottings are signed with the initials of my punk/poet *alter ego*, Out To Lunch. There's a list of books used at the end in case you want to know what edition of a book to refer to. This strategy was adopted to avoid recourse to footnotes, a textual device that seems inappropriate when dealing with improvisors and their disregard for the yawning archive.

OTL

1 CHILD AND TEENAGER, 1930–1951

Derek Bailey was born in Sheffield, Yorkshire, on 29 January 1930, into what he calls 'a sort-of middle-layer working-class family'. His father, George Edward Bailey, was twenty-nine, the youngest of thirteen children (many of them died when young, mostly the girls, which meant Derek only had two aunts on his father's side). George was a barber by trade; when times were bad, he would work on building sites, but reluctantly, because he was skilled as a barber and preferred that work. Derek's mother, Lily, was a housewife. She lived to a ripe old age, dying in September 1996. Lily's own parents both died aged forty-two, when she was eleven, probably of the flu epidemic that swept Britain after World War I. The eldest of three children, Lily was then taken away from school and made a ward of court; later she brought up her younger sister and brother.

> The whole family was incredibly close. Gladys, her youngest sister, and George, her younger brother and a guitar player, often used to live with us, in this yard. [8–ix–1997]

Bailey grew up in an area of Sheffield called Abbeydale. He points out that this was a respectable working-class area, similar to the area where drummer Tony Oxley was born eight years later. The two of them – prime movers in creating the unique and unprecedented music that is Free Improvisation – make jokes about the 'Sheffield sound', the industrial muscle and steel at the core of their tough, rhythmically decisive approach.

> I grew up in a four-roomed house in a yard with four houses which was reached by a passage. The passage, outside toilets, no bathrooms, no hot water – all the staples of working-class lore. There were worse

places. All the adults were keenly aware of that. They'd probably all come from worse places, edging their way up through the many strata of working-class society. [8–ix–1997]

As any working-class person brought up before the war will tell you, privacy was hard to come by. Derek was an only child, and so had his own room, but he was not always the only one sleeping there.

In the yard where there was a kind of open-door thing, they leave their doors open because there's no other fucking way of dealing with the situation. Those people were extraordinarily – 'communal' is not the right word – nosey! [8–ix–1997]

People were in and out of each other's houses?

Right. You didn't live in only your own house. You lived in the bottom half of the whole courtyard, and your own kitchen-type place was a public room, and weather permitting – and even if it didn't – you would move, generally speaking, between them. Or at least there were three houses that were constantly interchanging. There were six kids – one where I was, three next door and two beyond that. The fourth house was a chip shop, you didn't go in there because it stank like fuck anyway and they'd got this shed attached to the back where they'd chop up the potatoes. You could always get fish and chips. I ate quite a lot of fish and chips. People would stay with you. The passage was somehow significant. For kids, it provided, not privacy, but a kind of out-of-sightedness. Games can be played in a passage. You don't know what a googly can be unless you've played cricket in a passage. Mutual sexual investigations were carried on there, although they were a bit inhibited by the outside toilets, which were pretty much constantly in use only twenty or so yards away. And coming and going, *everybody* had to use the passage. All those houses had a front door that led straight onto the street. But front doors were opened only for dead bodies. Apart from a funeral, if anyone went in or out of a front door, the rest of the yard wanted to know why. And who with. [8–ix–1997]

In 1991, Bailey recorded an album with drummer Louis Moholo and percussionist Thebe Lipere. Moholo is from Cape Town, one of the many musicians who fled South Africa in the 1960s because mixed-race bands were persecuted by the apartheid authorities. Lipere is another South African exile, having jumped ship from the cast of *Ipi Tombi* in

1981. Called *Village Life*, the trio's record appeared with a photograph on the cover: not of the expected African village, but an early-century photograph of Derek's grandfather standing with five friends on a Sheffield pavement, in front of a pub where he used to play piano and banjo. They are wearing three-piece suits and flat caps. As far as Bailey is concerned, 'community' is by definition neither exotic nor pre-industrial.

After the advent of rock'n'roll, youth identities were supplied by the mass market. For baby-boomers and those who came after, discussions of early awareness of music invariably turn on record purchases. Growing up in the 1940s was different.

> There was a rather narrow sliver of music running through my family. My mother's father was a musician. I never met him. He used to play banjo and pub piano and paint pub signs. He was a decorator, but he also liked to paint pictures. In my mother's home there was a life-size portrait of Napoleon which he'd painted on one of the walls. They lived in a back-to-back. Three rooms, one on top of another, adjoining neighbours' walls on three sides. Percy Wing he was called; painter and decorator. He'd play his gig on piano, and sell his skills as a painter to the landlord. [8–ix–1997]

The guitar-playing Uncle George was an early musical influence.

> I was interested in what he did, I particularly liked his radio. Listening to his radio probably started when he was staying with us, but later – in the late thirties, I would guess – when he moved to a place about half a mile away, I would go over there quite a lot. I liked the atmosphere there, part of which was the radio being on much of the time. Then, when the war started, I'd listen to the American Forces' Network. I would be eleven or twelve then. My early musical impressions are very much associated with that guy, his life, because he was a musician – he didn't do what the rest of the family did, which was gruesome! The fucking steel works and all that shit. [8–ix–1997]

The unattractiveness of manual labour is a common theme with Bailey. One of the idealistic claims common to the artistic milieu receives a wry putdown.

When somebody says they would rather work in a factory than play music that they don't like or don't believe in, the answer's obvious. It means they've never worked in a factory. [8–x–1997]

In the mid-1940s, Bailey's father opened a barbershop.

I suppose he opened it when I was about sixteen, seventeen, but from that time onwards I was always partly away from Sheffield for different reasons. From the age of twenty it was music, but before that it was other reasons, like getting conscripted into His Majesty's fucking Forces and all that bullshit. He opened this shop which lasted until the early sixties and the struggle he had to keep it open kind of killed him in a sense. Very independent guy. Earlier, it had been an amazingly social place. Whenever I called in, for a free haircut usually, it always seemed full of people talking. My old man loved talk. He still remains for me one of the funniest people I've ever met. He came from a family of thirteen. My father's father, whose name was William – lots of Williams in the Baileys – I knew quite well, he died when I was sixteen. He'd been a cobbler, he lived near us, a place called Wolsey Road. [8–ix–1997]

Is the house you grew up in still standing today?

Oh yes, I only sold the house in 1994 for my mother when she went into an old people's home. It's full of students now. The whole area is pretty Pakistani now, fifty per cent. In recent times my mother's neighbours were black, which disturbed her for a long time, but gradually she actually came to think of it as being all right, maybe better than the other buggers she'd put up with all her life. They weren't nosey, anyway. [8–ix–1997]

Bailey's Uncle Bill was a regular in the army. He had fought in the Boer War.

He was very much a representative of the lower level, the one below this level which my father and mother had hauled themselves up to. He was an Old Contemptible – one of the regular soldiers before the First World War (when that war started the Kaiser called the British army 'contemptible', I don't know if this was to do with their behaviour in South Africa). They kept this name and they used to meet regularly – the Old Contemptibles. These guys had been in India, the backbone of the empire, etcetera. Anyway, they were an extraordinary bunch of people. I went to a meeting of them once with my old man. They virtually ignored us. They used to meet in this pub: by this time, around 1950, there wasn't one under seventy, I would guess. Huge white moustaches. As a group they seemed to last very well. Maybe it was the amount of beer they drank. Of course the group got smaller and smaller, weighed down with medals . . . but they lasted a long, long time. My Uncle Bill lasted until he was ninety-odd. [8-ix-1997]

After leaving the army, Uncle Bill kept a pub. It's worth listening to Derek Bailey discuss his relations: it's an improvisation that throws up motifs that aren't often encountered today.

One of my early memories is waking up in a pub lounge, sleeping on a bench, because we used to go up and stay with Uncle Bill at this place called the New Inn, it's still there on the outskirts of Sheffield. Just waking up in this strange smell, but it was a smell I was not unfamiliar with because my first home was in what they called a 'beer-off' (an off-licence or liquor store, but one which only sold beer). My mother's grandmother lived opposite my father's family on Wolsey Road. My mother had been bringing up her younger brother and sister but at some point they were split up, they were put in some kind of institution and my mother went to live with her grandmother. So, you've got the cobbler's shop, the beer-off . . . my mother and father met, they got married, and they went to live with my mother's grandmother at this beer-off. That's where I was born – licensed premises! My father's family go on and on and on, they were a very strange bunch, lots of men. My favourite was a fellow called Ben, Uncle Ben. He had a chequered career – he became a master baker. He was known for his audacity, there were lots of stories. You know in the Depression, the period of nobody working in the thirties, they'd hold sort of auditions for bakers. There'd be a job going for a baker and they'd go with something they'd baked and sit in a room. He had a technique for dealing with this, which seemed to be storming in with his cake and dismissing everyone else's stuff as rubbish – a somewhat forceful personality. He also worked as a tram conductor and gained a certain notoriety for never letting passengers go upstairs: 'I'm not running up and down after those buggers.' I remember him as being like that. He married twice, which for my father's family in that period was not known at all. [8-ix-1997]

Bailey is keen to press on his younger biographer the difference in *mores* that existed in previous decades.

I've been divorced twice and the first divorce I had – at the beginning of the sixties – even then was a hugely expensive and tortuous business. Now it seems you can more or less get one at the post office. One of the problems of talking about this kind of stuff is the background is missing – certain kinds of assumptions. To speak about someone being divorced, automatically meant they weren't working class. They were from a layer of society that could pay for it, it was very expensive and not guaranteed, you could go through the whole procedure and not get one. So for Ben to divorce in the 1930s . . . years later they were still muttering about it. [8–ix–1997]

The Baileys were not Catholics but Methodists, so it was not a religious taboo.

It was primarily economic but also social; rather complicated, they were pretty strait-laced. Mind you, there was a lot of . . . there was no overt amorality, but there was a bit of messing around going on, I can remember that from being a child. No shortage of adultery, I wouldn't say it was general, but given the opportunity, the adults were all over each other. It wasn't wife-swapping, there was nothing that could be seen. I suppose you could call it hypocritical, but it wasn't that: appearances were hugely important, strangely enough. My aunts were amazing characters, they all had bright red hair into their seventies. My mother was the only one who had natural red hair, and by the time she was in her seventies it wasn't of course, but she still had red hair. They hated old age! They weren't leaving anything to nature. My mother was quite a strikingly good-looking woman from photographs taken when she was young and she retained her good looks right into her old age. She brought two younger sisters up, but even the older sisters looked to her for certain things – kind of style in a way, but not on a level that would mean anything outside their own *mores*, class, you know. One thing was the red hair, and another thing was never being short of suitors . . . I don't think I can get into that! So I grew up in an eventful house as regards that, but then this yard was merciless in its scrutiny of what was going on. So if I didn't witness anything myself, I would find out immediately after it happened when having a meal – which hap-pened all the time – in someone else's house. Very public childhood, in a sense, semi-public. Public within very limited, localised bounds. [8–ix–1997]

Musicians who want to learn their instruments need privacy. Did having his own room help?

I always had my own room pretty much. There was a time during the war when I slept with my mother and an aunt, so I didn't have a room. Why was that? There were three sleeping rooms, two bedrooms and an attic. The attic was my study! [*laughs*] Full of junk and a bed which all visitors used, but I used to play up there – when I started playing anyway. Previous to that, yeah, I had my own room, it's just that very often I wasn't using it, someone else was. Difficult to lay claim to anything, in that sense. I was the only kid in the yard that could be said to have his own room – because brothers and sisters always shared bedrooms in the other houses. Three of them in one – two girls and a much older brother. I frequently stayed overnight in neighbours' houses for reasons which now escape me. And there were long periods when I would spend part of each night in an air raid shelter. We had one in the yard and when the sirens went we all crowded into it. A couple of times we were all shifted to other houses because of unexploded bombs in the vicinity, and on those occasions you would be sleeping on somebody's floor. So any concept of privacy was completely meaningless. [8–ix–1997]

FIRST MUSIC

Even before the Second World War, which left an intact and booming American capitalism poised to rebuild and rearm a shattered Europe, American mass culture was exerting a strong influence on the British working class. In the 1960s and 1970s, Bailey laid the foundations for an entire musical genre by reacting to the pervasive influence of America's supreme twentieth-century art form, jazz. But was film important too?

Yeah! Great – that was my education, like virtually everybody else from that strata of society at that time. It represented everything from fantasy to hope. I remember it changed my whole idea of what work might be like when I saw *Double Indemnity* for the first time and thought – like, hang on, maybe I could be an insurance man or something! The whole American thing . . . I got the same thing that everybody does from that period, and – I should imagine – still does. When I got to New York for the first time, I knew everywhere; I was more familiar with New York than I was with London. Maybe the cinema was a kind of privacy. There was a cinema within two hundred yards of the house. The biggest difference, though, between now and when I grew up was that there was live music all over the bloody place. There was no other kind of music. If you didn't have live music, you didn't have music. Including the local church where somebody was usually thrashing the organ. That was about a hundred yards away. [8–ix–1997]

Did the young Bailey attend church services?

Part of my social life was round this Church of England at the top of the street. I was in an organisation called the Church Lads' Brigade, a boys' brigade type of thing – uniforms, belts. I think of it now as being quasi-military. It had various attractions. Everyone I knew was in it. You got a place to go that wasn't your parents and wasn't the street, this thing attached to the church – a mission room it was called (and it did serve a missionary purpose, as one's early sexual experiences were often gained in the space between the mission room and the church which was very well sheltered). You'd go to this mission room twice a week and do physical things, boxing, athletics, that kind of shit. They had a band, a military thing – I worked my way through it, I played drums, I played the bugle, I played the big drum and I finished up waving the fucking mace around! That was the career pattern, there was nowhere else to go after that. The church was maybe a hundred yards from the local dance hall which was in the local cinema. That was it: home, dance hall, church, cinema – all within a two-hundred-yard radius. [8–ix–1997]

What about jazz? Was that supplying young Derek with any role models?

Back then, the distinction between playing in a dance band and playing in a jazz band did not exist. I remember Ronnie Scott talking about this – that it didn't make any difference about whether Ted Heath was a dance band or a jazz band. So I used to play clarinet, and the guy I liked was Artie Shaw because Artie Shaw was like . . . a star! He married film stars, he appeared in films – a young, good-looking guy playing 'Begin the Beguine' – I could play 'Begin the Beguine', sort of. That was when I was thirteen, fourteen. Before that I played drums. The band I played in – it was just a band, you couldn't call it a dance band or a jazz band – none of us could fucking play! We were trying to play. There was a guy with a saxophone who never got it anywhere near together. There was always a piano player who would turn up with piano copies of popular tunes and he'd play them and we'd all pile in – it was appalling! [8–ix–1997]

Was there a teacher in charge?

No, there was nobody. Not for that kind of music. It was kind of ludicrous. Later, we had a vicar who was encouraging. I think I may have been playing guitar by then, I was about fifteen. We were practising just to play, just to get through a tune without total chaos. The venue for rehearsals moved from this mission room to the vicarage, the vicar's study. This vicar turned up – he was a big fellow, about 6 feet 6 inches, he'd been in the army . . . this was the end of the war, 1945 – when he came there was a different regime. Most of these activities, like the band, had been frowned on earlier, we did it when we could get away with it. Apart from that, I also belonged to a Bible class that was religious instruction (I guess it didn't take too well). At some point I threatened the Bible class teacher, I said I'd punch him. The Bible class teacher left, just disappeared and came back with this fucking huge vicar. And the vicar said, If you want to punch anyone, try punching me! And I did not want to punch this guy at all. But he knew I was interested in – let's call it – music. I suppose at this time I was to some extent pushing this thing more than anyone else, I wouldn't say I was leading it, but I was insisting on it happening. He moved it to his vicarage, and it was much better, the rehearsals were much better. [8–ix–1997]

Did he have a piano?

He must have done. These bands had to have a piano because a pianist was the only person who could play anything, essentially. [8–ix–1997]

What about the radio and records?

That was a much stronger influence and went back donkey's years, the radio. Big bands were popular. They were popular with me anyway.

Popular music was Bing Crosby . . . some other early listening experiences came from the fellow who was married to Aunt Louie. They also kept licensed premises, they ran a club called the Artillery Club, and I used to go and stay there. He was a Bing Crosby fan, he liked to sing and he had lots of records, 78s – this is pre-war, late-1930s. And I can remember Louis Armstrong, and a fellow who was a Louis Armstrong imitator called Nat Gonella – and Jack Teagarden, he used to figure sometimes on these Bing Crosby records. That kind of strolling music was the thing. My Uncle George used to play records by the Hot Club of France, which I never got into at all – Django Reinhardt. It wasn't until he got into Charlie Christian that I could go with him, but then I was with him anyway because he was a musician and he'd go out at night wearing a fancy jacket and that and go and play. He played all kinds of music – Hawaiian guitar, banjo, electric guitar. I think he was the first guy in Sheffield to play electric guitar. He was into it very early, in the thirties. [8–ix–1997]

GUITAR 1

Lionised by his fans, the guitarist Django Reinhardt is sometimes credited as one of the few Europeans to have made a historical contribution to jazz. What was wrong with Django?

I just didn't respond. There would be a lot of guitar talk. My father hated it, though my mother didn't, she was very fond of her brother and musically she thought he was great. As far as she was concerned, pretty much all her life there was only ever one guitar player in her family. Even in the days when I was doing the work he never achieved, like working on television! It was always, 'George – he's a lovely player.' My mother didn't like jazz. She thought rock'n'roll was jazz – this noisy music and I'd always played noisy music. What I played when I was twenty-five was no different for her than what I played when I was fifty-five – all just noisy bloody music. I never played any tunes and she would like to play tunes: occasionally we would play together, but it's always been the same thing – you've got to play a melody. These are things that the mass of people recognise as music, it's no good, you can't argue against that. But the sound of the Hot Club of France for me didn't fit into this glamorous jazz idea. Maybe because it wasn't

American? Didn't sound American. From that period, the guitar player I was aware of was Eddie Lang. [8–ix–1997]

At the tail end of 1998, Derek Bailey was subjected to an 'Invisible Jukebox' for *The Wire*: played records blind, the only player he recognised was guitarist Charlie Christian. Credited by some as the swing supermind whose chordal innovations paved the way to bebop, Christian does not have the extensive recorded legacy that makes a name famous in a market dominated by albums. However, wherever you catch him, his comping has elements of the ever-changing, speculative zeal that Bailey made his hallmark: the inkling that harmony cannot quite be pinned down, that a song's 'changes' are not definitive, that a tune may be played many ways. And quite apart from musical considerations, Bailey insists that Christian was a star as far as an impressionable young musician in early-1940s Sheffield was concerned.

At first guitar was not – as how you might say now – sexy. It wasn't attractive to me, it was just this thing my uncle played. I never played piano really – my mother played piano in the house, and I used to mess around. I think I briefly took piano lessons, but it was completely uninteresting to me. All the people I admired didn't play piano – they didn't play guitar come to that, they played drums or they played clarinet. It was very much a fan thing, playing. The guitar had been there all the time, it wasn't a fan thing. [8–ix–1997]

So when you were young, wasn't the saxophone the sexy instrument?

No, clarinet, actually . . .

When was it that you got enthusiastic about the guitar?

I suppose it was Charlie Christian. At that time it was *new* – it was an *electric* instrument, the first electric instrument I think. [8–ix–1997]

Wasn't Christian quite hard to make out from the records?

Christian was a *featured soloist*! The Benny Goodman Band used to feature him as a featured soloist in the big band thing, and then in the sextet, he was one of the main voices. Nobody actually did it as successfully as Christian. Thereafter, it wasn't something that took. So when you got the big bands that followed, the really popular bands like

Dorsey and Charlie Barnet, Duke Ellington and Basie – although the black bands weren't the really popular bands very often – through to Woody Herman, you'd have a guitar, but they'd be there mainly for the rhythm and passages in unison with the piano and maybe a solo now and again. Charlie Christian wasn't there for that. He played rhythm of course, everybody played rhythm, but he was featured in a way where the tune is about Charlie Christian, like Stan Getz playing with Woody Herman, this piece is about this guy. Like Johnny Hodges with Ellington – the whole point of having the guy in there is to play these solos. Christian was a good rhythm player, but Goodman didn't need him for that. This was new, to have an electric guitar. [8–ix–1997]

Did school supply any formal training?

Oh yeah – totally irrelevant. When I was eleven, I went to a grammar school. I passed the eleven-plus. It was a stigma on me in my society, in the yard, because none of the other fuckers had passed it. Grammar school was a revelation to me, I really enjoyed it, that five years between 11 and 16. Because I didn't know what I wanted to *do* except I didn't want to do anything, I remember thinking soon after I got there, It's going to last for five years – that's forever, and that's fantastic. I used to walk to this school. My mother's district adjoins quite a posh area called Nether Edge. [8–ix–1997]

HOUSEBREAKING

Nether Edge is notable for its imposing mansions, built by Sheffield's wealthy industrialists over the course of the nineteenth century. When composer/bass-player Simon Fell needed space to rehearse *Music for 10(0)* (an orchestral composition for ten improvisors), saxophonist Mick Beck offered the front room of his Nether Edge mansion. Space was suddenly no problem.

All the houses round there are like that, they're castles. It's a beautiful area. I was walking around there recently. To say 'all' is an exaggeration, but I've been inside a large number of those houses! During the war many of them were empty. You would always be in their gardens because they had orchards. The police force was totally denuded, of course, just a few old guys, specials. They couldn't run or anything. To grow up during the war – well I don't know because I never grew up at any other time – but I didn't think of it as a hardship. First of all, I didn't go to school for about a year because they were closed down. It was freedom – and it was fantastic, and breaking into houses was a regular practice. Some houses we used to go into regularly, enormous houses – empty. But it wasn't to steal anything. Just to be in these strange empty, forbidden spaces. [8–ix–1997]

Where had the owners gone?

I think they'd fucked off to Canada or somewhere – a lot of the upper echelons did that during the war, apparently. I don't know. They were all detached, not with a small space in between, but detached with very extensive grounds. I became fairly adept – as all the kids did – at housebreaking. I used to walk through this district to get to this school, which was in one of these houses. There were a very small number of pupils – between two and three hundred. I really enjoyed it. An all-boys school. English was a favourite subject, English and French, languages. I was OK at that. I never paid too much attention, I just enjoyed being there. [8–ix–1997]

Who did he make friends with?

There were plenty of working-class kids there, but also plenty of middle-class kids, so that my closest friend from that time onwards was a middle-class guy, Anthony Barker Badger he was called. He was called Barker after his mother (I used to think, Glad they didn't do that with me: 'Derek Wing Bailey'!). He came from a different side of the tracks, really a different thing, but I got to know his family. They introduced me to all kinds of shit, the theatre, for instance. Though Badger wasn't interested in music at all. He was just someone who was interested in breaking into houses. He had a tendency to pick fights. Worse – worse for me, that is – he liked to get involved in other people's fights, total strangers'. He became a policeman. [8–ix–1997]

Though much of what Bailey wishes to impart about a pre-war childhood is unfamiliar, his dislike of music lessons at school has a familiar ring. They were horrible! He wanted to be a hip kid.

The music teacher was called C. H. C. Biltcliffe. He was the city organist in Sheffield. A strict man I will have to say. I took it for three and a half years before I managed to get out of it, but I finished up

hating music. When I started with him I studied singing, because that
was something I could do. His obsession was training the choir at this
place. It was intensive and sort-of rigorous. For instance, we had to go
to rehearsals of the Hallé Orchestra when they were in Sheffield. We
had to attend certain concerts which he'd arrange, and we'd all go in a
bunch. I finally broke away from it when I was approaching fifteen. We
were taught about the great composers. I hated it. If that had been
music, I would never have been a musician. Yet at the same time that
was going on there was this other stuff – listening to the radio, the
bands, playing. There was no connection, no connection. I don't think I
got into the band thing fully until I got rid of music at school. Then I
maybe started thinking I might be a musician like my uncle, but not
until I got rid of this other thing. If that was music I didn't want to
know about it. [8–ix–1997]

Was that because it was too abstract and technical?

Biltcliffe was a bad teacher. It wasn't just the sound of the music –
which I did not like particularly – there was such a difference with
music as I experienced it at school. Now, I enjoyed school, but as all
schoolkids know, there's a bad side to school. One of the lessons I did
not enjoy was music. Music at school was just part of school, whereas
the other stuff was magic – it was part of being a hip kid. Band music
in the early 1940s was supposed to be morally bad, dance halls too in
those days – dance band musicians were not thought of as members of
polite society. It was only in the sixties that they became figures of fun,
even in the fifties they were doubtful characters. For me, the music that
was outside school was a bit like breaking into houses. It was daring, as
well as being fucking great – you know, I loved the stuff. I never
collected records, strangely enough, but then again, we had no money.
I don't want to put it so bleakly, but we couldn't have had a record
player. Only Uncle George had a record player – and he didn't have
one, he borrowed one – when he was living with us. Later he didn't
have one, when he got married, but he had this great radio. [8–ix–
1997]

Did the worlds of school music lessons and radio ever collide?

I did make a mistake once. I can't remember the context, but I did say
in a music lesson that my uncle had told me that Johnny Hodges was
the greatest saxophone player in the world. I said this to Biltcliffe. He

didn't hit me, but he obviously would have loved to have belted me. The whole atmosphere went frozen: this authority figure was not pleased at all. He said something totally dismissive – We're not talking about that kind of nonsense – and that was the only time that the two worlds touched each other. There was no other connection at all. I got rid of it as soon as I could. I found it subsequently of no use either. [8–ix–1997]

In later life, Bailey was appointed musician-in-residence at a music gallery in Toronto for a few weeks. He noticed that many students were wearing T-shirts emblazoned with 'SMUCLA' or the name of some other prestigious educational establishment. He had one made that read 'Sharrow Lane Elementary School'. The memories of the band he had participated in between the ages of five and seven were more vivid than Biltcliffe's lessons on classical composition.

Between the ages of five and seven I played in a timpani band at the first school I went to. In this class they would put string round the classroom and hanging from the line were different percussion things, a triangle, a piece of metal, a drum, anything that made a different percussion sound. We would each have three or four which you whacked now and then at times, following some strategy determined by the teacher. That kind of thing is normal now, I'm told, but maybe not so usual in 1935. This was the first band I was in, and that's quite a strong memory for me. A stronger memory than all those years studying with Biltcliffe. Sibelius! In the war, they banished Beethoven, which was a bit of a problem for someone like Biltcliffe, who probably worshipped him. Brahms was tricky, Wagner was banned of course. But they found this great substitute in Sibelius. The Hallé was always rehearsing Sibelius. Nowadays, whenever I hear any Sibelius, I immediately start looking for an air-raid shelter. If there'd been no Sibelius, I can't imagine what they'd have got up to. They didn't get into any English things. [8–ix–1997]

What about Vaughan Williams?

No, I don't think so, it was a bit too romantic or something, too sloppy, not rigorous enough. What they really wanted, of course, was Beethoven, but, at the time, he was the enemy. [8–ix–1997]

GUITAR 2

As mentioned above, Derek's Uncle George was one of the first electric guitarists in the town. For a time, he worked in a music shop making pick-ups.

He would buy magnets and wire and wind them. I don't know how the hell he did it. The first electric guitars were Hawaiian, and he used to double on Hawaiian. I think the first purely jazz electric guitar player where I lived was a fellow called Ted Needham. Later he was a bebop player, which my uncle wasn't. Needham was a garage proprietor, middle class. Yeah, good player. After that, when I first played in bands, I'm not talking about the church band, but when I started actually doing gigs, I didn't play electric because I didn't have an amplifier, and I used to play into the vocal mic for solos. Most of the time I played rhythm – I've always loved playing rhythm as a matter of fact. Subsequently, when I came out of the forces, when I was twenty, I played electric. I think I must have been the third or fourth electric guitar player to have turned up in this town, a medium-sized provincial town, so it was still not common.

By the mid-fifties, big bands were using them hardly at all. There was a very brief period when electric guitars were used regularly in big bands, but after that it became a staple in small bands. An exception to this, perhaps, was a really interesting character, an American guitarist called Dave Barbour. He was a small guy who used to play a huge instrument, standing up. He appeared in at least two films. He had an eight-piece and also a big band. He married Peggy Lee. He was a nice guitar player, had a good sound – with the early electric guitar, there was endless shit about sound. Then he just disappeared: retired. He said he and Peggy Lee became too successful, made too much money. They got divorced and he opened an art gallery in Sausalito or somewhere. Retiring was a favourite career move for well-known musicians in those days. Artie Shaw was always doing it. They all did it. But unusually, Dave Barbour never came back.

After Christian, the guy who really established the sound for the electric guitar for guitar players who played in small groups was Oscar Moore, the guitar player in the Nat Cole Trio. He got a great sound and people used to struggle like mad to get this sound. With those big old guitars, you'd get feedback problems when they were amplified. In those days they'd think of feedback as a problem. People would get up to all kinds of strategies to prevent it. A regular thing was to fill the guitar with cotton wool. To some extent it was an early example of the impossibility of trying to reproduce recorded sound live. Later there were many nice guitar players around, of course, but there weren't any Charlie Christians. Actually, there weren't any Oscar Moores either. But my conduit to guitar playing was through my uncle because he did it and I could get an instrument from him. [8–ix–1997]

You borrowed his?

No. My parents bought it from him, and they paid him to give me lessons. But Uncle George was endemically impoverished, his sex life kept him running from door to door. He had maybe eight or nine children from three different women. I can't remember what my parents used to pay for lessons, maybe ten shillings, and I think I was meant to get one a week. They were usually about three months in front with the payments. If George had been, my father would say, 'Judd' – the standard abbreviation at that time for George – 'been today has he?' He wanted to know how much money he'd got out of my mother. So I actually didn't get too many lessons, which was very fortunate because as a teacher he didn't know what the fuck he was talking about. He played quite nice guitar, but teaching he was a total bullshitter. In fact, it'd only be a bit of an exaggeration to say I've lost jobs through putting into practice what he taught me, particularly about reading. He couldn't read. He insisted on teaching me to use a method that he used when reading music, perhaps successfully – though he wasn't a successful man in the music business – but it didn't work for me, and it wouldn't work for anybody else. So even at the late age of twenty-two, I'm still struggling to find out what you're supposed to do when you read things. Mind you, guitar was funny, nobody expected you to read until suddenly they wanted you to read, and then you were in the shit, and I had that experience. I lost my first playing job through that. [8–ix–1997]

Was that your first paid employment?

Actually, the first job I did when I left school was – and it sounds an exaggeration but it's true – digging holes in the road. Now I'd left school with a school certificate, which, as far as my parents were concerned, was specifically designed to avoid such occupations, but this was the end of the war and there was a great shortage of jobs and this was part of a training course. Throughout that winter, which was a bad winter, I worked in a road gang for the Post Office telephones, and that's fucking hard work, and anyway, hanging off a bloody telegraph pole when the temperature's about ten below zero is not a lot of fun when you're up there for about four hours, especially after you've dug the hole that you've put the telegraph pole in. That's what I did: dug a hole, put a telegraph pole in it and climbed up the fucker. That kind of experience puts everything into focus. I can't think of playing any kind of music that's worse than that. Delivering milk was not a bad job for my purposes: you get up in the dark, you go out, do it, finish by ten or eleven in the morning and practise all day if you can keep yourself awake. From that kind of thing comes the realisation that if you have the opportunity to do something that means something to you, it's absurd to be putting your main energies into doing something else. I knew I couldn't do it, I knew I couldn't push back this barrier of ignorance – both musical and in other ways – unless I did it exclusively. I wasn't entirely clear what I wanted to do, but I knew I couldn't do it part-time. [8–x–1997]

HMS NAVY

3 January 1949 – a date burned into my memory in almost every detail. I was called up to the good ship *Arthur* which, oddly enough, was somewhere in the middle of Wiltshire. A 'land establishment'. Stayed there a few weeks and after being physically and psychologically pummelled from all directions, got shifted to something called HMS – which stood for His Majesty's Ship I suppose, or Service, I never figured that out – to HMS *Raleigh*, which was in Cornwall, a couple of miles up the Tamar from Plymouth. Stayed there for a few weeks, got drafted onto various ships, big ships, little ships. During that period I was a stoker. I was offered two choices when I went in: I could be a cook or a stoker. I didn't know what either was, but I didn't want to be a bleeding cook, though as it turned out it was probably the wrong choice. Previous to that, in '48, I was playing regularly with a band. The last gig I did before I got called up was New Year's Eve, of course. I'd managed to borrow a microphone and an amplifier. I was in a trio –

drums, piano and guitar – and rather than thrashing and thumping rhythm most of the night which I usually did, I was playing the tunes, and – who knows – maybe a bit of improvising. Things were going fine until His Majesty needed me. No musical activity in the navy. Once, when I was on an aircraft carrier, I realised – even though I spent nearly all my time in the bowels of the ship, both working and sleeping and waiting to get ashore and get pissed – that they'd got a band on this thing. Because it was an aircraft carrier and had a flat top on which they could march around a bit. Marching around is a central feature of service life, and for that they like to have a band, a Royal Marine band. I'd got this frustrated hunger to do something about music, so I thought I'd try and infiltrate what appeared to be this musical part of boat life. There's a section dividing each ship, it divides the officers from the potentially rebellious crew – although that's unlikely. I think it's called the Key Flat. I thought I'd go and look up the bandmaster who was a Royal Marine officer. To find him I had to go across this Key Flat. I get to this Key Flat and I find this Royal Marine standing there with a rifle, just staring fixedly in a totally mindless way in front of him. I walked up to him and said, 'Excuse me, I've been a musician' – lying in my teeth – 'and I'm interested, if possible, to see the Marine bandmaster'. This guy just stood there staring straight in front of him, then his eyes flicked left and flicked right. Then still staring straight in front of him, he hissed, 'Fuck off!' That was the nearest I got to music in the navy.

I came out of the navy in 1950 sometime around the end of July or August, that was my reason for choosing the navy, it was a shorter period, eighteen months. I immediately went back onto this job I'd had before, which was working for the Post Office. I think I was fitting telephones. Towards the end of 1950, I got this gig in a pub, which was three or four nights, enough for me in those days to consider myself a full-time musician. I jacked in this civil service job as quickly as possible and embarked on my first professional role as a musician. In fact I became the bandleader. That lasted about three months and I got fired. I think we all got fired.

Next I got a day job. Between the middle of 1950 and the beginning of 1952, I did a succession of pub jobs interspersed by day jobs, each lasting maybe five or six weeks. There was a girl I knew through some youth club. I also knew her boyfriend, who had subsequently become her husband. They lived in a little estate in Sheffield, they had a nice little house, nice little baby, everything was just fine. In the course of a three-month period, I fitted their telephone, I read their gas meter and I delivered their milk, and she said to me, 'Listen – you'll have to stop doing this! Nigel just doesn't believe it, I say that you've been and you were here because of these different things. He just doesn't believe it . . .' I just throw that in as an illustration of what was going on at that time. [10–x–1997]

Someone who couldn't hold down a job was heading for trouble. But even a working-class misfit could turn to music as an escape. That is precisely what Derek Bailey did.

2 WORKING GUITARIST, 1950-1963

FIRST MUSICAL EMPLOYMENT

Like his Uncle George, Derek saw pubs as his first port of call as a guitar player. Sheffield was not much use for music in the early fifties, so the job required a trip to Bradford.

In 1951, I went to Bradford to play with a trio, in a lounge – a pub, but a rather smart pub. There I met one of the first musicians who was influential for me – I mean I learned quite a lot from him. He was a blind pianist which was quite significant for the approach to the music in the group, of course. Stan Hume, 'the Mayor of Bingley', as we used to call him. He lived in Cottingley, and the pub job was in Keighley. I was living in Bradford (the magic in these names!). I used to share this job with another guitar player called Laurie Steel, a friend of mine I'd first met in Sheffield. First when I went there I lived in his house, then I moved into a house in the Lumb Lane area, which even in those days was a black area. I lived with what used to be described as a 'mixed family' – black father and white mother. One of the children, who was twenty-one, was a fan of this band I played in. He was a phantom vibes player. He didn't play anything, he used to stand in front of the band and mime vibes parts to what we were playing. As a lot of the stuff we were playing was unison piano and guitar, it made more sense than it might sound, but it still looked rather surprising, especially to a room full of drunks. The other guitar player was a great guy. He drove a taxi as well. Additionally, we both used to sell polish door to door. But we did it via taxi. We would drive round in a taxi and then get out when we spotted a likely-looking area and try and flog polish. The patter went something like, 'I'm from Evod, Staffs, and I've been asked to call on you to demonstrate our new product, "Dove" . . .' This would produce a wide variety of responses. Another revealing exercise. Many of these jobs were significant for me in reinforcing what I already knew – that I did not want to know about the 'real' world. [10–x–1997]

How long did it take to reach the status of professional musician?

From my first three-or-four-night pub job in 1950 I considered myself a professional musician . . . but the first time it was economically justified was in early 1952. I got a genuine full-time job, working every night and two afternoons for a band that was resident in a dance hall, a fifteen-piece band. I played guitar in that. That went on through most of 1952, that was fine for me, I thought I was learning something, which I probably was. Anyway I didn't learn enough, I got fired from that. This was an occupational hazard if you were a guitar player in a big band, and also if you played bits of bebop – which was my inclination. Strangely enough, even as late as 1952, it wasn't generally recognised as being a part of popular music. I got sacked for playing 'Ornithology' in a quickstep melody. It was a contributory factor, anyway. [8–x–1997]

I asked Derek if he'd seen *Sven Klangs Kvintett*, Stellan Olsson's 1976 film depicting the tensions between professional musicianship and bebop deviance in a 1950s dance band in Denmark. It's often cited – alongside Bertrand Tavernier's *Round Midnight* – as one of the few films about jazz told from a musician's perspective. Derek had seen it. Was it romanticised?

I thought it was a pretty good film. Authentic, in so far as any film could be – to put that experience into an hour and a half. [8–x–1997]

The sax player launches into a bebop solo and the dancers grind to a halt . . .

That wasn't my experience. I don't know how the dancers reacted. The bandleader, though, definitely didn't like it! [*laughs*] [8–x–1997]

Musicians kept in touch with each other about possible employment, generally by letter.

In 1953, I went up to Glasgow, again at the invitation of Laurie Steel. I was doing some grisly job, delivering Walls ice cream I think. In

Glasgow I shared a flat with Laurie on Royal Terrace, a wonderful flat overlooking a park that led up to the university. I really liked Glasgow. Incredibly strong atmosphere at that time. That flat, in 1953, was where I first took part in what would have to be described as Free Improvisation. Three guitars, Laurie, me and another guy individually retuned our guitars and . . . played. The results? Can't remember. We didn't try it again. But that kind of exploratory episode, while uncommon, happened now and then, and my guess is that it has always happened. Nobody invented Free Improvisation.

I did some work in the Stage & Screen club, really a dump, with a trio. After a while they had a *change of policy* – what that meant was that one week they couldn't pay us and we got thrown out. I stayed in Glasgow quite a bit, and though it sounds like a melodramatic exaggeration, I got close, I think, to starving to death. I was living on virtually nothing as regards eating. Laurie was working and he was very generous to me, but I missed most meals. Finally I surrendered and went back to Sheffield and turned up at my parents' and they said, I told you so, we've had this in the family before. [10–x–1997]

AN INTERLUDE WITH CHARLIE APPLEYARD

As a variation in the programme of weekly interrogations, Derek Bailey recorded a tape of reminiscences at his home, without me being there. For this he adopted the alias of an out-and-about roving reporter on the trail of Charlie Appleyard, the senile and embittered musician who first made an appearance in the programme of Company Week 1990 (see Chapter 5), where he claimed to have 'invented' Free Improvisation. Derek's partner Karen Brookman was on hand to ask questions, too.

Investigative Reporter: And here we are at the 'Have You Ever Considered Euthanasia? Hospice', where we expect to find in the terminate ward of the one-foot-in-the-grave section a musician nowadays known as Charlie Appleyard, who you might remember, if you remember him at all, as Derek Bailey, the infamous serial killer who was accused of murdering – in a cold-blooded and horrific manner – the whole of the first generation, starting with Ego Park-It, of what used to be called the Free Improvisors, or some such ridiculous name. Ever since then he's been incarcerated, muttering to himself over and over again, 'These treacherous motherfuckers, treacherous motherfuckers . . .' For years, nobody has been able to get another word out of him. But we are hoping to reveal the whole history here in a series – I think it'll run to a series – entitled 'Is That All?' Meanwhile, let's check out Charlie D. B. Appleyard . . . [10–x–1997]

Karen has been drawing a wallchart of Appleyard's life: 'I've got to here – you're in Sheffield and your marital status is single . . .'.

Single, yes, free as a bird. I think my main sexual activity was masturbation. 1954, 1955 was a period that was pretty much doom and gloom all the way. I had very little playing work and during this time I stopped playing altogether. I'd never done that voluntarily before. For as long as I could remember I always seemed to be involved in playing music of some kind. But it was obvious things weren't working out too well, so I thought, Let's see what happens if I stop this nonsense. I learnt a lot from that hiatus.

Firstly, I realised that working or not, there was absolutely nothing else I wanted to do. Then – and this is difficult to describe – the thing I really missed was practising, and I realised the importance for me of simply working continuously on playing. Until that time, I'd practised regularly but usually for the realisation of specific ends, usually technical. But from that time my interest has grown in a wider view of practising. Starting around then, and continuing until now, I came to see it as something that served all kinds of purposes. Providing some sort of personal musical environment that you can constantly work on and develop. And if it's possible to think in a tactile way, then sometimes it's that. Is it a psychological need? You'll never be alone if you practise? Whatever . . . since that time, however much I'm working, I know there's more to playing than a string of gigs. There's a guy in Japan plays shakuhachi – Japan is always full of Americans studying with him – who practises, he says, for the good of his health. I can dig that.

Curiously, during this period I had my second brush with what could be described as free playing. A pianist called Eddie Barton had a trio – with bass and drums – and they invited me to play with them on a couple of occasions. They used to play pieces written by Eddie and then improvise freely – as far as I could detect – over them. I'd always assumed that improvising without reference to mutually recognised harmony was a sure sign of incompetence. But they gave every indication of doing this deliberately. It made no difference to me. I couldn't make head or tail of it. And I was probably too concerned to exercise my skills, as I thought, not to use them. It would be another ten years before I figured out that conventional skills are just as useful in free playing as they are in playing any music.

Incidentally, I don't want to set off a gold rush, but I have an impression that the E. Barton Trio made a record about that time.

My personal life had become extremely complicated. I'd met Frank Long and a Mrs Priest, who later became the first Mrs Bailey.

Karen interrupts Charlie Appleyard: 'When did you actually get married, Charlie?'

I think it was September '55. I don't know that it ever worked. I married this woman because at the time it seemed the easier thing to do than not marrying her. She got divorced from this guy – not entirely due to me – but before we got married it was sort-of obviously doomed I suppose, but anyway I went through with it, I didn't know any better really. Stupidity was always my ace-in-the-hole, I could always play that.

Then I got a playing job and from that time on – 1955 or so – I worked continuously, playing virtually every night, even in some periods days too, until 1968 or so, when I stopped doing commercial work altogether. But in '55 that job was with a trio in a restaurant; musically it was abysmal. I had to double on bass and piano. Of course, I couldn't play either bass or piano in any meaningful sense, but I did my best not to let on about that. Anyway, the requirements were so primitive – playing piano, for instance, all I was required to do was play a few chords while the pianist played a few melodies on the vibes. We were in this quite posh restaurant, maybe Sheffield's at-that-time most posh restaurant, located in a cinema, the Green Room it was called. Six nights a week and well paid. That went on quite a while until it was driving me nuts. At least it gave me a chance to do some work on the side. One of the things I'd taken up then – totally misguided – was studying arranging. As they used to say, 'I'm an arranger/composer' now. I started doing it for other bands. One of the bands I was doing it for offered me a job as bass player, guitar player and staff arranger. So I left this trio thing – this is '56 – and joined this big band. The first piece I had to arrange for them was the national anthem! Arranging, in my experience, wasn't a question of sitting up all night waiting for inspiration, the inspiration was delivered. Usually on a Friday evening, and in some detail. Like, 'I've heard so-and-so play this like this, I'd like a version that's similar.' I got fired from that. I finished back at the Green Room in this trio.

This job had certain secondary attractions. American touring bands used to eat there. English bands didn't because they couldn't afford it; the Americans could, and it seemed to be a policy of the management to get them in there. So I did meet a lot of American musicians. I got to know, on two or three occasions, the Basie band, for instance. Of course there was the terrible embarrassment that we had to play in front of these guys. Not only did we play to these guys, we would on occasions play with them. I wonder how many other British guitarists have played with Lionel Hampton? He sat in with us one night and, astonishingly, he played 'Star Dust'. I mean, 'Star Dust' had been his feature, even then, for twenty years, and he must have played it every night of the week for twenty years. He sat in and played 'Star Dust'! That was kind of instructive.

In 1957 I left Sheffield. I never went back to Sheffield until the Joseph Holbrooke saga started, which was the end of '63. I went to Leeds and I stayed there quite a while and worked in this dance hall, and that was a very good period for me. I met a woman there who I lived with. We had a very successful – the only successful arrangement with a female I've ever had other than my present one. [10–x–1997]

Karen must be blushing. 'You are ridiculous . . .'

I'm sorry! [claps] This is the truth, we have to give the truth to this man, he's a serious journalist and biographer. But I can't talk about this. It was a great time; socially and musically. I was working six afternoons and six nights: a quartet, good, and always at least one musician I could learn something from, we were doing occasional broadcasts, the occasional gig afterwards. Even, on occasion, before. It was possible to do morning gigs then. Say, for the opening of a furniture store. Something of that sort. If they wanted music, they had to have musicians.

I played in the jazz club two or three nights a week run in Leeds by a fellow called Bob Barclay, a black guy famous for his red beans and rice. So a lot of musicians – again, strangely enough, mainly touring American musicians – used to come in for the food. And be inflicted by us! I used to play there when I finished in the dance hall, this would be Thursday, Friday. Friday and Saturday the thing would go on all night and lots of people would sit in. It could be grisly, but Thursday was often very nice. But at that time, I thought it was all fantastic, great. I couldn't imagine anything better. [10–x–1997]

Karen: 'What happened next?'

I went to France, so I guess this was '58. I went to work with Stan Hume again. He had a five-piece there, a quartet with a singer. In France I lived in Orléans, then we went to Charente, I lived in Angoulême – shall I spell these? [laughs] – and I lived in La Rochelle, and then I lived in a great little place named Châtelaillon-Plage, which is on the coast, the Bay of Biscay, somewhere between La Rochelle and Bordeaux. This lasted maybe six months. We were working for the American forces who had bases nearby. There were French people there who claimed the Americans were worse than the Germans. They were still there, more than ten years after the war, and the whole economy of that part of France ran on the Americans being there. Working on the American bases is a special experience. You'd play to a six- or seven-hundred all-male audience that had just come in from a day crawling around with rifles in a muddy field somewhere. All they wanted to do was get totally pissed. Their musical taste . . . wow. Fifty per cent of it was 'Night Train'. To compound the viciousness of this situation they all came from Oklahoma. There's a special thing about Okies and music. For a start, they all play guitar, country. They all know how to play guitar, they think, and I'm sitting there doing my fucking Charlie Christian act, which they do not want to know about. Though he came from Oklahoma as it happens, not that they would know that – well some of them did. It's easy to underrate these guys just because their behaviour was so moronic. That's the soldiery, isn't it? You put a huge bunch of young guys together, throw a lot of drink at them, train them how to be aggressive, and what're they going to do? [10–x–1997]

Their main concentration was on our female vocalist, which is what she was there for, and she was great, she was fantastic at dealing with these fuckers. As a singer, she was quite good, and sort-of ambitious. But then again she knew that the only way she could survive in this environment was to have a relationship with an American in some position of authority. So all the time I knew her she had a boyfriend who was at least a sergeant or something. So it protected her a little bit, she made sure everyone knew about it. [15–x–1997]

Sounds like a Hollywood war film – the girl singer and the GIs . . .

But in those films they would be playing tunes like 'Don't Get Around Much Anymore', ballads. These bastards didn't want that. They wanted, at the most, six or seven tunes – all country – each repeated about twelve times a night. They also liked slightly *risqué* tunes. Stanley had a stock of these slightly dirty tunes which he sang, and the GIs loved them. It was always interesting working for Stanley, partly for his musicianship, but also the way he looked at things, if you'll excuse the expression, being the blind pianist I'd worked for in Bradford in '51, very good musician. Also, not surprisingly, a total cynic. He was funny. Stanley was a con man, and to see him working a con was a thing of beauty. His victims were the GIs. All Americans, according to Stanley, were incurably sentimental, a direct result of this being that they all suffered from 'momism': after a few beers they inevitably start talking about Mom. He seemed to prefer them in that condition. He operated a variety of cons; for instance, he would persuade some guys to play dice with him. He always won. He couldn't see anything of course, but they made sure he won. He had an additional income raking money off these guys. We all totally approved. These guys were getting paid more money for a day rolling around in the mud than we got for a month playing 'Night Train'. Anyway, through him, we never paid for alcohol; an absolute necessity in that situation. [15–x–1997]

We lived off the bases at Châtelaillon on the Bay of Biscay, and three of us shared a room in a hotel, a great place right on the front. A small holiday hotel in a small holiday resort. At lunchtime we used to eat at the hotel. It was summer and full of holidaymakers. Everybody ate the same, a *pension*-type place. The long tables were full of families, and the three of us were at a little table. We had more or less no money. Badly paid, we didn't always get paid on time. We were paid monthly, and we worked for a Paris agent. [*laughs*] I guess he was a one-hundred-percent crook. What money we had evaporated on our night off. Lunch was at twelve and everybody moved in there, it was festive. All the tables, with families and kids, were groaning with wine. Even the kids were drinking wine. Our table, the Anglos, were sitting there with – a bottle of water. Eventually, the people who ran the hotel couldn't stand it, they gave us a bottle of wine, just to start us off. And, of course, it did.

The first course every day – local thing – was twelve oysters on a soup plate. I hated oysters in those days, I could hardly look at the bloody things! Hung-over, every day starting with twelve oysters. Stanley loved oysters. But there were certain things Stanley couldn't do – it was amazing what he couldn't do and it was amazing what he could do – and somehow it became my job to prise free first his twelve oysters and then my twelve oysters and give them to him, loose in the shell. [15–x–1997]

The restaurant didn't open them for you?

No. I had to go through all that, and he just sat there like a big toad – glug, glug. That's a very strong memory. He was known as 'the Mayor of Bingley' due to a rap he had and was liable to produce anywhere. For instance, this bedroom we had – three of us, the tenor player, me and Stanley – had a balcony, and he used to go out and make speeches on the balcony. He'd start, 'I'd better introduce myself, I'm Stan Hume, the Mayor of Bingley. Now while you might not have heard of Bingley, I'd like you to know I've never heard of fucking Châtelaillon!' That kind of thing. Nobody walking about underneath knew what he was on about, of course. He was a funny man, and he was a real good piano player, maybe the first really good musician I ever worked with. Perhaps. Probably was. [15–x–1997]

How did you learn the country songs? Sheet music?

No, no written music, the band leader was blind! One of the skills you develop is learning tunes quickly, and they're not the most complicated tunes in the world. He would play it and he would expect me to be able to play it also – by the latest, third time round. If we'd played three choruses, he'd expect me to be playing the melody. Whereas he'd expect me automatically to play the right chords. In this kind of work, which at that time I'd been doing consistently for some years, if you can't get by without sheet music in most situations, you don't work. A fairly low level of work, but it does demand certain skills. Reading music is secondary. [15–x–1997]

How did you come to leave France?

I left France and went to this band in Glasgow – travelling from the Bay of Biscay to Glasgow by train and boat on a bank holiday weekend – the reason was that it was a twelve-piece band and there was no pianist in it, which was attractive to me. I'd never done it before, I had to take that role on the guitar. It was interesting for a while. [15–x–1997]

Because you had more responsibility?

You'd got more to play, yes. This was a pretty good job, but already by the late fifties those big-band jobs were moving on the skids. It had been gradually getting worse for years, but not to the point where it affected what I did. In fact, I was finding it easier to get work.

Now after that, things get complicated as regards movements. I moved from there – probably because I wanted to get back to a small group – to Edinburgh. Edinburgh was great, living in Edinburgh is something I've always retained as a possible reserve option. The group wasn't bad, and I had a lot of extra musical activity – I don't know if it was good, it was, I suppose, playing jazz and that. It was an amazing town for parties, I found, and I was there over a Christmas/New Year period, about three months, which was really fantastic. Opposite the dance hall was this beautiful little pub called the Fair Exchange. Terrific library there as well. So cold, in February, so cold, quite a special experience. [15–x–1997]

Where did you stay? Were there digs for musicians like the boarding houses that actors stay in?

Generally speaking I'd aim for a flat. When I first went to Edinburgh, I inherited the flat of the guitar player who had just left, which was a usual thing. You turn up, somebody meets you at the station, you go to the dance hall and do a rehearsal. Then they'd say, 'You'd better go to George's place.' I was taking over from George Firth, the doyen of dancehall guitar players. He'd been around for years. Apart from his reputation as a guitar player, he might have been even better known as a drinker.

I went into this flat. The curtains hadn't been opened for weeks, apparently. In the wardrobe there were lines of empty beer bottles going round and round in tiers, right to the top. Amazing construction. Next to the bed was a cupboard, opening it all these crisp packets fell out. I guess that was his diet. Interesting player. They used to call him 'the

Billy May of the guitar'. That won't mean anything to you. Billy May was an American arranger, arranged some Sinatra albums. [15–x–1997]

Actually, with the Easy Listening revival, Billy May's time has come again. He wrote the score for *Johnny Cool*, a 1963 throwback to film noir directed by teen-beach supremo William Asher, with the title theme – 'The Ballad of Johnny Cool' – sung by Sammy Davis Jr. However, the re-release of the soundtrack on Rykodisc (to the jubilation of loungecore fans everywhere) post-dated this conversation, so we're treated to Derek's description of May's style.

May's speciality was glissing saxophones, slurping and sliding all over the place. And George Firth (who was not doing it to copy Billy May) pretty much always glissed when going from one note to another. Quasi-Hawaiian, very commercial sort of sound. But he was very accomplished in certain ways. I remember asking him once if, as it appeared, he only played on the top two strings? He said, 'Yes, why bother with the others, there's nothing down there.' I said, 'Do you never play them?' He said, 'If I played them they would sound terrible, haven't changed them in years.' But George could work anywhere because of his busking abilities. He could play anything. This was in trio or quartet jobs where the guitar played the melody much of the time. He also, importantly, had a very good sound. On the top two strings, of course. [15–x–1997]

What does this have to do with finding a place to stay?

After a couple of weeks of George's place I had to get out. The place was suicidal. I went into digs – again, three of us in one bedroom. It was a workingman's digs, fantastic place, run by a Welsh guy who'd fallen off a scaffolding, his head was a strange shape, and his Scottish wife. The rest of the inmates used to work on building sites, one or two lorry drivers, and we all used to eat in the evening around one huge table. We were treated like fucking mascots, figures of fun – you guys are *musicians*?? [*laughs*] They were real nice guys. It was a great place. Stayed in lots of digs at different times. Not all of them were great. [10–x–1997]

Return of the Investigative Reporter: We now leave, as Charlie 'D. B.' Appleyard appears to have moved back to his 'treacherous mother-fuckers' mantra. This, apparently, is a sign that he wants to be fed. I think we'd better leave him now. So, bye. D'you think there's any chance he might get fed? [10–x–1997]

Karen: 'There's a chance. Thank you Charlie.'
The tape finishes.

DANCE HALLS

Bailey is keen to inform a younger generation about the conditions for a working musician in the 1950s.

One of the things missing in describing this stuff is context. It was a strange world. I liked it very much, maybe loved it. The idea of dance halls around today seems to come from television programmes made in the sixties, when dance halls as a social function had become completely defunct. The images of a bunch of ostriches leaping around in acres of space with a band in the background trying to keep up has nothing to do with the kind of places dance halls were [Bailey is referring to the tacky British TV series *Come Dancing*]. During the period I worked in them – from the beginning to the end of the fifties – they were slowly dying, I guess, but they still fulfilled a very special social role.

Essentially, the dance hall was a youth thing, this is the only fucking place they had to go to. The average age would go from fifteen, sixteen up to twenty-five. But these places might be open all day, and in the afternoons it changed, you'd get older people. Everything could happen in the dance halls. Primarily, everybody was there for sex. Looking for it or, in some places, getting it. A lot of criminal activity was centred on the dance hall. The afternoon was the time for the widest variety of people to use them. Many of them had balconies, alcoves – they were sometimes quite architecturally exotic places, vaguely oriental – some professional football teams seemed to spend most afternoons of the week there. Perhaps they considered it part of their training. Maybe they were just drinking tea. There was nowhere else to go, for fuck's sake, there weren't any drinking clubs. Of course they didn't sell alcohol, but all kinds of things were moving around the balconies. The dance floor would be almost empty. Musically, the afternoons were the best times. You could pretty much play what you like. Nights were completely different. These were often big, cavernous, sweaty, dark places and most nights they would be packed. Weekends were the time for fights. Fountainbridge Palais in Edinburgh, when I worked there, seemed to specialise in Friday fights. These were gangs fighting each other. You could see a fight moving round the hall. A favourite vantage point was the bandstand, and when they got to the stage you were supposed to carry on playing. You'd get a fight going between two bunches of lads – the toilets were deadly places sometimes to be in, if something was going off – and they'd work down the side, because there was a bit of room, and they'd get a kind of foothold on the stand if they could while they'd fight. Kids they were, kids. I don't know if anyone got seriously hurt. Nowadays, kids are into serial killing and so on, but I don't think back then that they'd thought about that. In some places a cage would come down and surround the band. [8–x–1997]

Like a fire curtain?

Yeah, actually a metal thing . . . this seemed to be a speciality of Glasgow dance halls, of which there seemed to be dozens. I think they were more concerned to protect the equipment than the musicians. There were all sorts of mechanical devices around. Particularly in the afternoons, the music had to be continuous even while the bands changed over, and they facilitated this by having revolving bandstands. In Belfast one time, I witnessed an amazing sight when a vibraphone, trapped between the revolving stand and an immovable wall, gradually got squeezed into an accordionlike contraption. And the band played on.

Socially it was, I think, an unusual life. There was no real separation between players and the people you played for. The musicians came from the same background, of course, sometimes still lived with them. And yet it was a completely separate life, almost a kind of secret society. A completely integrated alternative. There were no illusions about 'the people'. Unlike in art, there was absolutely no interest in what 'the punters' thought about what we were doing. All nonmusicians were alluded to as peasants. Nothing personal, just an acceptance that what the general public demands of music is that it's not demanding. They save their mental and sensual exertions for other things. And there was a kind of scatological approach to life. The obscenity count wasn't anywhere near as high as in the navy, but, for instance, more or less every song title would have accepted lewd associations, which could make requests intriguing. Some years ago, Emanem put out a record on which I'm talking about Margaret Thatcher ['The Last Post', *In whose*

Tradition?, Emanem 3404, 1988] and at the same time playing 'You Go to My Head'. In the extremely unlikely event of any of my former colleagues hearing this, they would immediately get the point of it, because they would have heard it used for the same purpose before. Don't imagine anybody else did. None of this seemed obviously cynical. Maybe it was a kind of defence against the unrelieved gruesome sentimentality of the stuff we were playing.

After Edinburgh, it was more of the same but more so. I was changing jobs every few weeks. Partly because I could do so, but also because I was finding it harder to find work that served what I was looking for. The only constant thing I can find about the music I play, from the beginning up to now, is that I can feel okay about it if I feel I'm learning something. If I think – however misleading the impression might be – that I'm moving a little bit somewhere. A new job would provide that for a while, but the periods when I could feel that were getting shorter. And although, strangely, I was finding it easier to get work, it was clear that the skids were under the whole enterprise. Dance halls were still open, but increasingly the requirement was that you play nothing but the top fifty. [8–x–1997]

Was this then a golden era of live music before records took over?

It had been, but I guess it was its last throw. We were moving into the era where live music's main justification was how successfully it could replicate recorded music. Whereas previously there had been a lot of freedom, if not in what you played at least in how you played it, now popular music seemed to be incomprehensible unless somebody had previously sold 50 million copies of it. At the present time, of course, it's all much more efficient. They've dumped the musicians altogether and they simply play the records. Perfect: they are there on time, don't throw up over the dancers, don't set fire to the TV in the bandroom and, best of all, sound the way they are supposed to sound.

But help was at hand! As dance halls closed, the club scene opened up. In some respects, better playing situations. All small groups, for a start. At the beginning of the sixties, cabaret clubs – as they liked to call themselves – opened up all over the country. The definition of 'cabaret' could be pretty loose. For instance, about this time – '60 or '61 – I took a job in the Potteries which involved playing in three different clubs each night. Primarily, accompanying the cabaret, which would be three or four acts, including wrestling. Incidentally, being confronted by some enraged monster ranting on about the way you've played 'Entry of the Gladiators' is the best argument against improvisation I've come across. In the early days of provincial clubs they were extraordinary places, some mixture of nightclubs and workingmen's clubs and often housed in cavernous places: converted back-street cinemas, very often. One of these Potteries clubs – Burslem, I think – was situated next to a slag heap. At night, the thing glowed red, as they do, or did. The bandleader – never been out of London in his life before – was petrified the first time he saw it. He thought it had just landed. And it was in one of those clubs that a well-known singer of the time, beautiful woman, called me into her dressing room to discuss a guitar intro or something. While we were doing that, she took a piss in the sink. I'd never seen a woman do that before. So, you see, there was an educational side to the work. [8–x–1997]

London was where touring bands were organised and where the agents operated. How come Derek only moved to London in 1961, after ten years of professional life?

I just loved the fucking provinces, I loved provincial life. One of the things I liked about it was you could work without travelling. I've spent a lot of my life travelling and I've always detested it: an appalling waste of time and anti-musical in some way. But I do like being in different places. That life – as a dancehall, nightclub musician in that period – provided that. I could live in different places but always working in residencies. I would never tour, for instance, except for short spells – there were lots of touring bands, I hated touring. After you'd achieved a certain competence and you'd achieved a certain reputation for that competence, you could move around, changing towns, let's say on average, three times a year. Maybe longer in some towns because I liked the music and the place. Between the early fifties and 1963, when I went up to Chesterfield and met Gavin [Bryars] and Tony [Oxley], I must have lived in every major town in Britain and much of it was, for me, fine. I enjoyed many aspects of it.

Those towns! It's beyond my abilities to explain how different those places could be from each other. Many of them had very distinctive features and atmosphere. It's disappeared so completely, I feel as though I'm talking about Atlantis. Now, if you were dropped down in the middle of Glasgow or Leeds or Birmingham, or for that matter Cologne or Rotterdam, you probably wouldn't know where the hell you were.

Maybe the best part was the amount, in time, you could work. Sometimes, it was possible to play for just about every waking hour of the day. Although I also found that through the sixties. But, as you say, as a musician you can't avoid London. I first settled, if that's the word, in London sometime in 1961. I enjoyed it in that period, '61 to '63. Later, when I returned in '66, it was, of course, drowning in bullshit. But the early sixties in London were just fine. I still worked mainly in clubs. Did a certain amount of jazz club playing in that time too. By this time, I'd realised that I didn't really understand what jazz was. What, since childhood almost, I'd taken to be some sort of exploratory process – a continuing development – turned out to be, in practice, more of a ritualistic thing.

There's another side to this, of course. My disenchantment with jazz stemmed from the realisation that I couldn't do what the people I admired had done. I'd started in the wrong place at the wrong time, possibly in the wrong race, a conclusion I'd reached much earlier. I wasn't going to be Charlie Christian. After that, it was about playing every fucking thing I could lay my hands to and looking to get rid of some of my musical ignorance. [8–x–1997]

You stopped doing commercial gigs when you found you could make a living by playing art music?

Let me try and explain this. I've never thought I could do anything – what I do now or playing commercial music – unless I did it full-time. This is a personal thing: however other people manage it, I couldn't play music part-time. It might be to do with what the alternatives might be but, mainly, whatever attention I can muster I need for this stuff, exclusively. [8–x–1997]

PRACTISING

Derek's pride in his instrument is evident as he explains the advantages of its low volume when unamplified.

The guitar is a very good instrument for practising on. You can play guitar in a room and somebody in the next room can't tell that you're actually playing an instrument, particularly if you play a solid guitar unamplified. I used to play my electric/acoustic Gibson, the same guitar

I use now – though that caused problems, because it could be heard. Sitting in the middle of a 16-piece band, the only other people that can hear it are the other musicians, the audience can't hear it, and usually they can't hear it on stage either. Imagine practising the trumpet – the limitations! You've got to do it out of doors I should think. You couldn't do it in a hotel, for instance. You can practise the guitar pretty much anywhere. [12–viii–2000]

Derek's habit of practising on the job got reactions from those around him. Playing in the orchestra pit for musicals and shows was particularly desirable – you weren't on tour and you weren't playing sets for dancers, both of which were exhausting.

A lot of these string players were ex-symphony, ex-orchestral musicians, the ones who'd play in the pit. I used to sit next to this violin player, an interesting character, a grey-haired small guy. He used to say, What is that stuff you were playing – Schoenberg? He at least knew what that was, the kind of exercises I was doing, what they were related to. [12–viii–2000]

In 1965, Derek Bailey played for the *Morecambe and Wise Show* at the ABC Theatre in Blackpool, a four-month season – two shows a night, six nights a week.

Morecambe and Wise were a very orthodox, traditional comic act. The season was booked up as soon as they announced it. This was before they became famous on TV. Ken Dodd was another one, he used to play in the opera house on the other side of the road, and that's a 3,500-seater. As soon as they knew he was playing there, for four, five or six months, whatever it was, every night would be booked up – twice a night. Morecambe and Wise had a particular method of working. A sketch would start off quite pared down, quite functional, and they'd develop it over a few nights.

They'd often start with a couple of sketches that were silent – I thought they were great actually – but they never left them silent. They weren't wisecracking comics, but the gags would develop out of the situation. I wouldn't say they were improvising, but the thing developed. If it turned out not to be great, they'd dump it, and put another sketch in. Generally speaking, they would feel their way for a little while. There was only one test as to whether it was good or not, and that was the audience. If the audience liked it or laughed more when they did a certain thing, it was in. There was no higher authority, it was strictly about audience reaction, but they knew their audience very well. [12–viii–2000]

You were backing the singers they had on as guests?

There was a whole show. I was booked as an accompanist for an ex-rock'n'roller called Mark Wynter – as far as I know he's totally unknown now, but he'd had a certain fame in the sixties – he came on and did ten, fifteen minutes. The whole show was a musical show in a sense, it started with music, finished with music, music between the acts. There was music in every sketch. There might be some conjuror act, and there'd be music all the way through – [*sings the 'Can-Can'*] 'da-da-datta-datta-da-da' – ridiculous music. You thrashed away for ten minutes. [12–viii–2000]

I asked Derek to tell me about the incident when his practising got a reaction from Eric Morecambe.

The sketch went like this. Ernie says to Eric, 'I've got these two birds, beautiful . . .' – I don't think they'd get away with some of this stuff now – 'I've got these two great birds, we'll be all right tonight.' In the theatre, they could be quite . . . [*Raunchy? Blue? How's-your-father? DB doesn't say*] Eric's saying, 'Great! Where are they?' and Ernie says, 'I'm meeting them, I'll bring them in to meet you.' So Eric's saying, 'What are they like?', and Ernie's saying, 'We'll be all right, they're beautiful.' This nonsense goes on a bit. Ernie goes off to get 'the birds', and he comes back on with these two quite good-looking young women, dressed rather scantily, both of whom are enormously fat, I mean *enormously* fat – and they didn't do anything else in the show, they were there for this sketch. Eric is appalled. The sketch then is Eric complaining to Ernie that he's fucked him up with these women, he's brought him these two ridiculous-looking women, but he can't say that because they're there, and he's saying, 'Yeah, nice, lovely . . .' [*DB makes exaggerated grimaces and waves his hands, utters squeaks of throttled horror*] It's gestural, see. Ernie's behaving as though they're perfectly all right, saying, 'What's the matter? What's wrong with them?'

I used to sit right under the stage, because I had a couple of spots where I played with somebody. I was down there practising, and during this, Eric leans over, and said, 'What's wrong? Well, there's a guitar playing in the middle of mine!' Nobody in the theatre knew what he was talking about, except the band. When the band laughs and the theatre doesn't laugh, that's bad news actually, they're only interested in the audience. He wasn't being nasty, he was just letting me know. They did ad lib to a certain extent, or Eric did, and Ernie would respond with some appropriate thing. It never happened again. I still carried on practising, I think I stopped for the rest of that sketch, but that particular one was a very quiet thing, with a lot of gestures. I really used to like the silent ones, but sometimes I would get off into what I was doing. You'd always know when time was up, there'd be a cue, anyway you'd got a conductor [*taps table like a conductor tapping his music stand with his baton*]. That's that story. [12–viii–2000]

THE STUDIOS

The career pattern for a successful commercial musician – Bailey was earning enough by the mid-sixties to buy a house in Rusholme, Manchester – was to end up working in the studios. This meant an increasingly straitened musical existence, with less opportunity to improvise, and less opportunity to learn, two things Bailey thinks of as synonymous.

Once I was working in the studios – because that's where the career I'd been following, if successful, eventually leads – I realised I didn't want it. Whatever I'd been pursuing all these years, it definitely wasn't that. Fortunately that coincided with meeting these characters . . . [8–x–1997]

These 'characters' – two musicians with musical horizons that extended beyond conventional success – were named Tony Oxley and Gavin Bryars. The three formed the Joseph Holbrooke Trio, playing music that transformed Bailey's musical direction, and laid the basis for Free Improvisation as a genre. Though it took another ten years – with opportunities to work in Germany and Holland with other free improvisors in the early 1970s – before Bailey could afford to drop commercial work completely, it was Joseph Holbrooke that opened the way.

3 JOSEPH HOLBROOKE TRIO, 1963-1966

The Joseph Holbrooke Trio was named after 'the cockney Wagner', a British composer discovered by Gavin Bryars in his researches on neglected and forgotten musics. There are doubts about Holbrooke's identity – sometimes his name is spelled Josef – and he died in obscurity in 1958, having composed, amongst many other things, an operatic trilogy, *The Cauldron of Annwen*, and orchestral variations on 'Three Blind Mice'. Bryars had been a jazz fan since his teens, but in the early 1960s was starting to explore the perverse avantgarderie* of John Cage: the choice of name for the trio was a typical example of his 'pataphysical satire on official cultural values and canons – especially since the trio never played anything written by the composer.

The three musicians of the Joseph Holbrooke Trio – Derek Bailey, drummer Tony Oxley and bassist Bryars – originally found each other through commercial work. When Bailey played in a Chesterfield night-club with Oxley and pianist Gerry Rollinson, he noticed something special about the band. In the summer of 1963, he had been playing guitar at the Winter Gardens in Bournemouth as part of the Winifred Atwell Show.†

---

* The term *avantgarderie* is one of Derek Bailey's contributions to the critical lexicon, and names the exhibitionist high jinks associated with bohemian circles.

† The idea of moving from Winifred Atwell – the 'wizardress of the ivories', born in Tunapuna, Trinidad, who had hits with 'Let's Have a Party' (1953) and 'Let's Have Another Party' (1954) – to the abstractions of John Cage may seem bizarre, but she was billed on her records as 'Winifred Atwell with her "Other Piano" and Rhythm Accompaniment'. This alternative to her consummate renditions of classical scores from Grieg to Gershwin was a 'battered old upright instrument she discovered in a junk shop' (according to Nigel Hunter, who wrote the sleeve notes for the back of *The Two Moods of Winifred*

This musician got in touch with me and said he was going to start this job in September, was I interested? I said, 'No, I'm going back to London.' He says, 'Well can you start it? I can't find a guitar player.' So I said, 'Yes, I think I can do that.' When I finished in Bournemouth, I went up to Sheffield and did the first two weeks. I realised that this was an above-average musical situation. Gavin wasn't in it then, there was another bass player, but there was a certain feeling about it, an attitude really. You know, in the commercial world, you can be playing with very good guys but there's not necessarily any freshness about it. If you're working six nights a week for six months with a bunch of guys who just want to improve, that's fantastic. If you're in a better band that's done it all, that can be dreadful. What I recognised with these guys – we were rehearsing all the time, playing, we immediately started a jazz club on Saturday lunchtimes – was that they wanted something better. A lot of it came out of Gerry and Tony, and then when Gavin came into it, it was really interesting. When he started, he wasn't the greatest bass player, but he got very good later, very good. So I was taken with the thing there, but I had to go back to London. It was curious. I said, 'I can't do the job – it's really promising and it bothers me to leave, but I've got to go back to London.' Back in London, the job I had to come back to was within four hundred yards of where I live now [in Clapton]. This place is still there, now it's a black club, but in the early sixties it was called the Regency Club and it was run by the Kray Brothers. That was the job, a quartet, which musically was OK – and working for the Krays was OK! But the club was ridiculous, totally worn-out, it was like some old cinema in there. Red plush and gold, but ridiculously tattered. So, that was it, back in London, living in Fulham, doing occasional sessions and one or two jazz gigs. During this time, my father's illness got worse – he died six months later from it. I was getting constant pressure from the woman who became my second wife, because she'd stayed in Manchester, she didn't like London, and I wanted to stay in London, so we'd separated. She knew about this Sheffield job, and she's on the phone, 'Why don't you take it?' She's on the phone. He, the Sheffield bandleader, is on the phone, because he still can't get a guitar player. My old man's sick, my mother's on the phone. So I thought, Fuck it – I'll go back! But a significant factor for

Atwell, Hallmark HM 527, 1966). Atwell's boogie-based sound rebuffed classical standardisation just as much as John Cage's prepared piano (itself, it should be remembered, devised to accompany dancing).

me was this music potential. I would have to have been visiting up there regularly anyway because of the situation with my mother and father – because my old man at this time had a barbershop of his own, and when he was sick she was trying somehow to keep it going, but there was no money at all. It was a mess when my old man died. So me actually moving back home – I lived with them throughout that winter – I think that was useful to them. I certainly hope so anyway, because I was never any fucking use in any other direction. [8–x–1997]

Although Derek acknowledges that one sign that the Chesterfield musicians were serious was that they wanted to organise a 'jazz' gig on Saturday lunchtimes, as he speaks his antipathy towards English jazz quickly surfaces.

I rarely did jazz gigs, I have to say I used to hate them in a way – conventional jazz gigs in London. I don't know why that was, I think it's more to do with attitude than anything, my attitude. Nobody ever seemed to be doing it full-time. The difference between London jazz players and provincial jazz players was that London guys earned their living playing in theatres and studios and the provincials earned it making penknives or something. And doing it full-time – whatever *it* was – seemed to me to be the prerequisite for doing the thing as it should be done. [8–x–1997]

During this period Bailey played summer seasons in Jersey, including one with Bryars, a period both recall with some fondness. To get a flavour of the times, I asked Derek about Frank Long, a friend who accompanied them to Jersey.

FRANK, DORIS AND JOAN

Frank Long went wherever I went at that period. Frank was a very close friend of mine. I'd known him in the early fifties. Although I used to consider myself a musician, I also did literally dozens of day jobs (the experience, I think, of most young musicians at that time). So I met Frank working in a shoe shop, a department store – or was it delivering ice cream? – anyway, I met him in one of these jobs. He was part of my education, Frank. My first wife – Doris – I met at the same time. She was a working-class intellectual with ambitions to become a middle-class intellectual. Frank was a playwright, also very much the working-class intellectual. He once had a play produced at the Little Theatre in Covent Garden about 10 Rillington Place, the mass murderer . . . no, no it was about Bentley and Timothy Evans, where they hung the wrong guy, all that shit. He was into that kind of thing too. [8–x–1997]

Did he read Colin Wilson?

Yes, he thought Colin Wilson was a wanker, he thought all those kitchen-sink guys were middle-class wankers, had no experience of what they were writing about, and were kind of voyeuristic. He liked Americans. He liked journalists. I don't mean [Ernest] Hemingway, he was suspect too. Frank could spend hours telling you about the dozens of ways in which Hemingway was suspect. Maybe his main objection to Hemingway was that he wasn't tall enough. A mere six feet or so. He liked Jack London, who was 6 feet 5 inches. Frank was 6 feet 4 inches. His background was, socially, rock-bottom. He'd been in the air force for seven years, he was about a year older than me. He'd devoured an enormous amount of literature, much of it late-nineteenth-century: Mark Twain, Jack London, the *Moby-Dick* guy – and the Russians: Tolstoy, Dostoyevsky. They often seemed to be big drinkers. I don't think Frank minded them not being tall as long as they drank a lot. He was enormously well read. Could give an exhaustive rundown on any aspect of this stuff. At the same time, I met this woman who was married to a painter, full-time painter in Sheffield, easel pictures, an artist. I didn't know him, but she was his wife. She didn't leave this painter because of me, but that was part of it. She was a few years older than me. She was also a literary type, had read everything under the sun, it seemed to me, though looking at it from this angle maybe I was mistaken. Although I had a taste in that direction, really I was totally ignorant. My whole life story is really a strenuous attempt to push back this colossal ignorance I've always carried around with me. She was a source of rather exotic mental life and so was Frank, and they were both good company and liked a beer. The three of us used to spend a lot of time together, particularly drinking, pub-crawling. We'd spend the whole night going from pub to pub and finish up somewhere totally legless and drag our way back to our flat. He still lived with his mother, which he did till he was about thirty. He lived in your genuine back-to-back house – that is, three rooms, one on top of the other. The other half belongs to somebody else. But nothing to do with music, neither of them. Frank liked Beethoven, opera, I think he used to collect classical records when he had a fixed address – he roamed around a lot. [8–x–1997]

You seem to have been pretty nomadic yourself.

The addresses don't change much in London. In the early sixties, I always lived in south-west London. In 1962, I was living in Putney with Joan who later became my second wife. We went into this local solicitor's and confessed – on oath! – that we're living in sin and could I get divorced? So Doris sued me for adultery. When it came to court the judge said, 'We can't have this! Who are these people? Anybody could do this. Certainly not!' So that was that. They threw it out. That was about six months' fucking wages down the drain. So what we needed, it seemed, was a witness. At that time Frank was living in Sheffield, so Joan and I went up to Sheffield and stayed the night at Frank's flat. Sometime later, the case is back in court. Doris is there, sitting next to Frank – they're friends you see. They called the first witness and Frank says to her, 'Excuse me . . .', and gets up and says 'Well, your honour, they came to my place about ten o'clock and they seemed to feel . . .' he's a wordy character '. . . some unutterable, irresistable urge, your honour, and they both went upstairs and all I heard from them after that was this creaking bed, so I would say I could vouch for what was going on, I think I know that bed.' I think he got reprimanded for being cheeky, which probably made his day. Anyway, we got the divorce. I don't think that mattered too much to Doris, but Frank's behaviour was a ghastly betrayal, this was her best friend. When he sat down again she said, 'You bastard,' and – apparently – the judge reprimanded her too.

Joan liked Frank, most people did, he was very likeable. In Jersey, he used to work for a car hire firm. Now Jersey's a pretty small place and the hire firm had a fleet of very little cars, Fiats I think they were. In order to drive them, he used to have to open the sun roof, and Frank driving around – with his head sticking out of the roof of the car – was a regular sight around St Helier. [laughs]

He was a failed writer, I guess, and he became a giant-tyre fitter, a job pretty much reserved for giants. Curiously, he was a skilled craftsman, trained as a carpenter. But he would never touch it after he left the forces. He stopped writing, which I thought was a real mistake.

Also I thought he aimed too low – what he wanted to write was a hit, any kind of commercial success. One time, he even tried to cajole me into writing songs with him. He had one or two plays produced, but it never seemed to lead to anything. He did a bit of journalism, but his writing seemed to peter out in the seventies. He just stopped it, he just thought I'm wasting my fucking time. By that time he'd been doing it for twenty-five, thirty years, written a mass of stuff, plays and novels. An interesting character, that's for sure, but he wasn't interested in the music at all. He was pissed off in general, his life was not working out.

Last time I saw him was 1979. Our relationship had come apart. I got him working for [Derek's record label] Incus. [laughs] He used to say, 'Have you thought about recruiting your mother for this?' He thought I was a total kind of user. I think a lot of my relationships have sundered at the point where somebody thought I was using them. I'd deny that was the case. But, more than once, I've changed the direction and way of my life quite radically, and when you do that your nearest and dearest don't necessarily want to change with you. This was particularly the case where wives and women I've lived with are concerned.

In the case of Frank I think he got on well enough with Tony and Gavin, but later he thought the people I worked with were, in general, a bunch of absurd poseurs. He had a strange faith in mainstream activity, and a suspicion of the notion of *alternative* activity. He thought of it as a particularly abject, self-deluding version of failure. In the late sixties, I dropped all my commercial work. At that time I was quite highly paid and, as Frank saw things, prestigious – so to throw in my lot with, as he saw things, a lot of hairy oiks with no detectable abilities was, to him, criminal lunacy. Our friendship carried on for a while after that but with increasingly little in common. That's how people can move apart. Why not? Seems logical enough. The real tragedy is when people stay together for no good reason, or for bad reasons. [8–x–1997]

You can tell that Derek is gearing up for a critique of his fellow musicians here.

A bit like musical relationships. Some appear to crawl on for ever immobilised by inertia, economic advantage and lack of imagination. Of course, some are perfectly wonderful, I'm told. [8–x–1997]

Back to Frank Long.

I only heard from Frank once more, and that was when I was living in New York. It was a postcard. There was no address on it, but it was posted in New York. That was in 1982. A great character. And I hope he's doing all right. [8–x–1997]

Although the sojourn in Jersey was in some ways perfect – Bailey fondly remembers playing in a lunchtime jazz club in 1961 with tenor saxophonist Alan Skidmore and a virtuoso spoons player – it wasn't without its upsets.

I used to have a lot of trouble with audiences in the commercial world. Having trouble with audiences in the commercial world is serious, it's not like in the art world. In the art world, you put it on your CV; in the commercial world, you get fired. I can't remember the ostensible reason why I walked out in 1964, I think I found the job becoming a little bit oppressive musically, although the guys I was working with were very good. And it was a nice spot, in fact it was idyllic. We'd had a problem with someone over the drummer who was Malaysian. Some racist thing, it was a posh place, right? Some drunk. It started like that, I don't want to give the impression that I walked out because of some racist remark, but it started like that. I finished up dragging my amplifier onto the dance floor and packed up on the dance floor and walked out. The dance floor was smaller than this room. Gavin offered to walk out with me, but I said, 'You carry on, I've had enough anyway.' They stayed the rest of the season, even though I was the bandleader. I didn't leave the island. There was a certain background to walking out – in that period I could always get a job. [8–x–1997]

Musicians who could play were in demand, they could call the shots?

To some extent. I could have stayed on the island playing somewhere else. I thought about it. I went there maybe three times, the last time was when I took Gavin, this trio. I used to like it there for all kinds of reasons, but after six months the reality of it being a small island presses on you. Whenever I was there, I thought of staying for the winter, you could work all year round. In Jersey, we were a fairly unusual restaurant group. We used to play Coltrane tunes as dinner music, 'Alabama' to accompany the soup. And you can get away with it, we got away with it for six months. Restaurants could be OK places to work. This was 1964. Later that year was the first time I found I couldn't reconcile what I wanted to play with the working situation. By then for some years, I'd always used jobs, at least partly, as practise grounds. For instance, I never, never played the same thing the same way twice. However limited the possibilities, I always found ways to change some part of what I had to play and, often, to adapt it to whatever my current interest was. Often, that was the job's main attraction: finding ways to do what I wanted to do within the requirements of the work. For the first time, playing at the Cabaret club in Manchester later that year, I found I couldn't do that. This problem, of course, arose because of the stuff I was getting into with Tony and Gavin. Primarily, the difficulty was that I'd started moving, investigating perhaps elements – such as serialism and non-time things – that couldn't be accommodated in tonal harmonic structures and song form. The customers did notice. Curiously, in the same club at the same time, the drummer – wonderful guy, Rex Denby – when in his frequent cups, would recite over the mic huge swathes of Dylan Thomas in a totally impenetrable Welsh accent. No, he didn't get away with it either. [8–x–1997]

Recordings exist of the Joseph Holbrooke Trio, the first recorded examples of his playing which Bailey acknowledges. A small segment of a rehearsal tape with a rendition of 'Miles' Mode' – ten and a half minutes – was released on CD-ROM by Incus in 1999.

> We used to (I say *used to* . . . I think on two or three occasions) record rehearsals, but it was to check out new pieces, many of them ours. The other pieces on the tape we have are mainly our compositions – a tune of Tony's, a slow modal thing, and one of mine, I think. Most of the free playing, such as it was, arrived when we played modally. None of us were really interested in modal playing much, and – like in this Coltrane tune on the tape ['Miles' Mode'] – we start playing modal, and then in the middle it goes into what is not modal, it's kind of free, you can tell there's something else going on, and then it goes back to the tune. Gavin became, I think, a really good bass player. There was nobody here doing what he was doing, it seemed to be years before any of the bass players in this country picked up on that kind of bass playing. This non-time playing – the time in this trio was ridiculous. It was very good actually – they used to practise together, the two of them. A lot of this came from Tony. Time was very much a thing between the two of them, I just used to fucking hope for the best, but I very soon got to feel that it wasn't difficult to play with. It wasn't a question of remembering where beats fall or something, it just felt okay.

It might have initially been some of that, but . . . I think Tony used to instruct Gavin in these areas when they were rehearsing. We used to listen to the Bill Evans Trio of the '61–'62 period – as far as I could figure, because I never had these records – two records, including *Sunday at the Village Vanguard* [Riverside 9376], almost two days that the Evans trio [with Scott LaFaro on bass and Paul Motian on drums] played that we seemed to pick on. It was a feeling of trying to stop the music. We were aiming for the opposite of *driving*, because everything was like that – this was the Oscar Peterson time – it was *all about getting it on* as Tony used to say. That's one thing we had in common. An impatience with the gruesomely predictable. Another thing we were interested in, it's the same thing – and it didn't, I think, come out of Cage, though Gavin will think that – was that we liked silences. We got to play silence. One of the reasons I like this rehearsal piece on tape, and it's related to the no-time thing, is that it seems to me to demonstrate one or two little things about transitional periods. [8–x–1997]

Were you you aware that if you tried to swing you'd be a pale imitation anyway?

I don't think Tony and Gavin were bothered about that kind of thing, they were too young for a start, but that was part of it for me, because it had been part of my playing for years – I'd assumed a long time previously that I would never be the kind of player that you'd have to be to make it meaningful to be playing jazz. For instance, one thing I used to find ridiculous was playing the blues. In a jazz club late at night, lights are low, palls of blue smoke around – and I'm sitting there playing the fucking blues. *Hilarious.* What is this shit? Wes Montgomery does it and it's beautiful, Charlie Christian . . . but me? It's ridiculous – and that's long before this stuff. I knew there were things I would never do in the only way that matters. I'd made an assumption, I think, quite early on, that in order to play jazz you had to do it at a particular level, and that the rest – you're labouring in the trenches. And only the stuff up there matters. It's *authenticity* we're talking about, isn't it? Don't hear much about that now. Is it obsolete? [8–x–1997]

Oxley plays free, but you feel he's completely certain about every beat.

He is actually a jazz player, by my definition. He is a very *fine* jazz player. It's a practical matter. He's done it, all those years at Ronnie Scott's produced something. There was no major jazz player during that period he didn't play with, night after night and for years. This is unique on the free scene. There are one or two who call themselves jazz players, apparently, but with them it appears to be some kind of philosophical position. I'm not sure philosophical positions cut it. Anyway, even before Ronnie's, he was a very fine player. And he has no time for it. That's the funny thing – his attitude towards it is very dismissive. While other guys genuflect before it, he's got no time for it. But most of the European free players are to me much more interesting than if they were jazz players. And Tony is a free player anyway, that's for sure. [8–x–1997]

What Oxley plays is so firm, so determinate, it's like rock even when it's free.

He's never going to be a chancer, is he, Tony? I mean, you've met him, he's not going to piss around. I used to run Thursday nights at the Little Theatre, and I'd play with absolutely anybody who'd turn up. Tony would sometimes come and check what was happening. I remember a violin player coming in one time and plugging into my amplifier. Afterwards Tony says, 'He's terrible. Why don't you stop playing? Why do you carry on playing?' To him, it would automatically cut off what he'd play. My view is more that if I go out to play, I stop playing too often. I think it's because there's too much non-playing in one's life. It doesn't bother me. I can stand to play a heap of shit sometimes. You try and make something: not regardless, but you're not going to give up because the other guy is playing what you consider a heap of shit. But stopping? What I do is not that precious. There are times when I'll play with more or less any fucking thing. Tony's different. Tony's very clear about what he wants to do – I don't know anyone who's clearer. [8–x–1997]

TONY OXLEY

Tony Oxley was born in 1938, making him eight years younger than Bailey. He jokingly describes the difference in their backgrounds by enumerating the number of rooms in the houses they grew up in;

> I lived in a two-up and one-down – he lived in a two-up and two-down [*laughs*]. [TO 25–ix–1997]

Oxley played drums in pubs from the age of fifteen, graduating to big bands at sixteen, playing 'the usual repertoire: Basie, Ellington, Kenton, Woody Herman'. Before he met Derek, he'd already worked his way across the Atlantic playing drums aboard the *Queen Mary*, with forty-eight hours off in New York to witness some jazz in the clubs. He served three years in the Black Watch regiment playing ceremonial and military music, and classical pieces in the regimental orchestra (Beethoven, Mozart, Handel, Dvořák and Prokofiev).

I was playing percussion – timpani, xylophone, glockenspiel, triangle if necessary, whatever needed to be played in the piece. With the traditional composers, Beethoven, Haydn and Mozart, it's mostly timpani, but with other composers, a bit more diverse, you've got to move around a bit. Having studied, or experienced, classical music in its structures and production, the diatonic system and the sonata form became for me like a second language. Moving on to Webern and Schoenberg, I felt that if that door's open, why isn't it possible to improvise? I'd already been playing the music of Art Blakey on the side when I came out the army and was getting a band together and doing a few gigs. It doesn't take you long to realise there's actually only one Art Blakey, and there's not much point in doing it. If you can't find something a bit closer to yourself, then it's going to be a strained kind of life. Particularly when I had an urge to do that, to move the thing and question: Why must the drummer always be clonking along behind keeping time for everybody else? – because that was really the pressure that was on drummers at that time. [*TO* 25–ix–1997]

So you didn't need Free Jazz to suggest the idea of being more ambitious musically? Joseph Holbrooke was an independent development from Free Jazz?

Well, there wasn't any at that time, was there? The closest you got – apart from Cecil Taylor, Bill Dixon and George Russell – was Coltrane and Dolphy, I suppose. And Bill Evans doing what he did, but none of that was really free at that time, 1960, 1961. I don't believe there is such a thing as Free Music, you see. These are terms from – excuse me – journalists that were adopted long before they decided to get interested or find out a bit more about it. [*TO* 25–ix–1997]

As already mentioned, when Oxley met Bailey, he was playing drums in a cabaret band in Chesterfield.

> Normal nightclub stuff. We had a singer. We decided to start to run a club on Saturday afternoons, which was our only free time. We were working six or seven nights a week, it was quite a long time. We both found our interests developing, and the only chance we had was to start a place in Sheffield on Saturday afternoons. It was mostly patronised by students from the University of Sheffield, which was where Gavin Bryars was. It was called the Grapes in Trippet Lane. It was a terrible room, upstairs, cold . . . you played by the windows. [TO 25-ix-1997]

I suggest that playing music inspired by John Coltrane and Bill Evans implies two very different models.

> It's so obvious we didn't think about it. It's like looking at two pictures, they're obviously different, but they're both good! It was quite dynamic, the music from Coltrane and Elvin [Jones] – particularly those two! – and Bill Evans was different. You can hear the French influence, the Impressionist period of music. I think Coltrane was closer to India and Africa. Bill was more Debussy. Consequently the music came out that way. [TO 25-ix-1997]

Though Derek accepted it when I cited it, Oxley dismisses John Shiurba's description of the Joseph Holbrooke pulse: 'playing the third triplet off-beat to disguise the pulse':

> I know what he means, but I wouldn't describe it like that. [laughs] I know what he means exactly.

Can you explain it a bit more to me?

> What he means – or what we did?

They are two different things, are they?

> Completely. That wasn't much to do with it. My idea was to . . . the feeling I had as far as the drums were concerned in the early days was to try – and later on, to not only achieve it, but do – what you've just described: get rid of it altogether. I thought the language had far more flexibility if you could find points in the bar (we're talking about bars now as you brought this up, keeping it in that box): just 1–2–3–4 and

subdivisions of 1–2–3–4, I didn't actually feel that that always suited the music. Sometimes I felt the way Derek was playing, that this kind of thing could be far more interesting if you could be more of a percussionist than a timekeeper and play a musical role rather than a functional role. I knew what I wanted to do in it, and I just sort of let that happen, and then analysed it afterwards: a more horizontal concept to broaden the bar. I found the eighteen-quavers-in-a-bar development as a fundamental very positive. Now when you've got a bar of 4/4 and you've got eighteen quavers in it, you haven't got a division of 4 in normal mathematical terms. That meant some of the things you could do without losing the pulse would neither be on the beat or off the beat because you've got 18 over 4. That gave you a wider spectrum, there's more possibilities. Of course, it used to throw people a bit. Not Derek and Gavin so much, because they knew what I was up to. [*TO* 25–ix–1997]

What's the difference between that and simply the time signature 18/4?

The time signature 18/4 is *not* the same, that would be eighteen crotchets in a bar! I could illustrate it to you on paper quite easily. The structure I found that coped was first to get the four crotchets, put over it six crotchets which means two groups of three, and on each of those individual groups of three put another triplet – so there you had eighteen over four, as a concept. But of course you didn't play eighteen beats every bar. You just played whatever musically seemed to be appropriate. Consequently, some of these things were not falling on the beat or off the beat. I could then make a musical decision, keep control of the time and widen the language. That's why Derek in the end decided – with me and with Gavin – that we might as well drop it altogether, we've just about got as far as we can. That's really what happened. It was actually published in 1965 in a magazine called *Crescendo*. I decided to publish it for the benefit of anyone else wanting to find a way through the dogma of the four. I published it, and I remember Charles Fox saying how interesting he found it, about the only one. That was how the spreading of the language developed, and eventually, as I say, we gave it up. [*TO* 25–ix–1997]

You say that 'absolute freedom' isn't possible . . .

I don't say that, because I wouldn't be that arrogant, I'm not a philosopher. What I'm saying is, that when certain musics are referred to by critics as 'free', I don't believe it's possible in the way they describe it. They use it sometimes just because it's not time. I don't think they know what else to say. The implication of free music is anything goes. You can say, Do what you like. But of course you are doing what you like, but what you like is not just thrown in because you yourself don't know what to do. You have what you're doing under control. You build a language and you work with that language, you improvise with that language. But you do have a language – hopefully it develops as you go along. [*TO* 25–ix–1997]

People associate not having a pulse with classical music – yet you're not going through any of the institutions of classical music . . .

Classical music mostly has a pulse.

Yes, but in the sixties, people thought there was jazz and rock'n'roll on the one side – music with a beat – and then there was music you sat down and contemplated.

Well, there was no drummer going bang bang through Beethoven's Sixth or Eighth Symphony, but of course there's a pulse in that music. I think where the critics make the mistake is that they don't know what's happening. In the sixties all this started, describing it as *free music*. One of the first records of Ornette Coleman was called *Free Jazz*, and that's what they sold it on, quite an adventure – the sixties was about knocking rules down. That was a way they thought they could sell it because it would be fashionable, but I think it's more a journalist's phrase. I don't think Ornette Coleman invented that, *Free Jazz* . . . I'm not sure who invented that. It came across as free, but what he was playing wasn't free, actually – he had melodies in his language and structure. I don't know what Free Jazz is really. If it means you can make decisions and not be tied down to a pre-determined pattern . . . up to a point, that is so. I think it gives an impression to some people of 'We don't know what we're doing'. By enemies, it's used very heavily. [*TO* 25–ix–1997]

Did avant-garde classical music have an influence on Joseph Holbrooke?

There was Stockhausen, of course, with his famous piece *Zyklus*, which I've got the score of – I could see how that was structured. I couldn't see the point in a way – though I could for a classical percussionist, who wasn't an improvisor. I knew about that. Gavin brought these considerations to the group. [TO 25–ix–1997]

Had you heard John Cage before?

I can't remember when I first heard Cage, but it was definitely when Gavin was there. I thought it was absolutely fascinating, but not necessarily for me. It was obviously very . . . *classical*, which meant that the improvisatory quality was not strong enough for me, but I felt – quite honestly – that that could be improvised, but that I as an improvisor did not want to improvise Cage's music, because then I as an improvisor would be doing the very thing I was trying get away from, which was imitating somebody else. But it didn't stop the respect for the pieces he produced, particularly the prepared piano pieces. Whilst I could understand certain classical piano players thinking it was sacrilege on the piano, I thought the sounds were quite interesting. Subsequently, we went to lectures in London. I found it really interesting, he was quite a rebel in his own way. It's a philosophy, isn't it, like Marcel Duchamp? – these philosophers using a musical language or a visual-arts language. For me, you quickly realise that. You don't expect to find a stamp so clear like you would Beethoven. [TO 25–ix–1997]

I asked Oxley what he thought of Derek's famous anti-jazz stance.

For him, he's talking about, and as far as he's concerned, he's not interested to touch it. But he was quite good at it, you know, there are tapes in existence of us playing with Lee Konitz and he was really good, and not over-playing – thoughtful. He played at the point during the sequence where it seemed to mean something. You know a lot of jazz players just go through their exercises and present them to the public. Anybody that knows can hear that. He was never that. He was a very thoughtful player. I wouldn't say over-intellectual, but over-intellectually gifted when you consider what guitar players at that time were doing. Even though they were perhaps more interesting than they are now, there were quite a few around. I think he liked Jim Hall at that time, maybe still does. So maybe that's one of the reasons, because *he's* forgotten about it, everybody else should. But I think he's only talking about it from his own point of view. It's something we don't discuss. [TO 25–ix–1997]

You became house drummer at Ronnie's. Did you feel you should stop
that work because you'd got to develop an entirely new language?

We'd done it by then, we'd developed it by then. It was a matter of
going to London. Derek went to London. I went to London and I had
the opportunity to work in Ronnie Scott's club. It was a living for
me. Considering that I'd only heard most of these people on record, it
was interesting to find out whether that's how it really was. Being
a drummer is being an instrumentalist, but rhythm is probably your
only weapon. Harmony is not that easily available to you. [TO
25–ix–1997]

Oxley was recognised as Phil Seamen's successor as Britain's top drummer. However, he did occasionally bring in some exotic new licks. An
old joke goes that jazz soloists were used to drummers whose basic pulse
– established in bebop on the ride cymbal – was 'ten-to-ten, ten-to-ten',
but that if you got Oxley at Ronnie's, it could come out as 'around
about a quarter-past-eleven'. Was the gig pleasurable?

Socially, very good. Not always musically speaking, but I don't know
whose fault that was, I suppose I was partly to blame if it wasn't
pleasurable, because I was trying to put too many things in that came
from the stuff I'd developed already with Derek. I suppose I was trying
to move that music as well when I went down there. I knew what could
come if you worked at it as we had done. I brought that with me. [TO
25–ix–1997]

Since Oxley had taken Bill Evans's music seriously, it must have been
gratifying when – after playing with Evans's trio on his 1972 European
tour – Oxley was invited back to the States to play with him. Although
Oxley wanted to develop his own music and refused the invitation,
there's always been a lot of coming and going between jazz and Free
Improvisation.

In my view, one led to another. I think it tells you what not to do, what
to leave out, how to get something that's more close to your personality.
When you know what exists, you know what to leave out. That's what
I call developing – not copying. Influence has quite a different meaning
in my view than imitation. I didn't find any conflict with it, it's my

personality. Derek went to London, Gavin went to America. I thought, I'm not sticking up here on my own because there's not much to do after they left. [*TO* 25–ix–1997]

Were you still playing conventional music during the week?

By that time we'd got the sack from Chesterfield because of our musical contribution and we'd been doing some work in Manchester, travelling every night over the Pennines. I don't think that was with Gavin. By then, Gavin had gone. The Chesterfield thing only lasted a year, by '64 it was over. [*TO* 25–ix–1997]

When you went to London, what sustained you?

I had my work in Ronnie Scott's quite a few months of the year. The rest of the time, I used to pop up at the Little Theatre. Derek and I had quite close contact still. I stayed with him when I first went down there. He was living in Fulham. Later of course came the period of amplification and electronics. That was sustaining. [*TO* 25–ix–1997]

Oxley stakes a claim for the originality of the Joseph Holbrooke Trio even more forcefully than Bailey. As far as he is concerned, isolation in Sheffield and regular practice allowed the trio to develop a musical language distinct from jazz.

The point I'm making is that with the three of us being so-called isolated in Sheffield – away from the jazz scene and jazz business – we were benefiting from a more objective standpoint. [*TO* 1–ix–2000]

If you subscribe to official histories that look at fame and record sales rather than the musical evidence, the English name that looks most significant for jazz guitar is John McLaughlin. Miles Davis flew McLaughlin over to New York to play on *Bitches Brew*, almost a declaration that jazz needed an English, rockist input. Tony Oxley played on McLaughlin's *Extrapolation*, a record cited by some as a pivotal moment in Free Improvisation's influence on jazz.

That was a job. John used to come to Ronnie Scott's when I was working there as a house drummer. On the first set, it was possible for some people to come in and play with the trio that would be working later on with the guest – the guest didn't come until the third set, because there were always two things going on: we'd do the first as a trio, then the next band would play and then we'd come on with the guest. John would make a point of coming in and using that first set to have a play. Then John had this chance to make this record, and he was having trouble finding someone who could play those time signatures. As I'd come from classical music, that was no problem for me . . . also I'd gone through that area of eighteen quavers in a bar: it was not difficult for me to work and do something with those time signatures other than just plonk out the time. And I was completely broke at that time, absolutely no money. John asked me if I'd be prepared to do it, and I said yes. There were certain people – in the musicians' court that we had, six or seven people – who thought it was perhaps a bit strange for me to be doing that. By that time, John was a friend, he came in Ronnie's – he always came to listen to the Americans, of course. I got to know him, and I thought yes, if he can't find anyone else who can cope with this. I would never misunderstand that record. I find it astonishing how many people like it. I call it a pop record. [*TO* 25–ix–1997]

Because it was very arranged and worked out?

No, because sometimes the tunes needed eight in a bar instead of swing, which for a drummer was . . . I actually never did that eight-in-a-bar thing, if I did I made it necessarily interesting in order to disguise it, in a way. I don't have the glorification of that record that many people do: if anyone asks me about it, I put it in perspective. I know what it is and what it was. At the same time I'm doing *The Baptised Traveller* [CBS 52664, 1969], *4 Compositions for Sextet* [CBS 64071, 1970], *Ichnos* [RCA SF8215, 1971] for major companies – that was my real work. The consequence of doing a record like *Extrapolation* is that it becomes more popular than your own work, and you're attached to it. You become part of that illusion. *Now* it might be quite clear; at that time many people wouldn't know I was doing something else. [*TO* 25–ix–1997]

To me, the critical function is a matter of ignoring illusions created by sales figures and looking at the music. But critics get taken by the glamour of success . . .

Yes, don't they.

I think Derek associates it with class. The working musicians are the productive side of things. Record company people and critics get in the way.

There is an element of that, yeah. In this sense: they don't give anything to it, they take. They take what's there and – excuse my French – piss it about. Our thing is to give to it. I think that's what he means, and there is this thing with class because he believes – up to a point, unless he's changed his mind – that most of the revolution comes from the working class. [*laughs*] I can't really say, I'm not a psychologist. The main thing for me is that I enjoyed life much better being a musician, a working musician, than working in the rolling mills or doing the ovens, even though I suppose I thought I was doing a necessary job at the time. I did have a feeling for music, that was always clear to me. Didn't matter, the instrument: it wasn't, I want to be a piano player, or . . . a drummer. I did play the piano when I was about eight for a while, until the piano disappeared. Music was quite important for me. [*TO* 25–ix–1997]

You're very blunt about class. Blunter than Derek, even.

My music is basically political by its existence, because it can't deny the background. If you come from such a place as we come from, you do understand the functions and the different strata of society. We know where we were – down there – doing more or less what we were told, or starve. We chose to – not starve – but put that in a very prominent position in our development, the thing that we thought was important. Whatever we participated in, like this Cabaret club, that was temporary. [*TO* 25–ix–1997]

How was the Incus record label founded?

It was after I understood that CBS were not to release my third LP, the one which would have been *Ichnos*. The recording outlet was disappearing – many musicians were not being recorded at all. I suggested to Derek we should start our own company. He agreed, but of course we needed money. A friend of mine – Mike Walters – offered to finance the idea. To start it off we had a meeting. He stated he did *not* want to be involved in the running of the company but would be happy to finance it. So, we needed a third member. Evan Parker was invited to fill the spot. I left Incus for various reasons a few years later. Subsequently

Evan Parker left. It's now run by Derek and Karen Brookman. [*TO* 1–
ix–2000]

The fallout over Incus and other matters created a split among the free
improvisors: Bailey and Oxley have remained deeply resentful of Evan
Parker's behaviour. Oxley told me:

> I haven't had much to do with him for years, but what comes to mind
> when this is referred to, is, in my opinion, 'the need for truth above
> personal gain'. [*TO* 1–ix–2000]

I brought the issue round to musical aesthetics. Having been the target
of a furious public dressing-down by Evan Parker for criticising the
romanticism of a Keith Tippett solo piano performance, I was interested
in hearing Oxley's opinion of musicians who bring tonal procedures
into free-improvised music.

> Of course, Keith Tippett is free to do what he likes, but there are two
> things – there's a bridge, we crossed that in the sixties – now we've
> found and developed what we have, I see no reason to bring that from
> the past into this language. [*TO* 25–ix–1997]

I mention that one issue that fascinates me is that Duke Ellington was
popular and Webern wasn't – yet I feel they're both aspects of modernism. Oxley's reply is succinct:

> That's not just the music, it's society, the way it's structured. [*TO* 25–
> ix–1997]

In this discussion, Oxley went beyond the bounds usually observed in
published discussions of Free Improvisation, but in doing so he touched
upon aspects of class and creativity that are crucial in understanding the
Joseph Holbrooke Trio's contribution to musical history. I reproduce
them without apology.

In 1997, Incus issued a two-CD set of duets by Bailey and Oxley. It
was an opportunity to inform people about an ongoing musical partnership that, because of Tony Oxley's later move to Germany and the

schism with Evan Parker, was little known in England. *Hi-Fi News* printed the following review:*

DEREK BAILEY AND TONY OXLEY
SOHO SUITES
INCUS CD29/30 (2 CDs, 105m 10s)
Guitarist Derek Bailey and drummer Tony Oxley pioneered Free Improvisation in Sheffield in the 60s. As house drummer at Ronnie's, Oxley has had more time for jazz than Bailey, but he's thoroughly attuned to his slashing, clashing soundworld. Indeed, his zinging compatibility actually suggests that Free Improvisation may simply be a name for jazz that's still alive and progressing. This double set comprises two performances in locations of the same name divided by the Atlantic (each disc is printed with an appropriate map): the first in Soho, London in 1977, the second in So Ho, New York in 1995. Bailey always shines with a powerful percussionist, and Oxley is one of the best: this is a chance to assess how both have developed.

On the London suite, Oxley builds firm yet elaborate metrical structures into which Bailey pours a dazzling variety of motifs. Oxley's playing his electronic kit, and the two players meld into fractal modernism, iridescent with fascinating detail. At the conclusion the musicians send out chimes as if to signal satisfaction with their work. They're right to be pleased.

On the New York suite, the two players dispense with any scaffolding and get straight to the dialogue. Oxley's acoustic kit sends woody rattles into the heart of Bailey's new zigzag vehemence. There are tense moments and risks (fifteen minutes into 'Rivington' they sound exposed and vulnerable). More peaks and more troughs than the earlier date. On 'Lafayette', Bailey teases an over-obsequious audience with a false ending, and the music explodes with helter-skelter mirth. Alternately sentimental and aggressive, this is very serious fun: musicians asking each other what the point is of it all, without relenting. Veteran players

---

* According to *Hi-Fi News*'s weird and wonderful method of rating, a CD is assessed for sound quality (A = 'Fine modern recording'; B = 'Good, some minor reservations'; C = 'Only moderately convincing'; D = 'Poor sound' and H = 'Historical source, *eg* 78rpm') and for performance (1 = 'Very Good'; 2 = 'Good'; 3 = 'Moderate'; 4 = 'Poor'; H = 'Historical'). Reviewers are allowed asterisks for exceptionally fine recordings and performances. Designed for rating classical records, these codes assume that the music itself is beyond criticism ('classic'). Since I was dealing with jazz and improvisation, I took 'performance' to mean the quality of the music in a general sense.

who risk *more* as they age? This bucks the clichés with vengeance. Shattering. A:1** [*Hi-Fi News*, May 1998]

Bailey's pointillist delicacy on the London disc makes a dramatic contrast to his scything metal attack on the New York one, where he seems to be raging against the idea of relying on any tried-and-true methodology. Likewise, it's strange to hear Oxley perform an acoustic version of his electronic drumming on the later recording: without those weird hinge-point flexitones and sizzling sustains, his beats sound gorgeously reverberant and organic. However, the way that time appears to stand still, opening up myriad extra pockets for fountains of variegated guitar and percussion sounds, has a similar quality on both discs, even though the two duos were recorded eighteen years apart.

GAVIN BRYARS

The presence in the Joseph Holbrooke Trio of Gavin Bryars, a philosophy student at Sheffield University, gives the lie to any accusations of workerism that might be levelled at Oxley and Bailey. Bryars brought in awareness of new developments in classical music. However, he had been fascinated by jazz since his teens.

I played piano from when I was about six. As a teenager, when I was still at school, I had a small jazz group, which actually used to play privately at my house on Saturday evenings. I don't think there was a bass in Goole – where I came from, I don't think anyone had a bass. My mother was a cellist and I loved the bottom end. When I used to listen to pop records, I would always know the bass line. I'd never follow the words or the melody, I would always follow the harmonic patterns. When I was doing the piano, it was the progressions that interested me. When I went to university I had free access to the resources there. In the loft there was a record player, and I remember spending hours listening to Hindemith and Stravinsky, stuff I'd never really heard before. Downstairs, in the basement, was a bass and some other instruments and no one was playing the bass, so I took it up and started practising. I got a book about technique and scales and started teaching myself, making a few mistakes, the angle of my hand wasn't right and so on. I got those corrected when I started having proper lessons. [*GB* 2–x–1997]

If Derek Bailey started out wanting to be Charlie Christian, then Bryars wanted to be Scott LaFaro.

There's a specific approach to improvisation I'm looking for: a Charlie Haden, rather mellow, Arild Andersen sort of sound, and that's very specific, the last ten, fifteen years sort of sound. You might find someone there who's all right playing Neal Hefti arrangements, but that's not the kind of bass I want – it's rather plodding, four-square, it won't sing, it would have that melodic sound. That's what I was always looking for, the ability of the bass to give sustained, legato sounds, not the short plops you get on some early recordings like Percy Heath and Tommy Potter, I used to really hate that stuff. So I was very involved with the bass as an instrument, and once I started playing jazz seriously, I really did get to know the approaches and the sounds of individual bass players. I wasn't very fond of Mingus. I found the way he attacked the beat – to me, he was pushing it too much all the time, a little bit forward. Richard Davis, too, though I admired his playing, he's always ahead of the beat. As long as you know that, it's not going to accelerate. I used to worship Scott LaFaro, that was the sound I wanted to make, so I had to work quite hard on the instrument because LaFaro's sound does have that beautiful legato sustain. It was quite hard to get that on the cheap instrument I had at the time. [*GB* 2–x–1997]

Bryars originally attended Sheffield University to study music, but found that music was part of a dual honours degree with a modern language. Although he had a French A level, he decided he'd had enough of languages, so switched to a single honours degree in philosophy. He remained part of the university music scene by playing bass in the university orchestra. He also played jazz in a trio with a student who later became a professional guitarist, Eddie Spate. This trio played during an interval break for Gerry Rollinson's quartet. Rollinson and Bailey noticed Bryars's playing and decided he'd be better than their current bass player, Len Stewart (who according to Bryars 'looked a bit like Arthur Askey and ran a music shop in Sheffield'). Bryars's first rehearsal with the quartet was in Derek's home, playing 'conventional jazz' – along with the conventional tests and trials.

The first thing I did, they were testing me to see how good I was. The piece they threw at me was actually John Coltrane, 'Moment's Notice', because it had a lot of changes, changes every beat in some cases, just to see if I could get my fingers round these changes. It was also in an awkward key – D flat, something like that. A real kind of challenge . . . it's also quite quick. It's just the kind of bastard thing that jazz musicians do. If you get on the stand they always throw 'Cherokee' at the fastest possible tempo to see if the bass player can keep up – and snigger if he has to go into two in a bar instead of four. It was a lot of that. It was also a genuine attempt to see if I could find my way around. At that time it wasn't Joseph Holbrooke, it was a jazz group, which was a quartet – with Gerry Rollinson on the piano. That was the group that used to play every Saturday at the Grapes. Until Gerry moved away and we played as a trio, and then started moving – through various devices – towards free playing. Initially, we were playing harmonic jazz, mostly the approach of the Bill Evans Trio at the '61–'62 Village Vanguard – which actually gave that liberated role to the bass and to the drums, a more melodic and less rigid format, a genuine interplay between the players. Gerry Rollinson was certainly using the Bill Evans voicings, but Derek would also try to do those on guitar, but he was also interested in Jim Hall, especially his sound – that mellow sound. I think Derek was convinced that Jim Hall did it by tuning his strings down, to get that rather rounded, almost flabby sound. It was that area of jazz – that melodic, harmonic and almost romantic area of jazz. We certainly weren't interested in hard bop or anything of that kind. The freer stuff arose out of exploring that territory. I was actively involved in jazz, and improvised music was a big thing for me at that time. I was still involved in music though I was ostensibly studying philosophy: I was more interested in playing bass. By the time I graduated, I had to fly back from playing a summer season in Jersey to do my finals. I lost interest in university life and became more and more interested in improvising. [*GB* 2–x–1997]

Although Bailey recalls Oxley and Bryars rehearsing together, Bryars reckoned that he himself was closer to Bailey.

I remember at that time when I was working with him, he used to read biographies, he was interested in political biographies, cultural biographies – and also the work of Samuel Beckett. He loved Beckett. That was unusual for a lot of people in the jazz world . . . Derek had a broader outlook and I enjoyed that. We did talk about other things, but more with Derek than with Tony. I respected and liked them as individuals. I'd guess that when I first started working with them, I was a bit in awe of them, because I was younger. At that time, I'd be nineteen years old, when I first played – that's quite young. They were working professionals. Derek was holding down regular playing jobs and doing radio sessions in Manchester. They were in a world I wasn't in. [*GB* 2–x–1997]

I asked Bryars if he had an opinion on the rhythmic side of the Joseph Holbrooke Trio. I pointed out that while Bailey had agreed with John Shiurba's suggestion, 'You were all tapping your foot, and somebody was playing the 3rd triplet offbeat in order to mask the pulse,' Oxley replied 'No, no – I was playing eighteen quavers in a bar.' What did Bryars think the time was?

That was actually in the conventional playing, when we were playing harmonic jazz. Tony and I would do some rhythm-section work, where he and I would rehearse at my flat, and Tony was trying these three-part subdivisions of the bar. I never thought of it as eighteen quavers and I guess Tony did, because the way I understood it was that each half bar was divided into triplets, triplet crotchets, and then each of those was made into triplets, which ends up with eighteen quavers – but I didn't hear it like that, that's probably how Tony was thinking of it and that's strictly what he did, but it sounded . . . I think he got some of that from listening to Elvin Jones. He found that there's this curious approach in some of the Coltrane recordings at that time, the early sixties, where sometimes you think, Christ, that's really sloppy, but in fact it's not. Tony tried to codify that and he came up with these quite tight systems. Rather than have to count it, in order to feel it, we did some rehearsing where we would simply play time and he'd do all this stuff and I'd have to be bang on the first beat, or he'd do a four-bar break and I'd be bang on, and ditto I'd play a little solo and he'd come back – so we were measuring each other's time in the same way. So we developed a kind of trust in terms of our rhythm-section playing. This was when we were still playing relatively conventionally, we were still playing time, but we were articulating time in a much looser – apparently looser – way. It wasn't always like that, it didn't become a routine. Anything could happen. We had to be ready for anything. Because we were developing those systems of trust and mutual confidence in the conventional playing, once we moved into the freer playing, that was already there – we were used to listening to each other very intensely. A lot of conventional players take it for granted that there will be that kind of cushion on which they will solo and they won't have to think about it, they know they'll get those kind of punctuations. They can just keep going in a steady four, whereas we were trying to think of other ways. Other things that we were doing – a gradual thing – was the idea of stopping the music, not always playing in time, but freezing the time at certain moments. We would try these as routines. One of the sources of that was actually the Sonny Rollins record *The Bridge* [1961, RCA LSP2527], where on pieces like 'Without a Song', he'd stop and go into a rather rhapsodic cadenza and just play through the changes in a very loose time, and then come back into it. We tried playing and then freezing on a particular chord, then playing in a free way, but over that as a single harmonic entity. That was a transitional thing, but sometimes within conventional tunes. We also tried other things. I remember slow pieces where we'd improvise on the *wrong* chord as it were, the chord ahead or the chord behind, so you had this dislocation – a way of vertically misaligning things. As a way also of being aware of where each other is, so we're not always in the same space, but we know where we are in relationship to each other. All sorts of things. I remember I did an arrangement of a Messiaen organ piece; occasionally there was a pianist called Bunny Thompson who used to play with us, who was also into that kind of stuff – but eventually it became basically just the trio. By that time, we were playing freely. There were other people who played with us from time to time. Barry Whitworth, a local trumpeter, and a student of mine, a guy who was for some reason studying composition with me, Geoff Cloke, a sax player. When Gerry Rollinson was around and Geoff was playing, he was baffled because Geoff didn't think he had to go back to harmonic jazz in order to play freely: he would say, Ornette Coleman is basic now, so let's take that as a starting point. And Gerry was saying, Geoff is nuts! So, odd frissons within that group, but essentially it was the three of us. [GB 2–x–1997]

Free music seems pretty conscious here – it's not just some kind of mystical intuitive thing . . .

By the end, long before the end, we were able just to play on these regular Saturday lunch times and just start and play and not think about anything or talk about anything and pieces would develop their own structures – and that was just down to close listening and reacting. It wasn't very clear who should start. I think I was pretty loath to start, myself. By then, there was that kind of absolute freedom that happens on the moment, but it was on the basis of having done all this stuff for so long that there were a lot of things we could take for granted, a lot of shorthands that you already knew. Also, you were aware that someone wasn't going to go off the rails, you had a sense of the parameters in which they were likely to play. [GB 2–x–1997]

And you had an audience?

Oh yeah, that was the remarkable thing. The audience which started out coming to hear us play conventional harmonic jazz stayed with us. You'd see the same faces week in, week out. Some people would miss odd weeks, but there was a regular audience and a reasonable-sized audience every week. And they stayed with all the changes that happened to the group. I remember Dave Holland coming along once, he was only starting to play bass, he was touring with Johnny Ray and playing rock'n'roll in some local clubs, just starting to play bass. Different people passing through town would come along. There was a steady local audience, absolutely, and they were genuinely intrigued and following our development, no question about that. [GB 2–x–1997]

The improvisors I've met who are influenced by John Cage (keyboardist Martin Hackett, for example, or tuba player Robin Hayward) tend to adopt his condemnation of a lot of improvising as adolescent, as showing off – not enough respect for unintentional sound. Steve Beresford once made the same point to Kenneth Ansell in *Impetus* [no. 6, 1977, p. 262]. Is that how you started to think of it?

That was part of it, but I think it went beyond that. I think you can have an interest in Cage and an interest in improvisation as well. [GB 2–x–1997]

Cage has a real animus against jazz, doesn't he? The session when he asked the jazz improvisors to stop listening to each other. It's almost like Theodor Adorno's philosophy of music: any form of collectivity is an oppression. Cage wants to break things up, achieve independence.

That's the ethos of Cage's music. In 1961 he said he had trouble with four things: Beethoven, jazz, the vibraphone and muzak. Gradually he came to terms with them individually, by appropriating them into music. I think jazz was the one he had most trouble with in the long term. Basically what I was doing – the earnings I was getting playing bass in this club – enabled me to continue studying composition after leaving university. I was studying composition with George Linstead, who was a good local musician. He was on the music staff at the university and had been passed over for the professorship. He'd written about Poulenc in the thirties, and he wrote the programme notes for the Hallé, and he was a local reviewer for concerts. He was a very open-minded man, aware of modern music. I used to study with him in a very strict way. I was using my money for that, but also to acquire music and scores. I would buy things like Cage and Christian Wolff, Morton Feldman. I remember buying that 1958 retrospective Cage concert album from George Avakian, you could only get it direct from a mail-order in New York.* We used to listen to that stuff. I remember Tony spending hours trying to bend the sound of the cymbals because in Cage's *First Construction In Metal* you hear this gong played and the pitch dips – 'Shit, how the hell do you do that?' That's because we didn't have the score. Cage actually dips it in water! But Tony didn't know that, we didn't know that. We were actively interested in those things, and I didn't see any conflict with them. For me, they were a way of enlarging my musical repertoire, my knowledge of music, my aware-ness of the possibilities of music in the late twentieth century. Little by little I started to compose things. Not particularly in the Cage idiom. We tried them with the group, graphic scores and things. We played some of those things. They were not ways of imposing things on the group, they were graphic representations of the way we played. Some of the first scores were in fact almost like me saying, 'Well, this is the way we play, and this is a map of it – and let's do this map.' It's a different format, but it was essentially what we already did. Those are some of my earliest compositions. They're gone now. I hope they've disappeared for ever. I think Cage took a couple of them, they're in a collection of his notations, so they'll be in some university in America – very embarrassing if those turned up, but I guess they exist. So there

* Currently available as the 3CD set, *The 25-Year Retrospective Concert of the Music of John Cage*, 1994, Wergo WER6247, one of the few really rewarding examples of Cage's music in recorded form.

wasn't particularly a conflict ideologically between the idea of composing and the idea of improvising at that time. Only towards the very end that happened. It was also tied up with other things too, things within improvised music which I encountered which made me feel uneasy. One of those was the first time we played in London at the Little Theatre club. There were aspects of that where I felt suddenly, this was not for me. I gave up the bass not long after that. [*GB* 2–x–1997]

In Derek's book you talk about seeing a bassist play who you felt was faking it. You don't name him.

Johnny Dyani.

He's greatly valued by some. John Stevens and Frode Gjerstad formed a trio with him called Detail. I love his playing in that trio.

Ironically, I found myself living in the same house as Johnny later, and Evan Parker was in the same house, we were all in Brondesbury Road.

You objected to Dyani playing something that 'sounded like' jazz bass, but wasn't structurally true?

It was more to do with his knowledge of the instrument. He'd got that kind of rather angular Richard Davis, Gary Peacock thing, where you'd leap from one register to another and you'd hit this note and you'd think, God that's amazing – but I could see the way his hands were going, that it was guesswork. It sounded all right, but I had a great knowledge of the instrument. Apart from rehearsing and playing with Tony and Derek, and playing every evening, I used to practise the bass up to four or five hours a day. Sometimes the bass would be in my hands for between seven and eight hours a day, even more sometimes. I knew the finger-board incredibly well. I knew exactly where everything was, I could do all kinds of things. I can't really say for certain, but I think I was a very good bass player at that time. And the very few recordings that exist I wasn't at my best, there's this rehearsal tape Derek's got that he wants to put out. I heard that, it was recorded at my flat in '65, so that's quite early, we were playing around with 'Miles' Mode'. I think at that time I'd just acquired my new bass, an old Simon Findt from the early 1800s – and I can hear on that I was feeling my way on the new instrument. It sounds reasonably competent playing, it's not flash, but it's reasonably assured. I could see when I watched Johnny playing that it was guesswork – inspired guesswork – but no more than that. And I just felt, What's the point? The other thing was the amplified bass being necessary, the bass guitar being necessary and replacing the bass – a lot of factors like that. [GB 2-x-1997]

Is it a tension between music as show and some kind of structural truth? Anyone who reads Samuel Beckett with enthusiasm is going to be prepared to make art that doesn't find an audience ... that idea of artistic militancy comes up, doesn't it?

Oh, certainly – and what we were doing in Sheffield had no relationship whatsoever with projecting or trying to find an audience or create something in order to attract people. We were playing it in a very hermetic way. Although when people quote that thing about there being a value in isolation, there's a sense in which that's slightly sentimental – like some old symphony composer living in the Lake District, Havergal Brian, chucking out his thirty-second symphony in his nineties, oh great, noble savage – but in the end, you've got to be in touch with reality. Although we were working away from London, we did listen to things. We did avidly find new recordings and listen to the radio. Tony taping stuff off the radio and bringing it along, I remember hearing some Morton Feldman on the radio for the first time, a piece for violin, tuba and piano, 1965, and we just loved that bizarre combination of instruments and the richness of the disjunctive harmony, which had completely no sense of progression but was entirely static. We could see a relationship between that and what we were doing. We would do things where things were very static and quiet for long periods – it wasn't the convention of Free Improvisation where it starts quiet, has a busy bit in the middle and then tails off towards the end. Quite often it wasn't like that at all – there'd be long periods of very very quiet music. Some pieces where we'd play for thirty minutes and it would never get above a *pianissimo*. There was a whole range of stuff going on. We were essentially hermetic, we were producing art for art's sake as a very pure activity. The fact that we had that loyal audience was very reassuring to us. We weren't just doing it in our front rooms. We were playing in public and we had that kind of following. [GB 2-x-1997]

You had difficulty finding out about new music?

Now, almost everything is available on CD. You have resources that cover everything, things like *Wire* magazine – for all its faults. Things like that weren't around then. The magazine that was most useful for jazz was actually *Melody Maker*. It was incredible that you could think of *Melody Maker* as a source for scholarship. One did have to actively seek things out. There were things on the radio. I remember as a kid in Goole hearing the Ornette Coleman Quintet on the radio, 1958 or 1959, and thinking it was fantastic. I also loved it because it was being so much reviled by the jazz press, I thought this must be great. I got to like it more and more. I tried to take that line, that if someone was putting it down, then it must be OK, to react against it there must be something there. That was just a mental tic of mine, so it didn't bother me that we were in a sense playing in isolation. One can over-romanticise the idea of us three ploughing our own furrow in this northern ghetto, because things were going on in London, independently of us, but probably a little bit later. I got to know more of that – John Stevens – later, but we didn't know about it at that time. We couldn't have known it. [*GB* 2–x–1997]

I think Derek got a lot of encouragement from the fact that Free Improvisation became a worldwide phenomenon.

If that sort of thing had been happening in '65, '66 – if there had been festivals in Holland and Germany for us to play – we may well have continued much longer, we'd have seen parallels, we would have found people doing similar things, and that would have been reassuring. [*GB* 2–x–1997]

But you didn't have that?

It wasn't there, and the very few things that we did hear on the radio were generally more conventional jazz. I remember Tony taping the trombonist Albert Mangelsdorff, which we found interesting, '65, '66, I guess. But that was the extent of it – no more than that. I remember meeting David Izenzon when the Ornette Coleman Trio was touring and talking with him and that was very useful – but they didn't know what we were doing. [*GB* 2–x–1997]

Is this why Cage and the classical route looked more viable as far as you were concerned?

We never got into the question of funding or recording with Joseph Holbrooke. The group stopped before it could become an issue. My move towards composed music was that I saw a bigger challenge there. I saw the horizons there as being infinitely wider. The number of questions that could be asked were far greater and far more complicated. This is what I expressed in Derek's book [*Improvisation: Its Nature and Practice in Music*]. When Derek interviewed me I was far more hostile to improvised music than I am now. [*GB* 2–x–1997]

You needed to separate yourself off.

That's right. I stopped playing bass in 1966. I didn't play my own bass again until 1983. For seventeen years my bass stayed in its case. I did some other playing, but not on my instrument, and not jazz. [*GB* 2–x–1997]

The end of the Joseph Holbrooke Trio was not the end of Gavin Bryars's involvements with Bailey (as we shall see in Chapter 4), but it signalled a divergence that turned out to be profound.

My disaffection with it came really quite late. It wasn't something that simmered there for a long time. We're probably looking at the last month or so, when we played together and it came to the surface. That's when I decided to stop working as a professional musician and take a teaching job, middle of 1966. I think the last time we played together as a trio was towards the end of '66, when we played a date in Northampton, which was where I had gone to teach. [*GB* 2–x–1997]

Interview over, Bryars wanted me to turn on the tape recorder again in order to recall a memory that was particularly poignant.

I do have the greatest respect for Derek. Apart from working together in this way, we also worked together in the commercial world. We played together in a cabaret club in Chesterfield and also in this quartet, a summer season in Jersey. In Chesterfield, there was a standing joke. Our first interval was just before the pubs closed. We used to go across to this pub. On the way back, I'd get – I wasn't a vegetarian in those days – I'd get a meat pie and chips, and I used to put it in the back of Derek's amplifier to keep warm until the next interval – they were valve amps . . . of course, they would heat up. You used to have the smell of pie and chips coming from the back of Derek's amplifier in Chesterfield. That was memorable. Also, when we were playing together in Jersey, we were really quite close then. I don't know if you've come across Frank Long, a really big guy – 6 feet 4 inches, big shoulders, not fat, but really big and partially deaf. He always used to come along to the Sheffield sessions. He was a specialist in fitting giant tyres: if a huge pantechnicon would lose a tyre, Frank would go and fit the tyre. He was always around us. He came to Jersey. Amazing man, he was also from Sheffield, he had that disarming thing – male thing – of calling you 'love'. We were close. I was very upset when Derek was fired from the band – the quartet in Jersey, with Gerry Rollinson and this local drummer, Benny Aaron, from the Phillippines or something, South East Asian, phenomenal technique this guy, could do single-stick rolls, but he couldn't keep time, he'd speed up, lose beats, but had incredible technique. I'd piss myself laughing working in this band. We were playing in this restaurant in St Brelade's Bay Hotel, beautiful spot, we were all living in St Helier for the summer. Derek got fired – by the management, not by the band – so we ended up as a trio for the rest of the year. I was very upset about that. I remember writing to my girlfriend at the time that, for me, Derek was the person in my musical environment who was most conscious of himself as an artist – not just as a working musician, he was actually thinking about art, in a very pure way. I was horrified that he had to go. It was a spat with the management. He'd sometimes arrive a little late. He'd come through the diners with his guitar and his amp and people would be dancing on the dance floor. It was a place where you'd get a lot of retired people, people with a bit of money. He'd say something like, 'Excuse me, would you mind getting out of the fucking way.' Quite a polite tone, then the word 'fucking' would come into it – and they'd complain to the management and he got fired. I was very upset about that. So Derek's someone I like as a person. We hardly see each other, but we've talked on the phone because of this tape of us playing 'Miles' Mode' he's found. I think Tony has some tapes from that time, but he keeps them close to his chest. We used to record a lot, not so much performances, more when we were working out in my flat. [GB 2–x–1997]

The Joseph Holbrooke Trio has acquired a legendary status.

There was this guy in California who tried to put us together in 1995, to play in Los Angeles. He went to great lengths, I was touring in Japan with my own ensemble. He was prepared to stump up for a ticket for me from Hong Kong to LA to London. It was going to cost him about £6,000, business class. For two nights – two sessions – at this place in Los Angeles! Then I was taken ill in Tokyo and my manager told me not to do it, particularly flying east. Coincidentally, Derek was ill too. This American guy tried to put it together, fly us all out from scratch, but in point of fact he couldn't raise the money for it. People keep trying! Maybe the best thing is if it doesn't happen. It's dangerous to keep going back down these by-ways. If we do play together, it's not going to be the same as playing somewhere in the sixties. I'm not going to be playing the same way and Tony and Derek have gone very different paths. It'll be interesting – a curiosity, no more than that. People will say, I was there, I got the photograph, the T-shirt, and that's it. People shouldn't read anything into it. What we did in the sixties was what we did. I valued it as an important part of my musical development, I learned a lot from it, especially from Derek. [*GB* 2–x–1997]

At the end of 1998, the Joseph Holbrooke Trio did meet and play together again – a broadcast for WDR Cologne in October, recorded live at the Stadtgarten and released as *Joseph Holbrooke '98* [Incus CD39], plus a London studio date recorded by Toby Robinson at the Moat Studio on 2 December. There was no rolling back the decades. The hushed drama evidenced by 'Miles' Mode' was the sound of musicians pioneering new spaces; now these moves are well known. The subdivided funk beat that was always there is much more audible, and, combined with plush recorded sound, some moments make one think of a Creed Taylor production. Bailey's guitar has a newfound metallic tinge (immediately recalling the spikiness of the releases with The Ruins and Tacuma/Weston), though there is a sense of humour in pitching this new, hi-tech violence into a music derived from Bill Evans. Bryars plays singing LaFaro-like notes, but also insinuatingly funky ones, adding a decadent touch. Oxley's drums have an oddly vocal quality. Throughout the performance, you do not know where the trio will go next. Although their sense of time is more confident and perhaps less exciting than the sixties unit, the musicians have extended their sonic palettes: this new, lush JHT is a surprising listen.

ANDREW SHONE

Malcolm McLaren said that to create a great rock band you need to find four people who hate each other. The members of the Joseph Holbrooke

Trio never hated each other, but my interviews with the three musicians showed that its creative differences haven't faded even today, thirty years later. To obtain another view of the Joseph Holbrooke Trio – this time from someone in the audience – I talked to Andrew Shone, who in the mid-1960s was studying architecture at Sheffield University, one year behind Bryars. A teenage jazz fan as well, he'd had his trumpet stolen while on holiday in Morocco. On his return to Sheffield, he mentioned it to Bryars, who said, 'Why not start something completely different – like double bass?' Shone borrowed one from the university, and Bryars taught him for a while.

> I became aware of Gavin because he was always involved in jazz things – whether in the students' union or in a pub somewhere. He worked his way through all the university Trad bands in the first year, then the modern bands, and then he was into all sorts of stuff. He left in '63. He told me he was doing this thing with Derek and Tony. [*AS* 9–ix–1998]

What was your own listening?

> At first it was a friend's Chris Barber and Humphrey Lyttelton records – knockout. I'd been searching in pop and skiffle and hadn't found anything particularly musical. My uncle played me a Charlie Parker record when I was ten. I hated it – like hating your first cigarette, and then twenty years later you're on twenty a day. Then I went through the whole canon, leaping back to where Barber got it from (there was a trad thing at the time, but we despised most of that, only liked the good bands), went back to Joe Oliver and Kid Ory and Johnny Hodges, then someone brought in a Gerry Mulligan record – that propelled us forward thirty years – then got to Bird and Dizzy. I learned about Benny Goodman and Dicky Wells, the whole gamut, in a pretty short space of time. By the time I got to university I was into the Rollins/Coltrane thing – you liked one or the other, I kind of liked both. I bought *Giant Steps* while I was still at school and that absolutely blew me away, fantastic. I bought *Kind of Blue* because it had Coltrane on it. I changed my mind then about Miles, I'd only heard bad Miles on Charlie Parker records before that . . . as a youngster I preferred Dizzy. Listened to anything, any live music that was going on. [*AS* 9–ix–1998]

For this writer, after dealing with Bailey's prickliness about jazz, Shone's enthusiasm was a relief (it's also pretty typical of Free Improvisation fans, up to and including audiences today). Shone heard about the Saturday lunchtime gigs from Bryars.

I knew Gavin because he was a student, but I wasn't aware of Derek and Tony until Gavin told me he was playing with them. His contacts were much better than mine, he knew the Manchester scene and the Leeds scene. When I first heard Derek he'd been a professional for ten years. At first it was more than a trio, they had a piano player called Bunny Thompson – he played on the ocean liners, sometimes he'd be around, then he'd disappear for two or three months. He'd heard everyone in New York. The fifth player was Barry Whitworth, already a well-established, well-known, very good trumpet player – the north of England's answer to Dizzy Gillespie. It was those five at the Grapes pub, upstairs. In those days there'd be a few regulars supping Tetleys downstairs. Outside lavatory, bloody cold in winter, a most unprepossessing place except it was in the middle of Sheffield. It was a neutral, blank canvas for them to start. There were no preconceptions about what sort of music would be played. It was just word of mouth, not a hell of a lot of people. I used to be on the door for them. Saturday lunchtime, one o'clock. If we got over thirty, it was a good day. Some Saturdays it might be down to ten. Some people were very loyal. Even if they were more interested in the rock scene, they'd come down regularly. The trio would do the latest Bill Evans that had come out, they'd have their own arrangement of that. That suited the audience, most of whom were into Bill Evans. Derek and Gavin and Tony were ahead of me, they'd heard this stuff – 'Waltz for Debbie'. Tony had heard Cecil Taylor back in 1959. This place suited what they wanted to do, miserable enough, blank enough. I did do a little bit of advertising, but if you'd put posters up all over town, you'd still only have got thirty or forty people anyway. Those people came nearly every week and developed an interest. It wasn't only Bill Evans, but everyone liked Evans at the time, and the three of them were very deeply affected by his music one way or another. Gavin completely modelled himself on Scott LaFaro for a couple of years. To a very amusing extent: he'd do his hair like Scott LaFaro! Evans had a more sophisticated approach to harmony, over and above what people had come to expect from a Bobby Timmons or even a Wynton Kelly or Oscar Peterson. And Paul Motian – I can see why they all liked it. They were very anxious to get out of the 4/4 time base. Because they played standards – I can still recall the feel of Derek sitting there playing Horace Silver's 'Song For

My Father', which was a favourite of his – they'd play that, and Monk and Coltrane, but the Evans stands out because they'd do so much of his material. People who were there dug this, and I think this was subconsciously a good ploy. It got them playing together in a well-understood format, with chord structure, then when they'd had a beer at two o'clock and everyone had a chat, they'd come back and do the freer, more experimental stuff, stuff they'd written themselves basically. It developed virtually week by week. They would rehearse for this sometimes, or try out something new midweek when they could fit it in. It was pretty well structured, but the way they improvised within this was extremely free. They really had started to listen. Of course musicians have always listened to each other, but what I mean is that the cue was purely taken on what was going on around them rather than any set structure to fall back on. I think they had to work hard at it until they got to that point where they were so familiar with each other that they could do this and make it sound good. [AS 9–ix–1998]

They held people's attention?

Absolutely riveted. As individuals, Gavin would jump up and down the bass like LaFaro, come up from the E string and rocket to the bridge and then descend in these clusters and carve something out in the middle – and meanwhile Derek would be playing very very quiet complicated chords behind, and then he'd suddenly punctuate something and the whole room would shake like someone had let a cannon off, metallic adrenalin! I was always surprised to see such a quiet, good-humoured, good-natured man as Derek sitting there crouched over his Gibson hardly moving and these incredible sounds would come out, quite arhythmic and very accented. This was in the context of people going home and putting on their latest Wes Montgomery, which we all loved of course. Against that sort of guitar playing – or Jim Hall – it was quite something else! [AS 9–ix–1998]

Why did he do it?

I never discussed it with Derek. The only person I ever talked to about aesthetic aspects was Gavin. I remember having a book about Cage and Marcel Duchamp which I gave him. That took him into a different direction. They were doing this virtually in isolation. Apart from playing Dolphy tunes, Trane tunes, Evans, they weren't *jazz fans*, they were musicians. They were basically interested in what they were doing themselves. After they'd absorbed Dolphy–Coltrane–Evans they wanted to move on, that was it. That was in their heads. I'm saying this in retrospect. As a member of the audience, I was behind them. A lot of my thinking has been retrospective. At the time, we just loved it, enjoyed it for what it was. [*AS* 9–ix–1998]

Did you have an idea that it was important, that people should pay attention to it?

I knew it was important – and certain other people. I never became disillusioned. There was a massive rock boom going on at the time. No one had ever seen anything like that before in popular music, I don't think. It was against that background – the whole jazz thing was against that background. I found it paradoxical. While a lot of my friends were going to rock concerts and buying rock records, I could come down to Ronnie's and hear these amazing tenor players every fortnight. The jazz scene in the 1960s was suppressed commercially by rock, but there was a fantastic amount of great music. I don't think it'd have made any difference at the Grapes. There was an elderly bank manager who used to come every week, who Tony knew, called Jack Crawley. Tony introduced me to Jack, and I used to go up to Jack's house once a fortnight. We'd sit and listen to Miles's records and he'd tell me how he got into jazz in 1926 on the radio. I never felt that what I was hearing was out of the tradition . . . it was scary – you thought, it'll collapse in a heap and nothing will happen in a minute – but you didn't feel that often. It was difficult to place what they were playing in a context of anything else, there weren't many people doing it anywhere. I think John Stevens was starting to do it in London a bit. [*AS* 9–ix–1998]

Why is Free Improvisation so despised?

Maybe because it's very hard.

Hard to do?

Yeah. You have to be a good musician to do it. You know – can Picasso paint? Yes, because you've seen his early stuff.

But Derek courted confusion in that area by being fascinated by what he calls the polytechnic 'art' people – he found that stimulating, but for people who want to see evident skill, it's disorienting.

Surely that's deliberate? They were striving even from those early days to be as free as possible. As Tony said, he wanted to get out of that jazz thing where the drummer had to *get it on* first and then everyone would come in on it. I could feel that happening at the time. They were deliberately making attempts to destroy the structure in order to get at what they wanted to do, which was as near to total freedom as you can get. I remember going to see Ornette Coleman at the Manchester Free Hall and running into Tony at the interval, and he says, 'They're still playing time, Andy!' – because he was desperately trying to get away from it. But he's one of the best time drummers I've ever heard, actually. [*AS* 9–ix–1998]

I think he always actually plays time, it's just very delayed and flexible . . .

The music was really swinging hard, in my opinion. Right through jazz history there have been different sorts of swing. I suddenly realised this is what they were doing and I could feel the whole thing, even though no one was playing the beat at all. Sometimes it was very powerful, like listening to the Basie Orchestra. [*AS* 9–ix–1998]

Derek doesn't favour comments like that – his whole idea is that the Joseph Holbrooke Trio dumped jazz as a model.

I know, but to me it's still in the tradition of jazz and it's shown an interest in, and written about by, the jazz community rather than the classical community, isn't it? [*AS* 9–ix–1998]

Derek talks about freedom in music, but every note he plays seems to be driven by necessity – there's nothing lax, it's always antagonistic, rigorous . . .

His conversation is like that actually. I always find it extremely pleasant and amusing to talk to him, but he comes out with surprising things, or complete irrelevancies. I remember taking a friend to meet him, years ago, when he lived in Thornhill Road in Islington, and instead of him telling Pete what he was doing musically, he said you must have some of this fruitcake, my mother sent it through the post this morning . . . He talked all afternoon about fruitcake! I understand that more now, but it was slightly off-putting at the time. I suspect he feels it's only if there's a certain discipline and a certain hard-edged quality that you can

Derek Bailey, guitar player, anytime: 'Where? I don't know. It's suitably enigmatic'.

Percy Wing, Derek's maternal grandfather (in centre wearing trilby) outside the
Sheffield pub where he played piano and banjo, 1918.

William Bailey, Derek's paternal grandfather, on his 90th birthday, 1946.

Freddy Francis and Derek Bailey: young bucks on Blackpool Pier, 1948.

Derek Bailey as conductor: 'I worked my way through the military band. I played drums, I played the bugle, I played the big drum, and I finished up waving the fucking mace around!', 1944.

Three sailors from HMS Illustrious at Stocksbridge: Derek Bailey, Unk., Slim Neate, 1949.

Derek works for J. Arthur Rank: 'You think I can play this thing, don't you?', 1956.

Harry Richmond Trio, with Derek Bailey on double bass and Count Basie on rumba shakers, at the Green Room: 'Sheffield's at-that-time most posh restaurant, located in a cinema. American jazz musicians ate there. Not only did we play to these guys, we would on occasions play with them', 1956.

Gordon Lee Trio: Gordon Lee (bass guitar), Danny Birch (accordian), Derek Bailey (guitar): 'I never saw Gordon carry his bass, always got someone else ... very clever man', 1958.

Derek Bailey: Charlie Appleyard's Biographical Wallchart, 1997. Coloured felt tips and biro on paper, 23" x 32". Crowndale Court, Somers Town (Collection Militant Esthetix).

achieve freedom. I can see that in an architectural context too. I tried Free Improvisation, actually. I used to play in a little group with a couple of guys, and we used to rehearse in Imperial College. We had two students who came in, and we were trying hard to master some Coltrane chords that were very difficult. They joined in, and it was a mess. To me it proves the point – you can't create out of nothing, you've got to come out against some kind of boundary. [AS 9–ix–1998]

What did you compare the Joseph Holbrooke Trio to?

Even as late as '64, I was finding some of the later Coltrane pretty difficult to come to grips with, I'd slip on some earlier stuff or '59 Miles and think I was an old reactionary. But through seeing these guys doing it . . . I think *that* was the important thing that happened at the Grapes as far as the audience went, because I think the audience, however small, has probably been fairly influential over the years – in a minor, low-key way – of spreading the word. The way they did known music – and even then it was fairly cutting-edge music – that people in the audience were listening to already or had heard, they were then able to have a twenty-minute break and a beer and move into this new area. [AS 9–ix–1998]

Has Free Improvisation changed since 1966?

I think people are better at it. I couldn't say exactly technically why, but I think the people practising it have heard a lot of it and are more used to experiencing it and playing it and they have developed their own – even if they're intuitive – their own ways of approaching it. It's more likely now you can put three or four established musicians together and get something interesting out of it than you could way back then. Then everyone felt they had to have the drummer playing four and the bass player laying down the rock-solid bass and so on, the piano player supplying the chords. I've never talked to Bailey about politics, but there's an element of 'three northern lads kicking out' with the Joseph Holbrooke Trio. There were certain things in the sixties that proclaimed a classlessness – okay, it didn't fully work and it didn't overthrow the system, but it attempted to – and I think jazz musicians were doing it on an even further-out level. To get involved with Free Improvisation was kicking against any respectability that jazz might just about have been getting at those stages. It's like Bird keeping the white guys off the stand with his difficult tunes and fast tempos . . . finding something new because it's overthrowing the establishment, though back in those days I never thought about it politically. It was just music and I liked it. [*AS* 9–ix–1998]

What about the high-volume stuff Derek is playing now, the blow-out gigs with the Ruins and Bill Laswell and Pat Metheny? Does that seem like a bizarre change from the silences of Joseph Holbrooke?

I heard Derek Bailey do feedback before Hendrix. I remember it because he started waving his guitar around in front of the amp. I was thinking – and I know other people were because I talked to them afterwards – what the fuck's Derek doing here, there's an awful noise coming out! He knew exactly what he was doing. It had happened by accident at home or whatever and he was going to use it. [*AS* 9–ix–1998]

THE 1966 LEE KONITZ TOUR

The Joseph Holbrooke Trio was one manifestation of the opening-up of parameters that occurred to jazz in the early 1960s. There are parallels to be drawn to contemporary recordings by Joe Harriott in London – *Free Form* (1960), *Abstract* (1962) – and Krzysztof Komeda in Warsaw – *Astigmatic* (1965). In Birmingham, Evan Parker was also working with a repertoire based on tunes by John Coltrane and Bill Evans. Joseph Holbrooke played regularly at the Grapes until 1966. In that year the trio toured with the American alto saxophonist Lee Konitz. Andrew Shone helped to organise the tour. How did that come about?

After one of these Saturday things, I remember standing outside the pub talking, and Derek said: 'Konitz is coming over, you know – he's playing Ronnie's. I think we should organise a tour – you can do it.' I found myself in this frantic three weeks organising a tour for Lee Konitz of northern universities, down to getting pianos tuned. Everyone was suddenly Lee Konitz mad for six months. That was very interesting. We did Sheffield, Manchester, Leeds, Liverpool, Hull. He was surprisingly into free music himself. He used to do strange things like carry a pocket radio in his inside pocket whilst he was playing on stage. He'd be listening to Radio 3 – or the Third Programme as it was called then –

through an earplug, and picking up bits of music he liked and incorporating them in solos! [*AS* 9–ix–1998]

Derek's memory is slightly different. According to him, Lee Konitz started the tour with Gavin and Tony and a piano player. Joseph Holbrooke were on the same bill at the Peel in Leeds. Derek's involvement came about then.

> After their first set, Joseph Holbrooke played. In the second half Lee asked me to play with them, so I played with them, and then he fired the pianist and we worked for the rest of the week as a quartet. I don't think it was the pianist that Lee objected to, it was the pianos he was being provided with in the clubs. [15–x–1997]

In 1987, Derek invited Konitz to play at Company Week. So was playing with him in 1966 a big deal?

> I always liked him from very early on – late forties, early fifties. When I was interested in jazz, I used to think he was one of the rare unusual voices. The reason I invited him to Company was partly to do with the set-up. I wouldn't have invited Lee as a matter of fact to any other Company but that one – it was more or less a jazz Company. Company often reflected, unintentionally sometimes, what was *going on*. One of the things that was going on at that time – '87 – was the jazz resurrection. He was the best possible guy for that Company. And also, he wanted to do it. That's important. He's an unusual character. Have you heard his stuff from the late forties? I was knocked out with that when I was young. I think his alto sounds like a guitar. [15–x–1997]

Derek's interest in Konitz is very specific. It stems from a certain period of experiment that Derek frequently mentions in interviews. Interestingly enough the American sax player Anthony Braxton, though he emerged from a Black Nationalist milieu, frequently does the same.

> Lee now – and also I found this when we played with him in '66 – plays far more kind-of beboplike than he used to when he was young. Lee has, as virtually all radical players do, gone backwards. It's usually described as 'maturity'. He's much more of a conventional player now than he ever was. Those tunes he used to play – Tristano's tunes – they weren't conventional bebop tunes. They were often faster for a start, and more complex. You should check it out. It's cool stuff, for sure,

they were the inventors of that Cool thing, but it had something *new*. It was one of those things that always seemed to be happening then, like first hearing Clifford Brown: 'Fuck me! What's this?' The surprise thing that jazz lost at some point. [15–x–1997]

I also asked Gavin Bryars about the Lee Konitz tour.

There's a published Lee Konitz discography and the second item on that is actually a recording of Lee Konitz with Derek Bailey, Tony Oxley and 'unknown bass player' in Manchester. That's me! It's nice to be 'unknown bs'. That's when Konitz was also interested in free stuff, but he would go in and out of playing free and playing tunes. I remember when we first played – I think it was the students' union in Sheffield – we didn't really rehearse, we just talked about things. I was aware of his music. Backstage, while I was tuning up the harmonics on the bass, he was watching and he said, 'Oh you're interested in bowed stuff?' I said, 'Yes.' He said, 'Would you like to start?' So to tune up I said I'd just play a very long A, and that's what we did. He came in, then out of the side of his mouth he said, 'Star Eyes' and broke into it – and I'd have to know, 'Shit! It's in E flat', you'd have to know that. That was part of the currency of being a jazz player. You'd have to know all the tunes and the keys they were normally in. At one point I was playing this rather angular two-in-a-bar and he goes, 'Four, play four!' So I had to play a walking line, because that's what he wanted. It was in and out of that sort of stuff, we did those things. [*GB* 2–x–1997]

Although Bailey is not especially keen that anyone hear it, there is a tape of the Lee Konitz–Joseph Holbrooke Quartet in existence, recorded in Manchester on 19 March 1966. It includes 'Carvin' The Bird', 'I Remember You' and 'Out of Nowhere' – all bebop standards – taken at a tidy pace, with Konitz playing knotty and introspective solos. Although it could become the *locus classicus* for disproving the contention that Bailey 'cannot play' – against socking cymbal work from Oxley and fleet runs from Bryars, Bailey plays delightful bop runs that have the all-important element of expressive phrasing – people who need such proofs aren't worth the music. Konitz's mournful tone is authentically moving, and even though the Joseph Holbrooke Trio were probably a little disappointed that he was in such a bebop bag, the gig sounds like it was great. A sizeable audience applauded each number enthusiastically.

ARGUMENTS WITHIN THE RANKS OF
JOSEPH HOLBROOKE

Mr Bryars, you're one of the few composers whose compositions Derek will admit to having played . . .

He asked me for a composition, he commissioned me: the second Incus release, 1971. Derek and I stayed in touch. Although I had this antipathy towards improvisation, it was probably to that type of improvisation we were doing with Joseph Holbrooke, whatever type that was – this mysterious genre that is the missing link in the evolution of improvised music! When I came back from Illinois having worked with John Cage, I'd been involved over there in some areas of improvisation, but with composers – within the idiom of the classical avant-garde. When I came back in late '68, early '69, I was involved in duo work with John Tilbury, the pianist, and we started working together, which eventually became the Music Improvisation Company – MIC – we started doing some things at the Little Theatre with a quintet that was me, John Tilbury, Derek, Evan and Jamie Muir. Those five used to play regularly at the Little Theatre, '68 and '69. But there was a clear split between the two classical guys and the three that came from the post-jazz/free-improvised world. I remember things used to break up and collapse because I would start fooling around. I'd do things like putting on gramophone records and turn on the radio, Derek couldn't handle that because it was too referential, you're bringing in another world, it wants to be sparking off between us. Once I started doing that sort of stuff, the music had to stop. [GB 2–x–1997]

A compromise was reached by evenings like that on Monday 24 November 1969, when the first part of a concert in the Edward Herbert Building of Loughborough University consisted of John Tilbury and Gavin Bryars playing Bryars's *Some of the Interesting Places You'll See on a Long Distance Flight* and Stockhausen's *Plus-Minus*, with the MIC (Bailey, Parker, Muir and Hugh Davies on 'live electronics') playing

'Improvisations' after the interval. Did the other improvisors consider Bryars to be some kind of dada nihilist?

Something of an anarchist, anyway. I was certainly behaving in an anarchic way, and an anti-social way. Being anti-social in a free improvisation is the antithesis of the free-improvisation situation: you have to co-operate. [*GB* 2–x–1997]

Is this what guitarist John Russell talks about [*The Wire*, no. 160, June 1997] – that the initial free improvisors decided, it was OK to go and let off a revolver at the opera, but don't do it here, we're creating something . . .

That's right. I remember Han Bennink coming along to one of these things. I used to use contact mics and a rather large guitar amp – I had two cymbals contact-mic'd – and had the volume up very loud. I remember doing a cymbal roll, very high volume, for five or six minutes, and everything had to stop. Bennink thought I was crazy – *he* thought I was crazy, for Christ's sake! So I did go back to improvising, but I wasn't on the bass then. I'd do things on keyboards, on toy instruments, collections of instruments, odd bits of electronics, and so on. We did that for about a year, regularly at the Little Theatre. There was an aspect of improvisation, but I was also aware of the post-Cage musical world, Fluxus and things of that kind, where you would get the anarchic element involved. You would also get the early La Monte Young territory of undifferentiated activity going on for very long periods. I saw that area of composed music as also being part of improvised music – and vice versa. It wasn't any different to me. I wasn't thinking, OK now I'm improvising, I'm going to do this. If I was doing some relatively free, text-based pieces with Fluxus composers, the same kind of activities would go on – early Christian Wolff, for example, La Monte Young prose pieces, all that sort of stuff. [*GB* 2–x–1997]

Did performance art interest you?

It didn't really exist then. That's a term that came later, but obviously that grew out of Fluxus and through Fluxus into things like the Scratch Orchestra, which I was never a member of, but I was involved in a lot of their activities. That kind of anarchic, disruptive element was something that was prevalent in that musical world. It was something that Free Improvisation couldn't handle. It was all right if one stayed within certain relatively polite bounds, one could actually be quite busy – things are flying about – but it's between consenting adults. Once you start over-stepping the bounds, suddenly the music falls apart. [*GB* 2– x–1997]

It's interesting, because Derek likes to cast himself as the rule-breaker, the critic of music settling into orthodoxy and the known. Yet you're saying the Fluxus agenda exceeded his brief . . .

At that time. Now, I'm sure [that the Fluxus agenda exceeds his brief] – and later than '69, the seventies – that's certainly true of Derek as a player. I remember hearing him in other contexts and he would be deliberately disruptive. He'd do things against the natural evolution of what's going on, in order to fundamentally change its direction. At that time I think he was too close to other more controlled areas of improvisation to take those risks. When I stopped playing in '66, Derek and I didn't stop working together, we continued over quite a long period – '68, '69. In 1971, when Incus first started, he asked me for a piece. I gave him *The Squirrel and the Ricketty Racketty Bridge* – for two guitars. On one side of the record he wanted three composed pieces: Misha Mengelberg did one, I can't remember who the other one was, another Dutch guy.* The other side was solo improvisations. What I wanted to do for that, was give him something to play that he would never ever do naturally in an improvised music situation, so it wouldn't sound anything like the rest of the album. That's why I got him to play two guitars, flat, and play them like keyboards – because he would never do that. And he did it and he recorded it, and it was fine. I did write some more conventional, Cage-type pieces for him in the mid-sixties, he's probably still got the scores of them – which would really embarrass the hell out of me. At that time, again, it was to challenge him, to take him out of his normal milieu. At that time, I was actually living in the same house as Evan Parker and Johnny Dyani and a few others in Kilburn, so I was aware of that Incus world going on. In '68, there was an exhibition called Cybernetic Serendipity: I put together a group to play some pieces by Herbert Brun, and Derek played guitar in that – and I played bass, though that was conventional written stuff [the performance was at the ICA, London, 29 August 1968]. In '75, when I did the first albums for Obscure, Derek played guitar on the first

* Willem Breuker.

recording of *Jesus' Blood Never Failed Me Yet*. Derek said that he's had more drinks bought for him on the strength of that than anything to do with his own playing! The second Obscure one, a piece called '1–2, 1–2–3–4', Derek's playing guitar on that – a little strumming part, and people like Cornelius Cardew are on there, Brian Eno, Phil Manzanera from Roxy Music, those people are all on this track and Derek was in all that. Later, we did another version of *The Squirrel and the Ricketty Racketty Bridge* for Obscure with four guitarists – me, [Brian] Eno, Fred Frith and Derek. We were crossing paths all the time. When I came back from America I had nowhere to live, and I slept on his floor in Islington for a time. We stayed close – not close, we just stayed in touch. [GB 2–x–1997]

It's as if you and Derek worked out your philosophies of music by contradicting each other . . .

And I counter that by throwing the gauntlet back at improvisors. When I'd stopped improvising and I was living in the same house as Evan, I used to refer to Derek and Evan as like these guys who're given false teeth and come out of the cottonfields and start playing Dixieland again. Are you guys still doing that? I'll buy you a new plectrum, maybe you'll start playing again. I used to take the piss out of them murderously. I viewed what they were doing as a lower form of life, like the Amoeba Brothers starting to swing again – like it was really history. There was a lot of banter between us, all the time. Actually, that conceals a certain amount of respect if you play that game, but if you really mean the insults to really hurt and go to the quick, then it goes too far. They were aware that it was banter. In the same way, Derek was against composers, and Tony Oxley used to talk about the stuff I did as 'nuts and bolts music' – that was the most adventurous thing he could think of, from Cage's prepared piano, nuts and bolts – I remember Roger Heaton telling me that there was a programme about Tony's stuff on Radio 3 once, and he was talking a little bit about the past and they mentioned my name and he said, 'Of course, Gavin's now a composer – nice one, Gavin.' On Radio 3 – it was such an incredibly crass thing to do. So there was a bit of animosity between us, but in quite a respectful way. But when Derek came to do his book, I thought I ought to articulate my views, because he was genuinely doing these interviews about all these approaches to improvisation. He was aware that I had been involved in a different way, so I set out some of my oppositions to improvisation. That was at a time when I was not improvising, in the seventies. I articulated some of the ideas that I had trouble with, that I grappled with when I was still in Joseph Holbrooke. The feeling, eventually, that there was a lot of redundancy, that there were things that were predictable. Even though now in retrospect I can see that there were also things that were not. I felt that certain things were coming out . . . I found that the boundaries of classical – composed – music were not so constrained as those of improvised music, ironically. In being free you actually were very very limited. [*GB* 2–x–1997]

But you have returned to your bass since then?

It was much later, in the 1980s, that I started playing bass again, when I was teaching. Some of the students knew I'd been a bass player, and a certain student was playing a transcription of an Eric Dolphy flute piece for his final recital and he needed a bass player to play with him. I thought, It's churlish of me to have my hang-ups about playing bass, for that to spoil this guy's experience, so I thought I'd play this part. It was straightforward. I could still play. I hadn't really been playing very much, but I could still get the sound. I knew what I was doing. People were surprised. Gradually more and more I got asked to do things like that. Eventually, there was another guy teaching, a sax player called Conrad Cork, who later got very involved with jazz education, who had also given up saxophone. He'd been a sax player in the sixties. He and I started doing some duo work together, it was actually quite rewarding because in a way we'd both come through the same sort of thing – moving away from it but in a way still having a kind of sentimental regard. What we did was not free, but conventional jazz, but a more austere version of it. I enjoyed doing duo work without drums, often, just bass and sax or bass and human voice. When Karin Krog came through, when she was touring with John Surman, we did a workshop, and also Sheila Jordan. I played bass with them and that was very nice because they had that kind of freedom. When I got more into that – in the late eighties – Derek got me and Conrad to play at Company Week at the ICA [Company Week 1988, 2–7 August]. I did a broadcast with Derek [*Music in Our Time*, BBC Radio 3, in 1988, with Cyro Baptista, Mick Beck and Alex Ward], so it had come full circle. I feel comfortable about it again. Ironically, when we did Company it was a situation where people were trying to throw together different pairings in order to challenge the situation, and it was Gregg

Bendian I think who wanted to try and get the Joseph Holbrooke group together – he named me and Derek and him to play. In fact he hardly played anything at all, because he just listened to me and Derek. The curious thing was that Derek found it really awkward, because he tries to avoid tonal reference in everything he plays, I would give a note that would make it have tonal implications, and he said he hadn't worked with pitch for so long and he found it very very hard work. I was being pitch-specific and thinking harmonically, even though he was trying hard not to. It's perfectly possible – someone can make the most complicated sound, and then if you put a particular root there you can make that sound like harmonic music. It's like you find in the music of Charles Ives – you get these kind of washes, but then you centre it with something else and it takes on a new meaning. But that's a composer's thinking. People found it very refined playing, but I think it was very puzzling. [GB 2–x–1997]

Some people say you can fit Derek's playing into an ordered system – that it's 25ths or whatever – that it therefore fits predictable structures.

I don't think it does, actually. I think Derek's stuff is very oblique and doesn't fit into those structures. I think I was being – again – malicious, and forcing it to. I remember hearing Derek in Leicester with John Stevens and either Kent Carter or Barre Phillips.* That was interesting, to hear another bass player being very interesting with harmonics and being very subtle, and I could see how they could work on the same plane as Derek and not challenge him in that way, and there was some lovely stuff on that occasion. I remember admiring what they were doing an awful lot – apart from when John decided to play the trumpet or bugle or whatever it was he started blasting out, but the other stuff was terrific. When I was teaching and started to play again, the curriculum was entirely my choice. There's a lot of practical stuff. Under no circumstances did I want people to have an education that was simply my choice. I thought there were things that ought to be there in order to make people rounded musicians, and there were things that I

---

* A recording of this gig (the bassist was Kent Carter) in November 1992 was released by Incus, *One Time* [Incus CD22]. Bailey gave it that title because it was the one time the trio had played together. When Emanem released *Fairly Early With Postscripts* [Emanem 4027] in 1999, it included two tracks played by this line-up. Bailey defends the Incus title by pointing out that the Emanem tracks were actually 'filched from a longer piece of a Steve Lacy group we played in' [27–6–2000].

didn't like that ought to be there – and one of these was improvised music. I then started running improvised music projects, a four-week period where people would do nothing but Free Improvisation, people who'd never improvised in their lives. I'd work with them to get them doing this, and I'd bring in people like Evan, in fact Evan was the sax teacher for me there. Paul Rutherford taught trombone there. I brought in Derek for some workshops, just to go through and work with people. When I first started working at the Haymarket Theatre, '87, '88, we did a music week where Derek came and played and we did some free things there. I did actively encourage that even though it wasn't my taste. Some of my ex-students are now working, playing Free Improvisation: I once saw on a programme that three of my students were referred to as 'having worked under the tutelage of Gavin Bryars'. They didn't say that, the organisers must have caught up on that, slightly embarrassing. But they did emerge as free improvisors from that environment. So my hostility to it doesn't extend to denying it to other people, because I can still see value. Ultimately, in the end, any musician that has had no experience of improvising is a poorer musician. All the people in my ensemble – who are essentially straight players – are gifted improvisors, they've all improvised in other contexts. They're also brilliant chamber music soloists – they're not there because they are improvisors, but the fact of them having improvised makes them richer players. More aware of listening – if they're the right kind of improvisor. If they're the wrong kind of improvisor, then they go their own way and don't notice what's going on. [*GB* 2–x–1997]

Does teaching save you from the isolation composers are heir to?

It's sort of the reverse. I took the Charles Ives line. Rather than try and work as a musician and compromise in order to earn a living and pay the mortgage, it was better to have a regular job and be free to do whatever else I wanted. In terms of composing I wouldn't have to compromise because the family were taken care of. I viewed teaching as that. I enjoyed teaching and I enjoyed the contact with students. A lot of the first period when I was teaching, the first eight or nine years, I was actually working in fine art departments, so I wasn't involved with music and I enjoyed that very much, because there was a lot of other thinking, an approach in art departments that was just way ahead of the thinking in music departments. They had a perspective on aesthetics that was incredibly rich and open-minded. [*GB* 2–x–1997]

THE DEMISE OF JOSEPH HOLBROOKE

In the Joseph Holbrooke Trio, three musicians worked out a method of incorporating silence and randomness into improvisation without breaking its sense of dramatic coherence – and without resorting to dictatorial methods of ensuring audience attention. Meanwhile, as the sixties progressed, a burgeoning avant-garde stemming from the arts schools was throwing up new possibilities. The relatively peaceful and constructive era of the lunchtime concerts at the Grapes gave way to controversies that were simultaneously exciting, hilarious and painful. However, it wasn't these disputes that broke up the trio, as Derek explained in a letter.

> The end of JH didn't come about through composition/improvisation ideological differences. We were all still writing pieces for the group until the end. All that comp/imp squabbling came up later, in different places. JH finished for geographic reasons. At the end, Tony was in Sheffield, Gavin in Northampton and I was in London. We couldn't make it work over that distance although, later in '66, I think, we did play at the Grapes in Sheffield, an art gallery in Northampton and at the Little Theatre in London all on the same day. That, I think, was our swan song. For thirty-two years, that is. [vii–2001]

As explained above, inspired by John Cage's theses about modern music, and uncomfortable with the 'muso solidarity' of the London scene, Bryars later became critical of Free Improvisation. His criticism of the 'predictability' of improvisations is shrewd: they do often begin quiet, work themselves to a climax and then dissolve into silence again (of course, one might counter that such reasoning might also be an argument versus the sex act, but this underestimates the zeal to discover the New that emerged in the sixties). At gigs, Bailey noticed that Bryars appeared to be turning against the idea of improvisation itself.

> The first live electronics player in the Music Improvisation Company – or what eventually came to be called that – was Gavin Bryars. Then it was John Tilbury. Then we got a more manageable character, which was Hugh Davies – when I say *manageable*, I mean musically. They

both had very strong ideological positions at that time, Gavin and John. What I'm saying is that I think they kind of hated it. Hugh seemed not to hate it. [8–x–1997]

I reported to Derek Bryars's words about contact-miking two cymbals and doing rolls on them for two minutes and Han Bennink being aghast. Despite the fact that the Joseph Holbrooke Trio were then planning an after-three-decades reunion, there was a touch of ferocity about Bailey's reply. These controversies have not been settled.

> One of the things about this kind of playing, as long as I can remember – as long as it's been identifiable as something or other – people have claimed to have 'gone beyond its boundaries'. I read a review recently about someone playing a melody and the guy saying, 'This is going to really offend the purists.' People have been playing fucking melodies in the hope of shocking somebody for as long as people have played this stuff. The Dutch school of the sixties and seventies was largely based on that. I can't imagine anything Gavin would do playing loud that would offend anybody, especially Han. Playing very quiet can disturb people, including other musicians. When Gavin was playing electronics, his main weapon to get up people's noses – and it worked – was the gramophone. He was an early DJ. He'd play records, and he had certain distinct favourites culled, usually, from the top ten of the time. [8–x–1997]

According to him, you couldn't handle that.

> What does (handle) it mean? You've got to understand, this wasn't an instrumental use of records, he used to play the one record over and over again. This is the old *avantgarderie*, isn't it? Some sensational event that blows everybody away. Composers have a weakness for this kind of thing. He had a record of Tiny Tim which he might play five times in succession – no gaps. Then there was this huge hit, a very slow sentimental song. He used to play this endlessly. I don't think I was particularly annoyed by this. Stunned, perhaps. Jamie Muir, who was heavily into rock'n'roll – a Stones fan or something – hated it, but it wasn't that it was a record, it was that it was a record of this garbage he couldn't stand. I just couldn't play with it. I mean, I was playing with that kind of shit during the day! I can imagine Gavin planning, with some relish, how he would shock the rest of us. It's amazing how some premeditated event such as that never seems to work. A similar,

unpremeditated, event – one that develops out of the playing – stands a much better chance. [8–x–1997]

Gavin also told me you did a session with Tiny Tim – that it was the one thing he really envied about your studio career.

I don't own up to any sessions any more – I don't admit to any sessions! Let's forget about the sessions. I did sessions throughout that time, particularly in the middle and late sixties. I didn't stop doing commercial work until probably '69, when I started working abroad. Their only relevance is that it was a quick way to make money. You couldn't work here playing improvised music then. In fact, it never occurred to me that anybody would pay us. Occasionally, art schools would book you. One lunchtime, I played with Gavin at an art school. The strangest of those gigs was when John Tilbury and I played for a group of pensioners at a coffee morning at Northampton Library. [8–x–1997]

On 24 November 1969, the Music Improvisation Company (MIC) with Bailey, Jamie Muir, Hugh Davies and Evan Parker played opposite John Tilbury and Gavin Bryars at the Edward Herbert Building in Loughborough ('playing opposite' is a danceband term to describe two bands alternating on the same night – rather than 'playing with', which implies playing together in the same ensemble – one of Bailey's contributions to the lingo of Free Improvisation). Bailey and Bryars were now pursuing different agendas. The MIC was focusing on the creation of meaningful music by using spontaneity, disjuncture and chance, whereas Tilbury and Bryars wanted to pursue Cage's inquisition into the composer-score-musician relationship. The latter required recognition of the classical tradition in order to appreciate its 'subversion', while Derek's band reckoned they could make significant music simply by playing it.

OTHER EVENTS IN THE HOLBROOKE YEARS

The great interest among *aficionados* in Joseph Holbrooke tends to divert attention from what else was happening in Bailey's life. Obviously the lunchtime concerts at the Grapes did not provide a living, and he was still working in shows and nightclubs. It was a commercial gig in

Chesterfield, after all, that had originally brought the three musicians together. Bailey put it to John Shiurba like this:

> But, of course, although music is everything, not everything is music, and for me this was a singularly intense period involving many other kinds of changes. Within this same period, my first marriage broke up, I married again, my father died, my son was born and my second marriage broke up. It would be extraordinary if none of that rubbed off on what I was doing. At times, the only thing that seemed to make any sense was the music. [26–i–1997]

This seems an appropriate place to allow Derek to expand on a personal philosophy – his view of the relationship between musical commitment and earning money.

> This thing I talk about, the necessity of doing music full-time, is not just a question of earning a living. Earning a living is essential because I've got no other way of living I can contemplate. By the time I got to my mid-twenties, I felt I'd had enough of the real world [of commercial work]. After my mid-twenties it was OK, I didn't seem to have to do it anymore, but it's always seemed to me to be necessary with music – either thinking about it or doing it – to do it exclusively. I can do this one thing, possibly, whatever it is, but not in combination with something else. You mentioned dilettantism. I've got nothing against dilettantes, because I've found, with the people I assume to be dilettantes that I've known, that they are totally involved. It's just that after a while they fuck off and become totally involved with something totally different. There's nothing wrong with their involvement. What I don't understand, and I can't bring myself to admire in any form, is hobbyism. Something that was rife in commercial music. Many commercial musicians were part-timers, and it was even worse in British jazz. The 'full-timeness', the complete absorption, I'm trying to describe is nothing to do with professionalism, which is a really suspect concept. The patron saint of professionals is Adolf Eichmann: 'I was only doing my job, guv.' The ultimate excuse for anything. That's why these contradictions arise, where, in fact, I can walk out on earning a living. The Show Must Go On is something I do not subscribe to. There's more to playing than a string of gigs. [15–x–1997]

LEAVING THE COMMERCIAL SCENE

This may seem a poor excuse coming from an attempt at Derek Bailey's biography, but chronology is really a lie. The older you get, the more you become aware that when you're preparing a CV for a prospective employer, you are spinning a story. Employment histories – besides being increasingly patchy and overlapped in today's climate of moonlighting, 'flexibility' and job insecurity – are just a scaffolding; they ignore emotional commitments, private developments, unpaid enthusiasms, the 'inner life'. Since this is what we are actually interested in when examining art, it seems crazy to plot Bailey's life on a bureaucrat's ledger. In the modern age, the pursuit of artistic truth has been a story of evading public scrutiny, of refusing public values, of subverting the dead hand of the spectacle. Show me an artist with a squeaky-clean, self-proclaiming CV, and I show you a craven puppet, a patsy for sponsors and grant-givers, someone utterly unlikely to deliver us from the ordinary. Going by the chronological dates – the gigs, the recording dates, the founding of labels, tours – breaks an account of genuine developments on a rack of particulars.

Derek Bailey's transition from danceband, pit orchestra and session work to Free Improvisation took place over a decade (as late as 1968, for example, the pianist Brian Dee recalls playing with him in the pit band for the musical *Sweet Charity*). The break was not accomplished at a stroke. Hence, Derek's pithiest comments on the difference between the two worlds are impossible to place chronologically. However, it would be a pity to lose them, as they help to explain his unique perspective on the music scene today.

Bailey emphasises the workaday solidarity and lack of pretention among the commercial musicians he worked with in the 1950s and 1960s. He evidently suspects his younger biographer – a critic on and of the bohemian fringe – cannot possibly imagine what this world was like. He compares it to serving in the navy.

In this one respect, it was a bit like being in the forces. If you were on the lower deck, people who didn't come from a working-class background stuck out, they were obvious. They weren't victimised in any way, fact is, you could be proud of them. In the navy particularly, if there was a guy in your mess with a university education he'd be called Doc or Prof and considered to possess some special, albeit useless, wisdom. Similarly, in the music trade, it was pretty much exclusively working class. Anyone not quickly seemed to gravitate into a bandleader. It was the last community I belonged to (sometimes the musicians in the free area speak of it as a community, but it's more of a political stance and, anyway has, I believe, evaporated in recent years). The community thing ... you know in London there used to be a number of streets where different trades would meet? Archer Street – where I also worked in a club – was where musicians met. On Monday morning, the place would be packed – the junction between Great Windmill Street and Archer Street, there'd be no traffic because it would be totally full of musicians. It was what would now be described as networking – you were checking out work. I never knew a musician to have an agent: nobody had a national reputation, the reputation was within the trade. That was important, actually, that was where your work came from – what other musicians thought of you, essentially, whether they wanted to work with you. By '61, say, I think that if I went down Archer Street I'd know pretty well everybody down there. But everybody seemed to know everyone. It was fantastic. In Manchester, there was a place called the Palace Bar which served pretty much the same purpose for the North. People used to come from all over the place for the Monday lunchtime drink in the Palace Bar, the bar in the Palace Theatre. Smaller affair than Archer Street, but the same thing. I didn't go there until I came up to Sheffield to work with Tony Oxley and Gavin Bryars, during which period I also worked in Manchester. I'd go in there, and I knew everybody. I think that was a common experience if you'd been in the business for a few years. It had the feeling of a community to me, I had a lot of friends, I exchanged letters with some of them for years after I no longer had anything to do with that world. [15–x–1997]

In order to explain what he means about the class nature of the trade, Derek describes the pianist Derek Sinclair, who in his phrase 'stuck out' because he was middle class.

When I was working in the gambling club on Archer Street in 1962, Derek Sinclair was playing solo piano upstairs. This place was on four floors – escalating levels of gambling risk. I was working in the basement which was the club, the social part: drinking, dancing, talking. We were a Latin quartet. Maybe I should try and give you the correct ethnic flavour of this group. We were two English guys and an Irish guy and the leader was Chico Arnez. He came from Streatham and was called Jackie Davis. Well, the club was the starting point for the punters, but Sinclair worked on the top floor, I never knew exactly what went on up there, but I gather that – gambling-wise – it was pretty rarified. That was the last time I saw him. During his time there he committed suicide, shot himself. He'd had bands all over the provinces and they were always very good bands. He used to play somewhere for six weeks and then get fired, this was on the Mecca circuit. It was a mystery how he could get fired – sometimes for the most outrageous behaviour – and start up again after a week or two, working for the same circuit in a different town. Turns out, he'd been to public school with one of the directors of this dancehall chain. He was the only person I've ever met who habitually carried a gun. Never heard of him using it, other than shooting himself, although I believe he shot up a bandroom dartboard one time. Derek played every instrument under the sun, good player, not particularly distinguished, but he could play anything, a good jazz player. He had exciting bands, big bands, though the best ones I saw were seven- or eight-piece, basically jazz groups, some Latin stuff. He always had good soloists. One of his distinctions was he always drove a white Jaguar, a somewhat hip thing in the fifties/early sixties, but not your average musician's car. When he was asked about it, he said it was his hobby: 'Some people grow pot, some collect train numbers, I drive white Jaguars.' Sinclair was unusual. [15–x–1997]

Were the musicians unionised?

You had to be to work anywhere except pubs. It was quite militant at that time but, like they say about prostitution, ruined by part-timers. People kept in touch by letter. Nobody was on the phone. Anyway, you were moving around. That's how you knew where the jobs were. I had three things: an amplifier, a guitar and one of those cardboard suitcases. I must have got rid of five or six hundred books – never took them with me after I'd read them. A lot of stuff got left behind, there was not much alternative. Most of this period I didn't have a car. [15–x–1997]

Were you expelled from the scene when you started playing free?

No, my exit from it was quite undramatic, and took a while. For some time – a year or two – I assumed that nobody in the business knew that I was involved in the free stuff. Surprisingly, some did know. Mostly, the people I knew were cool about it. When anybody referred to it, it was with incomprehension. When I played at the Little Theatre, I also worked at the Prince of Wales Theatre for a period, just around the corner. That pit band was full of jazz players. I used to sit next to the keyboard player, Brian Dee, he plays now on the jazz scene. Good player. I played with him a couple of times in jazz situations, but at this point I was seeing him every night – twice a night – in this theatre pit. His main criticism was on the lines of: 'What the fuck are you up to playing with these guys? They can't play!' I would say, 'It's a different thing, these are remarkable people, you don't assess them like, Does he know the changes to some fucking tune or other? I've learned things from these people which are outside our normal things.' His claim was, 'If those guys could play jazz they wouldn't be doing what they're doing.' In recent times I've wondered about that, because a lot of free players have moved back into a closer relationship to jazz. But, you have to realise, most conventional musicians thought that Ornette couldn't play. They weren't sure about Coltrane. [15–x–1997]

To illustrate the division between jazz and free players that existed in the late 1960s, Bailey tells an anecdote about an encounter between tenor saxophonist Alan Skidmore and drummer John Stevens.*

I don't know about the present younger ones, but the older jazz players, those of John Stevens/Evan Parker/Tony Oxley's age group, thought that free players simply didn't have the chops. There's a free player and he plays jazz too, some kind of local festival in London, and they're all in this boozer after time having a drink. The free player is on the piano, playing a few 'sounds' for his own amazement, and this guy – they've known each other for twenty years – who's a very good conventional jazz player . . . [15–x–1997]

You prefer to tell it as a generic story?

* Derek usually tells this anecdote without naming names, probably because it might seem a slight on Skidmore, but actually it can be interpreted quite simply as a clash of different methods. Anyone who can walk through an art gallery and appreciate both a De Kooning and a Dubuffet is not going to think this exchange implies having to make a choice between Skidmore and Stevens.

The names are beside the point and I'd prefer if you didn't use the names. But, anyway, Alan pushes John off the piano – 'Get off the fucking stool!' – and plays some changes, and he says, 'That's what you should play on piano!' There are certain movements which are standard movements in chord changes. He goes through a few of these and says; 'That's what you should play. You just don't . . .' What was the phrase? I was told this by John . . . 'You don't have the roots, you don't have the chops!' He goes through this list – 'You don't know the changes, you haven't done the tours, you haven't done the sessions, you can't play fucking jazz!' So all these things to these people are part of this thing – a rite of passage. And anyone who says, fuck all that is thought of as a cop-out. Possibly even now that generation thinks with great suspicion of anybody who plays free. As for the older players – Ronnie Scott's generation – I think the free stuff was totally irrelevant to them. [15–x–1997]

To Bailey, most British 'jazz' was a patrician raid on a form that had originally arrived through involvement in regular work.

None of the great players started playing jazz by standing in front of a rhythm section and improvising. They've always been in an ensemble – which used of course to be a big band – with other musicians, very often playing commercial music. Situations related to popular music – dances, lounge work. [15–x–1997]

The dialectic between commerce and art in American jazz was intimate and fertile. It produced a thousand variations.

It was a very volatile music. In the early fifties, there were lots of fashions, it used to change all the fucking time. You were always talking about, 'Have you heard so and so?' 'No – who's that?' That would happen all the time. Of course, Charlie Parker turned it all around, but there were other stories, and that includes Charlie Christian. But that was forties stuff. In the early fifties there was assumed to be a continuation of that, there seemed to be endless possibilities to the music. But eventually it seemed to kind of settle down. Then it appeared to start going backwards – with Blakey, I think. [15–x–1997]

Bailey parts company with jazz at Art Blakey, whose doctrine of neo-classicism – whilst a stunning opportunity for anyone lucky enough to see an edition of his Jazz Messengers before his death – finally became, via Wynton Marsalis, critic Stanley Crouch and CBS/Sony, a charter for the disastrous corporate embalming of jazz in the United States. Though Bailey is a stern critic of what he sees as sentimental and journalistic uses of the term 'jazz' – he subscribes to tap-dancer Will Gaines's argument that it is a glorious music, but one tied to specific social conditions, and effectively killed off by rock'n'roll – he continues to play with jazz musicians if he feels they have anything to teach him (it's been fascinating to observe jazz musicians who abhor Crouch's reactionary rhetoric – bassist Reggie Workman, clarinettist Don Byron, drummer Susie Ibarra, bass/drum team Jamaaladeen Tacuma and Calvin Weston – break ranks and join Bailey to engage in Free Improvisation).

The experience of the Joseph Holbrooke Trio in the early sixties gave both Bailey and Oxley complete confidence that their style of improvised music was a thoroughly integral development, something that really belonged to them. It is hard to avoid the conclusion that it is their working-class backgrounds – combined with unerring musicality – that gave them the confidence, not to say bloody-mindedness, to claim this music as their own.

4 SOLOISM AND FREEDOM, 1966-1977

RECORD COMPANIES AND FREE IMPROVISATION

During the latter half of the 1960s, progressive rock pushed past the restrictions of the pop song into extended jams. Though usually burdened with drug references and mystical claptrap, the term 'consciousness expansion' could justify instrumental freak-outs – that is, genuine extensions of experience. Cream, for example, progressed from the psychedelic pop of *Disraeli Gears* (1967) to the wild, fifteen-minute guitar marathons of *Wheels of Fire* (1968) and *Live Cream* (1970). The hallowed status of Eric Clapton paved the way for Carlos Santana, the only solo musician since the end of the Second World War to achieve chart stardom for prowess on his instrument. In Bailey's book *Improvisation*, Steve Howe, guitarist with Yes, mentions one of the technical and commercial preconditions for progressive rock: the corporate turn from promoting 7-inch singles to 12-inch albums. The longer format demanded more ambitious music. Rock was enmeshed with competitive technology: the art of the later Beatles and of Jimi Hendrix is inconceivable without stereo.

Enthusiasm for innovative sound was such that there was a brief period when the major record companies thought there might be money to be made from Free Improvisation. Before, that is, they discovered that the musicians were committed to a different ethic, more interested in regular playing opportunities than in being labelled as a saleable commodity for an album-buying audience (that was left to Fusion). Tony Oxley recorded three albums for corporate labels (*The Baptised Traveller* and *4 Compositions for Sextet* for CBS in 1969 and 1970, and

Ichnos for RCA in 1971). John Stevens recorded *Karyobin* for Island in 1968 and *Spontaneous Music Ensemble* for Polydor in 1969. Derek Bailey played guitar on all of them. In later years, the records became so fabulously rare that jazz shop elders would greet enquiries about them with bursts of wry laughter. In 1993, Chronoscope (distributed by Harmonia Mundi) reissued *Karyobin*, and in 1999 Sony acknowledged the growing interest in the roots of Free Improvisation by reissuing Oxley's two CBS albums – after a hiatus of thirty years. In other words, relying on corporate sponsorship was no way to proceed.

Derek Bailey recalls a 'double trio' being recorded for Island with John Stevens and Rashied Ali on drums, Evan Parker and Trevor Watts on sax, and Dave Holland and Peter Kowald on bass. It was recorded in a studio on 10 March 1968. Bailey is caustic about its fate.

> It never saw the light of day. Then I made one. These large labels were poking around to see if there was any use in this stuff. They didn't poke around for long before they found that it was exactly the kind of thing they wanted to keep as far away as possible from. This thing I did was supposed to be for one of these big labels. It got cancelled, actually, before they heard it. I remember the A&R guy gave me lunch. *[laughs]* Great! First time that ever happened. Not exactly posh, went into a boozer and boozed at lunchtime. This thing – an LP, of course – was made up of one side with Gavin Bryars's tape concerto: he'd put this tape piece together and I improvised a guitar part to it. We also recorded some trio stuff, that is, Gavin Bryars playing live electronics, Evan Parker on saxophone, and me. And then there was some solo stuff. That made up the record. Ron Geeson recorded it. I had the tape, I lent it to one or two people, including, I thought, John Stevens and Victor Schonfield, but when I later tried to trace it, neither of them admitted knowing anything about it. I've never found it. [8–x–1997]

Karyobin has become legendary. Recorded for Island Records at Olympic Sound on 18 February 1968 by Eddie Kramer, it was given a respectful review in *Melody Maker* (10 August 1968): this was a record 'to be heard by all who are interested in the current state of jazz', though Bob Houston did find its 'whispered intimacies' disappointing. He missed the individualised soloing of jazz proper (the headline asked, 'Can jazz get along without ego?'). *Karyobin*'s new species of sensitive, collective interplay has been claimed as an influence on Miles Davis's *Bitches Brew* and the first Weather Report album (though the intimate tone of *Karyobin* is totally different from Miles Davis's rock-arena grandstanding).

Derek Bailey, for one, was less than impressed by *Karyobin*.

It's a bit of whitey free jazz, isn't it? [15–x–1997]

He is also critical of its remix on CD, which reduces the role of John Stevens and separates out the different players to the detriment of the ensemble sound. In considering *Karyobin*'s exalted reputation, Bailey's scepticism about records and recording makes an appearance. He wanted to get his ideas sorted out on this controversial issue, and so re-edited his ad lib words (which explains the somewhat non-impromptu style of what follows).

'Whitey free jazz', is what I said to John when the CD reissue came out. It seemed to have undergone some tinkering. He was a bit cagey about it, but I got the impression that he liked the changes. I never liked the record much in the first place, as a matter of fact. That was more to do with what it was not, than what it was. Much of what that group had previously been about was missing. This often happens with recordings of Free Improvisation. Everything gets more 'musical' – tidy. But it was more than that. When I first played with these guys, they seemed to me to be unlike any musicians I'd met before. They would talk about a group concept, a shared open, generous attitude that was welcoming to any elements. There was talk of music 'growing, like the trees and plants', and, 'non-ego playing', elevating the group above one's personal contribution. I was all for it. It sounded like musical nirvana, and, man, was I ready for that.

Anyway it was talk, and what people say is not necessarily what they play, yet in the playing all these guys were, in my experience, quite special. I think I learned something from each of them and particularly from them as a group. This was as they were in '66 and '67. Primarily, there was John Stevens, Trevor Watts and Paul Rutherford; initially, I assumed it was *their* group. Certainly, it got most of its attitudes and dynamic from those three. John, of course, provided most of the energy and a truly passionate commitment. Trevor did most of the organising – keeping in touch with everybody regarding the rare gigs we had, things like that. The mysterious one to me at that time was Rutherford.

He could produce genuine surprises. If anybody at that point qualified to be called a free player, it was Paul. The rest of us – Evan, Barry [Guy], me and sometimes others – were more or less add-ons to their trio, and I was probably the most peripheral, something which suited me fine.

My main musical preoccupation during this time was in trying to work out – and this was mainly through solo practising/playing and writing pieces – a way to work within the free situation which didn't simply mean playing as before but dumping all harmonic and rhythmic restrictions. In those areas I was looking for greater possibilities, not fewer. Trees and flowers growing hadn't, so far, come into it.

Well, that's a different story. But due to the openness of the group at that time, I could work within that and that was invaluable to me. Having that number of different people coming together to find *something* made it a genuinely exploratory situation. The feeling was, it could go anywhere. Somehow, adding to all this was the setting, the Little Theatre, where, in fact, the setting, being a theatre, changed regularly. Great place to play. But, for me, theatres have always seemed the best places to play this music.

Anyway, back to nirvana. What happened next was rather dramatic. Suddenly – literally overnight, I think – this non-ego, all-for-one, one-for-all, open collective imploded into a duo. Exactly how this came about I haven't the faintest idea, it didn't smell too good but, at that time, the internal writhings of the SME were the least of my considerations.

My strongest memory of that time is driving. Endlessly driving through a fog of exhaustion. Although I'd moved back to London, there were bits of my musical and social life scattered all over the country. I had three jobs and the logistics were horrific. I had a six-nights-a-week job in a nightclub in the West End in London, I worked two, three or four days a week in a radio orchestra in Manchester, and I worked on a regular Sunday-night TV show in Blackpool. By virtuoso deployment of the deputy system and driving what seemed like a million miles a week, I managed to keep them all going through the second half of '66 and most of '67. In addition to that, I was trying to maintain some sort of contact with my estranged wife and my infant son in Manchester, and I was living in Fulham off the King's Road in a bedsitter in a house run by a 22-year-old woman, almost a parody of a sixties character – lysergic acid in the fridge, hashish cakes for tea: nothing unusual – who was a *couturière* to a succession of rock groups. Periodically, a Rolls would draw up in front of the house and rock'n'roll in all its hairy glory would burst through the front door and pose around the place for hours in its new costumes. I'd turn up my endless tape of Webern to full volume. The vocal pieces particularly would have 'em screaming for mercy. The power of unpopular music!

Well, this re-alignment, or whatever it was, took the SME in a very specific direction, a direction partly reflected in *Karyobin*. '*So, What Do You Think?*' was a more satisfactory playing experience than making *Karyobin*. Not that it would make any difference because *Karyobin* came *first*. The improvised music scene, at least in some quarters, seems to have sunk into an obsession with dates and who did what first. Of course, that's present everywhere, there's even an industry based on it. But for improvised music, in thirty-odd years, to have sunk to the level of the antiques trade is ludicrous. Essentially, what John did was take this amorphous mass and break a chunk off and fashion it to the shape he wanted. Primarily, he did this in the two duos, first with Evan, then with Trevor. Through them, he established the sound and a kind of aesthetic which informed all the other SMEs, such as *Karyobin*, '*So, What Do You Think?*' and umpteen other apparitions. Other people did the same thing: Trevor formed a group out of the '66/67 group, Rutherford formed Iskra out of it. This process – taking *raw* improvisation and giving it a more precise, recognisable identity, developing a *music* – is a customary procedure, although less so now than formerly, I think. When you get a largeish pool of musicians working in an unformulated way, small groups peel off and head for the shore: reputation, tours, festivals and all the doubtful benefits available to musical travelling salesmen. Personally, I've always thought there's a kind of fine balance between the amorphous situation and the fixed groups which produces the best playing. Semi ad hoc, is how I've tried to describe it, which doesn't say much but it's not a well-defined position: a degree of familiarity but retaining the shock of the strange. You know: 'What's THAT????'

During the original interview, I mentioned that I'd given *Karyobin* a whirl that morning (before catching the 253 bus to Clapton for the interview), and that the horns in particular seemed rather too trilling and decorative.

I find that too. You shouldn't play it in the mornings anyway. A very good record for playing in the morning is an early Willem Breuker record: all barrel organs – good for the bowels [namely, *Lunchconcert for Three Barrelorgans*, ICP003, 1968]. [15–x–1997]

Derek again resorted to a re-edit to put down his thoughts about John Stevens.

I'd like to say something about John. As is well known, he had many remarkable qualities but there is one which is never mentioned. Uniquely I think, he invented a style of playing an instrument other than his own. John was too committed to group activity generally to play solo, but I often thought his duos with Trevor and with Evan were his way of playing solo. The saxophone was a kind of extension of his drumming. I wouldn't go as far as describing it as a one-man band, but the direction of the music came so clearly from John that *duo* didn't seem right either. Maybe Trevor and Evan would have a problem accepting that now. But John was a messianic character and messiahs like – need, maybe – disciples, and I would have thought they would be happy to accept they were heavily under his musical influence at that time. Later, of course, they both played quite differently, from each other and from that particular role. But John's achievement in making that music was, I think, unique. It produced, at times, some fine music.

The most enjoyable playing I did with John came much later. Starting some time in '91 or so through into '93 we played together regularly, sometimes with others, sometimes the two of us. We had a whole string of gigs, for some reason, and he also used to come round to my place when we would play, eat, drink and talk. He loved to talk about music. That is unusual too: most musicians seem to view talking about music as a kind of weakness. Not John. And he was great to argue with. We disagreed on most things and always enjoyably. You can argue with some guys and it takes them twenty years to get over it, if ever. John thrived on it. One of the things we argued about, endlessly, was the relationship between this kind of playing and jazz – our different views of *Karyobin* are a good illustration of this. For me the connection between this kind of playing and jazz is umbilical: the real possibilities start once you cut the cord. John's view was diametrically opposed to that. He believed some connection was essential, however tenuous. He would speak of it as being organic. I loved it when John started using words like 'organic'. It meant we were in for a long night.

It wasn't all Free Improvisation, even at this date. On 29 August 1968, Bailey performed with Evan Parker and Gavin Bryars – and with Richard Howe (French horn) and Bernard Rands (cymabalom) – at the Institute of Contemporary Arts, an event called Cybernetic Serendipity Music. The quartet were billed as playing a 'composition': Herbert Brun's *Infraudibles*.

More significant from the point of view of documenting where Bailey and Oxley had got with their music was the album *The Baptised Traveller*, which Oxley recorded for CBS on 3 January 1969. The thirty-year gap in its availability has allowed all kinds of misconceptions about the true origins of Free Improvisation to arise. The record has a manifesto-like quality. By beginning with themes reminiscent of bop and modal jazz, Oxley was portraying the origins of the new music. The album culminates in 'Preparation', by which time the syntax known as Free Improvisation has arrived, a glorious ball of noise with the musicians inserting more notes than seems humanly possible.

According to Oxley's text on the sleeve, the opener – 'Crossing' – 'illustrates the impatience with one's present environment' and 'setting forth for new horizons'. Written by Oxley in 1964, the tune has two blasts of discordant, spooky unison followed by a burst of high-energy scribbling and a fast piece of bop-like melody. Everything stops for an unaccompanied bass break by Jeff Clyne, then it's back to the spooky discords to introduce a fantastic Evan Parker tenor solo. He is straining at the outer edges of sax timbre in the manner of Trane followers Pharoah Sanders and Archie Shepp, but the sound has a severe definition that is all his own. The musicians develop Oxley's written theme into freer, more speculative playing with complete assurance. Like contemporary work by Joe Harriott and Krzysztof Komeda, Oxley disdained the flurry and blur of much European blues and jazz, preferring to outline his ideas with clarity and precision. Kenny Wheeler's trumpet sounds stunningly articulate, though perhaps a little too cool and collected for the particular ruggedness Oxley is after.

For 'Arrival', Oxley scored a slow, haunting unison over a bowed-bass drone and drum rolls, introducing the kind of folkish flavour later favoured by Ken Hyder's Talisker, John Surman and Jan Garbarek. However, here this isn't a stylistic finishing point, but a static episode designed to set off more dynamic parts. This is still jazz, but the modal openness is inviting the omniresponsive internal dialoguing peculiar to Free Improvisation. 'Stone Garden' is an arrangement of a tune by Charlie Mariano (Mingus alumnus and pioneer of Indo-Jazz). A hymn-like resignation and mournfulness suggest Coltrane tunes like 'After the Rain', but Bailey's guitar – highly amplified, but brought up with the foot pedal so there's no attack – provides a glinting strangeness, a straining towards harmonic light and colour. The stereo mix is crude, with Bailey's guitar isolated in the left channel. If one listens to the right channel alone, everything sounds straightforward: Bailey's contribution is his brashly electric sound and his indifference – even hostility – to the prevailing harmonic atmosphere. In contrast to the surrounding mix of blues and pastoral, Bailey's guitar is an alien light. Like Sun Ra with his dadaistic electronic-keyboard solos, Bailey is exploring the bizarre nature of electricity itself – dodgy contacts, finger fumbles, current leaping between frayed wires – rather than delivering a stable, processed image. What sleevenote writer Bob Houston (evidently more impressed with Oxley's direction than that of John Stevens) calls Bailey's 'intelligent and strikingly original use of harmony clusters' breaks open the atmosphere of the piece, something the horns are not doing. As on *Karyobin*, Kenny Wheeler plays almost too assuredly, his suave, horizontal lines indeed making his accompanists sound like 'a particularly untogether rhythm section' (Bailey's description of how Wheeler made the SME sound). Jeff Clyne's sonorous bass feature is reminiscent of Charlie Haden, but Bailey's chimes and fidgets are unprecedented. Clyne and Bailey conclude their duet with a flamenco flourish, then Bailey performs a single-note electro-interference solo that is really like no previously attested music at all. At the end, Bailey's guitar sustains 'fits', but he gets perilously near leaving the planet music altogether.

According to Oxley, the final track, 'Preparation', has as its concep-tual basis 'the necessity for decision'. A ten-note quasi-serial row launches a stop–start improvisation of extraordinary density and vitality. After what's gone before, its syntax is utterly comprehensible – detailed, swinging and involving – but it's also Free Improvisation in all its scary, arbitrary, everything-goes-here glory. Wheeler and Parker disappear into strained squeaks, and then Jeff Clyne brings everyone back to the tune with some hefty bowing. If people say that British jazz has produced no masterpieces, it's an illusion created by the fact that CBS had no idea how to market this album.

CBS did, however, know how to market a guitarist named John McLaughlin – especially after he'd played with Miles Davis and formed a band named Mahavishnu Orchestra. Interestingly enough, McLaughlin's 1969 debut on Polydor, *Extrapolation* – the record Tony Oxley drummed on but dismisses as a 'pop record' – was conceived as an expression of the British avant-garde. Yardbirds manager Giorgio Gomelsky wrote a puff for the album sleeve. In *Jazz: The Essential Companion*, Ian Carr called *Extrapolation* 'one of the classic albums of the decade . . . a virtual summary of current small-group playing techniques, it anticipated the jazz-rock movement of the 1970s and it showed that McLaughlin was already a very fine composer, as well as being a sublimely original guitar stylist'. Unfortunately, Carr has his eye on chart placings rather than musical facts. The flashes of brittle modernism McLaughlin displayed on the record – set among his banal and harmonically restricted runs and tunes – were actually pure Bailey. On the back of the album, McLaughlin was shown wearing glasses, hunched over his guitar. The side-lighting – emphasising his jawbone and look of concentration – made him look distinctly Baileyesque. Comparison between the two guitarists was not so absurd: as late as 1973, they were both staged by the same Edinburgh promoters, Platform. Speaking to *Time Out* of the challenge to audiences represented by Bailey's playing, Evan Parker used McLaughlin as the obvious counter-example.

> So who do they all like, John McLaughlin or somebody? To me it's just hot licks, that style of playing. And when you know that the consciousness of the guys involved goes beyond it, you can't help but feel that what they're doing is playing down to people, and that's hard. But most people would probably find that a fantastic idea, that John McLaughlin might be playing down to them, because they've been hyped into believing that it's an incredible move up for them, that if they can dig that then they must be really into something. Nowadays the policies of the major record companies seem to originate in the accounts department. [Evan Parker to John Fordham, *Time Out*, 6–12 October 1972, p. 23]

The mismatch between the reputations granted Bailey and McLaughlin by the industry and the actual artistry of their playing is a graphic proof of the alienation of the public from genuine musicality and the illusions generated by commercial systems. However, before waxing too indignant about record manufacturers favouring saleable appearance over musical essence – a perfect illustration of Marx's observation that the commodity develops exchange value to the detriment of use value – it should be recalled that for improvisors, live music is where the action is, and live music depends upon venues.

THE LITTLE THEATRE

The Little Theatre in Garrick Yard, 23 Garrick Street, St Martin's Lane, situated in London's Covent Garden, was a space opened up for free and experimental music by John Stevens. An early flyer sets the scene:

THE LITTLE THEATRE CLUB

SPONTANEOUS MUSIC

This Club opened for music on January 3rd, 1966 and was the first regular venue for free music in London. Since then the Club has been an important meeting place for the younger generation of jazz musicians. Among those who have played in the Club in the past are:

GRAHAM COLLIER   MIKE WESTBROOK

CHRIS MCGREGOR   JOHN SURMAN

The purpose of this handout is to confirm that the Club is still functioning regularly. Naturally, the Club is not able to advertise extensively and so this leaflet will reach people who perhaps do not see the advertisements. The musicians who still play at the club include:

DEREK BAILEY   TREVOR WATTS   EVAN PARKER

KENNY WHEELER   NICK BRYCE   PETER LEMER

and JOHN STEVENS

Open on Thursdays, Fridays and Saturdays from 10.30 until 1.00 a.m. A telephone call can determine who is playing on a particular night.

THIS LEAFLET ENTITLES HOLDER AND ONE GUEST TO ONE EVENING'S
FREE ADMISSION.

Cost of membership - 10/- year (students - free)
Cost of admission - 4/- members, 6/- guests

The music that was played at the Little Theatre produced powerful reactions. In 1973, *Melody Maker* hosted a four-way discussion between altoist Bruce Turner, pianist Keith Tippett, drummer John Stevens and Derek Bailey. Questions were posed by Steve Lake. Tippett declared that audiences were less fashion-conscious in Europe and more serious about the music. Steve Lake asked if there wasn't also better coverage of new music on European radio.

DB: Yes, there probably is, but there's various sides to this thing. I'd rather play in the Little Theatre Club than anywhere in Europe.

JS: Oh wow, Derek Bailey. What a fucking lovely thing to say. He's a star, and he'd rather play at the Little Theatre Club than anywhere else!! [*Makes strange whooping noises and then lifts up Bailey's trouser leg and begins kissing his calf.*] How do you tip this table over? What do I have to do?

DB: I played three days at the Little Theatre Club with Jamie Muir, and each day we had an audience of one, and it was always someone who'd come in from the rain while he was waiting for a bus, or something like that. It was never someone who wanted to actually hear the music. And this audience reacted in the same way every night. They'd listen, frowning, for about 20 minutes, then they'd shout 'bullshit!' and storm out of the club again. So, some nights there were really horrible, but even so, the best nights were there too.

KT: That's interesting, because the best buzzes I've had have been in Europe playing to large audiences.

DB: Yeah, but the atmosphere down the Little Theatre Club at the moment is a creative one, the audience is mostly made up of young musicians.

JS: Right. [*Melody Maker*, 15 December 1973, p. 42]

Like Bailey and Parker, the messianic Stevens was convinced that music is something to be played rather than marketed or even 'enjoyed'. He and saxophonist Trevor Watts and Paul Rutherford had met in the Royal Air Force in 1958, where they managed to turn a spell in Germany into a musical education, learning from German musicians such as Manfred Schoof and Alexander von Schlippenbach and organising a cellar jazz club in Cologne. It's indicative that the most revealing Stevens interview did not appear in a music magazine but in *Radical Poetics*, a journal published by disciples of the (equally messianic) poet and critic Eric Mottram. Stevens's anecdote about Chick Corea, the avant-garde pianist who in 1971 discovered Scientology, bossa novas and mass sales, is illuminating (despite the fact that Bailey thinks it pretty much a tall story). A critique of 1980s postmodernism by veterans of the counter-culture, this comes at you through a thin drift of marijuana smoke from Stevens's Ealing pad in the early 1990s, as Michael Hrebeniak and John Stevens discussed the politics and meaning of the music.

MH: So many young jazz players are fascinated by marketing, using a phrase like 'reaching out to communicate with an audience'. The implication is that 'compromise' is synonymous with 'democratisation' of art. That attitude is patronising and humiliating – a product of the Stalinist/capitalist attempt to undermine the role of the artist in society. It disallows any aspiration to change consciousness. It's as if the need to train people into artistic appreciation and participation is now unnecessary. What passes for art no longer challenges established thought, and as a result, power structures are preserved through a cultivated mediocrity.

JS: Yeah! I hope you won't assume I'm name-dropping, but this story will hopefully prove that I understand what you're saying. Before Chick Corea formed Return To Forever, he was playing with Anthony Braxton, Dave Holland and Barry Altschul. I'd played with Dave in my group earlier, and they all came down to the Little Theatre Club. Chick had a play and we had a nice time. A year later, Chick was in town again. So I went down to Ronnie Scott's, and saw him in the foyer. I said, 'Chick, how are you doing?' and he went, 'Oh, John, let's go for a walk.' So we walked down the road and he said, 'What are you doing then, John?' I said, 'Well, I'm doing what I always do – Spontaneous Music Ensemble, work in youth clubs, blah blah blah.' And he said to me, 'Look, John, with all your skill, why aren't you, like, out there projecting it? Because I'm out there and we're reaching the people and they feel like dancing . . .' and all of this stuff. And I went, 'Well, Chick, that's not really what I do, or what I'm about.' Anyway, we carried on walking and he kept stressing this point: 'Get out there with us. Join us.

You can do it, I know you can do it.' So this goes on and on, and we're walking back towards Ronnie's, and I said, 'Chick, why do you think I came out to see you this evening?' And he said, 'To borrow money?' And I went, 'Chick, for Christ's sake, I came to see if you wanted to have a play while you're here.' To me, that sums up a lot of what you're saying. And that's early days. Now it's reaching extreme points. And again I get back to the fucking profession as the biggest limitation of music, which buys people out of the freedom to collaborate with each other and cross-fertilise towards fresh music. New music does not only come out of the mind, but develops through relationships manifesting themselves in a certain sound, an agreed way of playing. And it carries on evolving. It never stays static. [*Radical Poetics*, no. 1, 1997 – copies available from 23 Broadcroft Avenue, Stanmore, HA7 1NT, UK (the interview is followed by an extensive John Stevens discography)]

Disappointment with Chick Corea's turn was not restricted to free improvisors such as the now much-missed Stevens (he died suddenly from a heart attack on 13 September 1994, aged fifty-four). Rich Underhill, alto saxophonist with Toronto's Shuffle Demons – a street-busking outfit that inspired Xero Slingsby, another late-lamented anti-commercial messiah – was similarly disappointed.

When I was sixteen, me and my friends went to Vancouver specifically to hear Chick Corea, and we were really disappointed. During the concert we wrote this stupid note and passed it to one of Chick Corea's people, just full of teen angst: 'How could you do this, Chick, you were so great and what's all this electric stuff?' (*RU* 15–ix–1990)

Enthusiasm for John Stevens's legacy – during his lifetime he led countless educational workshops, the initial training for such mid-eighties jazz-boom stars as Courtney Pine, Steve Williamson and Claude Deppa – has resulted in posthumous releases that obscure rather than clarify his virtues as a player (Stevens's laudable attempts to emulate the thrill of rock and dance records proved peculiarly difficult for someone committed to realtime performance). *Playing* [Incus CD14], a 1992 duet with Bailey, and *One Time* [Incus CD22], with Bailey and bassist Kent Carter, are the most effective memorials of John Stevens as an alert and provocative drummer.

Bailey saw possibilities in the inchoate 'experimental' music of

Stevens's early ensembles. However, this potential was threatened by the musicians' growing proficiency. To his ears, the Spontaneous Music Ensemble began to sound less radical.

The first Music Improvisation Company came out of Thursday nights I used to run at the Little Theatre as an alternative to what was happening at the SME. So I used to play with all kinds of people on this Thursday night, an early Company-type thing I suppose. Later, the guy I played with more or less consistently at that time was Jamie Muir. But, before that it was with a variety of people – anybody. I've even played solo all night on my own there – this will sound absurd – to nobody. [8–x–1997]

Nobody at all? No audience, just musicians?

No audience – no musicians!

You went down there . . .

You don't go down to the Little Theatre, you go up, four flights. You don't carry an amp and a guitar up four flights and just take them down again! Anyway, it was a good place to play. I was living at that time in a flat where I could not practise electric, so I didn't care. If anyone had turned up, there'd only have been three people, Richard Leigh and two others. The audiences were always in single figures, except occasionally there'd be some jazz journalist who'd come to sniff it out. Jamie and I played one or two nights to no people, or one or two musicians. One night we played and the audience – for a certain amount of time – was Tony Oxley and John McLaughlin. They'd come over from their interval at Ronnie's. That was the basic thing, Jamie and I, and then I used to invite people. He became the first regular and then it gradually built up, through a number of people, and finished up as MIC. [8–x–1997]

ART SCHOOL FREAK-OUTS

Eager to escape the restrictions – and second-rank status – of being a Yorkshireman playing jazz, Bailey was intrigued by developments in the art schools. Conveniently forgotten by today's art scene – eager to applaud every kindergarten 'outrage' by Saatchi's generation as a spur to Brit Art's new-found saleability – the sixties saw unrest and experimentation on an unprecedented scale.

You'd never play in music departments . . . come to think of it, you still don't. Not in this country. That fine art scene in the sixties – totally alien to my previous life. The music they liked was rock, it wasn't that we were doing what they liked, it was just that somehow it was 'art', and it was art that was outside – so they'd kind of let it happen. I can't remember working anywhere at that time but art schools and art situations. We used to work at the first Arts Lab on Drury Lane, that was quite a place, they produced a magazine – Tom McGrath edited it. I didn't know what an art school was, but it turned out that half the guys who played this music came from art schools, particularly in Germany and Holland. Han and Brötzmann came from art school – I think most of them did. Here, Jamie Muir, John Stevens . . . I don't know what they learned. It provided some kind of basis for employment for certain people. John Tilbury used to teach in an art school, Gavin taught in an art department at Portsmouth. They automatically slotted into the art schools as teachers, doing 'projects' – that's the word you'd use now, I don't know what they called it then. I never saw anybody play a guitar in a conventional manner in an art school. I'll put that another way. I never saw anybody play a guitar except laid flat on its back – in the way Keith [Rowe] plays it, who I'm *sure* went to art school. If anybody was playing a guitar in an art school it was lying flat on its back. I played – a fantastic gig this – when they moved the Arts Lab to Roberts Street, they produced what-not there, what d'you call that paper, underground? [8–x–1997]

International Times?

IT, all that stuff. I had a gig there once, playing this composition for four guitars, all of which had to be laid flat on their backs. There was this obsession. [8–x–1997]

The mid-seventies recording for Obscure?

No, this is mid-sixties. Gavin's idea of the guitar comes out of that thing, he probably prefers a guitar played flat on its back. Which is a change from the rock'n'roll world, where they like the *player* to be flat on his back – as you know. There was this piece, the composer – Lloyd-

Baker – played bass guitar. I played with him in the original stage version of *Hair*, in the stage band. A rock band. It wasn't my job, I played there once or twice as a dep. I knew him because I'd worked in *Hair*. I'd got him to come to the Little Theatre one Thursday night, and we'd played a guitar trio with Keith Rowe. So he played free bass guitar – must have been the first guy to do that. He'd written this piece for four guitars, his part was probably bass guitar, and we all sat and had our guitars flat on their backs, and we had a box which he provided full of bulldog clips. You put them on the strings. It turned it into a sort of gong sound. Wherever you put it, it was a slightly different gong sound, quite different.

Like John Cage's prepared piano?

Exactly. We had a box of bulldog clips, these highly amplified guitars lying on their backs and at some point he said 'Go' – and we went, bulldog clip, *bong*!, another bulldog clip, *bong*!, take it off. And there were four of us doing it, quite pretty for an hour or so. [8–x–1997]

Was it all written out?

Probably, but I never used to look at these things. That's when I found out I'd better improvise, because I couldn't read these bloody scores anyway. Some of them were monstrous things. I found relating the performance to the score . . . I felt I was playing a minor part in some major absurdity. Either the composer was having me on, or he wanted me and him to have someone else on. I didn't doubt the musical intent or sincerity, I just thought that this way of achieving it was ridiculous. At least it was for me, because I couldn't actually read the scores in any musical way. I could admire the scores, and I did. When I lived in Islington, I had this basement flat, and the wall was covered with them. I might have discovered the best use for those fuckers. I found the verbal or typed instructions a little bit better, but it never really made sense to me – I was too much of a conventional musician, like when Gavin said, I couldn't stand him playing records at gigs, that's because I actually knew what to play with the records. I could play something that was meaningful in my terms, but what I couldn't do – and I don't think I could do it now – is play along for three or four minutes with some tune and *not* play the tune. I'd have to find a conventional role with a conventional piece of music. That's my particular hang-up I suppose, but then I'm a conventional musician. So there was all this stuff. [8–x–1997]

Time for the big question. Did you have long hair?

No. Then I was thirty-five, thirty-six. Far as I can remember, my hair has always been short – maybe a bit longer in the seventies, and that was more to do with economics. Then virtually all the people I worked with were ten, fifteen younger than me. Now, they can be forty years younger – but playing with Switch and Alex Ward, I don't feel as I felt then. It never bothered me that much, it was a comfort in a way, but I used to feel like an alien in those days in that environment. Not with the free players. Although they adopted all the appearances and all the rest of it, they somehow seemed separate from the sixties stuff. They were, of course. [8–x–1997]

Growing your hair and being signed to a corporate label was the dream for progressive rock bands. Long before punk, Free Improvisation scorned that strategy. However, Derek Bailey and John Stevens were not the only ones to think there must be other ways to proceed.

OBSCURE RECORDS RECONSIDERED

After wowing the music press as support act for David Bowie at his Rainbow Theatre Christmas concert in 1971, Roxy Music made substantial amounts of money for Island Records: who knew what a label initiated by its flamboyant keyboardist might deliver? Nowadays celebrated as a trail-blazer for the Ambient genre, Brian Eno's Obscure label allowed the experimental avant-garde to reach an album-buying public. Obscure No. 1 was by Gavin Bryars, who contributed a masterpiece of disorientation and cultural shipwreck, *The Sinking of the Titanic*. Side two contained *Jesus' Blood Never Failed Me Yet*, a tramp's drunken and lachrymose rendition of one line from the Salvation Army hymn looped on tape, with creaky accompaniment by Derek Bailey on guitar, Michael Nyman on organ, John Nash on violin and John White on tuba. Bryars signalled composerly *hauteur* by conducting; double bass duties were taken care of by Sandra Hill. John Bonis designed covers for the series: a coarsely screened colour photograph was almost obliterated by a black overprint, apart from a single small aperture, whose position and shape differed on each. This aesthetic of obliteration came from contemporary fine art, where Gerhard Richter's grey monochromes were considered the zenith of anti-bourgeois nihilism. The very name of the label implied resistance to commodity culture.

> The name Obscure was a name Eno and I had. Originally we didn't want the records to be available in the shops in an easy way. People were going to have to get them via mail order and acquire them in the same way that we'd had to seek out things in the sixties. I took the line that when you're doing any research, one of the greatest pleasures you get is after hours of going through some series of indexes, you finally see a reference to the one name you've been looking for, and it's such a pleasure to encounter something – to have to seek – that when you get it, you value it the more. It was not a commercial way of thinking about marketing at all, the very name Obscure militates against that. That was a kind of wilful idea we had. Later, because Polygram got involved, they were distributed, but not very well. People found them and valued them. They had – they still do have – a kind of cult status. [*GB* 2–x–1997]

The little chinks in the black overprint implied each record was part of a jigsaw (a device also used by Oliver Bevan for the covers of the first ten volumes of Frank Kermode's early-seventies Fontana Modern Masters book series), though the picture that would be revealed was actually a banal English cityscape: stare through the keyhole of Modern Art and discover the Everyday.

Eno had attended concerts by free improvisors and experimental composers at the Purcell Room on London's South Bank. He enjoyed what John Tilbury and Bryars played, and ended up moving into Bryars's flat when Bryars left (Roxy Music's original bass player, Graham Simpson, lived in the basement of the building). Eno also worked for a printshop that printed some of Bryars's scores in the early 1970s. What had caught Eno's ear was the minimalist music at the Purcell Room. He believed it had commercial potential.

> When he got involved in rock music and achieved some success, he had this idea of some areas of contemporary music that he felt were actually

incredibly accessible and would not turn off the normal pop listener. He was particularly interested in the idea of ambience – things you could listen to on two levels, either closely or almost as background, because they didn't have the kinds of peaks and troughs of a lot of the more spiky avant-garde music. He wanted the tranquillity, the static quality. [*GB* 2–x–1997]

With the victory of minimalism in the concert halls in the nineties, and Ambient and Chill Out sections appearing in the record shops, the philosophy behind the Obscure label appears to have won out.

Seems to have – more and more. It does seem like the spiky avant-garde has been a little bit of a cul-de-sac, certainly in commercial terms. And also maybe even, in many ways, in the way written music is evolving, the spiky guys are thinking in other ways now. Eno perceived that. [*GB* 2–x–1997]

Back in 1975, however, the tenebrous and disquieting surrealism of *The Sinking of the Titanic* was not quite so marketable. Island could stretch to Stomu Yamash'ta's Red Buddha Theatre, Rico Rodriguez's trombone dub and Klaus Schulze's synth symphonies, but this music must have seemed almost deliberately dour and unappealing. Obscure was taken over by Polydor, who distributed the same records with stickers covering the reference to Island.

Some of the composers aired on Obscure – Michael Nyman, John Adams and Bryars himself – have gone on to become big names in contemporary classical music. Naturally such composers feel their success reflects the victory of their 'experimental' approach over the 'modernist' virtues of previous composers such as Harrison Birtwistle, Elliott Carter and Pierre Boulez. We are in the topsy-turvy world of postmodernism, where pastiche and simulacra are deemed more innovative – or at least more chic – than innovation. And, unsurprisingly enough, the 'experimental' composers seem to have conquered without any change to the system of orchestras, publishers and reviews-in-the-broadsheets that had originally been threatened with destruction.

In 1989, *The Sinking of the Titanic* and *Jesus' Blood Never Failed Me Yet* were re-recorded, the latter with a performance by Tom Waits replacing the original documentary tape-loop. This substitution was indicative: a camera-ready Hollywood celebrity replaced an upsetting document of penury. *The Sinking of the Titanic* itself became a harmless montage of sound effects. Clean recording deprived it of the disquieting mournfulness of its first recording; the strings were 'well-played'. In reviews, no one referenced the original, just as no one remembered the intense debates about composition and improvisation – and revolution – that had surrounded it. Cornelius Cardew's Scratch Orchestra, whose manifestations Bryars took part in, had promised to bring down all the divisions and hierarchies of capitalism. Gavin Bryars's Portsmouth Sinfonia may have lacked such political ambitions, but it still translated amateur performance into something provocative and satirical (the 7-inch single 'Classical Muddly' released by Springtime in 1981 proved that inept musicianship could debunk classical pops just as hilariously as punk trashed quality rock). However, by the late 1990s, with Gavin Bryars writing a requiem for performance at Westminster Abbey – Tony Blair in attendance – and Michael Nyman wrecking the political thrust of David King's Trotskyist photo-essay *The Commissar Vanishes* at the Barbican, it was revealed that the political radicalism of the 1970s was simply the noise of artists courting the attention of the establishment.

Brian Eno's Obscure series brought into the mass sphere music that would otherwise have been confined to one-off recitals. Unlike the later Editions EG on Virgin, by which time experiment had been honed into ingratiating lifestyle soundtracks, there was still a residue of thought-provoking music: notably *The Sinking of the Titanic*, but also Jan Steele's *All Day*. This latter came out of the 'quiet, repetitive form of improvised rock-based music' played by F&W Hat, a Yorkshire strain of Canterbury Rock (like Cornelius Cardew, Steele suffered from the peculiar self-hatred induced in radical intellectuals by Stalinism; he won *Melody Maker*'s 1976 Student Rock Essay Contest with a polemical attack on 'bourgeois' progressive and experimental rock – his own *métier* – in favour of the proletarian authenticity of the Who). Like Egg and National Health and Robert Wyatt, Steele's music had a poignancy and intimacy lacking in the strident ironies of the Obscure composers who later conquered the classical scene.

Obscure's quietist retort to rock hegemony was intriguing. However, its alternatives – hermeticism rather than display, silence rather than noise, intellectualism rather than animal heat – finally suggested a classier consumer option rather than any fundamental or galvanising critique. As punk was soon to prove, what was wrong with rock was not its noise and populist appeal, but the way marketing deprived it of immediacy, humour and politics. The exploitation of the avant-garde as a musical 'style' meant misconstruing its aims. Having a recognisable star – Robert Wyatt or Carla Bley – sing a song by John Cage effectively cancels its disruption of classical performance logic and converts it into an exercise in sentiment. This was the version of the avant-garde that the Kronos Quartet subsequently brought to market: rather than a culture of debate and experiment which resists passive consumption, the 'avant' becomes a smorgasbord of exotic comfits proffered to well-dressed yuppies.

Obscure No. 8 was shared between John White and Gavin Bryars. Bryars's piece occupied side two, and was the new recording of *The Squirrel and the Ricketty Racketty Bridge* with its all-star cast of Bryars, Eno, Fred Frith and Derek Bailey. The pleasing aspect of the Obscure recording is the live indeterminacy created by the four players, and its throbbing layers of acoustic and electric guitars. The compositional framework is deliberately banal (in the vein of Steve Reich). Played by less obstreperous personalities – or 'more accurate' musicians – the piece would be far less striking. Of course, both the chosen personnel and the playing handicaps were part of Bryars's intent, and (though less power-fully than *The Sinking of the Titanic*) it does show what telling music can result from Cagean interrogation of the parameters of musical production – provided that the composer uses improvisors rather than jobsworths.

IMPROVISATION – THEORETICAL EXCURSION (BRIEF RETURN)

Consideration of the Obscure series in the light of the music subse-quently produced by its composers forces one to take Bailey's anti-composer argument seriously – though maybe as a criticism more of the composers who emerged from this milieu than of composition as such.

Proceeding from a highly politicised critique of bourgeois art practice, Cage and Cardew opened the door to a host of practices. However, Cage's particular virtues only work within the frame of concert music, with its formality and rituals. This is why recordings of his music are usually unsatisfactory. Whereas his compositions are invariably surprising and concept-busting – Kant's 'sublime' – when experienced at classical concerts, his negations have little meaning at informal pub gigs where there is no dead weight of respect and tradition to subvert. When composers from the 'experimental' tradition – the term coined by Michael Nyman in his book *Experimental Music* to distinguish the post-Cagean, postmodernist approach from the modernists and serialists at Darmstadt – stop experimenting and subverting, and start delivering 'proper' music for performance by classical orchestras (as Bryars and Nyman have done), the bankruptcy of the aesthetic is revealed. The experimental composers made interesting music in the early 1970s because there were audiences prepared to negate bourgeois concert practice; when more reactionary times set in, it was revealed that the 'composers' from this milieu had not absorbed this negation into the technology of their scores: as positive music, its failings are blatant. The Joseph Holbrooke Trio, in contrast, built an audience at the Grapes on the basis of the musicians' *positive* virtues: Oxley's post-Elvin drums, Bryars's LaFaro-like bass, Bailey's dramatic guitar, and the trio's ability to hear and respond to each other. Joseph Holbrooke Trio music still bursts from the speakers with the vital, unapologetic quality of a side by John Lee Hooker.

Eno's Obscure series also brought in another factor, one derived from blues and rock, which is the *album*: the commodity that elevates the mere musician to 'recording artist', someone affiliated to a well-known label, implying fame, fortune and a connection to corporate capital. The album bristles with all the contradictions of commodity production: it introduces alienation and exploitation, yet also suggests the universal accessibility of cultural forms. The album separates musicians from their product and turns their labour into a means of making profit: but it also provides the generalised experience that allows music criticism to be something more than reports of specific concerts or technical analyses of scores. With the album, music is converted into part of the social environment: as punk understood, to criticise pop music is actually to criticise everything about capitalism.

Different forces within our fragmented culture set up well-defended forts at different places in this much-disputed terrain. Purist free improvisors decry the album form – until that is, they're pushing their own CD, in which case they become righteous petit-bourgeois label owners selling you items untainted by 'corporate compromise' (like nineteenth-century handloom weavers hawking a sample of their wares). Record collectors resent the implication that they are disempowered morons salivating over other people's place in the spectacle, and point out that without vinyl records and CDs musical history would be the private domain of an elite of contemporary-music concertgoers. Someone who believes in the authenticity of the super-difficult scores written by the likes of Brian Ferneyhough and Michael Finnissy might argue that the Obscure composers derived radical chic by association with Free Improvisation, but failed to carry Free Improvisation's superfine rhythmic and microtonal granularity into their objective scores; as soon as Nyman, Bryars and Adams got the chance to write for straight orchestras they did, ditching the 'spiky' soundworld of the improvisors, and helping the official concert scene to regress to neo-classical kitsch. An Obscure recording might have a certain charge – deriving from the collective *ésprit* of those involved at the date of recording – but it was not in the *score*, a product of the scientific organisation of sound, and hence the composer's work is unrepeatable and inauthentic. In so far as Obscure records sound good today, it is because of the unique time and place of the music – in other words, their *improvised* quality.

Different approaches pack different virtues. Take the issue of silence. Rather than a nihilistic erasure of meaning or a trivial background 'ambience', Free Improvisation makes silence part of a collective event. It's interesting that Brian Eno favoured Tilbury and Bryars in particular, both classically trained: their silences were not collective and lived, but vacant and conceptual. According to Eno, here was avant-garde music that 'would not turn off the normal pop listener' (the opposite of Frank Zappa's belief that hearing Varèse and Nancarrow might turn *on* the *abnormal* pop listener). This normative concern stems from marketing rather than from music making; it abandons the idea of new music transforming listening habits, and instead proposes accommodation to conventional taste. It obscures the fact that the 'normal pop listeners' are themselves historical products, and forces musical possibility into a commercial straitjacket. Eno's aesthetic is decadent, a knowing accommodation to capitalist pressures. No wonder his bachelor-pad installation at Sonic Boom – a sound-art exhibition staged at the Hayward Gallery on London's South Bank in 2000 – suggested the funeral parlour in *Soylent Green*, where ageing citizens go to have a last draught of 'pleasure' before they are put down and recycled for foodstuff. The Obscure series cultivated the aspects of the informal avant-garde that were reactionary, strategies designed to give bourgeois values a new lease of life, rather than bring them crashing down.

One reason Bailey resists the term 'jazz' is that it is used to stuff the gap between pop and classical with a known repertoire, when it is precisely the unknown potential between the two that provides a space for innovation. Bailey likes the fact that the music he plays has no settled name (he finds the term Free Improvisation, capitalised in this text, slightly ludicrous); people more concerned with distribution than musical production, on the other hand, deem it a victory when a term they're hawking – Brian Eno's Ambient, Johnny Black's New Age, Tricky's Trip Hop, Edwin Pouncey's Weird – is granted a slot in the racks. The recent inflation of these terms is a perfect illustration of the tendency of the rate of profit to decline: all the speculators pursue the same policy of profit maximisation, yet drive the system inexorably towards slump.

Once it's grasped that Derek Bailey's musical production is not 'pop' – and sits uneasily with attempts to grant it commercial visibility or cachet – the usual assumption is that it is therefore 'classical' or 'art'. However, it is equally hard for fine art institutions – music publishers or art dealers – to get a grip on something as evanescent as Free Improvisation. Unlike John Cage and the pioneers of the graphic score, Bailey's interactions with fellow musicians produce no tangible objects for the art dealers and music publishers. He is the seventies anti-commodity conceptual artist who really did leave the bourgeoisie with nothing to grab.

The problems do not stop there. The very evanescence of Free

Improvisation also represents a challenge to rational analysis. Absolute insistence on the specificity of a musical event abolishes the historical imagination and sociological perspective necessary for materialist-aesthetic comprehension and judgement. Occasionally Bailey adopts an unhistorical humanism which characterises score writing and recording as bourgeois deviations that hardly dent the centuries of improvisation that existed in pre-capitalist times – and will presumably be reinstated as capitalism reverts to barbarism or ascends to socialism. Marxist musical analysis, which depends on a historical understanding of artistic form, is made impossible by such Zen insistence on the anthropological *hic et nunc*. Sometimes it feels as if Free Improvisation is the result of musicians who believed John Cage's rhetoric and, forgetting to put their own trademark opus numbers on their versions of silence, played themselves off the horizon of history. We're the real thing simply because no one has heard of us.

This is where a triangulation of Bailey's practice – from the point of view of the art aspiration of Cage and the pop positivism of Eno, as well as the drive to innovation of jazz – can define its position on the world historical map and gauge its real value. It is axiomatic to any philosophical consideration of the aesthetics of jazz and blues that it was recording technology and the commercial circulation of records that allowed a 'folk' art to become a mass phenomenon. Mechanical recording allowed individualised instrumental approaches – and particular, non-standardised voices – to become historical actors. Though it seeks musical events unbounded by the commercial logic of record promotion, Free Improvisation likewise proceeds in a web of recording technologies. Bailey is probably one of the most documented musicians playing regularly today: since the early 1980s, it hasn't been unusual to see several tape recorders running at gigs where the actual audience was scarcely in double figures. The uncommercial nature of these recordings is no reason to doubt their significance: they are an extension of the democratic and anti-hierarchical thrust of Free Improvisation. However, they do allow for historical study, providing opportunities for judgement and distinction. For example, the instant recognisability of Bailey's guitar – whatever the context – provides a line in for listeners who might otherwise reject anonymous experimental chaos.

It must be admitted that making a fetish of Derek Bailey's contribution can offend the democratic ethos that marks Free Improvisation. Paul Buckton, founder member of the Leeds Termite Club and its indomitable organiser during the 1980s, once accused this author of being a 'nameist' because he expressed excitement that Lol Coxhill was coming to play in Leeds. However, Free Improvisation does retain a competitive and critical edge, resisting moves to turn it into community art, feelgood seance or audio-therapy. Inability to recognise the need for leaders when waging struggle condemns radical politics to armchair anarchism and moral stricture. Likewise, in radical music: Frank Kofsky's understanding of the key role of John Coltrane in the struggle for freedom in jazz remains one of the great gifts of Trotskyism to music criticism (see Kofsky's *Black Nationalism and the Revolution in Music*, reissued as *John Coltrane and the Jazz Revolution of the 1960s*). It is not a matter of elevating Bailey's contribution to unapproachable 'genius' level, but of understanding *how* his particular approach enables musical dialogue to happen. He is a leader, not because he dictates, but because his example can be learned from. Let's think once again about *what he plays.*

Like a truly interesting conversationalist, Bailey's guitar-playing does not flatter the musicians he plays with, or attempt to make them sound good in a facile way: he attempts to understand what they are playing by contradicting them. He 'tests' their musical utterances just as Socrates tested the statements of his contemporary Athenians. The source of his 'spikiness' is this interest in repartee; his negations are productive because they are grounded in musical comprehension of his interlocutors' logic. Bailey proposes a new music in which answers are only valued as answers to concrete questions. There is no transcendence parachuting down from the skies. All there is is you here talking – so, now, get on with it. *Contra* Bryars and Eno, without this 'spikiness' all dialectic – all genuine communication – ceases.

Solo Bailey is different: more strained, more problematic and existential and bleak, definitely harder work. However, at its best it echoes back the myriad dialogues which Bailey has engaged in. Like all the greatest literature, it is a composite of many voices. When Bailey and Zappa suspend obvious time in their music, it allows them to make their instruments speak. Zappa spoke a low-down argot full of blue innuendo and blasphemy. Bailey's discourse is authentically English, and recalls the blank-verse rhetoric of the Elizabethan stage, where dramatic tension is achieved by the contrast of big, loud, resonant phrases and hushed and intimate reflections. The mistake many solo improvisors make is to forget that all musical utterance – even that dreamed or heard only by the inner ear – is social. Bailey's blurting, jilted phrases are a riot of rhythmic invention because they forever turn on the contradiction between public rhetoric and private conscience – as farctate with dynamics, unlikely contrasts and neologisms as a soliloquy in a Shakespeare play.

BAILEY AND COMPOSITION

Like his turn from commercial work to Free Improvisation, Derek Bailey's turn against composition wasn't instant. On 6 October 1972, for example, he took part in a 'Composers' Weekend' sponsored by the Society for the Promotion of New Music, playing alongside bassist Barry Guy in an ensemble billed as the 'London Contemporary Chamber Players'. Conducted by Henry Ward, the concert included pieces by Roger Marsh, Dallapiccola and Richard Steinetz. On 6 December 1972, Bryars and Bailey were billed as playing a 'Concert of Contemporary and Electronic Music' at the John Clare Building in Northampton. Bryars was in America, and John Tilbury took his place. In the first half, Tilbury played from *Sonatas and Interludes for Prepared Piano* (1946–48) by John Cage, and then Bailey played what were billed as *Guitar Pieces *1, *2, *3* (1967). The programme note ran:

> These pieces all derive from the same series, technically, and owe much to the music of Webern. The 2nd piece is in song form and is specifically designed for the guitar. They are all concise pieces which attempt to compass a high degree of emotionally expressive sound within the confines of the miniature.

Bailey committed these pieces to tape (the same reel-to-reel he had used to drive the rock *couturière* to distraction with Webern). In 2002, miraculously restored through the combined efforts of Toby Robinson (who made a digital recording of the original tape) and Scott Hull (who mastered the release), they were issued on John Zorn's Tzadik label: *Pieces for Guitar* [TZ7080].

Given the caustic comments Bailey makes about the classical fetish of the score, some fans believe he is an intuitive player, hostile to the analytical thrust of Western music since Bach codified the tempered system. Not so. Rather like the anarchist anti-intellectuals who applauded Lenin's break with the Marxist Second International in 1914 (when he called for international proletarian opposition to the imperialist war), only to find that he'd reached that position by an intense study of Hegel's *Greater Logic* and Marx's *Capital*, intuitivist Bailey fans may be shocked to find that in 1966, in formulating his theory of permanent improvisation, Bailey was obsessed with the works of Webern.

Bailey's critique of musical academia is not that it cares too much about the precise position of each note, but that it confuses means and ends. Hypnotised by the legacy of Bach, Mozart and Beethoven – all of whom were more famous in their lifetimes as players than as composers – classicism places the score on a pedestal and ignores the creative, practical musician who is really the source of invention. However, when Bailey looked to extend the freedoms he had been exploring with Gavin Bryars and Tony Oxley in the Joseph Holbrooke Trio, the example of Webern was crucial – and Webern's music is inconceivable without the score. Bailey needed to sketch his own scores to work out how his guitar could accommodate Webern's break with tonal restrictions. However, the point was not a finished 'work', but the ideas that could allow a musician's fingers and ears to enter a new dimension.

Pieces for Guitar is centred on six written pieces, but 'Practising: Wow & Stereo' and two improvisations on 'Piece No. 1' and 'No. 2' show what kind of playing they were designed for: free improvisation. Bailey plays electric guitar exclusively, immediately taking the sonic a million miles away from classical models. He plays soft, separate, undistorted notes, evoking the atmosphere of Brian Eno's Discreet Music series of the early seventies (as revealed by the battle with the *couturière*, Derek was likewise reacting against the high-volume commercialism of rock). So novel and various are Bailey's note choices, that one has the impression that he's playing not guitar, but some kind of multi-stringed microtonal harp.

Bailey did not adopt atonality as a formalist straitjacket, but as the key to a post-Einsteinian universe of note relations (when he called a release *String Theory* – Paratactile PLE1109 – in 2000, it was because, in common with the new cosmogeny, he understands the universe to be made of vibrating strings). The new freedoms enabled him to access musical ideas as old as biology: 'Bits' has a dialogue between an upper-register stream of motifs and a sequence played on lower strings. Recalling both Punch and Judy and Wagner's pitching of banks of double basses versus the soprano voice, such high/low gender role symbolism helps conceive of music as urgent dialectic rather than stasis and hierarchy.

As the name implies, 'Practising: Wow & Stereo' emphasises sonority, one so strange it's like watching microbes on a moon of Jupiter improvise a jig. Bailey's ripping changes in dynamics – his sudden loud notes that make you jump out of your skin – could not arrive from someone trying to be dramatic, because any theatricalism would frame the gesture. It is Bailey's concentration on innovative clusters and stretched intervals (often using two octaves and a seventh as a springboard) – devices which, he declares today, still occasionally demand to be noted on scraps of paper – that makes the outcome so raw and inspiringly unexpected. Free Jazz was not created by the flamboyant saxophonists who made their names with the style, but by technical advances in terms of overlaid tempi made by the composer Charles Mingus. Bailey occupies a similar role in Free Improvisation. In other words, his fierce commitment to unwritten improvisation is more a defence of the only environment in which his playing can thrive than an outright condemnation of written analysis.

In the second half of the Northampton concert, Bailey and Tilbury performed improvisations and pieces by Morton Feldman. When Bailey later developed his theory of improvisation – in a BBC radio series in 1974, and culminating in the book *Improvisation: Its Nature and Practice In Music* (1980) – it wasn't out of ignorance of the possibilities of twentieth-century composition. Indeed, a founding release of the new genre included the word 'composition' in its title.

SOLOISM AND FREEDOM, 1966-1977

4 COMPOSITIONS FOR SEXTET

On 7 February 1970, Tony Oxley made another record for CBS. Whereas *The Baptised Traveller* had a weathered boulder on the cover, a study in moss and lichens, *4 Compositions for Sextet* had just the title in ornate script, its flourishes suggesting the gravitas of classical music. Oxley had Bailey on board as a player, but Oxley's references were different. The titles – 'Saturnalia', 'Scintilla', 'Megaera' and 'Amass' – sounded a note of high seriousness, though on listening each prove to be precise descriptions of the music. 'Saturnalia' opens with what Michael Walters's sleeve note called 'a brief fanfare of melody'. It still bursts on the ear like a wake-up call to the senses. The brownwood solemnity of modal jazz has erupted into iridescent jags, atonal intervals allowing the different sounds of the instruments to shine raw and unhomogenised. Oxley's musical concept is a challenge to the skill of the players, who have to think in finer metrical calibrations than any music heretofore. The musicians are pioneering an improvised art music cognisant of Webern and Stockhausen, giving a sense of a static grid to be stained by their sound gestures. The power of this interstitial leakage derives from the ensemble procedure rather than from the individuality of the players.

On 'Scintilla', speedplay exuberance is held in check by tentatively assayed clusters that ache with the pressure to squeeze new moods from the diatonic system. Whereas Ornette Coleman's free jazz seduces the listener into a mental (or, when occasion permits, a physical) dance out of sympathy with soloistic subjectivity, this has a contemplative serenity, like watching an abstract painter lay down shapes. Once this contemplative moment has been attained, the pace hots up, whirling the instruments into the multicoloured density that is the Bailey/Oxley contribution to ensemble music. A closing, preplanned chord seems to be there to assure the listener that all this has been utterly deliberate.

'Amass' begins with a trilling motif from Evan Parker's tenor, fraught with tension. Bailey's glancing clusters are so alien they sound like experimental electronics – which is what they were mimicking. Paul Rutherford's wittering trombone mimicks Parker, a perfect example of the way creative illusionism allows European improvisors to drag them-

DEREK BAILEY AND THE STORY OF FREE IMPROVISATION

selves out of tired harmonic and rhythmic patterns. Bailey says, 'That's one of the great playing pleasures, to not know whether you've played it or someone else has played it. You don't get much of that nowadays.' [27–vi–2000]

Rutherford's use of throat and voice distorts legitimate timbre, giving the sound a physical quality more appropriate to Oxley's anti-transcendental concept than the fleet suavity of Kenny Wheeler's contributions to *The Baptised Traveller*. Oxley was intent on avoiding bop cliché, and this included the vocalised blues licks that sound like pastiche coming from Europeans, yet he wanted something more than cool 'head' music. He wanted, in fact, the total physical immersion – no part of human experience excluded – that marked Beethoven's revolutionary universalism, and which John Coltrane and Cecil Taylor rediscovered for the twentieth century. However, Oxley saw that this totality could not be achieved by borrowing superficialities from either classical music or jazz. In the noises of the animal body, improvisors find a vocabulary untainted by 'sounds-like' sophistication, free of the social hierarchies implied by historically attested sound (or 'music').

That is not to say that technical advances – genuine additions to musical science – are not evident. 'Megaera' uses serialism to keep simultaneous voices apart. The idea that the twelve-tone method opened the way to a democracy of sound (no key in charge) has always had a paradoxical twist in the hands of art composers dictating to (often unwilling) musicians. Here, the democracy is evident: if these players abandoned atonalism their contributions would congeal in a harmonic lump and lose their individuality. However, unlike the vocalised expressionism of jazz, the individuality of Oxley's music on *4 Compositions for Sextet* relies on an abstract system rather than life-into-art personality: despite the debunking, visceral nature of much of the playing, the classicising album cover was no idle threat.

ICHNOS

Sometime in 1971, Tony Oxley recorded *Ichnos* for RCA Victor, his last brush with the corporates until the re-release of *The Baptised*

Traveller and *4 Compositions for Sextet* by Sony in 1999. He again used Bailey, Wheeler, Parker and Rutherford. Bassist Jeff Clyne was replaced by Barry Guy. The record appeared on RCA Victor's standard orange label, the one used for Lou Reed's top-selling *Transformer* album: it's fascinating to consider that in 1971, reeling from the success of progressive rock, record company executives had no idea that Tony Oxley's music was in a totally different category (that's because in the context of Jimi Hendrix and Soft Machine and their incursions into pop's business-as-usual, it wasn't).

The cover sported a photograph of Oxley's augmented drum kit, with its cowbells, inverted aluminium casserole, saucepan lid, metal ciné reel, corrugated washboard and row of miniature cymbals bolted to a length of self-assembly bookcase girder. It was photographed from the drummer's point of view rather than the audience's. The record included a percussion solo – 'Oryane' – that showcased Oxley's extraordinary ability to inhabit the serial world of Stockhausen, giving his astral soundworld an expressive fluency never achieved by classical performers.

The record opens with a new version of the *Baptised Traveller* opener 'Crossing' that replaces the bop melody lines with what Oxley called 'textures'. The lack of harmonic order means that even Kenny Wheeler sounds appropriately manic and unhinged. The fleet violence and detail of the music is still more stunning than that of *The Baptised Traveller*. Behind the flurry there is an inexorable power – the triumphant surge Oxley's understanding of time brings to all the music he plays. 'Quartets' opens with cartoon sax quacks and continues with a fast-paced array of motifs from metal percussion, electric guitar and trombone. By seizing the timbral serialism of Webern and performing it with the expressive velocity of jazz, Oxley's group heralded almost everything new in music for the next three decades – from fusion to punk, from John Zorn's *Parachute Years* 'game' pieces to drum'n'bass.

In contrast to the piety with which art music is presented to gullible publics – from holy minimalism to ecstatic jazz – what characterises *Ichnos* is the wit and pomp-pricking savagery of the interactions. It revives Edgard Varèse's project of a music that would organise itself according to the dictates of timbre and the impact of noise rather than overarching systems of harmony and rhythm. Intense, high-speed syncopation – a novel sense of swing – allows the musicians to emphasise the sounds of their instruments as never before. It makes all previous music sound grey.

GAVIN BRYARS VERSUS FREE IMPROVISATION

Gavin Bryars's rejection of improvisation and his success as a composer have not deprived him of his ability to make shrewd observations. He explains why Free Improvisation resists passive listening.

> It's a very dramatic activity. You're watching people think quite intensely in public. In a way, you can't relegate that to the sidelines. That's why it has to be done in places where you are focusing on that activity. It can't be dinner music. But some things, Evan Parker's playing for example, the solo soprano sax stuff – that for me can be very easily acceptable, where you're not forced to follow an argument in the same way as you are with a group of people improvising together. [*GB* 2–x–1997]

In interviews, Derek Bailey frequently compares Free Improvisation to conversation, pointing out to puzzled interrogators that really nothing is more natural than improvisation: 'Isn't that what we're doing now?'

> I really believe there's a unique compatibility between music and improvisation. The only other area where I think improvisation is in its right element is conversation. There are so many parallels between music and conversation. [*Melody Maker* 2 August 1980]

If Free Improvisation is conversation and repartee (what Socrates called 'dialectic'), the fondness of New Age and Ambient and Trance for held chords would correspond to the collective catatonia of the more tedious and alienated examples of drug use. The influence of La Monte Young on the Velvet Underground – via his pupil John Cale – established inevitable connections between amplified drones, drug use and transcendentalist impatience with dialectical reason. Like Dada, Free Improvisation is conversational, here-and-now, aggressively banal. It is not automatically 'sublime': sublimity must be earned through playing intelligence. It creates a genuine connection between sublimity (the One) and the everyday (the Many): that's its point.

To the mainstream, all avant-gardes look the same, but the avant-garde is actually bifurcated by a struggle between transcendental idealists and dialectical materialists. Free Improvisation is not simply another 'avant excess' which Marxists can indulge or not as it suits them (or as it suits their concept of the conceptual limits of the working class): it is the manifestation of socialist revolution in music – practical, collective, anti-ideological and humanist. It stomps on myth and insists that music is played by people (even if not in circumstances of their own choosing). Free Improvisation is no more recuperable by class society than revolutionary Marxism; and it is no less riven by debate, polemic, destabilising exaggeration, awesome self-consciousness, shocking treachery, bloody apostasy, brilliant moments, and noise.

People who are sceptical about the political significance of artistic form point to the successive recuperation of avant-gardes by the establishment. As Trotsky pointed out, avant-garde 'protest' is usually the noise of those who most crave admission to the academy. The careers of John Adams, Michael Nyman and Gavin Bryars are relevant: they emerged from an 'experimental' milieu loud in their scorn for an antiquated establishment, but they now occupy precisely the positions they once criticised. To broadsheet reviewers whose coverage is restricted to the famous and successful, the editorial purview provides a self-fulfilling prophecy: anyone visible is always a sell-out, which proves that all rebellion is phoney. Indeed, the invert situationism of declaring that unrecuperable art is impossible – and hence not worth attempting – is one of the principal planks of postmodernist collusion and reaction.

The question remains as to the status of the thousands of recordings on which Bailey has played. This depends on the state of music and society in the twenty-first century. Like the player-piano compositions of Conlon Nancarrow or the albums of Frank Zappa, Bailey recordings are a resource for anyone genuinely interested in forging a universal musical language that shows respect for the specificities of cultural diversity. However, both Bailey's record label and his scattered tapings have evaded capture and exploitation by either music publishers or corporate labels. Bailey himself finds the idea of listeners in thrall to old recordings as repulsive as any charade presented by music industry agents and promoters. If Free Improvisation is to prosper, it will be in the care of free improvisors defining their own soundworlds, not tapeworms burrowing into the archive. However, as Tharg said in a reply to a letter in the esteemed sci-fi comic *2000AD*,* those who ignore history will be condemned to repeat it (or as Misty In Roots said on their first John Peel session, 'a man without knowledge of history is like a cabbage in this society'). Free Improvisation represents a practical attempt at a universal musical language so far unsurpassed. Like *Finnegans Wake* or the writings of Karl Marx, the legibility of Bailey's *oeuvre* is dependent less on its finely wrought and conscientious inner structure (which undoubtedly exists, and which no doubt academia will one day try to unravel), than on the potential of society to recognise the substantial freedoms capitalism's conquest of nature implies – but which its social relations deny.

THE MUSIC IMPROVISATION COMPANY

Having performed at the Institute of Contemporary Arts the previous summer, Bailey occupied another bastion of the establishment, in the form of BBC Radio 3, when he recorded for a broadcast with Evan Parker, Hugh Davies and Jamie Muir on 4 July 1969. Though later called the Music Improvisation Company, the group was announced on air on 23 July as the 'London Instrumental and Electronic Improvising Group'. This temporary name was an apt description: Parker and Bailey were both practised instrumentalists, whereas Davies and Muir emerged from art school experimentalism. Though Davies also used an electronic organ on this date, he was essentially interested in the qualities that electronics – close-miking, amplification and echo – brought to sound. At the same time, his input was rather more musical than that of some experimentalists Derek was familiar with from the Little Theatre.

* Prog 599, 5 November 1988.

Everybody was walking around with contact mics they were sticking on things to see what it sounded like. I'm not quite sure how this evolved, we thought we needed somebody a little more, let's say, instrumental – these were all geniuses who were coming up and playing and you know the trouble with geniuses, they get these fucking ideas all the time. Well, any fool can get ideas, we wanted somebody who could play. [*laughs*] We thought for some reason that Hugh would be more group-minded and it turned out to be so, I think. So this was the Music Improvisation Company. [16–xii–1997]

Bailey used a foot pedal to alter his volume, and at high volume his plectrum's attack on the string frequently mimicked Davies's amplified fidgets and scrapes. It is worth examining the music they played in detail, because Bailey thought enough of this BBC session to release it twice (*The Music Improvisation Company 1968–1971*, Incus LP17 in 1976, and Incus CD12 in 1993).

'Pointing' begins with a sustained, high-pitched tone on soprano, recalling a practice often employed in the Spontaneous Music Ensemble. It takes the saxophone out of the orbit of jazz: instead of a vocal argument it becomes an abstract sound colour. Bailey and Davies then hang an astonishingly varied series of processed noises on this sonic line. In an aesthetic where so much depends on the active contrast of different qualities of noise, the clarity of CD sound is particularly revealing: though recorded in mono, the detail and presence are ear-pricking. As Parker starts to respond to the others, he becomes an enquiring subject: a sensitive, rather nervous rodent nosing among rustling leaves and loose wires.

On 'Untitled 3', the musicians' eagerness for musical material is palpable as they leap on any random opening motif with analytical knives and forks sharp and ready. The four contributors whirl into a single entity. The word 'vortex' is too reminiscent of natural forces to be accurate here; rather, the Music Improvisation Company resemble the conglomerate monsters that erupt from urban bric-à-brac in Manga animations. However, this entity is a Velcrose snowball comprising wire rakes, garden hoses and rusty hinges. Davies's organ provides a dim memory of chordal propriety, but it is the electronic distortion he's interested in. Jamie Muir's drumming has abandoned metre for responsive flurries that underline his colleagues' gestures; Bailey is so rhythmically graphic, it is as if every note he inserts between Muir's snare rolls comes prepacked down the fast-food chute. Parker develops his exploratory snuffles into a squeaking continuity, turning the solo voice of the saxophone into the breathed equivalent of rhythm guitar. The music has the abrupt arbitrariness that characterises all unapologetic art invention. 'Untitled 4' again whirls everything round a single point of energy, Davies's electronics and Muir's cymbals suddenly opening up spatial vistas. In 'Bedrest' the musicians' vibrating sonics appear to reach out like sensitive antennae. The musicians have broken into an expanding musical universe where, rather than submitting to *a priori* parameters of key and tempo, sound gestures themselves define the structure.

On 18 June 1970, the 'Music Improvising Group' was again recorded by BBC Radio 3 for broadcast, providing the last two titles for the *Music Improvisation Company* album: 'Its Tongue Trapped to the Rock by the Limpet, the Water Rat Succumbed to the Incoming Tide' and 'In the Victim's Absence'. If anything, the music has gained in power, though on the first of these additions Parker is intent on a funny-sounding squeak that suits the title (whose whimsical humour sounds like something from Lewis Carroll, immensely popular in the late sixties underground).* A sparse beginning unfolds into an ensemble roar, the musicians using pitch to keep their instrumental effects separate rather than gain consonance. Rather than exchange motifs, the players evince awareness of overall mood and tension.

On the sleeve Bailey appended a learned citation. Its anthropological focus on playing activity – rather than listener association or official musical history – made it a favourite resource of Bailey's.

The original concepts of vocal and instrumental music are utterly different. The instrumental impulse is not melody in a 'melodious' sense but in agile movement of the hands which seem to be under the control of a brain centre totally different from that which inspires vocal melody. Altogether, instrumental music, with the exception of rudimentary

---

* Derek Bailey insists, 'That actually happened to Mal Dean [*Melody Maker* caricaturist and critic and trumpeter in the Amazing Band] on his holidays . . . I don't mean *he* was trapped to the rock by his tongue, but he saw it, or at least he claimed that.' [i–2001]

rhythmic percussion, is as a rule a florid, fast and brilliant display of virtuosity. [Curt Sachs, *The Wellsprings of Music*]

It might seem weird that Bailey should cite a defence of 'brilliant displays of virtuosity' while playing music so little suited to crowd-pleasing. However, it does beg the question, What is it about Bailey's style that denied him the plaudits showered on fusion players? As his innovations are absorbed by less contrary talents – Bill Frisell, Thurston Moore, Eugene Chadbourne – and punk and grunge make skronk guitar a desirable commodity, there are signs that recognition is glimmering on the horizon, but in the seventies any comparison of the status of Bailey and, say, John McLaughlin would have been laughable. What is the real difference between the 'florid, fast and brilliant' guitar playing of Music Improvisation Company and *The Inner Mounting Flame*?

The basic difference is harmonic. John McLaughlin's music is pressed into dramatic modal arpeggios designed to represent the spirit rising towards transcendence. The return to a particular note, the leap of an interval, a dazzling run through a scale, can all be measured next to the framework set up by bass and keyboards. With *Music Improvisation Company 1968–1971*, there is no framework by which to judge Bailey's virtuosity: this is suggestive play rather than calibrated sport. It is possible to cite a battalion of theorists of radical modernism – Theodor Adorno, Clement Greenberg, Asger Jorn – to argue why this shows Bailey is free and valuable in a way McLaughlin is not. One can also play his music next to that of the Mahavishnu Orchestra and ponder the difference.

The comparison highlights something the supporters of Free Improvisation tend to forget. In refusing the public spectacle, in insisting on the dramatic nature of private sound, Bailey and Company undermine the sublime. In comparison to the sweeping virtuosity of the Mahavishnu Orchestra – which evokes traditional virtues from Liszt to Ravi Shankar – the kind of virtuosity proposed by Bailey is so shockingly physical that the listener is forced to think of such acts as armpit-scratching and nose-picking. Its return of music to the physical act debunks civilisation itself. That is why there are so many correspondences between the primitivism of punk – which negates the achievements of history and culture in favour of existential confrontation with social limits – and the musicianly expertise of Free Improvisation. Bailey and Company are musical inhabitants of Diogenes' barrel. Woof woof!

When Hugh Davies is pursuing a close-miked scrunch and Bailey is signalling his involvement with a series of rasped pings – or Evan Parker is pushing overblown soprano saxophone sound into glottal regions of nose-blow anguish – we are witnessing the pursuit of instrumental ability beyond civilised elevation. The unconscious basis of curiosity – the child's interest in the products of the body – is foregrounded in these sounds, refusing the transcendent beauty of staged virtuosity. In citing Sachs, Bailey is criticising styles of playing that transcend the physical instrument, using time-honoured harmonic signals to evoke immaterial values: he wants to ground music-making in its played actuality. To the transcendent – or Mahavishnu – ear, this will sound bathetic, even disgusting; however, to listeners who suspect that the evocative mechanisms of the past can only be recycled as kitsch, Bailey's return of music to physical actions of scratch and sniff sounds like the voice of truth. That which appears retarded and ridiculous from the point of view of transcendence actually reveals transcendence as a lie. The key system and counted-out metres are unmasked as a fixed-point perspective required for an illusion of beauty; a more robust beauty is found in paying attention to the combinant materials themselves.

At the end of August 1970, Manfred Eicher paid for the Music Improvisation Company to record an album for his label ECM. This was before the development of the notorious ECM sound which – though strenuously denied by those employed by the label – is actually a transcendent aesthetic acutely uncomfortable with sonic realism and productive actuality. (Due to ECM's powerful advertising budget, this is not an easy observation to make in music magazines: having had many spats with editors over this issue, I was pleased to see critic John Corbett make this point, though it was naturally in a Marxist art journal rather than a commercial music magazine (*October*, no. 54, reprinted in his collection *Extended Play*, p. 43.)

Even at this early date, Derek was uncomfortable with record company assumptions about the best methods of achieving brilliant music.

SOLOISM AND FREEDOM, 1966-1977

We went to the country for five days, recorded in a large mansion. We recorded it ourselves, or maybe Evan recorded it. We used to go out there. They used to stay out there, I used to drive back, the thought of sleeping in this damp bloody baronial mansion. No. It was at Redhill. This is what rock groups used to do, go to the country and make a record. So we went out there and recorded for five days. Hopeless. I think the music on the record is the first forty-five minutes of Monday morning's recording. The five days just went on and on, it became worse and worse. It's hopeless, that system, too much time. You can't have too little time – how can you have too little? we're improvising – but you can certainly have too much. This abandoned house, it had a swimming pool outside. The house disappeared because it was where the motorway to Brighton was to go. I think we had a dog there – one of the tracks is named after this dog. By this time we'd recruited Christine Jeffrey. [16–xii–1997]

It is a tribute to singer Christine Jeffrey's musicality that it is hard to distinguish her contribution. It is easy to make a vocal sound stand out in front of musical instruments (this partly explains Derek's animus against the saxophone), but on her two tracks Jeffrey mixes her vocal with the soprano sax and the whistling electronics to great effect.

The song titles seemed designed to offend the aggressive tastefulness Manfred Eicher would later make his hallmark. The opening 'Third Stream Boogaloo' guys Gunther Schuller's fusion of avant-garde classical and jazz; the closing 'Wolfgang Van Gangbang' manages both to name the aforementioned studio dog and make a lewd joke on the names of Mozart and Beethoven. A similarly scurrilous attitude pervades the playing. A spirit of boisterous hooliganism makes the musicians so keen to grapple with each other's musical ideas that they immediately dive into impossible knots. These compacted scrums of hard, dense, writhing energy are separated from each other by stringy sections where instruments strain at the edge of audibility, like the thin paint streaks connecting complex blotches in the lines Asger Jorn dripped over Guy Debord's words in *Mémoires* (1958). Sounds hang in the air as gestural acts, but any hint of reverence is trashed by the speed and avidity of the musicians' ripostes. Parker and Bailey have an extraordinarily congruent sense of harmony, sputtering together like a single firework. The untempered electronic noises thrown out by Davies force Bailey to hear his guitar notes as brute electronic sounds, giving his high-note pings near physical force. Parker's tortured-duck gargle is the only possible reply to Bailey's metallic finger-scrabble. This music is a continuously evolving sonic junk-sculpture which redeems all kinds of ugliness – rust, jagged tears, waste fragments, garish scraps, acid flecks and burns – by its liveliness of placement and contrast.

'Packaged Eel' proposes a new music comprising tense waiting, sardonic anticipation and musical interpretation of the sounds of movement and fidgeting. Muir's drums follow up the others' phrases with an erotic sense of consequence. The sensation of risk and violence is stomach-knotting. Bailey's guitar demarcates Davies's sounds like a draughtsman sketching wall stains; Davies retorts with baby tantrums, his electronic outbursts rejecting this swaddling of sense. Everything the Music Improvisation Company play refuses the 'gorgeousness' offered by electronics – echo, automatic harmony, consonant shimmer – instead foregrounding manual intervention, human decisiveness, collective activity, repartee.

On 'In the Victim's Absence' – recorded by the MIC two months before (without Jeffrey), and released on *The Music Improvisation Company 1968–1971* – everything seems to stop before it starts, everyone listens more than they play. Small sounds appear in the silence as if the musicians are observing sonic matter appearing in the distance. Musical resolution – closing harmony or rhythmic finish – isn't abandoned but delayed, held in mind throughout the piece. Hugh Davies's electronics create a stretched field across which Bailey and Parker motifs squiggle like automatic calligraphy in surrealism (Ernst, Klee, Michaux).

The Curt Sachs quotation that Bailey printed on the Incus release of the Music Improvisation Company concluded with the words 'Quick motion is not merely a means to a musical end but almost an end in itself which always connects with the fingers, the wrists and the whole of the body.' This relates to the emphasis on the human hand – with its opposable thumb – to be found throughout the history of materialist and oppressed-class philosophy. In the manner of Wilhelm Reich, the unrepressed delights of auto-eroticism ('wrist jobs') are wielded against mysticism and cant.

As the gods are thrust into the background, the interplay of nature and mankind comes forward more prominently and more powerfully. This can be seen in the Milesian speculations on the problem of biology and the development of mankind. Aniximander said that mankind arose from the moist element and was once like a fish. Anaxagoras, his successor, made a no less noteworthy contribution to materialism. He attributed the superiority of man over the other animals to his technological activity. According to him, man is the most intelligent of the animals because he has hands, the hand being the tool par excellence and the model of all tools. [George Novack, *Origins of Materialism*, p. 105]

Novack's conclusion can also be applied to the Music Improvisation Company:

This observation is wholly in line with the first principles of historical materialism which singles out the hand as the most important single biological organ responsible for the transformation of the primate into man because it made labour possible. The hand was the biological handle, the parent and prototype of the tool and made possible both tool-using and tool-making. [George Novack, *Origins of Materialism*, p. 105]

As the most thoroughly socialised form of energy known to mankind, electricity works at both physical and symbolic levels. This explains why its application to music is so hotly contested. Although dunderheads debate the matter as if it were a controversy between old and new, there is a far more interesting contradiction at work. As a staple of modern urban life, electricity suggests universal, non-privatised provision, a socialist possibility denied by class property relations (charging for domestic usage is an illustration of a capitalist confusion between electricity as a means of production and electricity as a means of consumption). On the other hand, the invisible character of electricity (in comparison to, say, sacks of coal or drums of oil) occludes the labour that goes into its creation and maintenance, suggesting the immaterialism of pure spirit. These issues surface in musical aesthetics: electricity can amplify the productive body, or conceal it. Electric sustain on a guitar string can focus on digital actuality as never before possible, or it can suggest transcendence of hand and instrument in washes of disembodied harmony.

With subsequent releases by electro-bassist Eberhard Weber, saxophonist Jan Garbarek and guitarists Terje Rypdal and Bill Frisell, ECM took the path of glossy transcendence, forging the parameters for New Age (it was only when Frisell forsook ECM that his touch-sensitive immediacy as a guitarist began to be documented). Derek Bailey used electronics to take music in a totally different direction: in Free Improvisation, sound is nothing more or less than a register of the physical manipulation of instruments. Transcendence and shimmer are rejected as a repressive disguise, an illusion of depth requiring compression and echo and stereo. Improvisation finds a more robust beauty – and humour – in the physical act of music-making itself, and hence does not fetishise 'quality' recording. Though it has been compared to Ambient's lulling absences, Lo-Fi could only have emerged from a free-improvising milieu. The Music Improvisation Company showed the way.

The approach of the Music Improvisation Company was not simply an 'experimental' one as opposed to that of 'jazz'. Nor was it the crass celebration of electric modernity versus acoustic antiquity that cyber-boosters find in *Bitches Brew*. It was a dialectical operation that used electricity to foreground the physical act of music making, the very opposite of the dream of ungrounded omnipotence that characterises bourgeois notions of power and technology (which reach hysterical levels in cyber theory's fantasies about computers). Tony Oxley provided a typically down-to-earth explanation of the improvisor's approach when he described why he built his own drum kit.

> To me, electronics as they're sold in the shop, I'm not interested in at all. I use them basically for amplifying natural sound, so really it's a very sophisticated method of amplification. And then in certain situations I'm prepared to use, on top of the basic sound, a ring modulator or an oscillator or an octave divider. Very primitive things like that, where I can still improvise. But the difference between the electronics you buy and the way you use them is: they've got a signal which is the same signal all the time, then you manipulate that signal into the particular shapes and texture you want. I, on the other hand, don't have one signal, my feed-in range is very wide, so I put in many different

signals and only need a few things at this end to manipulate them. I'm not relying on patching it up and patching it down. I'm feeding in cymbals and wires and motors – maybe I've just lost a million pounds by telling you that.

My reasons for doing it were as simple as this: a cymbal, for instance, has a lot of possibilities to do with sound. It's not one pitch, it's made up of many pitches. So I thought, wouldn't that be nice to have a cymbal that you could actually capture this thick cluster of sounds with and be able to move it up and down? Why be satisfied just to hit it? And the same with any of the other things that I feed in. It was developed in a very natural way. Of course, it sounded a bit crazy, but it was a complete extension of the kit and I can now bend it around.

[TO to Brian Priestley, *The Wire*, October 1986]

The hands-on instrumentalist refuses the standardisation of shop product. Anyone who dismisses this as nostalgia for craft production has never heard a fully motorised solo by Oxley: this is flesh meets machine in forensic glitterbang, an audio reminder of the industrial substructure that undergirds such consumer froth as laptops and mobile phones. Bailey and Oxley are not *craft* – a luxury alternative supplied to those living off surplus value, a comforting image of unalienated wholesomeness – but necessary *art*. Unlike the sterile virtuosity of fusion with its drum clinics and 'how to' guitar videos (playing as demonstration of new product rather than an end in itself), the instrumental dexterity of the free improvisor foregrounds the human labour at the heart of capitalist power. Instead of buying the drum set and then finding you can't actually drum like Vinnie Colaiuta, an audience for a Free Improvisation learns how creativity works. Free Improvisation is not a redeeming add-on or wishful afterthought to the business of shifting commodities, but a struggle inside musical production. Instead of being a surplus siphoned off and used to glamorise and gild, electricity becomes the material object of investigation.

Even after he'd been discovered by Miles Davis at Ronnie Scott's and played on *In a Silent Way* and *Bitches Brew*, bassist David Holland continued his involvement with the London avant-garde. In January 1971, he recorded with the Spontaneous Music Ensemble – 'So, What

Do You Think?' – and made a tape of duets with Bailey at the Little Theatre Club which was issued by ECM as *Improvisations for Cello and Guitar*. *'So, What Do You Think?'* made explicit the musical dialogism of collective Free Improvisation. John Stevens asks the title question verbally, then his four musicians reply with customised phrases: 'Yeh! When's that?' (Bailey); 'Sure! Of course I will' (Holland); 'I suppose, it's all right' (Trevor Watts) and 'Yeh! I'd like to' (Kenny Wheeler). Then Stevens taps out the question on his snare and the others play phrases that are meant to represent their replies (notations for these appeared on the back of the album). This garrulous introduction sets the tone for the rest of the piece, which is restless, agitated and chirping, the musicians continually interjecting and pausing. In a sleeve note written in 1973, Max Harrison compared the music to the 'seamless continuity' of a kaleidoscope. According to Bailey, one of Stevens's favourite words was 'organic', and there is something very moving about the way individual contributions feed into the intricacies of the whole. Unlike *Karyobin*, the horn players break their lines in order to achieve equality with percussion, bass and cello. Towards the end, the other musicians fall silent and John Stevens drums alone: 'drum solo' would be an inadequate expression for an extraordinary example of percussion as interrogation (Stevens warps his snare sound with an elbow, a device learned from Art Blakey, gives his beats a questioning lilt): it is as if he's summarising what has been played and coaxing the others for some concluding statements. *'So, What Do You Think?'* is a near-perfect statement of the courteous collectivity that distinguishes English improvisation from American jazz.

The record is also an opportunity to compare the drum styles of Stevens and Oxley. Stevens is fluid and responsive, lacking Oxley's monumental quality. Stevens described the difference in these terms:

> I think his rhythms were perhaps more linear than mine; he was more into adding details on top of other details, where I was interested in making things disappear into other things. [JS to Brian Priestley, *The Wire*, October 1986]

Oxley had found a way of subdividing time so that he could deal with almost any kind of randomness a band member might throw at him (watching him deal with the antics of wildman guitarist Hugh Metcalfe has been one of the joys of his later groups), whereas Stevens was more interested in warping time itself. With *Improvisations for Cello and Guitar*, ECM had music strong enough to take advantage of its purist aesthetic. Holland contributed a striking image for the cover, making maximal use of simple black and white by using negative shapes: an Arp amoeba is duplicated and rotated into framing symmetry. On the back, a sonnet by e e cummings pondered the paradoxes of doubling, reflection and unity – an appropriate meditation considering that Bailey and Holland seem to be abandoning the traditional identities of their instruments for a dialogue in which string sonorities echo each other. Both players are evidently conversant with the twelve-tone method, but that breakthrough merely supplies the foundation for a new music that pays as much attention to the distance between string and bridge and sounding board as it does to official notes. On 'Improvised Piece IV', Bailey forces the exchange to a climax of compacted clusters that explodes received wisdom about the virtues of acoustic instruments. As Holland's cover design indicates, this music is as much about measuring space as it is about positive sounding. You can hear the two musicians find new ways to relate sound to sound, and their excitement is palpable.

PAUL RUTHERFORD, BARRY GUY AND ISKRA 1903

The first release by Incus Records was *The Topography of the Lungs*, a trio between Derek, Evan Parker and Han Bennink recorded on 13 July 1970. Its second was a solo Bailey album in which he improvised on one side and played compositions (by Misha Mengelberg, Willem Breuker and Gavin Bryars) on the other. The third was a double album – the only way vinyl could achieve the playing time of the modern CD – by a group named Iskra 1903. It comprised Derek, bassist Barry Guy and trombonist Paul Rutherford. Its two records were housed in an imposing gatefold sleeve, and documented two performances: live at the ICA in August 1970, engineered by Hugh Davies, and in the Colourtone Studios in May 1972, engineered by Bob Woolford.

It was in July 1903 that Lenin argued that keeping useless people on the editorial board of *Iskra* – the newspaper and collective propagandist, agitator and organiser of the revolutionary party – 'out of pity and injured feelings' endangered the socialist movement:

> We have gathered here for the purpose of creating a party, and not of indulging in mutual compliments and philistine sentimentality . . . our only consideration should be the interests of the work and a person's suitability for the post. [Lenin, quoted by Tony Cliff, *Lenin*, Vol. 1, p. 113]

Lenin won the debate, forcing a split in the Russian party that later manifested itself as the gulf between Bolsheviks (revolutionaries) and Mensheviks (liberals). Inside the gatefold of *Iskra 1903* [Incus 3/4], Incus printed grainy blow-ups, details from the famous rooftop-view newsreel of insurrectionary workers rushing across St Petersburg's central square in 1917. There were also choice obscenities, jokes and statements from subversives as diverse as Lawrence Durrell ('It is the duty of every patriot to hate his country creatively; England cries out for brothels'), Ludwig v. Beethoven ('I haven't eaten since yesterday noon'), Hugh McDiarmid ('All government has the monopoly of violence'), Willie Rushton ('Take courage Britain, it's going to be funny') and an uncredited anarchist ('All hate to the state'; 'Women! Close your legs and you'll strangle Mankind'; 'Britain is an embarrassment to the 20th century'). The one quote contributed by Bailey – 'You can pick your friends/You can pick your nose/But you can't pick your friends' noses' – was credited to 'Traditional' (Derek later discovered it derived from R. Crumb). A newspaper headline reproduced on the gatefold reads 'Critics proved wrong'.

Derek Bailey tends to avoid political postures within Free Improvisation: the brain behind these images and quotes was Paul Rutherford's. Nevertheless, the promise of sonic Bolshevism conveyed by the cover is apt. Iskra 1903 *were* musical revolutionaries: unsentimental, principled and vanguardist. As evidenced above by Derek's remarks on the Spontaneous Music Ensemble, he holds Paul Rutherford's playing in particularly high regard. Sceptical about records – and musicians' judgements regarding them – he rarely comments in print on releases by fellow musicians. However, in 1987 *The Wire* magazine persuaded him to write about Paul Rutherford's *The Gentle Harm of the Bourgeoisie* (Emanem 4019), a re-release of his solo trombone album from 1974. Characteristically, Derek used it as a platform for a polemic. He hailed the record as an exceptional document of *real* improvising: 'no apparatus between the idea and its appearance' (none of T. S. Eliot's 'falls the shadow').

Then faithful to his own doctrine of the poverty of historicism, Derek used the review to air a contemporary grievance: he curses the fad for solo improvisation as a miserable product of 'the Thatcher Winter' [*The Wire*, no. 36, February 1987].

Rutherford of course had technique in abundance; what Derek valued was his ability to sound as if the way he played was 'invented on the spot to fit his immediate needs'. Derek was parting company with Evan Parker, who was then making a name for himself by his lengthy solo saxophone excursions, which use circular breathing and freak notes to create a dense wall of trilling multiphonics. Fans of systems music (as minimalism was then known) were impressed, those committed to free-improvised spontaneity less so. Bailey was using Rutherford to define what he thought of as genuine improvisation: a musician prepared to deal with the contingent.

He had a point. On 10 November 1989, for example, playing to thirty people at the Adelphi Hotel in Leeds courtesy of the Termite Club, Rutherford engaged in two solos. During one of them he outlined the pub room's fireplace with his trombone plunger, a site-specific device that couldn't be more graphic. And 'solo' is perhaps not quite the right word anyway. Rutherford's unaccompanied recital was sandwiched between playing by saxophonists Lol Coxhill and George Haslam: all three were showing us what they could do, but also listening and responding to each other's discoveries. The sense of engagement and mutual learning was obvious.

In interviews, Evan Parker claimed to be pushing his circular-breathing gambit as 'far' as he could – pressing himself up against a brick wall and pressing further – but the totalitarian afflatus of his technique steamrollers specific ambience, turning his music into the kind of dependable commodity required by promoters and applauded by the general public (promoters Serious Music – not known for their support for Free Improvisation – booked Parker to open for Ornette Coleman at the Town and Country Club in 1987, for example). The audience for Free Improvisation may be small, but it is committed: part of this commitment stems from the way free improvisors respect the specificity of the audience. Deprived of that, you might as well be twiddling your thumbs as some pop act or classical orchestra goes through its well-rehearsed show.

As part of the Spontaneous Music Ensemble, Paul Rutherford played with Bailey as early as 1966. On 20 March 1967, he participated in a BBC Radio 3 broadcast of the Spontaneous Music Ensemble, along with Bailey, Wheeler, Watts and Guy. In June 1969, he joined Bailey and Parker in an encounter with a raft of European players – including Peter Brötzmann and Han Bennink – in Bremen, and broadcast for Radio 3 again as part of the SME (a grouping that was effectively a collaboration with Chris McGregor's Brotherhood of Breath). Rutherford gigged with Bailey in groups with Stevens and Oxley, and also in international groups assembled in Frankfurt and Rotterdam. However, it was his trio with Derek and bassist Barry Guy that was deemed worthy of a group name – and Incus's first double-LP release.

Barry Guy studied bass and composition at the Guildhall School of Music and Drama, graduating to play in a number of London's most prestigious classical orchestras. In the early seventies, he became professor of his instrument at the Guildhall. At school he'd been a jazz fan and studied with Graham Collier. As the crucial string players of jazz, double bassists seem to find it easier to cross over into classical music, giving them a special view of jazz orchestration (following Charles Mingus, many bassists – including Gavin Bryars, Simon H. Fell and Guy himself – have thrown themselves into ambitious composition for large orchestras). Unlike Bryars, Barry Guy never relinquished his instrument. Capable of glowing, LaFaro-like sonorities, he has a modernist sensibility at odds with the harmonic simplicity required to make such notes really sing. Guy is a virtuoso player with an excitable temperament, making him an ideal improvisor. He and Bailey lock into the kind of intense delvings into illegitimate timbre that bring to mind someone thrusting a screwdriver into hard-to-reach recesses of an electronic soundboard, a sense of frustration and urgency predicated on extracting the unpredictable note from a mutual flurry. Digital dexterity is forced to a crisis as wit supersedes the playable, resulting in ragged and unfinished textures that can then be contrasted to more lyrical sections.

From his opening notes on *Iskra 1903*, Bailey demonstrates his intent to make us hear sound as the result of physical action rather than as the in-filling of a preconceived rhythmic or harmonic scheme. Barry Guy uses close-miking to amplify the scrape of his bow along the strings of his bass, recalling the brute precision of the mason's chisel rather than the romantic surge of the cellist. Rutherford begins by playing piano, conjuring the twinkling outer space of indeterminate tonality. When he picks up his trombone, another procedural innovation becomes evident. Both trombone and bass are large instruments, giving extended technique and close-miking much scope for making a music of variegated noise rather than legitimate notes. Rutherford and Guy exploit this, making us hear Bailey's guitar too as a vast sounding board, a site of sound production rather than a 'proper' instrument.

In other words, the musicians immerse us in the soundworlds of their instruments. Yet because it's an improvised trialogue, this retreat into the immediacy of their productive medium – which in Samuel Beckett is perceived as existentialist, ontological and asocial – remains collective. The insides of trombone and bass, and the space between guitar string and magnetic pick-up become the entire universe, all the atoms merely vibrations. Instead of being presented as fusion's glossy athleticism, ear-to-hand fleetness is used to comprehend and humanise contingency, noise and accident. It intimates what a world might be like in which everything was as resonant and responsive as these squeaks and squeals and bongs: the socialist vision of human activity as an end in itself, rather than merely a means to accumulate capital.

The three shorter improvisations on side two are even more effective than the twenty-minute epic on side one. Bailey used a foot volume-pedal to introduce his abrasive, unclean electronic sounds. They loom like astral lights. There is still some of the flying-saucer unworldliness of his playing on *The Baptised Traveller*. On the eleven-minute 'Improvisation 3', Guy's long-bowed drone creates an atmosphere similar to Oxley's slowly evolving chord sequences on 'Crossing/Arrival' (that listening tension that was *The Baptised Traveller*'s bridge between modal jazz and Free Improvisation): a tenebrous landscape strafed by lightning fidgets from 'bone and 'tar. As the rhythmic intensity increases, it seems impossible that so many contrasting sounds can be whorled together, so many musical pleasures referenced by fleet iconic suggestion.

Record two of *Iskra 1903* consists of seven studio improvisations recorded two years later. Again, the music is highly dramatic, milking the contrast between long, low notes and sudden, violent stabs of sound. John Cage's theory of the nonexistence of silence encouraged audiences to listen until their ears ached. Here the pieces seem to start from that engagement, then the musicians' eagerness to respond seizes on random scraps to create dense-packed musical events. On 'Improvisation 5', Bailey plays acoustic: thin, spindly pluckings quite different to his electric bongs and scrunches. Occasionally you spot the serial runs that often become the substance of his solo improvisations, but here these are lyric threads scattered amongst the bump-you timbrism of the trio.

The closing piece, 'Improvisation 11', starts as a tight trombone/ guitar duet, the two musicians using the super-divided beat pioneered by Oxley to twirl the music about each other's statements. Bailey hits upon a repeated high note which gives Guy space to enter. His bowed notes make Bailey switch to electronic effects, his metallic sustain resembling cymbal percussion. Guy finishes the album with bowed harmonics. His scrapy, interwoven semitones recall field recordings made of descendants of the Incas, where the episodic flute-playing of circles of men – wearing broad-brimmed hats and multicoloured scarves – merges with the whistling wind of the Andes to desolate effect.

As well as corporate labels, the Free Improvisation scene of the early seventies had hopes for recognition by the classical establishment. After all, no lesser an authority than *Melody Maker* critic Richard Williams had pronounced in *Radio Times* that 'these men accomplish every night what Stockhausen has been trying to do for years'. One of the more prestigious coups was the inclusion of Iskra 1903 as one of three ensembles in a box set called *Free Improvisation* issued by Deutsche Grammophon in 1974. The cover showed a photograph of a score indicating the key of B flat major and 3/4 time – with a match setting fire to it. The stave lines are fraying and unravelling. Free Improvisation, in other words, promises to incinerate the classical heritage. However, the Deutsche Grammophon logo remains unperturbed in its gilt frame: whatever the indignities inflicted on classical music by these art icono-clasts, the proud record company can issue the results. Each group included in the box set appeared on a separate long-playing record. Since Free Improvisation has been cast in a role of terminal unsuccess and unpopularity in Britain, it's interesting to con-sider the backgrounds of Deutsche Grammophon's other improvisors. New Phonic Art 1973 were an improvising quartet comprising: Carlos Roqué Alsina (piano and electric organ), who had studied with Luciano Berio, conducted at the Deutsche Oper and lectured on contemporary piano literature at Buffalo University; Jean-Pierre Drouet (drums), prize-winning trumpeter, composer, drummer in André Hodeir's jazz group and student of Indian classical percussion; Vinko Globokar, prize-winning trombonist, also a Berio student, and from 1974 director of the instrumental and vocal department at IRCAM, Pierre Boulez's lavishly funded sonic research centre; Michel Portal, prize-winning clarinet player and leading musician in both avant-garde classical and jazz circles. All were members of Karlheinz Stockhausen's 'intuitive' music ensemble, recording *Aus den sieben Tagen* in 1973. New Phonic Art were volatile and occasionally creative, disconcerting the listener with insulting sax squarks, eruptive drums and moments where the musicians chatted to each other. Globokar found thoroughly nasty noises on his trombone, against which Portal played with an irrepressible sense of swing. At the end of 'Improvisation Nr 2', Portal played his 'bando-neon', a humorous reference to European street music. 'Improvisation Nr 3' occupies the whole of side two. It becomes rather tedious, as if the musicians have not yet transformed gestural transgression into a viable musical method.

New Phonic Art were less free improvisors than brilliant musicians creating 'events' in concert halls. Some of the more cacophonic sections resemble the provocations David Tudor used to play under the guise of interpreting John Cage; when Drouet and Portal demonstrate the kind of control of the instant associated with jazz players, it's as if the group do not know what to do with this alien tongue. The humour of the bandoneon section was an obvious – though rather crass – way out of this quandary. New Phonic Art were asking a lot of questions – they declared they had given 'about seventy concerts in Europe, North and South America' – but answers were thinner on the ground. Wired was another quartet. Karl-Heinz Böttner (guitar, zither, electric bass) had studied with Bernd-Alois Zimmerman and lectured at Darmstadt; Mike Lewis (Hammond organ, percussion) had studied composition in Toronto and trombone and percussion in Munich, but was described as 'an outstanding connoisseur and exponent of the pop scene'; Michael Ranta was an orchestral percussionist who had worked with Mauricio Kagel and Karlheinz Stockhausen; Connie Plank disdained to supply a CV, describing his role as the 'diabolus in musica, live electronics, sound control and recording supervisor' – though he later became famous for his production work in Krautrock (Neu, Time, La Dusseldorf, DAF) and English synth-pop (Ultravox, Eurythmics, Killing Joke), Plank was not present when Böttner and Deutsche Grammophon's Rudolf Werner mixed down their improvisations from 140 minutes to an LP-length 53 minutes. Wired's music is dire: feeble-minded surrender to the 'wonders' of electronic noise, a premonition of the cyberscapes that would be blessed with the name of Electronica in the nineties. Liberal use of echo blurs any sense of concrete utterance, suggesting the interminable boredom of Stockhausen's *Stimmung*. When any hands-on playing is heard – such as Michael Ranta's glockenspiel – it is bathetically inept. Lacking either the skill or the will to dialogue, the players wallow in whatever crude evocation they stumble on. Böttner's sleeve note – 'There is no past and no future, only Now, and so, breathless, we face up to each sound . . .' – supplied the Zen hokum that seems to be the inevitable condiment to such artless 'experimentalism'.

Sandwiched between these two slices of European avantgarderie, Iskra 1903 present a strong argument for Derek Bailey and Free Improvisation as a determinate answer to the crisis that shook classical music in the 1960s. There is no embarrassment about the players' ability to control the sounds of their instruments, no iconoclasm. Despite Michel Portal's best efforts, New Phonic Art have the somewhat desperate air of post-1945 gallery nihilism (Armand Fernandez's burnt pianos, John Latham's incinerated books and violins, Diter Rot's foodstuffs rotting beneath perspex laminates): artists who sense the spiritual vacancy of bourgeois institutions and derive energy from destructive postures, but cannot propose any material alternative. In this context, and despite the fact that Bailey saw himself as a refugee from a dying form (jazz), hungry for the freedom and open-ended speculation of the art world, Iskra 1903 feel like a breath of fresh air: a blast of positive, demotic music-making.

In conversation, Derek will shrug his shoulders about the alleged difficulty of his music, saying that he's almost embarrassed to confess how simpleminded his approach actually is. Wary of grand artistic gestures, he proposes a music where all thoughts are directed into the details of playing. Just as some dadaists criticised Kurt Schwitters for his 'bourgeois' concentration on artistic production, one could accuse Iskra 1903 of being too polite. However, that would be a superficial judgement, born of reluctance to expose one's subjectivity to these sounds. As when listening to a conversation, one discovers that level tones and polite pauses can actually convey concepts of pressing import. The musical logic is so self-conscious and fleet, it is as if it is already commenting on itself faster than the mere critic can do. In Iskra 1903, Bailey, Rutherford and Guy found a way of making their sounds variegated and responsive without recourse to any known musical style. There is provocation, but no bluster. The musicians sustain a dialectic between sonorous sustain and high energy, the responses so quick that homogeneity is ensured.

'Improvisation »5012«' is Bailey unaccompanied, playing a 'nine-string acoustic guitar'. He sounds as if he has developed another pair of hands. This track sits in the midst of the avant-garde rhetoric of New Phonic Art and Wired like a piece of flamenco busked to the queue for the opera. On 'Improvisation »5010«', Guy answers Rutherford's trombone snuffles with a brilliant vocabulary of bass rattles and plunks. 'Improvisation »5020«' is again a miniature, but like a copperplate by William Blake, it has a concentrated energy lacking in the gestures of public art. There's a resigned and haunting section of bowed-bass harmonics, Salvation Army brass melancholy, the guitar notes strained and scrapy. Notes are sounded with drama and decisiveness, but linger strangely. The listener has an edge-of-seat intimation that the musicians have broken into new vistas of emotional resonance with no plan . . . and no route back.

'Improvisation »5021«' reinforces the realisation that Iskra 1903 is far from the 'anything goes' of Free Improvisation as popularly misconceived. The trio are working on distinct sets of notes, working through particular rhythmic impulses. Although there is no jazz flavour, the music is true to Coltrane's sense of harmonic investigation, of wringing the changes to discover how a musical mood is constructed, working on a motif until its outlines explode: the idea of persistence earning reward and release. The trio aren't provoking anyone or making a statement, but asking our imaginations to accompany them on a trip. The way they close the improvisation feels immensely satisfying, though there is no recourse to classical formality or jazz logic. Of course there is an anthropological basis to this syntax: intimations of inhalation and exhalation, of muscular tension and relaxation, of sexual arousal and relief. Like the heroic abstract art at the opening of the twentieth century, Iskra 1903 play this way because they scorn the sectarianism of traditional genres and yearn for a universal human language.

In line with his 'heads-down, no nonsense, let's improvise' concept, Derek Bailey rejects the idea that recording for Deutsche Grammophon represented any kind of high-cultural ambition. When he talked to critic John Corbett, Bailey's reply was reminiscent of Don Preston, the experimental keyboardist who explored free improvisation in LA in the early sixties, met Frank Zappa, joined the Mothers of Invention – and then looked up to see that thousands of people were watching, and thought, 'that's incredible', but most of the time was too busy playing to notice.

> To me it was like Paul Rutherford ringing up and saying, 'Deutsche Grammophon are putting out a triple box record of Free Improvisations and we've gotta go to Berlin and record some music for it.' I said, 'Well, that's amazing.' But I didn't assume there was a career going to blossom out of that, no. If I thought anything other than '*What a nice gig*, I assumed they'd made some kind of mistake.' [v–1992, interviewed by John Corbett, *Extended Play*, pp. 244–5]

However, there were other musicians around Free Improvisation who thought the stakes were higher.

IMPROVISATION VERSUS COMPOSITION, ROUND 23

Paul Rutherford's ambition and cultural politics manifested themselves in compositions for an ensemble he called Iskra 1912. The project resulted in two studio recordings, the first in September 1972 and the second in October 1973. Like Gavin Bryars with *The Sinking of the Titanic*, Rutherford signalled his composerly seriousness by conducting rather than playing. He used two singers (Maggie Nicols and Norma Winstone), three trombones (Malcolm Griffiths, Paul Nieman and Geoff Perkins), reeds (Trevor Watts, Evan Parker and Dave White), tuba (Dick Hart), trumpet (Kenny Wheeler), piano (Howard Riley) and bass (Barry Guy). On the 1973 session, Trevor Watts was absent and Tony Oxley was added (his contribution was described as 'live electronics' rather than percussion). Derek Bailey overdubbed guitar a week later. When the two sessions were released by Emanem in 1997, they were named 'Sequence 72' and 'Sequence 73'. Thereby hangs a tale.

On 13 May 1974, Paul Rutherford performed a piece by Luciano Berio named *Sequenza V for trombone*, one of a series of compositions written by the Italian composer featuring single instruments. Berio's *Sequenzas* were designed to acknowledge and extend traditional approaches to particular instruments. *Sequenza V* asked the trombonist to both play and sing ('it's no easy matter coordinating these two actions, and for the piece to work, the intervals between voice and instrument must be scrupulously respected . . .'). Rutherford began by following the score, then took off on his own. Applause and favourable reviews showed that no one – least of all the 'experts' – could tell that the genius on show was Rutherford's rather than Berio's. The incident has entered Free Improvisation folklore as an inspirational example of musicianly rebellion.

The Emanem release of *Sequences 72 & 73* [Emanem 4018] includes four minutes of Rutherford's improvisational hijack. It makes an intriguing comparison to the version of *Sequenza V* recorded by Benny Sluchin of the Ensemble InterContemporain (released in 1998 by Deutsche Grammophon). Sluchin was taught by Vinko Globokar, whose New Phonic Art contributed alongside Iskra 1903 to the Deutsche

Grammophon box set and who was himself a student of Berio. Avant-garde music is a small world: given the disparity in respect and funding between academia and Free Improvisation, comparisons are inevitably controversial, not to say invidious.

Rutherford's free version of *Sequenza V* – renamed 'Non-Sequence' on Emanem 4018 – resembles his playing on *The Gentle Harm of the Bourgeoisie*. The trombonist completely inhabits his soundmaking, pursuing an expressionist continuity familiar from free-jazz saxophonists since Albert Ayler. The use of vocalese, harmonics and bubbling saliva contribute to its guttural animality. In his *Wire* review, Derek Bailey said, '. . . imagination is the engine, and he keeps it unencumbered by forward planning or systematic devices'. That is the great contrast with *Sequenza V*; indeed, compared to the visceral individualism of Rutherford's line – unrelieved by any dialogue or ensemble collectivity – Berio's soundworld is refreshingly clean and objective: the opening, with its passing references to different tempi, evokes the multiplicity of the external world. To go from Rutherford to Berio is like fleeing a bawling baby and stepping out onto a balcony overlooking a city: one notes pedestrians, bicycles, cars, trams and clouds all moving in different directions and at different rates, but all somehow related.

However, that wasn't Berio's specific intention in the piece. Interweaving different tempi is, after all, elementary for a composer. *Sequenza V* is dedicated to 'Grock' (Adriano Wettach), the 'last of the great clowns', a neighbour when Berio was growing up in Oneglia. Aged eleven, Luciano saw Grock perform at the Teatro Cavour at Porto Maurizio, and was struck by a tragi-comic moment when, in the midst of some ludicrous routine, he fixed the audience with a disarming stare and asked '*Warum?*' Sluchin, too, asks 'why?' during the course of *Sequenza V*. Berio's intention was to move from the disciplined abstraction of classicism towards the contingent and personal. The piece does become more expressionist as it proceeds, but as an attempt at what Berio calls 'vocalization of the instrument and "instrumentalization" of the voice', Rutherford – by drawing upon blues and free jazz – is infinitely more advanced. In this sense, Free Improvisation already occupies the territory that the academic avant-garde craves.

In his sleeve notes to *Sequences 72 & 73* – as befits a heroic small-label owner facing the big guns of Deutsche Grammophon (current corporate owners: Universal Music) – Martin Davidson argues for the superiority of Rutherford's *extempore* version. However, playing the two pieces back to back does not necessarily result in a complete victory for Free Improvisation. It is questionable whether Rutherford's refusal to follow the score really proves anything about the 'superiority' of improvisation as a musical method. The objectivity created by the score – the sense that Sluchin is sounding out a pre-prepared pattern – actually creates space for reflection, for the listener's own thoughts. Indeed, there is something suffocatingly mono-dimensional about Rutherford's 'Non-Sequence': Ayler without the gospel populism to make him something more than an oppressive subjectivist.

In this context, one understands the remark Gavin Bryars made in 'Objections' in Bailey's book *Improvisation: Its Nature and Practice in Music*:

> One of the main reasons I am against improvisation now is that in any improvising position the person creating the music is identified with the music. The two things are seen to be synonymous. The creator is there making the music and is identified with the music and the music with the person. It's like standing a painter next to his pictures so that every time you see the painting you see the painter as well and you can't see it without him. (Moorland edition, p. 135; Da Capo, p. 115)

It is characteristic that Bryars should appeal to painting, the art form most in hock to bourgeois property relations. His argument runs counter to a whole vein of Black Studies that makes a virtue of the *griot*: the jazzman as the in-person embodiment of tradition ('in jazz, the musician is the treasure', as Archie Shepp puts it). In general, the materialist aesthetic of Free Improvisation sides with jazz against the transcendental idealism of fine art and its fetish of product over producer. However, in art, generalities rarely provide answers (rather, they stifle examination of particulars by reference to ideology).

While it is true that Rutherford has in abundance what Berio is after – tragi-comic ontology, vocalised contingency, expressive poignancy – *Sequenza V* was not the only kind of piece that Berio is capable of. From the recorded evidence, Rutherford's *Sequences 72 & 73* – squalling and knotty – could learn from the lightness and molecular scintillation of *Laborintus II*, Berio's composition from 1965 for three voices, poet (Edoardo Sanguineti), magnetic tape and 17 instruments (including close-miked double bass). While it is true that composers who admire the interstitial interactions and timbral subtlety of Free Improvisation often end up with something rather plodding and simplified in comparison, it is not true that free improvisors always make superior records.

In Rutherford's *Sequences 72 & 73*, directions about overall shape put a brake on improvisor responsibility and invention without putting anything salient in their place (similar problems occurred with Barry Guy's scores for the London Jazz Composers Orchestra). A lugubrious pomp descends over the ensemble, a cavernous echo of the very classicism the music is meant to be subverting. Although the playing is electrically sensitive, the effort to keep the piece afloat gives it a rhetorical air. Directionless skitter is not the same as freedom. The decisive events and sonic efflorescences of *Laborintus II* – notably the delightful moment when the delirious sounds of the magnetic tape burst into the performance – suddenly seem incredibly valuable. Although the balance sheet of twentieth-century music making hardly argues in favour of establishment procedures, vaunting Rutherford over Berio, as some champions of Free Improvisation do, is not especially convincing.

Sun Ra, Frank Zappa and Simon Fell have all shown that scores can keep detail and complexity alive in improvising ensembles. However, these composers share a cabbalistic fascination for the letter of the code (inversion, retrogrades, xenochrony, reference). This dialectical close-focus results in rehearsal and performance methods that acknowledge and harness musicianly resistance to discipline. Blows against fetishism and hierarchy are necessary, but less at the level of ideology (Cage, Fluxus, SME, AMM) than at the level of the material mediation of the musical idea. There is more truth in watching a classically trained musician struggle with an 'impossible' score by Luigi Nono or Brian Ferneyhough than in watching La Monte Young or Keith Rowe present a ritual spectacle of 'freedom' to a stunned audience. The notion that scores invariably subjugate the musician to blind obedience ignores the social dialectic that produced the masterpieces admired today as classics. It leads to transcendental solutions to in-place social blemishes that actually produce still more mystification. As Freud pointed out – a devastating pre-critique of all such evasion – you may seem unconstrained, but if you are *bored*, you are not free: you're repressed.

COMPOSING FOR IMPROVISORS

Barry Guy's involvement in orchestral playing naturally led him to consider the possibility of scoring for players from the improvising scene. As the presence of compositions on side two of Derek Bailey's solo-guitar release *Incus 2* demonstrates, Bailey's later antagonism towards composition (and solo improvising) was the fruit of experience rather than a readymade ideology. In his sleeve note to *Ode* [Incus LP6/7], Guy explains that the idea of the London Jazz Composers Orchestra arose from conversations within Iskra 1903, and with Evan Parker, Tony Oxley, Howard Riley and Kenny Wheeler during a trip to Hamburg in 1970. The London Jazz Composers Orchestra premiered at Ronnie Scott's on 3 October 1970, with compositions by both Guy and Oxley conducted by Buxton Orr. Iskra 1903 played support.

The name of the ensemble was borrowed from composer Michael Mantler. Having moved from Vienna to New York in 1962, Mantler composed and recorded in 1968 a series of concertos for leading free-jazz players – Cecil Taylor and Don Cherry, Roswell Rudd, Pharoah Sanders, Larry Coryell, Gato Barbieri – under the name The Jazz Composer's Orchestra (the London variant omitted the apostrophe, a useful ambiguity when, in later years, musicians beside Guy came to write for it). Mantler's concertos – or 'Communications', as they were called – vie with Peter Brötzmann's *Machine Gun* as an adequate musical response to that revolutionary year. Issued on a label run jointly by Mantler and Carla Bley, Mantler's work was inspirational for its massive sonic force, but also for the demonstration of what a grant-demanding co-op and self-run label could achieve.

As far as Barry Guy was concerned, it was less a matter of improvisors requiring the discipline of the score, than of applying their innovations to a large-scale ensemble. Improvisors were far ahead of classical musicians in pioneering new ways of playing – Guy cited Heinz

Holliger (oboe) and Cathy Berberian (voice) as two exceptions – and their 'new sound textures' could be used to invigorate composition. The logistics of organising large ensembles are daunting, nowhere more so than when refusing 'commercial enterprise or musical compromise'. Taking as his model Olivier Messiaen's *Chronocromie* and its use of the strophe/antistrophe dialectic of the Ancient Greek chorus (hence *Ode*), Guy wrote music for specific players, 'sometimes complementing, sometimes almost dictating a direction which the soloist may follow or react against'. Each movement was named after a Surrealist painting. The Arts Council of Great Britain funded several days of rehearsal and the recording itself, which was done in front of an audience at Oxford Town Hall on 22 April 1972 by the Pye Mobile Recording Unit. The concert was part of Lina Lalandi's English Bach Festival (which, despite its name, had been premièring work by the likes of Iannis Xenakis). Audio quality and balance were exemplary, and the music is still ear-alerting today (as Incus's commitment to pure improvisation has become more obdurate, CD reissue has been left to the Zurich-based Intakt label).

Given the complexity and passion of the arguments surrounding composition among improvisors, it is worth giving the music of *Ode* a close listen. Writing in the *Penguin Guide to Jazz*, Richard Cook and Brian Morton concede that it is perhaps 'a little hard-boiled for most of the critics', but its reissue on CD reveals it 'as a grand triumph, in some respects a more satisfying work than the more exploratory and sophisticated compositions that have followed in recent years. Unheard for some time, it has been possible to think of it as a 'prentice essay. It is, in fact, one of the masterpieces of European improvisation.' The *auteur* approach of the *Penguin Guide to Jazz* means that *Ode* is discussed in connection with later recordings by Barry Guy and the London Jazz Composers Orchestra, rather than in terms of the aesthetic debates and performance possibilities of the time.

As purveyors of 'quality ratings' whose purview includes the whole recorded history of jazz, Cook and Morton have a responsibility to the consumer. Their judgements are often shrewd, but because they start with the end result of the musical process – the product – they can obscure the real relations of production. Allergic to politics, they rarely deal with artistic controversies, tending to smooth over famous points of contention with phrases that speak volumes to the initiated, but protect vested interests from criticism. About Guy's later work they say:

> *Portraits* [Intakt, 1993], as we have suggested, sits more than comfortably alongside *Ode*. It is of its time – as was its predecessor – but most obviously in the decision to allow the inclusion of some quite explicitly melodic material (which did seemingly confuse and antagonize some of the more dogmatic improvisors). In the fifth of the main sections, which are interspersed by portrait subsections, there is a ballad, written for Simon Picard. Alan Tomlinson is given a blues (words by Paul Rutherford, recited by the players), and there are other identifiable outlines.

Morton and Cook are being disingenuous here, castigating as 'dogma' misgivings they actually share. Like mouldy fygges who turn judgements of modern music into the 'acoustic *versus* electric' debate, postmodernist defence of melody versus serialism rarely aids criticism – whose aim should be to tell us whether or not a particular piece of music has succeeded. Their 'it is of its time – as was its predecessor' is evasive, borrowing the conservative/liberal myth that 'the sixties' were quite naturally a period of revolt, whereas today such ideas are 'inappropriate' (that is, NATO was monstrous during the Vietnam War, but is a virtuous force when dropping uranium-depleted missiles on Serbia or Iraq). Of course such points will sound irrelevant and outrageous in the apolitical clubrooms of *Penguin Guide* connoisseurship, but without them one is never going to get a grip on a form as revolutionary as Free Improvisation.

It is not that blues and ballads are 'bad things' in themselves (as anyone who has heard a recent Hammond organ CD by Mel Rhyne, or some free jazz by Sabir Mateen will know), but whether the musicians of the London Jazz Composers Orchestra, with their backgrounds and their particular sensibilities, can render them with conviction. The answer has to be no. The retreat of free improvisors to 'acceptable' public music – the big-band pluralism of the Italian Instabile Orchestra, the blurry harmonies of Guy's later LJCO recordings, the sweet orchestralism of Butch Morris's recent conductions – is all about funding and grants, and very little to do with musical necessities. In the teacup of musician-dominated circles (where big-band projects generate income and exposure), such remarks provoke ire, but the aesthetic facts are evident to anyone capable of comparing one recording with another. *Ode* still has a striking impact, but it derives from a particular era of playing: Guy's 'score' contributes little. In later decades, battered into submission by commercial and institutional scorn for their genuine musical inventions, improvisors' recourse to 'blues' and 'ballads' is sad – the musical equivalent of former revolutionaries confessing their crimes at a Stalinist show trial or a McCarthy hearing. Those who point out that Barry Guy's turn to traditional devices produces poor music do not do so because of 'dogma', but because it's true: he's betraying the fantastic things he's capable of as an improvisor.

The bursting horns at the start of *Ode* recall the high-stressed intensity* of the Mantler compositions (derived from Cecil Taylor), though it is immediately apparent that Trevor Watts – the first soloist – is not receiving the level of harmonic challenge supplied by Mantler's writing. He plays well, but it is a line superimposed on the whole, not a vector within a field of forces. The ensemble *tutti* lack the self-antagonistic tension that cleaves Mantler's writing, veering towards flabby pomp. However, the expressive irony of the playing still leaves the listener gasping.

'Exact Sensibility' has echoes of Carla Bley's irony (a twist she derived from Kurt Weill), with Mike Osborne's alto playing an Aylerish dirge. Unlike Weill's politically sussed satire, Guy's intent is confusing. A similar problem is raised by the ecumenical usage of tonal and post-serial devices by what Tony Oxley calls 'the Westbrook clique': the negative logic of modernism is omitted. Instead of a break with the past – and hence a criticism of tradition – modernism is presented as an add-on, an extra. 'Exact Sensibility' bristles with borrowed motifs – there's a Mingus-like 'quickening-pace' section, voices and flutes that recall Berio's *Laborintus II*, there's free-jazz sax gargling reminiscent of Coltrane's *Ascension* – but, contrary to Guy's intent, these feel like impositions on the players rather than strategies derived from the way they improvise. A section of woodwind plaintiveness summons up the wist-

* A 'pitch too high for the burner', J. H. Prynne, *Not-You* (1993).

fulness of an Ealing Studios film score. Despite its hectoring quality, Mantler's extremism gave unity to his music: here, Guy's eclecticism results in bathos (in answer to accusations of 'dogma', it should be pointed out that eclecticism can work, but the eclectic needs to be keenly aware of the social implications of the styles mobilised, which is why Zappaesque eclectics such as Eugene Chadbourne, Billy Jenkins and Paul Minotto do not produce this species of bland, cherry-picking positivism).

'According to the Laws of Chance' benefits from fantastic scrabbled amplified interference from Bailey, who should almost be credited with 'electronics' rather than 'guitar'; on 'Presence of Mind', Alan Wakeman plays strong tenor and Karl Jenkins exorcises the pastoral Englishness of the oboe by overblowing it so it sounds like a North African musette. However, it's hard to see how these statements might relate to any aesthetic of improvisation and its confrontation with contingency: these are more like jazz solos – coherent and forceful – though once one hears them that way, one misses the propulsion a jazz rhythm section might provide.

'Indefinite Divisibility' was originally scheduled as part three of a seven-part suite, but appears as the closing side of the two-LP box set. It is inaugurated by a titanic drum salvo from Oxley, metallic scrap and frazzle emitted through his oscillators and octavidors. Guy's split-prism chords are appropriately Varèsian, a montage of luminous elements creating a martial, Birtwistlish attack. The tenebrous depth of three mighty trombones – Rutherford, Mike Gibbs and Paul Nieman – contrasts well with the pipping highs improvisor extended-technique had discovered for reeds. However, the undoubted power twinkles off into indeterminacy, as if composer and players aren't sure who should be responsible for developing the musical argument. Paul Lytton's percussion section sounds more like conventional drum soloing, lacking Oxley's serialist/surrealist ability to open up jagged abysses of resonant silence. Mantler gained coherence by making the music an epic confrontation between soloist and orchestra; here we too often witness a head of steam dissipated into yet another arbitrarily chosen composerly idea. However, low groans from bowed basses, acidic reed attacks and sprinkles of Messiaenic percussion do set up a tense and shimmering environment for Bailey's pluckings. His lack of interest in linear harmonic coherence allows him to relate to the Boulezian delirium better than the horn players have done, commenting on what's around him like an enthusiastic geologist at the edge of a volcano. A Bailey/Rutherford/Guy trio allows a glimpse of Iskra 1903, supplemented by some dazzlingly bizarre electronic squiggles from Oxley. In this context Karl Jenkins's oboe begins to sound like a sine wave. The acoustic instruments weave into the resonant electronics of Bailey and Oxley to create an intriguingly differentiated sense of space. The ensemble quietens to reveal Bailey scrabbling away obliquely without amplification, for all the world like the practising guitar player in the pit of the Morecambe and Wise Show. After this welcome piece of serendipity, melodic lines from the horns seem like a reassertion of 'real music' ordinariness, though one is hard put to explain the composer's rationale. Pianist Howard Riley is left to wrap things up, which he does with commendable zeal, though he has been put in the unenviable position of inviting comparison with Cecil Taylor's contribution to Mantler's Jazz Composer's Orchestra release. Nevertheless, drama is built but cataclysm isn't reached. The listener is left with the rhetoric of the avant-classical opus, but with no structuring logic to support the rhetoric. The tolling bell at the end – now the end of the entire piece – sounds overly portentous ('. . . Clangs/The bell' as T. S. Eliot has it in 'The Dry Salvages'), evoking a retrospective, religious nostalgia singularly inappropriate after the futurist sound-making we've been hearing.

The Joseph Holbrooke Trio and Iskra 1903 proposed a new music that would apply all the virtues of blues and jazz – music predicated on the concrete utterance of the working musician – to the freedoms won by Anton Webern and John Cage in the 'classical' world. This rebuttal of the divisions of class society was formally consistent and artistically vital. In the 1980s and 1990s, the music world was swamped with a thousand-and-one 'solutions' to divisions between high and low culture, all of which were as virtual as the postmodernist philosophy that provided the buzz words. Barry Guy's attempt to scale the heights of classicism using the new tools of free-improvisor musicianship had to be made: however, the composing was insufficiently rigorous – too reliant on 'sounds like' rather than process – to succeed. Its net effect seems to have made Bailey deeply sceptical about the use of composition at all. Although two months after the recording, Derek Bailey and Barry Guy both attended a 'composers' weekend' sponsored by the Society for the Promotion of New Music at Hatfield College, Durham University (20–23 July 1972), *Ode* did not pave the way to commissions from the straight world.

Derek made some concise points about the use of scores to *Guitar: The Magazine for All Guitarists* in 1978. Demonstrating that he knew about the stave and its dots, the magazine printed a 'Study' from 1967 featuring some typical intervals and clusters.

Writing music only really adequately covers pitch organisation and rather crude time, and I think the various avantgarde notation systems of the last 20 years are quite useless. Anything I want to write – and I haven't written anything for years – if it goes beyond standard notation, then I consider it can't be written. How do you write this? (*said Derek, playing something simultaneously before and behind the bridge*). The main constituent is the bump of the string on the fingerboard, plus some of the harmonic, the old drum rattle against the finger-nail, and the very high note plucked behind the bridge. Just one item like that is more or less impossible for any notation to reproduce, so when I did write things down they were only things which could be represented by standard notation. [DB to John Dalton, *Guitar: The Magazine for All Guitarists*, vol. 6, no. 10, May 1978, p. 22]

Such a no-nonsense approach cuts through the mountains of mystification that have grown up around the score – equivalent to all the useless post-Duchampian art-gallery games with the category of (is it or isn't it?) art. Although Bailey will not credit the next part of my argument – committed as he is to the collective, anti-individualist ethos of John Stevens – it also shows why Duke, Ra, Zappa and Fell compose as they do and did: charts for where it's necessary (pretty much conventional ones, showing 'pitch organisation and rather crude time'), while working with improvising *personalities* for untranscribable contributions and driving rhythm. It also shows why their vital, communicative music has had such a hard time being recognised by the musical academy: their efforts are directed to how music actually *sounds* rather than fetishising an antiquated means of preserving musical history.

HAN BENNINK

The Dutch drummer Han Bennink has been one of Bailey's more colossal collaborators. When I first saw them together – in Leeds on 21 March 1986 – the Termite organisers had promised great music, but nothing prepared me for the scorching energy, dishevelment and 'now' shock of the encounter. New York jazz critic Kevin Whitehead correctly put a photograph of Bennink on the cover of his account of the Dutch music scene, *New Dutch Swing*. Bennink's influence extends beyond music to haircuts and graphic design (see London drummer Steve Noble). In 1964, Bennink and pianist Misha Mengelberg played on Eric Dolphy's album *Last Date*, the songbird's only successful European barbecue. Bennink has drummed for Ben Webster, Sonny Rollins, Dexter Gordon and Cecil Taylor, though it is with European free improvisors that he reveals his most special gifts. Despite this, Ian Carr devoted just two sentences to him in *Jazz: The Essential Companion* – further evidence of the incapacity of the bureaucratic mentality to gauge great music. Han Bennink adds a violence and impatience to jazz drumming that makes every performance an event, creating perfect occasions for Bailey's eagerness to respond to the unexpected.

On 30 July 1969, Bennink and Bailey recorded an album for the Instant Composers Pool, the organisation set up by Bennink and Mengelberg. The word *lijm* – in loopy letters dripped in transparent PVC glue – appeared on the LP cover. The first track was titled 'An old woman is shelling beans inside her privy parts. It sounds "like the deep croaking of a frog"'. The title wouldn't suit an ECM release, and nor does the music: it is visceral enough to make the celestial spheres blush in embarrassment. Guitar and drums appear to grunt and gargle at each other. Bailey is ridiculously inventive and responsive: when Bennink starts bashing something metallic laid across his snare drums, Bailey alters his timbre to something appropriately brittle straightaway. The speed is cartoonlike and relentless, chasing bourgeois depth and sanctimony out of the room and down the alley. On 'Suki', Bennink's drumming is so damn fast you check your turntable to see if it isn't running at 45rpm. Bailey's nineties affinity for the sped-up surreality of jungle is predicted here, as the duo evoke mice on speed stashing individually wrapped gorgonzola titbits between the wires of a stainless steel egg slicer. On 'Gachi', Bennink fools with his voice, throwing his whole body into the performance; 'Kst, Kst' is rubbish collage of gangrenous infection and colloidal beauty.

The way that music of such evident technical and creative power as *lijm* has been buried by jazz criticism as currently constituted gives one pause for thought. What is it about this music that makes it unacceptable? It resembles the problem straight music criticism has with Frank Zappa: as soon as humour and the body emerge in music – however undeniable the musicianship – the guardians of cultural seriousness close ranks and deny that anything has happened. Two of the best acts in modern music – the duo of Roger Turner (drums) and John Russell (guitar), and Ascension (with Stefan Jaworzyn on guitar and Tony Irving on drums) – sound like derivates, if excellent ones, of Bennink/Bailey. It becomes clear why materialist authors as diverse as James Joyce and William Burroughs speculate about art as prophecy and time travel. When art is as technically proficient as this – and disinclined to use that technique to reproduce acknowledged moods and emotions (the subverbal, attitudinal, unconscious bedrock of the status quo) – it creates pockets of resistance to complacency and boredom. The objective necessity of technical innovation is proved by subsequent usage by other people.

Bailey and Bennink play the way they do because there is nowhere else for musicians who have absorbed what they have – who know what they know – to go. It is the very opposite of the calculated manner in which merely clever musicians cop styles and mix genres. The necessity that drives Bennink/Bailey proves its objectivity when its discoveries are attested by new formations – like drum'n'bass – that came from no direct influence at all. Ian Carr draws the map of 'jazz' via ascertaining visible fads and record sales (a highly questionable practice in a qualitatively defined musical genre). He cannot gauge the significance of art like this. Resistance to pomposity and pretension burns through the dialogue, making it one of the rare musics that have a political and critical thrust simply by dint of high spirits and honesty.

In spring 1970, Bailey toured with Mengelberg and Bennink and the

Danish saxophonist John Tchicai on the European continent. Between 13 and 17 June 1972, he toured England with Bennink. Performances on the last two nights, in London at the Soho Poly on Riding House Street (near Oxford Circus) were issued on LP as *Live at Verity's Place* [Incus 9]. Verity, who lived opposite the Poly, ran a lunchtime theatre in the Poly and let musicians use the space in the evenings. It was she who suggested to Derek that 'Company' – with its suggestion of a theatrical troupe – would be a good name for what he did. The Bailey/Bennink duo was exciting, if not quite as awe-inspiringly insane as *lijm*. Mal Dean's cover – drawn in the style of Lewis Carroll's illustrator Sir John Tenniel – showed two combatants, left ankles tethered to pegs in the ground, right ankles tied together across an abyss, blindly flailing at each other with fearsome bio-weaponry (a swordfish and a crane). Their helmeted heads were represented – in singular Anglo-dada fashion – by a radish and a hot cross bun.

When Derek Bailey formed Company, he borrowed an image from Mengelberg and Bennink and their Instant Composers Pool: 'Company is a pool of improvisors,' ran Bailey's description, 'from whom different groupings are drawn for different occasions and settings.' *Company 3* [Incus 25] was a duet with Bennink recorded at South Hill Park in September 1976. The album came clad in an intimidatingly enigmatic sleeve. It used banality as a kind of aggression. A drawing by Iain Patterson of two Dutchmen steering a sailing boat was presented like a silkscreen print, the sails pink, the picture framed in cool eggshell blue. As a sleeve note, Bailey printed a routine by Woody Allen concerning epistemology, and named one track 'Umberto who?', doubtless referring to Umberto Eco (before his success with the bestseller novel *The Name of the Rose* in 1984, Eco was known to *cognoscenti* as a formidable structuralist and semiotician). On the soundtrack, mutual provocation has pressed beyond speed and surprise into the realm of the concept. Bennink resorts to ludicrous evocations of Ayler and Bechet on clarinet; he plunks a banjo and pummels 'home-made junk'. On 'The Song is Ended', Bailey stoops to recalling jazz chord progressions, while on 'Tether End 1' and 'Tether End 2', Bennink scratches away at a violin: since chafing and scraping comprise so much of his drumwork, this abuse of Europe's most esteemed instrument seems highly appropriate.

Titles like 'A Fine Mesh' and 'Stanley' reference the silverscreen slapstick duo Laurel and Hardy. Though it's doubtful that anyone looking for laughs would have bought this album, these song titles convey the cumulative violence and anything-goes absurdity of the duo live. Bailey and Bennink toured England again between 15 and 22 March 1986. Bailey called it his 'favourite bout'. When Incus Records began issuing CDs, its second release was *Han*, a selection of duets from this 1986 tour (the Leeds venue is erroneously listed as 'The Camarthen', it was actually upstairs at the Cardigan Arms, a pub on Kirkstall Road frequented by trade unionists and socialists). *Han* was so energetic and pullulating, you didn't regret that Incus wasn't reissuing the earlier classics. On 14 March 1998, always ready for a rematch, Bailey and Bennink fought it out once more in Edinburgh. In 1999 they inaugurated 'post improvisation' – by sending each other digital audio tapes (DAT) to improvise to by post. *Post Improvisation 1: When We're Smilin* [Incus CD34] has Bailey improvising on guitar in London to a tape of hectic drumming by Han Bennink recorded in Amsterdam; *Post Improvisation 2: Air Mail Special* [Incus CD35] reverses the process, with the Dutchman responding to Bailey's tape of riffing, intervallic atonalism and irrelevant spoken word. Though the speed and irritation of the playing still glitters with cunning malevolence, the open-ended violence of the live jousts now sounds squeezed and two-dimensional. Indeed, the first CD more closely resembled the albums Bailey had recently made by improvising to pre-recorded rhythm tracks: *guitar, drums 'n' bass* [Avant] and *Playbacks* [Bingo]. The DAT Bailey sent to Bennink is more provocative and broken, with sudden silences and spoken word. There are some gorgeous congruences between Bailey's low strings on acoustic and Bennink's bass drum. This author's review concluded:

> So, two veteran purists of Improvisation ditch the genre's historical insistence on immediacy to explore the paradoxes of time and consequence thrown up by recording technology. The pair seem to have taken on board Theodor Adorno's dictum 'art would perhaps be authentic only when it had totally rid itself of the idea of authenticity'. Perhaps they'll flog some copies on the lo-fi/experimentalist racks. [*Hi-Fi News*, February 2000]

However 'post', Bennink and Bailey are always prepared for another bout. They played a duet together at the Palais des Beaux Arts in Brussels ('a monstrous nineteenth-century place') on 9 March 2003. Bailey was looking forward to playing with Bennink at the Bimhuis in Amsterdam in June, but had to cancel because of an injured finger.

STEVE LACY

International contacts are the elixir of Free Improvisation, giving musicians at loggerheads with local audiences hope that they are not merely perverse and crazy, that they are indeed part of a necessary historical development. The money helps, of course. Talking of the early 1970s, Bailey put it like this:

> All of my paying work was outside England, which was how I started doing this all the time [*that is, dropping commercial work altogether*]. Brötzmann was the key figure of getting people together, that was how I played in Germany and met Breuker and Han. Throughout the seventies, I spent 85% of my playing time in Holland, then, at the end of the seventies, it switched to the States. [27–vi–2000]

Backing Lee Konitz had been a break for Joseph Holbrooke, but though Konitz used his radio earphone to fold-in unexpected ideas (and later accepted an invitation to play at Company Week), he was not committed to Free Improvisation as an ethos. Soprano saxophonist Steve Lacy was different. A New Yorker, aware of the debates among Abstract Expressionist painters about chance and expression, Lacy went through his own existential confrontation with indeterminacy in the course of the sixties. It was trumpeter Don Cherry who first suggested to him – in 1961 – that one could play freely, without any plan or preconception, but it took 'four years of really hard work' for him to get there. Lacy reckons that his 1966 recording *The Forest and the Zoo*, made in Argentina with Enrico Rava (trumpet), Johnny Dyani (bass) and Louis Moholo (drums), was 'the first completely free LP'.

> Freedom is hard won and then you have to fight for it again. You can never rest for very long, you have to take it further, or it's no longer free.

SOLOISM AND FREEDOM, 1966-1977

We were playing 'freely' but it didn't sound free any more! What is this?
I couldn't believe it – it sounds the same every night. What are we going
to do? That's what we were trying to get away from. [*SL* 18–v–1998]

By the next year, free improvisation was finished for this quartet: 'we
couldn't work that way anymore'. However, Lacy was intrigued to find
European musicians still at it.

Derek plays every note so that you can't pin it down, and that's fine.
It's a good way. We used to work like that too. The reason he and I get
along so well is that I know the way he works. On *The Forest and the
Zoo*, we worked that way. Anything that we ran up against that
smacked of that thing we were running away from, we would run away
from it. It was like touch-and-go, you wouldn't let this happen because
that's what you wanted to get away from and you would go and do
this. 'No, no! That sounds too much like . . .' A constant touch-and-go.'
A very exciting process because it was pure improvisation, there was no
preparation, no rules, nobody knew what the other person was going
to do. We tried not to let it get pinned down. It worked, it worked like
a charm, very exciting music. [*SL* 18–v–1998]

Lacy first encountered Bailey in 1968 at the Free Jazz Workshop in
Hamburg. Musicians later associated with the Jazz Composer's Orchestra – Don Cherry, Carla Bley, Michael Mantler – were also in attendance, as well as drummer Paul Motian. Lacy duetted with Derek, and
had him play in a piece he 'got together', his *Precipitation Suite*.

I loved his playing right away, it was great, never heard anything like
it. I don't know any guitar player in the world who can play like Derek
and keep it interesting, keep it alive. Keep the time alive, keep the
audience alive, keep yourself alive. Every stroke of so-called free music
is only about that. It's like calligraphy – is it lively, is it happening? [*SL*
18–v–1998]

He played your piece? He's famously hostile to composition.

He doesn't like rules, he's obstreperously intransigent about that, yes. I
tried once to put a piece of paper in front of him and I found out right
away that he doesn't like paper [*laughs*], so I gave that up! We've
worked since in the way that's most comfortable. You've got to turn
musicians on, one way or another, and if paper turns them off, you've

got to remove the paper. We're all very flexible, we can work in many different ways. The so-called Free Revolution was done by that time, and we were into the post-free. We were arranging, experimenting, trying out different things, it was very, very interesting. I like it to be organic, music that we grow. I've been working on some pieces for thirty, forty years, and that's the way something happens. Derek doesn't work on pieces, he's not a piece man – I'm a piece man. When we get together, it's always been wonderful. He's the only one in the world I can play with in that fashion . . . well maybe not the only, but one of the few. [*SL* 18–v–1998]

After a spell in Rome playing with Musica Elettronica Viva (1967–1970) – whose interest in improvised playing and electronic equipment ran parallel to the Music Improvisation Company – Lacy returned to the traditional jazz dialectic between composition and improvisation. In the 1970s, he continued to play with improvisors – the most memorable encounters being with Bailey and the Dutch contingent (Misha Mengelberg, Maarten Altena, Michel Waisvisz) – but he no longer considered Free Improvisation as viable as a method for his own music. In fact, he declares that he finds most free improvising today highly predictable, and sympathises with audiences who suspect free gigs will be a drag. He makes an exception of Derek simply because his musicianship is so extraordinary.

As someone who has played with Cecil Taylor, Gil Evans and Thelonious Monk, Lacy inhabits jazz comfortably – and rejects Derek's condemnation of Monk for relying too heavily on composition (between 1961 and 1964, Lacy and trombonist Roswell Rudd led a quartet dedicated to performing Monk's compositions).

> Free Improvisation would absolutely not exist if there hadn't been the history of jazz before that, in my opinion. There was no way in the world that people were just going to start noodling around freely, spontaneously like that, if there hadn't been the whole history of jazz. They should acknowledge that. I think most free players do acknowledge that. Derek is a curmudgeon, you know. [*SL* 18–v–1998]

But the curmudgeon did invent a 'language', just as Cecil Taylor did. Lacy uses this word – a favourite of Tony Oxley's – to sum up Bailey's achievement.

The word *language* is very important. Derek has his own language, he made it up. It's an original spoken language and he can really deal it. He knows exactly how to speak it and it fits with many many other musics. It fits very well with my music. I had everything written out, and he could do whatever he wanted and it sounded great, man, wonderful. [*SL* 18–v–1998]

In July 1973, Steve Lacy was invited over from Paris to London to play at concerts celebrating an exhibition of Val Wilmer's jazz photographs at the Victoria and Albert Museum. He brought Steve Potts (alto) and Kent Carter (bass) from his band, planning to work with Bailey and John Stevens. Martin Davidson recorded the quintet at the 100 Club on Oxford Street, and it became a release on his label Emanem: *The Crust* (reissued in 1998 on CD as *Saxophone Special + (1973–4)*).

The idea of an accomplished, successful jazz player like Lacy using heretics like Bailey and Stevens for his pieces is compelling simply from the point of view of perversity. Titles like 'The Crust', 'Flakes' and 'Revolutionary Suicide' imply that Lacy knew what he was risking. According to his sleeve note, '38' was 'a self-portrait dedicated to, and in the manner of, Coleman Hawkins, who taught me something about aging', while 'Flakes' 'features Derek and is an ice-skating piece written for Mark Rothko'. When this mixed quintet play Lacy's intricate, jagged themes, it is as if bebop had suddenly regained its dotty freshness. Clanging discords from Bailey chase away the linear mournfulness that too often shrouds 'jazz' on British soil. Though Stevens and Bailey make hilariously unruly interventions, they cannot upset bassist Kent Carter's fabulous sense of swing: Bailey's mad solo on 'Flakes', as it dips in and out of harmonic congruence with Carter, is a delight. As Ronald Atkins put it in his review, 'Hearing one of Bailey's astringent guitar solos played over a straight tango rhythm from Carter's bass proved how many mansions there are in the domain of musical liberation' [*Guardian*, 31 July 1973].

On 19 December 1974, Lacy performed a concert at London's Wigmore Hall, this time with a soprano sax quartet (Lacy and Potts, plus Trevor Watts and Evan Parker) and a 'noise section' comprising Derek Bailey and synthesizer player Michel Waisvisz (these tracks also appear on *Saxophone Special + (1973–4)*). If anything, the importation of composed material makes the proceedings still crazier than straight Free Improvisation, as earnest-sounding saxophone charts careen over BBC Radiophonic Orchestra twiddles and splurges. Showing he was fully conversant with the dadaistic proclivities of the London avant-garde, Lacy became a DJ; he had Davidson supply him with two public-library gramophone records. Hence the contributions a steam train and symphony orchestra make to 'Dreams'. Again, one senses that the provocative spirit of bebop has been saved from the drones. The music is nervous, jumpy and even swinging, the combination of rigorous musicianship and sheer silliness just right. Bubbles of sax twiddling separate off from the central washtub and create a delightful multiplicity of bulbous, soapy rainbows. Music as keenly articulated and delirious as this escapes all too rarely.

In 'Swishes', the ability of a score to regulate musicians – the pumping of a saxophone chorus – is guyed as mechanical and meaningless. The riff turns round and round like a cog in a Dada collage by Marcel Duchamp or Cal Schenkel. In 'Snaps', the saxophones parp and prattle at the bleeping electronica like cartoon-caterpillar leaf-munchers faced with midget aliens sporting ray guns. Emotive reeds tremble in the face of Day-Glo plastic debris driven on a consumerist wind. Categorical commitments to 'composition' or 'improvisation' are incapable of measuring the critical intelligence of Lacy's spiky surrealism. His arrangement voices the contradictory impulses provoked by advanced technology (fear of soulful stupidity, dread of soulless novelty). Sax riffs quiver like mosquitoes over the fleshpots of artistic communion. Although Soft Machine and Henry Cow came close, there would be nothing quite as piquant in this vein until the advent of Martin Archer's Bass Tone Trap and Hornweb Sax Quartet in Sheffield in the 1980s.

ANTHONY BRAXTON

Like other Americans who had forced jazz into dialogue with modern art – atonality, chance and happenings – Anthony Braxton saw opportunities in Europe, where definitions were not so rigid. Paris was particularly hospitable. Echoes of the revolutionary upheavals of May

1968 resounded. A stark sense of confrontation pervades the free-jazz sessions recorded in 1969 and 1970 and issued by Jean Georgakarakos on the BYG label (the 'Actuel' series). Braxton's *This Time* [BYG ACTUEL vol. 47] is a typically chill and absolutist statement. The penultimate track has the musicians – Braxton, Leo Smith and Leroy Jenkins – out on the street, playing to the sound of passing cars and running motors: the explosive sense of expectancy recalls the magical moment that precedes 'Moonlight on Vermont' on *Trout Mask Replica*. The record concludes with a poem. Metrical stress on arbitrary syllables makes the gentle Braxton sound like the severest exponent of black rage against imperialism. If society thinks anything can happen, art where anything can happen suddenly makes sense.

In February 1971, a Parisian performance by Circle (Braxton with Chick Corea, David Holland and Barry Altschul) greatly impressed critic Bernard Loupias [*Jazz Hot*, April 1971]. The ructions of '68 had shaken up received opinion about jazz, prodding audiences to investigate new developments. The American Center, always on the look out for opportunities to prove that the United States had something to contribute to the capital of European Old World culture, promoted Braxton throughout December 1971. For a brief spell, this steady work made it possible for him to compose and begin his three-volume, 1,700-page *Tri-Axium Writings*.

David Holland played records of Bailey's playing to Braxton. In 1971, visiting London to perform at the 100 Club with Mike Osborne, Braxton saw Bailey at the Little Theatre. 'He did a solo gig and, boy, his music excited me,' he told Graham Lock. 'I felt I could really play with this man' [*Forces In Motion*, p. 129]. Then twenty-six, Braxton's rounded musical education meant he could see at once the significance of Bailey's innovations. In 1972, Val Wilmer reported:

> Braxton, always an avid listener, spent many nights of a previous visit here checking out Yorkshireman Bailey at the Little Theatre Club. He never misses an opportunity to enthuse about the man he feels is 'the most important guitar player on the planet right now. I think he's significant enough to say that his not being heard is criminal. I really would like to have a whole period of coming to London just to listen to

Derek and hopefully play with him. I think he's that important.' [*AB* to Val Wilmer, *Melody Maker*, 30–xii–1972, p. 30]

On 24 March 1973, at the Salle des Fêtes in Bourg-la-Reine, Braxton duetted with Bailey for the first time ('vieux rêve de Braxton de deux ans' according to Philippe Cardat in *Jazz Hot*, May 1973), before bringing on Cesare Massarenti (trumpet) and Peter Warren (bass) for a quartet (dedicated to composer–pianist Masahito Sato) and then the mighty Daniel Humair (drums) for a quintet (dedicated to composer–saxophonist Sam Rivers). On 30 June 1974, Braxton and Bailey played together at the Wigmore Hall in London, a concert immortalised by Martin Davidson's various releases on Emanem records under the name *First Duo Concert* (and by Val Wilmer's famous photograph of the pair seated on folding chairs in a back garden). Although the *Penguin Guide to Jazz*'s negative judgement on the Braxton/Bailey partnership ('divided by a common language') has gained currency amongst the deaf centrists of jazz criticism, the music tells a different story.

Davidson's sleeve note in the CD issue points out that some negotiation was necessary: Braxton's commitment to composition meant he was not prepared to 'improvise totally' (in Bourg-la-Reine, the pair had played a Braxton composition called 'Duet [dedicated to the composer–guitarist Derek Bailey]'). In 1969, Braxton had released *For Alto* on Delmark, a set of compositional strategies for solo performance that had been invented to address the 'void' he had experienced when trying to improvise off the top of his head. Braxton and Bailey ended up with designated 'areas' for staccato sounds, sustained sounds, repeated motifs and solo playing (really a rationalisation of what improvisors do anyway). There were also 'open' sections ('Area 3' and 'Area 11'), where the players could explore what had occurred to them as the concert proceeded. 'Area 4' was for solo guitar, 'Area 9' for solo sax.

The disagreements about improvisation as a total method were differences about emphasis and direction, not substance. True, born in 1945, Braxton had a rock'n'roll adolescence rather than Bailey's jazz one (Braxton liked Elvis, Little Richard and Bill Haley, plus Chicago's own Chuck Berry and Frankie Lymon). But his background as an active musician was similarly wide-ranging. Braxton enjoyed playing Neal

Hefti and Henry Mancini in the school orchestra, as well as hard bop
and soul jazz in after-hours sessions. Like Tony Oxley, he used army
service to broaden his musical horizons: stationed at Fort Sheridan, a
few miles north of Chicago, he joined the Fifth Army Band, one of the
leading marching bands in the Midwest, playing composers as diverse as
Richard Wagner, Richard Rodgers, Ferde Grofé and John Philip Sousa.
As a teenager, his two favourite records were Ahmad Jamal's *Live at the
Pershing* (1958) and Dave Brubeck's *Jazz at College of the Pacific*
(1953). Like Bailey and Oxley, Braxton's interest in music was ecumenical and questing.

In early interviews, Braxton named Paul Desmond, Dave Brubeck's
ofay/gay alto player, as his primary inspiration. This contravened Black
Nationalist dogma about the racial roots of jazz, but it didn't stem from
conservatism. Braxton's debut album *Three Compositions of New Jazz*
may quote him saying 'you can list my influences as being Paul Desmond, first, and then Ornette . . .', but the sleeve note still has Braxton
declaring 'we're on the eve of the complete fall of Western ideas and
life-values'. From 1959 to 1964, he took private lessons with Jack Gell
at Chicago's Roosevelt University. His intention, he told Ronald Radano
in 1982, was to 'lean on the piano' to play, like the cool, nonchalant
Desmond did in the Brubeck Quartet [Ronald M. Radano, *New Musical
Figurations: Anthony Braxton's Cultural Critique*, p. 51]. Gell introduced Braxton to Lee Konitz, Warne Marsh and Lennie Tristano,
musicians Braxton admires to this day. It was only hearing Roscoe
Mitchell in person that turned Braxton around to the more demonstra-
tive freedoms of Coltrane, Ornette and Cecil Taylor.

Far from being 'divided' musically, Braxton and Bailey heard in an
astonishingly similar way. They were both products of independent-
minded musicality, a truly global aspiration for a music beyond racial
cliché. Both were scornful of compromise with vested interests, which is,
after all, the real acid test: tyros of the first art movement since
Malevich's Suprematism that wished to be 'firmly planted in mid-air'
[Radano, p. 28]. Though, as a result of the treachery of the French
Communist Party, 1968 was not to be a 1917, Bailey and Braxton did
have one advantage: unlike painting, mid-air is where music materially
occurs.

With hindsight, even those who find Bailey's insistence on improvisation idiotic, or who (like this author) deem Braxton's semi-composed quartet music superior to much Free Improvisation, have to concede that the most effective tracks on *First Duo Concert* are the 'open' ones. Derek said this about his set-up:

> I used to play with a volume pedal and a fuzzbox, and at another period I used two volume pedals plus the fuzzbox for playing in stereo. But I used to get complaints from other musicians. Somebody said it was like playing with a guitar that was 30 feet long! [to Mark Lockett, *Ear* magazine, April 1990, p. 25]

The Wigmore Hall was a perfect soundspace for Derek's stereo system. Coupled with his emphasis on low sustain and high pluckings, the impact of his guitar is stunning, neo-orchestral. On 'Area 1' he surrounds Braxton's reed ballet with a panoply of sonic effects, like some artful stage designer conjuring up sun-dappled meadows and leafy glades for a lone dancer. 'Area 2' was designated for 'staccato' sounds, but if one were told that it was freely improvised, one would not be surprised. Certainly the compositional rubric seems more like a mnemonic for Braxton than anything Bailey is paying attention to.

'Area 3 (open)' is where the duet flowers, a graphic application of ideas latent in Eric Dolphy's stretched intervals. Both Braxton and Bailey push the extremes of their instruments – Braxton's ability to squeak on his reed while honking in the bell of his horn is astonishing. The pair sound like four players. You can hear Bailey mimick on his guitar the emphatic 'phuts' of Braxton's sax. Braxton plays a halting melody while Bailey comps, though each phrase is broken down into a fragment so that it becomes an event in itself, a timbral motif. They twinkle off into silence, the quick scrub of their attacks sounding like erasure rather than assertion.

'Area 4' was designated for guitar only. Bailey's stereo system presents each note as a vector within space, Suprematist spheres and arrows which are finally swept into a swirling Tatlin Tower of energy; when Braxton enters on contra-bass clarinet ('Area 5') – a lowering sea whale rumble – the net effect is no longer of instruments, but of surrealist cinema. Bailey ornaments Braxton's livid presence like a demented electrician screwing light switches and bulb sockets into the prosthetic tentacles of an alien apparition. 'Area 6' demanded sustained tones, and both musicians obey, stretching out their sounds with timorous sensitivity.

'Area 7' and 'Area 8' introduced Bailey's 'nineteen-string guitar', which included 'contra-bass strings' wrapped around each foot. On flute, Braxton blows so softly that his instrument does not resonate, yet even then sounds fierce and pressured; he maintains the same sense of an ineluctable slipstream that characterises all his hands-on music. His intelligence makes time buckle over on itself, introducing extra pockets and tucks by anticipating later developments. Far from failing to communicate, it's evident that Braxton and Bailey are discussing the same topic – the diatonic system – clambering about on it, testing it, busting its struts, restructuring it. Braxton's jazz training is evidenced in his velocity, a Trane-like need to ask a set of questions about a particular chord, except that he trills and slides all round the problem until it careens off a precipice (while Trane mines inside and explodes the matter from within).

'Area 10' was designated for 'repeated motifs'. Braxton fixes on a folkish tootle. Bailey strums around without finding anything determinate enough to engage him in dialogue. It's a rest, really. The composer in Braxton might think of this as providing variety, but skronk-hounds will prefer to skip it. 'Area 11 (open)' shows us what we've been missing. It's as if Bailey has been frustrated by the instruction for 'Area 10' and he's been waiting for this moment in order to engage seriously. His entry is like someone dispensing with small talk and getting stuck into serious argument: his air of confidence that his musical ideas will be understood – the surge of curiosity about what Braxton will play in reply – is exhilarating. 'Area 12' climaxes in an awe-inspiring fountain of splurge and grunge: a tarry, clotted, hitherto-unattested texture that is proof of the duo's starry invention.

It might be argued that Braxton's 'restraining devices' give *First Duo Concert* an overall shape – light and shade – it would otherwise lack. However, that wouldn't explain why Braxton's later duets with Bailey dispensed with them. It is more likely that, in an appearance at a prestigious venue, Braxton needed to protect himself: he did not yet trust the duo's ability to improvise music from scratch. However, it was the 'open' passages that showed the way forward: like Tony Oxley's with Cecil Taylor, the duo's musical understanding is so deep that compositional strategies could only hold back the dialogue. When musicians press beyond what sounds like 'music' into this kind of sonic immersion, the process is self-structuring, immanently logical. Free Improvisation is revealed as the kernel of the revolutionary idea: when we have nothing to lose and nothing to hide, the future can be improvised.

Two days later, on 2 July 1974, Bailey and Braxton played another duo concert, this time in the somewhat less hallowed surroundings of the Royal Hotel in Luton. The first part was issued by Incus ten years later as *Royal Volume 1* [Incus 43; the hopeful title has never been consummated by a second volume]. There's no 'compositional' agenda, and the two players dive straight into the knotted tangles that their agility and high-pitched instruments invite. Perhaps Braxton had some plan in his head – there's a distinct move from staccato assertions to slurred, bent notes – but the transition feels less forced than on *First Duo Concert*. After grappling like boxers in a huddle, Braxton and Bailey separate and bob alongside each other without engaging in explicit note doublings or discords, but there's some mutual understanding of tempo as the pace never relents and they recombine without a moment of confusion. As the dialogue deepens and Bailey's accompaniment starts to sound orchestral, the clarinet/guitar pairing suddenly seems classic (the jazz buff's brain goes spinning through the archive for precedents: did Pee Wee Russell ever record with Lonnie Johnson? Perry Robinson with Jim Hall? of course, it must be Benny Goodman with Charlie Christian Derek's thinking of . . .). As Bailey and Braxton reach a mellifluous congruity – though not via subservience to any known music – it's evident that they'll soon delight in picking it all apart again. This is music as purest thought; each affirmation is pursued by a denial or question. Like reading *Finnegans Wake*, it takes a few passages before the mind adjusts and starts listening in the right way; suddenly there are glimpses of a world where pure intuition could speak, transcending established vocabulary and grammar. Braxton's unaccompanied outing reaches back to the so-ugly-it's-beautiful honks and skronks of *For Alto*.

There are fewer dead patches than *First Duo Concert*, though perhaps the lack of 'compositional' goading explains why Bailey's contribution is slightly less fierce. One awaits the release of *Royal Volume 2* with impatience.

In May 1977, Anthony Braxton and Leo Smith – trumpeter and fellow member of the Association for the Advancement of Creative Musicians – played at the first Company Week, both by then prepared to risk total improvisation. Braxton played with Bailey five times, including a duet at the Roundhouse matinée on the final Sunday. This wasn't released, though a great trio with Bailey and Han Bennink – the opening of Friday evening at the ICA – appeared on *Company 6 & 7* [Incus CD07], a burst of sheet-metal petals.

On 4 October 1986, Bailey and Braxton played a duet at the Musique Actuelle Festival in Victoriaville, Canada. The forty-eight-minute concert was broadcast by SRC Radio (part of the 'Jazz Sur Le Vif' series) and was released by Michel Levasseur as *Moment Précieux*, catalogue number two on his Victo label (Levasseur's festival and label have since gone from strength to strength, the latter with over 70 releases). *Moment Précieux* is a fascinating set, though it lacks the untrammelled enthusiasm of the best of *First Duo Concert* and *Royal Volume 1*. Bailey was in his *intimiste*, quandary-about-harmony period, and only occasionally hints at the forcefield suprematism of his Little Theatre stereophonics or the hi–volume blow-outs of the 1990s. Braxton plays superbly as ever, but is quite prepared to lead Bailey into orthodox harmonic areas. There are none of the dazzling strides into the collective unknown that occurred in 1974. However, the resorts to harmonic safety have none of the smarts of postmodernist irony, sounding more like careful soundings-out of treacherous sediments that have swamped the streams of creativity. When left alone, Bailey's mouse-on-a-wheel non-progressions – agitated, restless, trapped – are as claustrophobic and obsessive as an Escher print. Braxton's re-entries are experienced as a relief. It's seemingly only against Braxton's saxophone that Bailey can free himself from the headache of note systems and can conceive of his guitar playing as *sound*. Braxton, in contrast, is content to weave in and out of regular chords and make sad and plaintive gestures.

Set two is far better, and is really all that should have been released.

Braxton and Bailey are clearer about what they want to do, making space for each other's felicities. A mellifluous, melancholic section now sounds deliberate, though Bailey sounds distinctly strange: picture someone twanging a sad melody on the torture apparatus of Franz Kafka's 'In The Penal Colony'. When guitar is played in a way that foregrounds timbre and physicality, it sounds grotesque as a chordal device. Braxton justifies his melancholy by tipping his solo into a caterwaul, pushing the music to the brink of artlessness required to keep improvisation from preciosity. Braxton's familiar strategy for upping tension is to bob and weave through the harmonies like a boxer in training: Bailey begins to sound engaged, and even bends his strings (a rockist twang that is usually anathema); Braxton's overblown distortions receive appropriately muddy clusters in reply.

At 17 minutes in on set two, Bailey starts playing a chiming, nostalgic nocturne; Braxton responds with a folkish lament on sopranino. Like rhyme in a late poem by an ultramodernist poet like J. H. Prynne, this traditional consonance signals exhaustion rather than beauty; whenever Bailey approximates to 'proper' harmony, it sounds surreal and hollow, the chance consonance of the tickings of a mad old clock. Off-the-cuff ornaments and flashes of exchanges towards the conclusion suggest where things might have led if the musicians had persisted, perhaps in less public circumstances; the final fireworks are sign-off flourishes rather than true grapples. When the applause bursts out, it is as if the audience is clapping the idea of the two great men playing with each other, rather than anything that's really happened musically.

If the *Penguin Guide to Jazz* needed an example of being 'divided by a common language', then the harmonious passages of *Moment Précieux* provide it: it's precisely when the players haven't the energy to improvise a duet from here-and-now timbre and split-second timing, and fall back into 'music', that communication ceases. The 1980s were a hard time for radicals, cultural as well as political. This account of the 1986 Braxton/Bailey duet is not an attack upon the musicians involved: indeed, the sincerity with which they measure out their reduced potential for invention at Victoriaville is rather moving. What needs to be criticised is the surrounding hype ('everything is melody', declares Art

Lange in his hyperbolic sleeve note). If every confession of quandary and failure is greeted with a burst of applause, it is small wonder musicians turn their backs on audiences. For new listeners, *Moment Précieux* might constitute a life-changing introduction to two utterly unique – and unbendingly honest – musicians; but next to *First Duo Concert* and *Royal Hotel*, it's a sad song they're singing.

JAMIE MUIR

Characteristically, the British musician whom Bailey cites as having had most influence on him in the years between Joseph Holbrooke and Company isn't a big name in either jazz or Free Improvisation. It's Jamie Muir, quintessential 1960s art school rebel, painter and Buddhist. Bailey spotted him playing drums in a free-jazz quartet in Edinburgh, and played a duet with him on the night. He liked his non-jazz, rock-tinged sense of time, his extended kit and his recklessness. In the programme for a gig with Muir, Jeffrey and Rutherford on 28 October 1971 at Goldsmiths College in New Cross, south London, he put it like this:

> Perhaps it's the post-Cage ear, something to the effect that everyone's hearing has changed. It hasn't, of course, but sometimes you do find people with a completely different sensibility to music. Christine Jeffrey and Jamie Muir are very good examples. I've got quite a conventional ear, actually, but the other stuff interests me. Rightly or wrongly, I feel as if I've played all the other music, and what I'm doing now seems to be logical. I'd have thought it would be an attractive area to work in, but the only one of my contemporaries who's doing it is Kenny Wheeler, I suppose. But people like Jamie and Christine, who've never played anything else, now that I'm really interested in. It's fascinating, don't you think? [October 1971]

What did Muir look like?

> Classic sixties guy, hairy – not facial hair, long blondish hair, very good-looking guy I imagine, a bit of a scruffy dandy. I've seen him with a silk handkerchief up his sleeve. You don't see them very often, the sixties would produce these people. [26–vi–2000]

When Bailey initiated Thursday nights at the Little Theatre – in part to avoid the strictures and struggles surrounding the Spontaneous Music Ensemble – Jamie was 'the only guy who fitted in perfectly':

He seemed to be able to provide a different playing experience every time. He was the first guy I met who turned up with his kit in a bag and started playing from the moment he opened the bag. This was standard, I might be playing already. He'd come with it in a bag or a suitcase. He'd regularly pack up like that, the end of the show was him packing up, all that shit. I'd not seen anyone do that before. He fitted into this idea of having no particular preconceptions. Not an easy guy to play with always. I've been playing with him and he'll stop and say, 'What the fuck is this?' I don't know anyone else who'd actually stop and say, 'What is that shit you're doing, you're doing that all the fucking time!' He was a highly reactive person, one of the things I really liked, there was the impression that he was slightly uncontrollable, on an edge. I don't think any of the stuff we did at the Little Theatre was of any significance to *him* at all. What he wanted to be was the drummer in the Stones. We never talked about this much. We weren't trying to put a group together, 'it's getting better', none of that shit – it was tonight, Finish. You're as good as the next time you play. [26–vi–2000]

What Bailey particularly relished was Muir's sense of event, his focus on the moment, his lack of anxiety about 'musical quality'.

After Joseph Holbrooke, in the period 1966 to 1973, Jamie and Han [Bennink] were the two most significant people for me – it was about attitude, the way they approached playing, a disregard for the results in a sense. There's always been a mix of the exploratory side and the setting-up side* in this music – the setting-up side gradually devours the exploratory side. During that period they were both uninterested in the setting-up side, which was fine for me, because there was nothing I wanted to set up. Both were highly reactive – what they were after was a certain kind of *playing* experience. When it's finished, it's over, and the next opportunity you start again. Neither express through their playing any preferences about other people's playing. There's always been this tendency, for the last thirty-five years, to franchise a bit of this

---

* DB later subsequently defined this impromptu term as the 'getting-it-together' side.

music, to chop bits off and turn it into a *music*. What's unique about this area is the freedom to do what the fuck you like. I've tried it in other areas of music, you can't do it. [26-vi-2000]

Bailey once again expresses his concern about his biographer's 'over-valuation' of the current scene (an opinion derived from reading my CD reviews in *The Wire* and *Hi-Fi News*).

Most of the types of music and bands and groups and soloists that come out of this music seem to me – it's difficult to say this to you as you're an enthusiast for this kind of thing – but I don't think it justifies the activity. What does justify it is this possibility to do anything with anybody at any time in front of nobody. Maybe I'll have that put up on the wall. [26-vi-2000]

Although I know it'll receive a put-down, I cannot resist pointing out to Bailey that this is sinisterly like the slogan used by the technicians at Frank Zappa's Utility Muffin Research Kitchen: 'Anything, Any Place, Any Time, For No Reason At All'.

From what I know of his music, that really surprises me. Zappa knew exactly what he wanted other people to be. [26-vi-2000]

On 30 January 1970, the Music Improvisation Company with Bailey, Parker, Rutherford, Davies, Muir and Oxley played a gig at the Purcell Room on London's South Bank (sponsored by the ICA). Writing in *Melody Maker* [7 February 1970], Richard Williams thought Muir's 'sound and fury' upset Oxley, and fellow reviewer Michael Walters regretted that his 'rattling and clicking' destroyed the quieter passages 'in marked contrast to Tony Oxley's attentive and constructive efforts'. Actually, Oxley calls Muir 'one of his favourite drummers – quite original and amazing logic, almost undetectable in influence' (to Trevor Taylor, *Avant*, no. 2, Summer 1997, p. 48). Cartoonist Mal Dean, reviewing ECM's release of the *Music Improvisation Company* [ECM1005] in *Records and Recording* in August 1972, called 'highland kamikaze percussionist Jamie Muir' 'a bag of laughs'. Like Dean, what Bailey seemed to value most about Muir was his lack of regard for Free Improvisation: it left the guitarist freer to play what he wanted.

When Jamie went with King Crimson [Muir played on *Lark's Tongues in Aspic*, 1973], he shook off this scene with disgust. He did an interview where he said, they're all playing bloody solo, it's ridiculous what they're doing, ego maniacs. He kicks the ladder away, but I don't think he had any great commitment to it in the first place. He was a rock'n'roller. He thought I was a lost cause, some creepy old danceband player who didn't know how to grow his hair long and was totally suspect in every direction. We used to get drunk together sometimes. [27–vi–2000]

Bailey emphasises those aspects of Muir's 'attitude' that he found most liberating (as we shall see below, Muir's commitment to Free Improvisation in the 1980s was not to be doubted). Muir's interest in Tantric Buddhism led him to spend most of the 1970s in what Bailey calls a 'monkery'.

I've stayed in this monastery on a number of occasions, I used to go and see him. I once went there with Steve Lacy. [*laughs*] You know what Lacy's like, classic fifties American-in-Europe, long leather coat, the haircut, he's a version of Frank Sinatra in some respects. We're sitting in this foul boys'-school sports pavilion, it smelt of mud and it's cold, everyone's dressed in these gowns, we're eating this very doubtful porridge with hunks of dried bread. Lacy's sitting there . . . it was beautiful. It's near Lockerbie, where the plane crashed. [27–vi–2000]

When Muir emerged in 1980, after spells in Buddhist retreats in France and India, he re-engaged with Free Improvisation. Muir and Bailey played together again many times: with cellist Georgie Born at the Gallerie Nachts St Stephens in Vienna on 13 November 1980; with Christine Jeffrey, saxophonist Tony Coe and experimentalist David Toop at Goldsmiths College in Deptford on 14 February 1981; with Born, bassoonist Lindsay Cooper, trombonist Radu Malfatti, Steve Lacy and bassist Maarten van Regteren Altena on 20 May 1981; and with Christine Jeffrey at the Half Moon Theatre in June 1981. Muir also played the 1981 Company Week, the Company tour of England in January 1982, and the 1983 Company Week at the ICA.

In August 1981, the pair recorded a duet album together – *Dart Drug* [Incus LP41] – at Crane Grove in London. Though Bailey thought Muir had matured, and actually missed some of his old volatility, he was still an excellent improvisor: his percussion is timbrally varied and unexpected, extracting a weird pentatonic orientalism from Bailey's guitar. When reissued on CD in 1994, the album received the following review from *Hi-Fi News* (closing joke courtesy Kristen Hersh of the Throwing Muses, a line from her song 'America').

JAMIE MUIR/DEREK BAILEY
DART DRUG
INCUS CD19
Elegant, airy interchanges between the master of the f-hole (Bailey) and a maverick percussionist (Muir). Muir provides a ceaseless array of new timbres, opening up delicate spaces between distant rumbles and in-yer-face pops and clicks. He boils up noisy squalls out of which Bailey's notes sail like slo-mo silver bullets. Derek Bailey is truly the guitarist's guitarist. Although recorded way back in 1981, this is so far ahead of what most deem possible on the guitar that it's ridiculous. And sublime, simultaneously at the same time. [A:1] [*Hi-Fi News*, January 1995]

The CD arrived wrapped in images of glass-curtain buildings, photographs by Jamie, sporting bizarre wobbles caused by imperfections in the glass. He also drew the album's title, a bizarre scrawl like some mescalin-induced vision notated by Henri Michaux.

In June 1972, Nigel Rollings's *Microphone* – a duplicated monthly – asked percussionists Tony Oxley, Frank Perry, Paul Lytton, Peter Britton and Jamie Muir to set down their thoughts. Oxley answered tersely ('The most important activity for me is the enlargement of my vocabulary'), Muir at greater length. He anticipated many of the positions adopted by anthropologist Michael Thompson in his classic 1979 work *Rubbish Theory*.

> Improvising percussionists are primarily concerned with effecting alchemical changes over rubbish. The changes can be directed towards objective ends – a conception of beauty/purity/music – or subjective ends – an essentially organic interest in the process of change/transmutation itself.
>
> To make something out of 'it' – or 'it' to make something out of you. I am interested in neither of these – heroes – antiheroes – raspberry. I am just interested in rubbish . . . rubbish rubbish rubbish rubbish . . . in fact if I wasn't surrounded by it . . . wallowing in it guzzle I'd spludge

go MAD – Oh God . . . But I am, that's to say, I am surrounded by it, so I have no fear you see, no fear at all. London's made of rubbish – the only thing I can aspire to in the environment is rubbish. If there was no rubbish there would be . . . efficiency. We live in rubbish, we breathe it, we drink it, we earn it, we talk it. The minute you take off all the hygienic layers of wrapping from food – FOOD – it's rubbish, throw it away – tons and tons of it. [*Microphone*, June 1972]*

Muir went on to say he reckoned drummers Elvin Jones and Milford Graves had 'filthy lavatories'; that he preferred junk shops to antique shops, but above all he preferred rubbish dumps ('neither found nor collected'). He attacked percussionists who 'stake a claim', create value and so tame the wilderness. Slow people admire Buddy Rich or Peter Clayton, middling people Miles Davis or Stomu Yamash'ta, he said: 'but if you are fast and you're still looking, then THE RUBBISH DUMP IS THE PLACE FOR YOU . . . and believe me I play absolute rubbish' [*Microphone*, June 1972].

Jamie Muir: rubbish theorist, timbral extendor, weird catalyst.

PETER RILEY ON DEREK BAILEY

In October 1973, *Great Works* – a duplicated poetry journal edited by Bill Symondson and Peter Philpott – published an essay on Derek Bailey by the poet Peter Riley. Away from the hurly-burly of the music press, Riley's cool historical assessment still rings true today.

> You would have to refer back to the sound of the clavichord, in a European context, for a plucked string of such expressivity and rigour; to material like Byrd's folk-song pieces for such sustained imagery, such energy within control and substance. [*Great Works*, no. 2, October 1973, p. 34]

Riley had evidently watched Bailey play in the flesh, and paid attention.

---

* Bailey quoted different paragraphs from Muir's extraordinary text in his *Improvisation* (p. 96).

The guitar is fully realized in its entire range of modes, every possible kind of vibration of string and of the wooden hollow (which is not a mere amplifier) by every manner of plucking and otherwise manipulating the length of gut or wire. A range extending from melodic/contrapuntal to percussive is there present, *at each moment* of the course of events, and it is this simultaneity which, with its sources, removes the music from the 'familiar' into the exploratory. In it, rhythm is no longer a separable entity from pitch/timbre, and 'harmony' occurs only as the overlapping of independent existences and the reverberations set up among them. There is no prior structure for these non-fortuitous coincidences and no-one is accompanying anyone, ever. [*Great Works*, no. 2, October 1973, p. 34]

The fierce assertion that 'no-one is accompanying anyone, ever' works well as a description of the soloism and rebarbative dialogues of the period. In defence of descriptions like 'there's a great moment in "Domestic 1", where Alex Ward unleashes an astonishing circular scrape-fest and Bailey is momentarily non-plussed, then pings along an inspired accompaniment' [review of *LOCationAL*, Incus CD37, *Hi-Fi News* November 2000], these are not meant to imply a fixed role for the guitar, so much as dramatic moments of domination and submission within the tussle. Another caveat: Bailey does like to play rhythm guitar (see his words on recording *Harras*), though this is conceived not as accompaniment to a 'soloist', but as a spritzer to the ensemble's total effect.

According to Peter Riley, Bailey's turn against jazz did not distract him from its positive virtues. Free Improvisation is not academic nihilism. Riley correctly divines the motives behind Bailey's use of Webern.

Webern has been studied, but the social context of this music makes it clear that such study has not been a means to instant contemporaneity, nor a step towards the high-brow, for much shorter routes to those undesirable ends are available. Nor has it resulted in a complete abstract – the base layer is a rich resource of part-reference whether conscious or not: mandolins & Balalaikas strumming in the distance, George Formby's banjo, Leadbelly's steel 12-string, koto, lute, classical guitar ... and others quite outside the field of the plucked string. [*Great Works*, no. 2, October 1973, p. 34–5]

But can you hear the jazz? What became of the jazz? 'A record of delightful chamber music which has nothing to do with jazz' one reviewer said of ECM 1013, though it apparently took a 'jazz-man' to find 'delight' in it, or even note its existence. If you can't hear the jazz, perhaps you should listen to Cornelius Cardew's A. M. M. Music of improvised bullshit (theoretical ineptitude of planned purposelessness) and then turn back to INCUS 1, and you'll hear the jazz. After that it sounds like a ragtime band. [*Great Works*, no. 2, October 1973, p. 35]

Riley points to the way that Bailey controls his notes all the way through, a practice that leads to the quality of focus and presentness that characterises Free Improvisation.

There is an assumption of responsibility for the sounds produced. Perhaps evident in the style by which a note need not necessarily be abandoned once it has been struck and left to its dying fade-out. The initiation of the note is not the principal focus of sequentiality. At times, the note once struck, it can be quite playfully cajoled into second or third upsurges of energy by delayed fingerboard pressure, or foot-pedal, or allowed almost to die out and just at that final moment, the edge of departure, slid to a new pitch which is momentarily definitive. Handled the way it is, as perhaps by the best sitar-players, it seems like a vision of life-span and the possibilities of old age, a clear notation of hope. [*Great Works*, no. 2, October 1973, p. 35]

Having defined Free Improvisation as materialist and nominalist (' "Substance" in that sense ("form") is found in the exploration of occasion ("matter") as inherent in it as that particular juncture'), Riley goes on to distinguish Derek Bailey's dialectical treatment of the contingent from John Cage's attack on human intention.

Cage-type pseudo-Zen sequences of nothings can also be totally improvised, of course, hence superficial resemblances to this music. But that is an exploration into a rarefied atmosphere wholly dedicated to the business of finding nothing and running shrieking in horror from the merest glimpse of something – thus 'chance' as willed inertia, as if it were not actually fortune (quite understandable in an American situation). 'Chance' with Mr Bailey occupies a range from imposition to liberation, and is something worked with rather than abandoned to. [*Great Works*, no. 2, October 1973, p. 36]

Peter Riley's observations make such sense, it's a pity that they did not inform more discussion of Free Improvisation in the decades that followed.

DEREK BAILEY AS THEORIST

Derek Bailey has not always depended on Cambridge poets for theoretical armature. Reacting against some regular evening-slot two-hour broadcasts of semi-light music on BBC Radio 3 – 'I thought that if they had that much time to spare, they ought to use it' – Bailey proposed interviewing improvisors from around the globe. In 1974, Radio 3 broadcast a series of programmes about improvisation by Bailey. 'They weren't a drop in the ocean,' Bailey told *Melody Maker* later on, 'they evaporated before they got to the ocean' [*Melody Maker*, 2 August 1980]. Stimulated by what Viram Jasani (sitar), Paco Peña (flamenco guitar), Lionel Salter (baroque organ) and Stephen Howe (rock guitar) had said, Bailey turned the radio series into a book, adding contributions about composition and improvisation from Earle Brown and Antony Pay, an 'objection' from Gavin Bryars, and notes on the Joseph Holbrooke Trio, the Music Improvising Company, solo playing, and improvisation in the classroom. Called *Improvisation: Its Nature and Practice in Music*, the book was published in hardback in 1980 by Moorland Publishing, and received glowing reviews. It was revised and republished in paperback in 1992 in Britain (by the British Library National Sound Archive, an organisation that had been documenting Company Weeks at The Place Theatre), and in 1993 in America (by Da Capo who, doubtless thinking of Louis Armstrong, put a trumpet on the cover, even though Bailey didn't interview any trumpeters). *Improvisation: Its Nature and Practice in Music* has been translated into Italian, French, Japanese, Dutch and German, and was the basis of a terrific TV series, for Channel 4 by Jeremy Marre, called *On the Edge* and broadcast on Sunday evenings in February 1992. It included revealing footage of the

Grateful Dead, John Zorn conducting *Cobra*, Buddy Guy playing with Junior Wells, the improvising organist at Sacré Coeur, Max Roach leading a percussion workshop with Harlem schoolkids, George Lewis improvising with his computer, Butch Morris conducting conservatory students, country session players in Nashville, tribal rituals in Zimbabwe, and folk singers in the Hebrides. It also demonstrated that Bailey has one of the most ear-alerting talkover voices to be heard anywhere in the media.

5 COMPANY WEEKS, 1977–1994

The Music Improvising Company was a group, a unit with a particular personnel. When Jamie Muir left for King Crimson in 1972, it was effectively over. The years that followed saw Bailey playing an increasing number of solo gigs. This is what he told Michael Walters for *Sounds* in 1975:

> Now I get fewer gigs than before, because over the last three or four years I've mainly been solo, and I no longer get to work in bands so much.
>
> It's alright though. I get enough gigs to feel involved, and there is a further advantage that playing solo actually lets me play with a wider range of people. It is a basis from which I can always work – I can play on my own without a gig, and I'm free to play with anyone else.
>
> Solo work is very useful for certain things – particularly in allowing me to work out certain musical problems. I don't think of it particularly as an end in itself, but it is better than the other alternatives open to me. I prefer it to playing in a small group for years on end – it's a freer situation. [*Sounds*, 14 June 1975]

Solo playing allowed Bailey to present his musical ideas in a pure form, intimating a Beckett-like poverty of means. The joke of a book like Beckett's *Malone Dies* (1956) is that the writing 'degree zero' of shrugging off 'content' – characters, plot, *mise-en-scène*, local colour – to concentrate on the act of writing itself is not actually puritan at all. It's more like a riotous act of self-gratification, Diogenes masturbating in his barrel, Proust's Swann reminiscing at ridiculous length about his childhood. What happens is that allowing the writer to focus on what really interests him – writing – unleashes a lurid energy which is far more charged than realist novels that dutifully 'represent' scenes other people wish to read. The prospect of boring the reader becomes an aggression artfully deployed, a new weapon at the disposal of the writer. The profundity of bourgeois drama is replaced by stand-up comedy, monomaniac and self-lacerating.

Solo playing was also suitable for someone whose hands 'think' faster than his brain, whose immediate impulse is wittier than anything his consciousness could devise (in this, Bailey's approach has the proletarian lack of depth exemplified by the pop-modernist poet Tom Raworth when he ascribed his liking for Kurt Schwitters's collages as a need for immediate gratification, art that renders its pleasures faster than the concept, what he calls his 'low attention span'). When given a chance to record an album for the Italian Cramps label – a project bankrolled by the progressive rock group Area, and produced by *avantiste*-about-town Walter Marchetti – Bailey recorded fourteen stunning tracks on the first day (16 September 1975), then spent the next three days drinking wine on studio time. However, Bailey gradually began to consider solo *performance* (that is, 'the presentation of musical ideas' rather than the 'pursuit of musical ideas' which is solo practising) as diminishing the unpredictability of collective improvisation.

Widespread interest in solo playing led to bizarre programmes like the following, a concert sponsored by Music Now at Notre Dame Hall, Leicester Square, London, on 15 June 1976:

```
EVAN PARKER QUARTET
solo: Evan Parker, wind.
solo: Derek Bailey, strings.
duo: Paul Lovens, Paul Lytton.
percussion quartet.
```

Reacting against this rather lonely situation, and as a way of formalising his interest in selective promiscuity rather than group commitment, Bailey started calling aggregations he worked with 'Company'.

One of the reasons it came about was because I was spending a lot of time playing solo and it actually came to seem ridiculous. Playing and improvising solo has certain usefulnesses to do with language and working things out, but after that it is ridiculous. So a lot of it is to do

with me playing in the company of other musicians. If I didn't do
Company gigs I'd be playing solo again. [DB to Kenneth Ansell,
Impetus, no. 6, 1977, p. 244]

The first time Bailey used the Company name was in 1976. With
characteristic canniness – parallel to his whole philosophy of 'improvisation' – he was naming the unnameable, trademarking the unsaleable,
creating a hiccough in assumptions about music, bands, records and gigs
generated by an industry geared to marketing commodities.

The strategy worked, and Bailey's concept was highly influential.
When this writer encountered Free Improvisation in the form of pub-
upstairs promotions by the Termite Club in Leeds in the mid-1980s, it's
no exaggeration to say that the entire format derived from Company
(though it took me several years to trace its provenance). Bailey's term
for the way he liked to work was '*ad hoc* groupings', part of his general
critique of the way that once musicians have established ways of
working with each other, their music becomes more predictable.

'*Ad hoc*' is Latin for 'to this', meaning 'to this particular end'. The
Oxford English Dictionary defines the verb 'to use *ad hoc* measures or
contrivances' as 'to improvise', which returns us to Bailey's central
concept. The phrase links improvisation to particularity, connecting to
the anti-universalist nominalism of the Middle Ages, which Theodor
Adorno resurrected as Negative Dialectics (the hippie troupe Here And
Now who toured Britain with Alternative TV in 1978 also referenced
this anti-authoritarian heresy). 'Company' put the focus back on ensemble interaction.

Like any band name – or poetic coinage – worth its salt, the term
had many resonances, some from the past and some yet to arrive.
Anthony Braxton's trio with Leroy Jenkins and Leo Smith had been
named the Creative Construction Company, like some imaginary building firm, and the billing 'Bailey & Co' also suggests a business (one in a
northern city, no doubt, gilt capitals glimpsed on the signboard of a
tricyclist delivering groceries). In 1982, Bailey said in the brochure for a
tour that Company 'took its name from a theatrical repertory company
... the closest approximation to its method of work'. In 1992, the
rubric ran:

Music in recent times has tended to be an activity that has been totally directed, presented like a flower show, in the best, most flattering way. In that context, improvisation is a muddy ditch: it's where things can grow. [DB to Nick Kimberley, *City Limits*, 16–23 July 1992]

In 1993, a building metaphor – proletarian constructivism versus bourgeois consumption – surfaced again: 'Company Week is not a festival,' read a note in the programme, 'festivals are fashion parades; a sequence of exotic creatures cat-walking their stuff. Company Week is a building site; we get together and make something that wasn't there before.'

Of course, without a score, what's played won't be there afterwards either: whatever Bailey's scepticism regarding records (and writers who review them), they are a crucial means of putting a viable group on the map. So Company was established by three releases on the Incus label, named – logically enough – *Company 1*, *Company 2* and *Company 3*. The first was recorded on 9 May 1976 at Riverside Studios in London, with Evan Parker on soprano and tenor, Tristan Honsinger on cello, and Maarten van Regteren Altena on bass. For the string players, Bailey called upon musicians from the Dutch improvising scene, contacts made through Bennink. *Company 2* [Incus 23] was recorded on 22 August 1976, a trio record with Evan Parker and Anthony Braxton. *Company 3* [Incus 25] was the duet record with Han Bennink described above (see page 180).

The musical and political tensions underlying the use of Honsinger and Altena might be best illuminated by considering the music from a gig that occurred at the Cambridge Poetry Festival in 1977, a result of contacts made by the poet and publisher Anthony Barnett (who generously supplied me with a tape of the event). Barnett had known Bailey for some time. He had organised gigs for the Spontaneous Music Ensemble in the basement of Better Books when he worked there in the late 1960s, and performed a guitar/poetry event with Bailey at the Cambridge Poetry Festival in 1975. From 1969 to 1972, Barnett had played percussion with John Tchicai's Orchestra Cadentia Nova Danica, broadcasting for Radio Danmark and recording for MPS. John Tchicai was originally a discovery of Archie Shepp (whom he met at a jazz festival in Helsinki). Tchicai gained legendary status by playing on John

Coltrane's *Ascension* [Impulse!, 1965], universally hailed as the mightiest blow-out session in the annals of free jazz. In 1968, Misha Mengelberg and Han Bennink honoured Tchicai by recording a trio with him as their second Instant Composers Pool release [*Instantcom*, ICP 002]. The pair's fifth release, recorded on 3 March 1970 in Rotterdam, was recorded during a European tour, featuring Tchicai and Bailey playing in a quartet with Mengelberg and Bennink.

Naturally enough, given Barnett's illustrious contacts, the Cambridge Poetry Festival organisers had the idea that a Tchicai/Bailey gig would be a great idea. However, as Barnett tried to explain to them, things were not that simple. Reviewing the quartet album [ICP 005], Michael Walters had written, 'Tchicai often appears rather intimidated by it all.' Walters had put his finger on a real problem. Nor were the differences simply musical. According to Kevin Whitehead, 'Each (Mengelberg and Bennink) recalls, independently, fondly, a quartet tour where Derek Bailey and John Tchicai argued endlessly' [*The Instant Composers Pool 30 Years*, p. 7]. Tchicai and Bailey hadn't played together since, a split that could only be aggravated by Bailey's continuing discomfort with the rhetoric of Black Nationalist Free Jazz – both saxophonic and philosophical (any close associate of Braxton was likely to share his dim view of the showy militancy exhibited by Archie Shepp and his camp). Such antique animosities are forever the fault lines lying in wait to trip up promoters.

Barnett managed to parlay the original proposal into a compromise. Bailey would play with his own accompanists, and then Barnett and Roy Ashbury, both playing percussion, would accompany Tchicai for a set. After that, who knew what might happen? Barnett would have liked Tchicai and Bailey to play together, but he thought it most unlikely. The gig occurred on Sunday 17 April 1977, at the New Court Theatre in Christ's College. In the first half, Bailey played a trio with Honsinger and Altena. After an interval, Barnett, Ashbury and Tchicai played a set. Then, to Barnett's 'great and pleasant surprise' [letter, 9–viii–2000], everyone played together.

Barnett and Ashbury had played a brilliant trio gig with Bailey at the University of Essex on 24 February 1977. Sensitive to the spatial aspects of percussive sound, the duo's playing recalled both modern classical pieces (Cage's percussion pieces, Harry Partch and Steve Reich) and jazz, from Baby Dodds's snare rolls to the open-field work of the likes of Milford Graves and Rashied Ali (Barnett subsequently established himself as the world's leading authority on swing violinist Stuff Smith). During his set, Tchicai deliberately summoned the ghosts of Coltrane and Ayler (in the last number he actually played Ayler's theme tune, 'Ghosts'), making Barnett and Ashbury sound initially like an 'untogether rhythm section'. Once they accept Tchicai's lead, though, the music gels. In contrast, Bailey's playing with the duo had highlighted their specific qualities (timbral variety and spatial sensitivity, rather than a jazz drummer's musical flow), achieving a chill focus on the musical instant.

If Bailey had wanted to signal his disdain for free jazz, he could not have chosen more apt musicians than Honsinger and Altena. Though active in Holland, cellist Tristan Honsinger was American, a conservatory-trained cellist who'd dropped out of academia. He'd played in Jazz Libre du Québec, a free-jazz group that gigged in prisons and hospitals. However, he was unhappy with the group's political bent ('they were more into talking about politics than playing', he told Kevin Whitehead, *New Dutch Swing*, p. 189). Honsinger liked the music he heard on ICP and Incus releases, and relocated to Europe in 1974. After busking on the streets of Amsterdam and Paris, he met Han Bennink and bassist Maarten Altena. Altena, too, was classically trained. He appreciated jazz (in 1970 he played with US bop legend Dexter Gordon), but believed that Europeans couldn't master the real thing, and so found the move towards free music liberating. Like Honsinger, Altena believed that humour belongs in music. In 1973, he'd released *Handicaps* [ICP 012]: a plaster cast on his left wrist was duplicated by a cast on the fingerboard of his bass. A music theatre duo with Teo Joling saw Altena brandishing Christmas tree branches, wearing model battleships, and pacing on a treadmill. Although he did not employ such devices in Cambridge, his approach had the same provocative edge as Honsinger's.

The concert in Cambridge began with a typical outburst from Honsinger. Accompanied by moans and stomps, the cellist delivered a violent and impassioned mixture of angular folk motifs, sarcastic memories of Bach and Dvořák, and vocal-sounding bow rasps. Reviewing the concert in *Musics*, poet John Hall noted that Honsinger's approach was 'physical', contrasting it to Bailey's more 'contemplative' attitude. Treating the performance as a physical phenomenon rather than 'music' led Hall to some pertinent observations:

> The cellist was energetic, *physical*, witty and allusive. By *physical* I mean that, in contrast to the detachment of Derek Bailey's playing which made his guitar seem an object of – more than a *means* to – contemplation, Honsinger was engaged in a dance with his instrument, his whole body moving to a rhythm his playing assumed, and it seemed a casual accident that the strings were actually only sounded with fingers and bow – since any part of his body might have served. The term here seems to be *control*: Bailey seemed to be in control over the sounds he made and therefore to eschew allusion, whereas Honsinger and – to a lesser extent – the bass player, with their greater bodily engagement were playing within an area of greater risk, where *control over* is confused with *in control of* or *surrender*, so that the instrument itself seems constantly to be suggesting to the player all the other modes available to it. And this is what I meant by allusion: the moving into moments of emotional security – secure because they were previously shaped and have acquired poignancy through familiarity. [John Hall, *Musics*, no. 13, August 1977, p. 28]

When attacked with Honsinger's exhibitionist abandon, the cello became an anti-art paradox as graphic as John Latham's incinerated books and musical instruments. Deploying Honsinger was part of Bailey's strategy of *tabula rasa* creation, a nihilistic assault on tradition. However, Hall's review does pinpoint a problem. In his eagerness to jettison any trappings of jazz, Bailey welcomed post-conservatory players who came laden with their own baggage. In truth, Honsinger's resort to folksy and romantic cliché is every bit as distracting from the music to hand as saxophonists who quote Coltrane or Ayler. His energy can fire an ensemble, but the clichés stick in the throat. Altena, who has greater control of timbre (particularly when bowing), provided much more musical and suggestive moments, evincing (dare one say it?) a jazzman's sensitivity to the sonic environment.

In criticising the gross-out rock band Brain of Morphius, Pence Eleven's Nathan Blunt once asked, 'Why must rock singers always pretend to be epileptic?' In seeking to overcome his conservatory-trained repression, Honsinger also exhibits something rockist – epileptic and infantile. His is an assault on bourgeois repression unconditioned by trans-African rhythmic grace. You can understand why some cringe and say this kind of 'freedom' is all too predictable, a *conservatoire* tantrum as 'twere. However, Honsinger does supply a cataclysmic challenge which Bailey thrives on: at one point in the opening trio, you can hear Bailey echo the folk reel Honsinger has been plucking, picking out the notes he wants in a moment of instant analysis.

With Honsinger and Altena, Bailey pursued irrelevance and disaster as a new form of musical continuity. Though he had hinted at this by working with art school experimentalists in the Music Improvising Company, the process now went beyond electronic novelties into degraded classicism, sarcasm and pastiche. In a musical version of Samuel Beckett's end-of-tether tramps, Bailey picks through Honsinger's garbage, providing a kind of atonal counterpoint to his accents and rhythms. Music as obedience to an overarching harmonic or rhythmic order is trashed in favour of music as activity – energy and attention. The high point of the trio came when Altena abandoned some irritating folk-out-of-Bartók rhythms and started plucking in response to Bailey, slurring his notes to make them talk, with Bailey pausing and hurrying in turns. By the interval, Altena and Bailey had broken into the magical realm where sonic textures seem to unfurl as simultaneous dialogue.

At the close of the concert, all six musicians did play together. However, Bailey signalled a certain reluctance to acknowledge his role in the group by inviting audience member John Russell on stage to play guitar too (it was a general come-all-ye: poet Denise Riley's son Jake assisted Barnett on percussion). As usual in Free Improvisation, differences were worked out in practical music making. To start with, Altena echoed Tchicai's phrases on bowed bass, providing a kind of harmonic hands-across-the-genres greeting. In turn, Tchicai took up Honsinger's high cello wittering: the two high lines sounded brilliant in the midst of the percussive clutter of Barnett and Ashbury. However, when Honsinger resorted to a deconstructed sonata and Tchicai referenced Ayler's 'Ghosts', a chasm opened up between the musicians. It was a perfect illustration of the correctness of Bailey's insistence that 'idiomatic' playing has no place in Free Improvisation: it's actually a break on the thrust towards musical community, a regress to possessive individualism. In this case, Bailey merely had to strum some of his characteristic harmonic ambiguities and the sense of the music's focus and possibilities returned.

> Tonality is like an argument, and the answers to the questions are always the same. Play Gmin7, C13, and the next chord has to be one of three or four things. If you're looking to get away from that kind of thing, you have to use a different language. Atonality is a way of moving from one point to another without answering questions – almost a sequence of isolated events. Atonality has a non-grammatical quality, a non-causal sequence to it. [xi–1987]

Bailey's playing shows that, rather than the punishing negation feared by conservatives, atonality is the open door to real communication: the cosy fug of individual memory is dispersed, and one sniffs the chill air of collective action, risky and uncharted.

COMPANY WEEK 1977

Bailey's annual Company Weeks were a way of making Free Improvisation public and visible. They were intensely involving events, allowing audiences to follow processes that are usually kept out of sight. Bailey has described them as 'emotional, musically intoxicating experiences; pretty much my ideal way of working' [*Improvisation*, 1992, p. 136]. The first Company Week was held at the Institute of Contemporary Arts (ICA) between 24 and 29 May 1977. In retrospect, after Company began including dancers, moonlighting classical players, rock guitarists and turntablists, the 1977 line-up looks distinctly jazz. At the time, though, it was an international summit meeting of free players from three countries. The four British hosts were Derek Bailey (guitar), Steve Beresford (piano, guitar, 'etc.'), Lol Coxhill (soprano sax) and Evan Parker (soprano and tenor saxes). America supplied Steve Lacy (soprano), plus two musicians from Chicago's AACM (Association for the Advancement of Creative Musicians): Leo Smith (trumpet and flute) and Anthony Braxton (reeds and flute). The Dutch scene supplied Maarten van Regteren Altena (bass) and Han Bennink (percussion), along with the American Tristan Honsinger (cello). Bailey thought enough of the music to release three LPs [Incus 28–30] and – in 1994 – a facsimile of a 'dummy book' written up from notes made *in situ* by the poet Peter Riley, and given to Bailey because Riley hadn't managed to repay his complimentary tickets by getting anything into print: *Company Week* [London: Compatible Recording and Publishing, 1994].

Peter Riley's account insists on the ineffable unknowability of the musical in-itself. This allows him to focus on many poignant details – the holes in Steve Beresford's socks glimpsed through his sandals, or the ducks in St James's Park which Riley passed on his way to the concerts – but tends to postpone critical judgement. Working with guitarist John Russell, another devoted member of the audience, Riley came up with a somewhat disappointing description of what Braxton and Parker played on the Wednesday night: 'jolly interesting' (Riley's psychogeographic descriptions of the City, on the other hand, show that the 'London' commonly ascribed to Iain Sinclair is just one example of a modernist vision vouchsafed to Olsonites and Prynnians). About the music, Riley wrote: 'What we "think of it" is our problem. What I "thought of it at the time" is as faultlessly irrelevant as my complete non-recollection of it now. From Thursday on we were all more-or-less besides the point.' Riley's aphasia allied Black Mountain poetics to Bailey's fear that any consideration of music outside the act of playing will end up as promotional duplicity or composerly diktat. Decipher the handwritten text, however, ignore the Zen/Heidegger/Wittgenstein metaphysics, and Riley's *Company Week* is fascinating: a snapshot of the quandaries raised by a week of Free Improvisation.

Company Weeks are love affairs, brief and intense episodes that affect relations between musicians and audiences for life. Speculation about underlying tensions during a Week is like Freud's primal scene: fascinating, but extremely dangerous. However, unless one is going to dissolve everything in a saccharine solvent of 'lovely music', it is these tensions that make Company Weeks electric. Pondering the way in which Bailey hones in on music that is not so much pleasing as interesting, Riley reached the formula: 'there is a kind of music which

breaks pleasure into all its unrecognisable components', a parallel sentiment to James Chance's 'sex is better than pleasure' on the song 'Contort
Yourself' [*Buy*, Ze Records, ILPS7002, 1979]. For the radical Freudian,
sexual pleasure is related to curiosity and enlightenment rather than
comfort and the known; the free improvisor approaches music in the
same way.

Eugene Chadbourne, who played at Company Week in 1990, put it
like this:

> It's interesting when Derek creates situations in which he might not
> even be playing. He's not only creating situations for himself to get
> involved with, he's creating it for the situation where he can sit back
> and hear something new or special. I remember a Company thing at
> the Victoriaville Festival in Canada [3 October 1987], the most
> unlikely combination of people – it was the first time they'd ever gotten
> together – there was Derek, Gerry Hemingway [drums], Steve Beres-
> ford [piano] and Tom Cora [cello]. I walked in the dressing room and
> thought, How are these people going to play together? They can barely
> hold a conversation among themselves! Derek brought them together,
> but on their own they didn't have that much in common. I remember
> Gerry Hemingway was playing with Steve Beresford and they started
> to lock in and get something going, it was kind of an Afro-Cuban jazz
> groove, and they're getting into this. Then I hear this voice from the
> side of the stage: [*Eugene's Charles Laughton accent*] 'Hey now, I'm
> not paying you cunts to get together and play this kind of rubbish!'
> So Beresford started freaking out on piano, and it turned into some-
> thing else, like a whip from the sideline. I thought it was great. [*EC*
> 28–ix–1998]

If you're interested in what happens before musicians gel into bands,
you'll not be squeamish about 'incompatible' elements. At Company
Week 1977, Steve Beresford's interpretation of freedom – very much in
the vein of the performance art antics introduced by Gavin Bryars –
didn't suit the high seriousness of the AACM delegates. On the first
night, during the third act – a quartet with Coxhill, Bennink and Altena
– Beresford poured water from a hot-water bottle into his trumpet, and
paddled in the resulting puddle. He then set fire to a piece of paper.
Riley wrote:

Realism? Referring us back to the glories of trivia. The metaphorical pool, the far longed-after surface of tension/ease, becomes actual in downright present tense: a hotwaterbottle emptied into a trumpet (horizontal, then rain). We are all suddenly aware what time it is. He wears no shoes or socks. He paddles in the pool under his trumpet – infant urination delights: seaside flesh-eaters (with chips). From there to fire-breathing dragons in one hop. [Peter Riley, *Company Week*, 1977]

Six nights gave ample opportunity for every one of the ten musicians to play with everyone else. Anthony Braxton and Leo Smith sedulously avoided any grouping with Beresford, as did Evan Parker (the only other unconsummated permutation was Bailey/Coxhill). Although Beresford must have felt woefully misunderstood – his act was destructive only in so far as it was perceived as such – he'd raised a banner for a certain species of improvisor. Eugene Chadbourne, for one – proud inventor of the 'electric rake' (a garden rake with a contact mic attached, which is used to rake the walls and floor of a venue to produce highly entertaining noise-fests) – pricked up his ears.

My introduction to Steve Beresford was that Anthony Braxton and Leo Smith had gone to this early Company thing, and in my dilettantish way I was really interested. I liked both their music and the English improvising scene, and I liked to see them coming together. I really liked the record with Braxton and Bailey, I thought that was great. I was waiting for reports. This was at a time when I was talking a lot to those guys, so I get this report: 'Well there was this one guy who was a *complete* lunatic, don't ever play with him,' I remember Leo saying. 'He doesn't have his musicianship together.' That was Steve Beresford. I think a whole aspect of my music is based on the fact that I'm really rebellious. I don't like anyone to tell me what to do. If they tell me not to play tunes, I'm like, 'You think! I'll play tunes if I like to!' So I thought, I'll play with Steve Beresford if he bothers those guys so much. I always like the outcasts. Right away I made contact with him, because I was trying to find somewhere to lock up my instruments and he was the phone number to call. We started playing together. He'd gone through this experience where people had rejected him. I remember one of the Company performances I was at as a viewer, Han Bennink was being used to create this kind of belligerent energy on stage. Braxton and Leo Smith were so cool, presenting things in a certain kind of way,

Bailey put them together with Bennink, and Bennink was kind of lampooning them. They were playing this very serious-sounding thing that sounded like a composition and he got out this tenor sax and got in between them, towering over them, starting to play 'Misty' with this honking tone, like an embarrassing drunken saxophonist in a sleazy bar and they're making these faces, so embarrassed to be caught in this situation. Derek was creating this mini drama, this mayhem using these different people. He'd do it to you too. One of the ones I was involved in [Company Week 1990], I had a really busy day, because I played a little gig in this store during the day – the old Rec-Rec store – and I hadn't had a chance to eat anything. I was there at the Company thing and I asked Derek, when am I going to play – I want to nip out for a curry. I think that sort of pisses him off. You should be hanging around the whole time. While I was out getting the food to bring back – I thought I'd relax and eat while I was getting ready to play – he shifted the order round, so as soon as I get back with the food, it's, 'Oh! you're on stage!' So I put the food down and rush out there. I think he likes to see people under pressure, he fiddles with people's expectations. [EC 28–ix–1998]

Audiences were so successfully shaken out of their expectations that a 'barger-in' made his appearance. Han Bennink spoke about the incident with a sensitivity that belies his wildman image.

The playing was very good and he found a way into it, which I think was a very positive thing. But after five minutes we realised that he had no material and he was sitting there turning feedback on. He was playing with the feedback and he just went on and on and on. I tried various things to let him stop in a normal way, but . . .

And then time came to play my second set with Anthony [Braxton] and he was sitting at the side staring at the instruments with a strange atmosphere around him. I went up to him and said, 'Anthony and I are going to play a duet now; if you want to play with me we can do it afterwards, but not now.'

It was very strange because I can produce the same tone that he had on Steve Beresford's little amp on the megaphone. It was like he was programmed: when after five minutes playing with Anthony I played the same tone he stood up and started to join in again. They got him and tried to throw him out.

That tension then, the whole atmosphere was terrible. You can decide to stop, or continue to blow, but it doesn't make any sort of difference. I played some low, soft notes to try and calm them down. And then this long scream came, this beautiful, but also terrible, scream. It was like daily life. When you go to work by underground or bus lots of things can happen: it can rain, or the bus can have gone, or there's a strike, or someone stands on your toes or whatever. That must happen in music too. [Han Bennink to Kenneth Ansell, *Impetus*, no. 6, 1977, p. 254]

The first record that resulted from the 1977 Company Week was *Company 5* [Incus 28], cut at a special recording session held after the Thursday night concert. It included all the musicians apart from Beresford, Bennink and Coxhill (thus excluding all the 'humorists' except Honsinger). However, the concept of Company as a pool of musicians meant that this was no slight: though you didn't hear all of them, the names of all ten Company musicians were listed on each record.

Lol Coxhill made some pertinent comments on the humorous aspects of Company Week 1977, revealing a commitment to music that explains why his presence on stage – whatever his reputation as a comedian – so often ensures that great music is played.

Kenneth Ansell: It has been suggested that during the Company Week your attitude and playing seemed to indicate that you were at pains to align yourself with the musicians rather than the 'clowns'. Would you say that was true?
Lol Coxhill: I would say that to say I was aligning myself with them was wrong. It was natural for me to be like that. My sense of humour and my performance-art attitudes come into play in certain situations. The only humorous things I did during that week were with Han Bennink, Steve Beresford and Tristan Honsinger with them as the instigators. They're the ones who set people up and create the confusion. Han will do things that are very amusing visually, but if you don't watch they are very beautiful musically. These were the only times my sense of humour would come into play. The rest of the time I never even thought of it. I was involved in what I was doing and in that situation I reacted naturally. Which is all I do anyway. It was a very rare opportunity to play with people who I consider to be very important and very creative musically. So I certainly wasn't going to waste it through being silly. I was there for that week to grasp every opportunity

going to play with people I care about. [Interview in *Impetus*, no. 6, 1977, pp. 246–7]

One can reflect on Company gigs one has attended (or eavesdrop via live tapes) and speculate about artistic tensions and directions, but a release on the artistic level of *Company 5* is nothing less than a manifesto. 'LS/MR/DB/TH/AB/SL/EP' (Bailey named the tracks after the initials of the musicians) occupied the whole of side one, a pushing-at-the-vinyl-limit twenty-five minutes. It's a rare example of a collective free improvisation by more than five musicians being completely successful. Though its atonality, unrestricted instrumental palette, woven complexity and lack of percussion make it resemble modern classical music, it has a rhythmic toughness and vehemence that score-readers rarely achieve. Leo Smith's trumpet flurries and Derek Bailey's stinging electric guitar provide a metallic spritzer to the reeds of Braxton, Lacy and Parker and the strings of Honsinger and Altena. Altena's busy bass and Bailey's instant-answer guitar provide the kind of active foundation that provokes great playing (in other contexts, this is called 'swing'). Rather than indulging in the sarcastic sonatas invited by solo recitals, Honsinger plays his strong suit on cello: his rhythmic insistence acts as a dynamo for the musical machine. Energised sections fold seamlessly into poignant evocations, making the listener wonder why rhythmic laxness ('gorgeous echo' etcetera) is so often equated with aural poetry. Bailey's twangs and pings sound like the reverberations of some wire mesh the other musicians are pushing their sounds through. Manual tweaks and jolts that are literally local and private suddenly open up into cosmic infinitudes: music as sex. To anyone who uses their ears to evaluate modern music (that is, not that many), *Company 5* makes a powerful case for Free Improvisation as the supreme method.

When it came to CD re-release, Bailey chose to combine *Company 6* [Incus 29] and *Company 7* [Incus 30]: the first lost three tracks, the second one. He neglected what was arguably 'better music' for a rumbunctious taste of the highs and lows and clashes and hokum of the first Company Week. With such a level of drama and invention, it's easy to see why so many musicians wanted to play at Company. The sound of the playing is so personal-sounding and affecting it gives every musician a larger-than-life aura. In the same way that John Tchicai became legendary for his part in *Ascension*, the sound of Leo Smith's trumpet – a lonely, austere blues cry – or Lol Coxhill's soprano – a homely yet questioning chirrup – exalts the player in the imagination. Despite Derek Bailey's irritation that Free Improvisation is relegated to the jazz section of magazines and newspapers, and despite his rejection of the musical forms and techniques of 'jazz' (a never-ending task, given jazz's flexibility and penchant for vocalisation and mimicry), this emphasis on the sound of the individual musician gives Free Improvisation a sociological correspondence to jazz. Eugene Chadbourne makes this point:

> Jazz always meant to me that you learned all the styles, and a good jazz musician should know something about all the different styles of jazz and be able to play some of it. That's what it meant to me. It's a music of tradition and of history, a music with heroes in it, and if you're going to play it you bought into that. It's a heritage – you can't just play the music and ignore the heritage. [EC 15–vi–1993]

A current of anarchism in Free Improvisation disagrees with this approach, claiming that the form should be 'non-hierarchical', and that critics and audiences should refuse to acknowledge heroes or leaders. Anything tainted by the will to power is evil, so we should all lie on the floor and 'deep listen' while Pauline Oliveros squeezes her postmodern accordion. Buttressed by John Cage's Zen homilies about vanquishing human desire, such blandishments are frequently echoed in musicians' magazines. The idea that ego can be transcended is obviously a convenient ideology for collectives. The problem is that, in a highly competitive scene, it's invariably absolute humbug.

As against this universalising moralism – a feature of anarchist thought from Mikhail Bakunin to John Cage, from Michel Foucault to Gilles Deleuze – the Marxist asserts that tradition and leadership are not *necessarily* pernicious. It all depends which traditions and which leaders. As against anarchist irrationalism, Marxists argue it's possible to distinguish between the different social forces at work in society and culture. Power is not irredeemably evil, some original sin: it all depends on who holds the power and what social relations it implies. Focusing on concrete historical conditions and possibilities, the Marxist has a place for both historical awareness ('heritage') and leaders ('heroes'). This was the thesis argued by Frank Kofsky when he explained the defeat of free jazz in terms of the early death of its 'leader', John Coltrane.

As with Kofsky, it's Chadbourne's socialist – as opposed to anarchist (or 'lack of') – politics that lets him insist on tradition without becoming reactionary. The question facing music today is not just an abstract question of tradition versus innovation, but a question of *which* tradition we're seeking to sustain and develop: the musical corollary of *whose* side you're choosing in the class struggle. Jazz is the voice of the oppressed, it's in essence a tradition of resistance. Without that social awareness – that is, class consciousness – one is left with a bleak choice between conservative neo-classicism (Wynton Marsalis's concept of antique jazz as objectively 'fine' Black music which can be preserved in aspic by a middle-class elite) or pseudo-revolutionary iconoclasm (post-modernist and cyber-theory denials of history and struggle).

In a special issue of *Impetus* devoted to Company Week 1977, editor Kenneth Ansell interviewed the musicians involved. Steve Beresford – the performative 'anarchist' of the Week – introduced the abstract 'critique of power' by which contemporary feminism (using arguments from Michel Foucault) was separating itself from Marxism, class struggle and any concrete understanding of history. If everything can be blamed on a ubiquitous and inevitable 'will to power' (or 'patriarchy' or 'sex drive'), then politics is reduced to a never-ending – and, as the Thatcherite eighties proceeded, increasingly 'ironic' – twinge of guilt.

Most people who play music love showing off, they might show off in a very subtle way but it's all to do with showing off. It's very adolescent I think. The point is that what I do is a lot more adolescent than what they do in appearance. But I think you like impressing the girls and you like to be admired and all those motivations are a bit silly, but I'm sure that's why most people do it. At least that's the original motivation, they might since have found out a lot about the music and got into it a lot deeper. I think most men, because it's nearly all men who play this music (which is another question that is very vexing), have adolescent motivations. [*Impetus*, no. 6, 1977, p. 262]

Any fan of Elvis or Hendrix or Iggy Pop is likely to retort to this kind of hand-wringing with a two-word expletive (thus conveying a vigorous Reichian critique of the repressive individualism and vestigial-Christian body fear motivating bourgeois-feminist sex denial). Beresford drives Bailey's critique of showbiz – musical essence *versus* appearance – into a morass of hopeless, unresolvable moralism. However, in Beresford's defence, both Eugene Chadbourne and Mark P (of *Sniffin' Glue* and Alternative TV fame) praise him for raising questions about adequate musicianship and instrumental 'macho', and so encouraging their own 'punk' versions of Free Improvisation. Whatever the failings of Beresford as political philosopher, Derek Bailey required his affront to professionalism.

Company Weeks did not so much develop a musical style as promote a set of 'names' – musicians known to have played at Company Week gained a certain status. However, though organisers like the Leeds Termite Club's Paul Buckton might complain about such 'nameism', in making heroes of free-improvising musicians, Company Week did not create stars *à la* Hollywood – super-rich fixtures in a celebrity spectacle – so much as pivots for dialogue about music and society. Anyone who's played Company Week has taken part in an intense social microcosm, one with symbolic resonance for how things and people could be organised. Such hero status does not accrue to the musician cost-free: subsequent involvements and musical activities are likely to be examined with the same heightened sense of attention they received at Company Week.

Free Improvisation was a response to sixties concepts of freedom engineered by a musician who had played in dance orchestras, who abhorred the 'let's get it on' ethos, and who warded off hairies and posers by playing the *Lieder* of Anton Webern at full blast. Company Week 1977 was a major event, and established Free Improvisation as a rhetorical stand. It became a point from which to criticise the way the music industry – both pop and classical – had immersed past and present music in commodity fetishism, a market of competing 'geniuses' rather than an arena of collectivity, co-operation and construction – of active music-making.

The symbolism of the first Company Week happening in 1977, the

Year Punk Broke, means little to Derek Bailey. Someone who never credited the Beatles or Stones in the first place was hardly going to be impressed with Joe Strummer telling everyone their day was done. But to anyone who was inspired by the raw situationist disdain of the Sex Pistols and their 'assault on the music industry' in Jubilee Year, the congruence is striking.* With the later emergence of Hession/Wilkinson/Fell, Rudolph Grey and the Blue Humans and Stefan Jaworzyn's Ascension/Descension, genuine links were forged between rockist excess and Free Improvisation, but in 1977 they felt as different as football and ballet.

Why? The format of Company Week discourages the kind of musical *thrust* associated with subaltern protest and affirmation (from hard bop to rap, punk to drum'n'bass). The Company concept is of musicians listening to each other, engaging each other in duos and trios, exploring how their different ways of playing could be welded together. The emotional atmosphere is closer to that of an intelligent dinner party than a night getting hammered down the pub. The idea is that audiences might find this activity of interest, thus exploding the distinction between the musician's consciousness and the listener's. The Impressionists shocked Parisians by proposing that their *plein-air* sketches could be bought as finished works: why should musicians deny audiences the intriguing pleasures of music *not* fitting together, and always stage 'shows' where everything has been worked out, so that the signs of passionate interest and creativity are brought out on order? Bailey's radical suspicion of musical impact – a suspicion nurtured through decades of live playing – suggested giving audiences a taste of musical thought as it arises first time: fresh, uncut, uncensored. Free Improvisation goes beyond Impressionism into Abstract Expressionism, where the artist's own pleasure in handling the materials becomes the main event.

Bailey says music is a different beast from visual art, and such comparisons don't help. However, reference to past art movements does

---

* By touring with the Damned, Lol Coxhill demonstrated that the punk and improv categories were not impermeable. Questioned by the music press over punk *shtik* about 'not being able to play', Coxhill replied, 'Well, it's a funny area isn't it?' He concluded that because the audience gobbed on him as well as Captain Sensible, they must have liked what he played.

alleviate the pressure on the music writer to become an apologist and booster for a clique of musicians. Instead, one can begin explaining various objective tendencies in modern art. Aware that his status as 'godfather of improv' means his opinions are taken too seriously, Bailey is wary of expressing judgements about other musicians in public. However, he does have an impressively objective view of the aesthetic import of Free Improvisation as a moment in musical history.

I really did think it would be like Cubism – a strong thing that would last six, seven years and then carry on as an influence on other things. Which might be the case. We got six, seven years, which is great – I never thought it would happen at all in the first place. The fact that it's continued and turned into a kind of scene is nothing that I anticipated, I don't even feel that it's anything to celebrate. This end of the music, to leap into the present, for me personally, my relationship with the music is not one that I like now. I'm not talking about the music, I'm talking about me, this elder statesman kind-of grandfather of Free Improvisation that comes out of this journalistic approach. I don't like that, but that doesn't matter, that magazine approach to it, but as it exists, it's not as stimulating as it used to be, it's less unknown. [2–xii– 1997]

From the recorded evidence, Free Improvisation had a trenchancy and power in its period of innovation (1966–73) which it lost in later years. In *The Baptised Traveller* and *4 Compositions for Sextet*, in the first duets between Bailey and Parker, and between Bennink and Bailey, the excitement of a music built out of illegitimate sonorities yet driven by musicianly gesture was so strong that the music had both integrity (no note played by rote) and impact (no vagueness or confusion). Despite his scepticism about the judgement of history, Bailey has a shrewd sense of musical quality, and all the strategies that journalists and promoters find so vexing – the elusiveness of his musical production, the championing of unknown names, the reluctance to make positive statements about current trends, the perversity of his venue choices – are intended to prevent mediocrity congealing around himself. It is an unapologetically modernist aesthetic. It grates against practically every tenet of cynicism, accommodation and pragmatism in the rubric of postmodernism.

Although to mention the word 'jazz' to Bailey is to step into a minefield, he actually adheres to principles established by jazz. To cite a deliberately banal example, when *Melody Maker* reported on Earl Bostic's pop success in the mid-fifties, it conceded that 'die-hards' would not call his music 'jazz', adding, 'For it was when he left the legitimate fields of jazz improvisation and progress that Bostic made his money' [Jack Hutton, *Melody Maker*, 4 September 1954]. 'Improvisation' and 'progress' were the *sine qua non* of jazz criticism of the fifties, and they have remained Bailey's watchwords, even if commitment to them has forced him to abandon what is called the 'jazz scene' today.

Free Improvisation has a distinct aesthetic. It has never been a matter of anything goes. If you compare the early-seventies releases of Tony Oxley and the Music Improvising Company to the floating neo-classical Euro-jazz released on the ECM label, it's evident that they are both indebted to the rhythmic disassociation pianist Bill Evans achieved with Scott LaFaro (bass) and Paul Motian (drums). However, there is a world of difference between the rugged sonic thrill of Oxley and Bailey music – its intimation of crisis, its Varèsian thunder, its Leninist constructivism – and the smug, bourgeois, all-labour-screened-off languor cultivated by Manfred Eicher at ECM (which one wag dubbed 'the sound of the middle classes falling asleep'). Free Jazz and Free Improvisation can be contrasted, inviting a replay of 'Hard Bop versus Cool'. Actually, Bailey/Oxley versus ECM is a better debate: it supersedes American racial distinctions with the more fundamental struggle over social vision and class allegiance.

Company Week was a challenge to musicians and listeners, a proposal about music that jettisoned any reliance on past achievement, but it had no built-in guarantees. Theodor Adorno said it about Schoenberg, but it applies to Bailey too: 'There is perhaps no single factor which distinguishes Schoenberg so basically from all other composers as his ability to discard and reject what he has previously possessed' [Theodor Adorno, *Philosophy of Modern Music*, p. 122]. If the birth of Free Improvisation coincided with a high point in terms of mass resistance to capitalism – the Watts and other riots of summer 1965, the Tet Offensive of February 1968, the mass strikes and occupations of May 1968 – Company was inaugurated for a period of massive downtown in struggle and consciousness, the Reagan/Thatcher-dominated eighties. As Adorno also said: 'No artist is able to overcome, through his own individual resources, the contradiction of enchained art within an enchained society' [Adorno, *Philosophy of Modern Music*, p. 105].

As it embraced classical players, rock renegades, electronic experimentalists, turntablists and dancers, Company Week was more like a forum for an international avant-garde than a specific kind of music. The tessitura of the music shifted upwards towards soprano saxophones, violins and pipping electronics, a sonic corollary of it becoming 'head' rather than total-body music: a mesh of stringlike statements to *comprehend* rather than an integrated wave blast to *feel*. Although this might seem to reflect some 'essential' Bailey (the guitarist who admired the cool saxophone of Lee Konitz and the elegant guitar stylings of Jim Hall), such refinement served to limit the scope of the music. In the eighties, Company Weeks were certainly interesting events, but they did not have the messianic fervour – or invite the kind of critical crusades – of Free Improvisation in its classic period.

In short, Company Weeks did not result in uniformly great music. At worst, they resembled academic seminars, where critical ideas flare up only to be deflected from their revolutionary conclusions by a seminar politesse that insists that everything is merely speculation, and that organisation and action are off the agenda (organisation and action wouldn't be 'improvised'). An ideology of endless research and experiment replaces the determinate statement, a musical version of the Althusserised pseudo-Marxism of the 1970s academy. And in the late 1980s, the swamps of postmodernism – edgeless pluralism, universal tolerance, snobbish consumption of anything-goes as high-class entertainment – beckoned. Free Improvisation always feels best when played in the teeth of scepticism and disapproval, where its silences and tensions are hard won, an achievement on the part of musicians and audience, an immanent development inside a genre that means things to its audience (why the years of Free *versus* Jazz sound so heroic). The 'respect' won by Company could also work against it.

Company Weeks became flagship events for Free Improvisation, and hence prone to preciousness, competitive exhibitionism and lame jokes (even if they were intended to break the 'respect'). Certainly, this author would explain his commitment to Free Improvisation as resulting from regular attendance at provincial clubs in the north of England, where small groups of musicians played sincerely and at length, rather than by his Company Week experiences. This is not to criticise Bailey's particular decisions regarding venues or personnel: the prestige that accrued around his activities as 'godfather of improv' became an albatross that had to be dealt with. He acknowledged as much in 1988, when he invited musicians from Leeds, Manchester and Sheffield to Company Week and made polemical assertions about the relative strength of Free Improvisation in the provinces compared to the metropolis.

If one attempts to map aesthetic positions, social circumstances and political developments need to be recognised. For this writer, an exemplary contrast between strategies developed in different epochs was provided at Company Week 1991. Keen to publicise his new CD *Ya boo, reel & rumble* [Incus CD06], drummer Steve Noble set up a stall and was selling T-shirts (he gave me one, a budget production that became a bizarre indecipherable rag on the first wash). They featured the same image used on the CD, an African ritual dancer in a feathered skirt, from the same stable of images as those used by the post-punk band Rip Rig & Panic with whom Noble had played. The Incus release, duets between Noble and clarinetist/alto saxophonist Alex Ward, signalled Bailey's recognition of a new generation of improvisors (the pair were born in 1960 and 1974 respectively). Nevertheless, I remember Bailey shaking his head in bemusement at Noble's promotional device. He did not say anything beyond that, but the ideological contrast was further cemented by a brief exchange I had with Alex Ward about Zappa. Unlike Bailey, Ward adores Zappa's music. I mumbled something about Zappa's critique of commodity fetishism. 'But I like commodities', Alex replied. 'One of the reasons I like buying Zappa's records is that they're so well packaged . . .' Ward's point was undeniable, but suddenly the media term 'Thatcher's generation' took on a lurid reality.

Only the moralist judges actions without reference to the circumstances in which people act. The appreciation of Noble and Ward for the marketing strategies of groups like the Mothers of Invention and Rip

Rig & Panic was forced upon them, a reaction to two things: the eclipse of revolutionary left politics caused by the Reagan/Thatcher onslaught of the early 1980s, and the increased rationalisation and commodification of cultural life, which had effectively wrecked 'the jazz scene' as a serious arbiter of good music. If innovative improvised music is pushed out into the margins, there to consort with every species of home-made experimental endeavour (from the inspired to the wack), it is hard to recall a time like the early 1970s, when Columbia released Joe Harriott's *Movement* and Tony Oxley's *The Baptised Traveller*, both accompanied by sleeve notes that argued authoritatively for the music as contributions to jazz history; a time when *Melody Maker* could print discussion articles about Free Improvisation as a viable genre, and Richard Williams could boost ICP and Incus releases *and* talk intelligently about the technical problems facing improvisors using rock metre [7 February 1970]; or a year like 1972, when the members of Iskra 1903 snatched first (trombone), second (bass) and third (guitar) places in the *Melody Maker* Jazz Poll [11 March 1972]. As the recession of the 1970s bit deeper and Thatcherite economics became the commonsense of management, jazz departments at the major labels were forced to justify themselves by reference to the 'bottom line'; the anxiety that refusing to back innovation might mean missing the next Charlie Parker or Jimi Hendrix meant little compared to the threat of personal redundancy. To many musical rebels, the only answer was the counter-strategies and devil-may-care brinkmanship of punk.

Neither Joe Harriott nor Tony Oxley could be described as corporate-friendly. They took Columbia's contracts as their due, fruits of recognition by an authentic jazz scene with powerful representation in the industry. The musicians hadn't despaired of establishment recognition. Although he now lives off the proceeds of his own tiny label (and regular performances abroad), Derek Bailey and the other members of the London Musicians Collective originally put their hopes in Radio 3, the Arts Council and the South Bank. The idea that public money should not be 'wasted' on the arts had not yet been driven home (either by punk's demonstration of the nihilo-aesthetic superiority of scummy commercialism over funded worthiness, or by postmodernist neo-liberalism). In selling T-shirts, Ward and Noble were adopting strategies from rock music, where literate judgement always takes second place to a sense of what's hip and hot and saleable.

By interpreting everything as competition, the commodity system trivialises what we do. Our ability to resist depends upon the demonstrable possibility of collective endeavour. Free Improvisation – one of the most radical proposals about musical organisation in history – could only have occurred against the background of the Vietnam Solidarity Campaign and the miners' strikes of 1972 and 1974. Just like those on the left who seek to retain revolutionary convictions in times of reaction, free improvisors were subject to extraordinary pressures as the Thatcher years proceeded. There were splits, betrayals, denunciations. There was no way in which, single-handedly, Derek Bailey – or anyone else – could maintain the high tempo of the heroic years. Company Week became Bailey's forum for attempts to prevent the music congealing into a style. As with Frank Zappa's *oeuvre* – but using entirely different methods – Bailey made sure that no single species of connoisseurship (whether of the jazz canon, of twentieth-century orchestral modernism, of punk-rock *événement*, or of modern dance/physical theatre) could definitively judge a Company performance. Every time, audiences had to make up their minds anew what could constitute the act of observing musicians at work – though that did not necessarily mean that everything was wonderful. If you create an oasis for direct communication in a world mediated by commodity glamour and reassuring boredom, it isn't inevitable that everything you hear will be brilliant. But it does *matter*.

COMPANY WEEK 1978

Company Week 1978 took place at the ICA between 30 May and 6 April. The musicians who took part were Leo Smith (trumpet), Maurice Horsthuis (viola), Johnny Dyani (bass), Misha Mengelberg (piano) and Terry Day (percussion). Unlike Company Week 1977, Incus did not release music from the Week. There was no Company Week in 1979.

COMPANY WEEK 1980 AND 1981

In his book *Improvisation*, Derek Bailey says that 'more theatrical tendencies' surfaced in Company in 1980 and 1981. Riccardo Bergerone, who published a twelve-page listing of Company dates in 1984, does not register a Company Week for 1980. There was, though, a two-day engagement at the ICA, where Bailey and Altena played host to different musicians on different nights: Georgina Born and Tristan Honsinger (cellos), Tony Coe (clarinet), Evan Parker (saxophones), Lindsay Cooper (bassoon) and Frank Perry (percussion) on 29 August and Han Bennink (drums), Larry Fishkind, Maurice Horsthuis (viola), Misha Mengelberg (piano), Radu Malfatti and Wolter Wierbos (trombones) on 30 August. Bailey's view was characteristically sceptical:

> By this time there was a sort of impetus to this thing which came from the funding. After doing '77, I didn't want to do it again, but it was successful in terms which everybody could recognise and the pressure to do it again was quite amazing – and particularly from the people who'd given me the money, the Arts Council. So I did a Company Week in '78 that I thought was not particularly successful, so I tried a different format in '79 and that was a weekly concert for four or five weeks. It was cumulative. I started solo, then some duos and trios and it built up to an eight- or nine-piece. I thought I'd try it that way. I didn't like that much either, it was just concerts. I tried it again in '80. [xi–2000]

Company Week 1981 was held at the ICA between 19 and 23 May. The musicians who took part were Steve Lacy (soprano sax), Min Tanaka (dance), Christine Jeffrey (voice), Maarten van Regteren Altena (bass), Georgina Born and Tristan Honsinger (cellos), Jamie Muir (percussion), Toshinori Kondo (trumpet), Radu Malfatti (trombone), Lindsay Cooper (bassoon) and Charlie Morrow (trumpet, horn, voice, flute, bells and assorted 'small instruments').

In January 1982, Bailey organised a Company Tour, which was like a Company Week except that (with the exception of absolute fanatics, groupies and other camp followers) audiences changed nightly. The participants were Evan Parker (tenor and soprano sax), John Zorn (alto sax), Steve Lacy (soprano sax), George Lewis (trombone), Misha Mengelberg (piano), Jamie Muir (electronics), taking in the Roundhouse in Chalk Farm, London (24 January), the Arts Centre in Darlington (27), the Arts Centre in York (28), the Playhouse in Leeds (29), Phoenix Arts Centre in Leicester (30), Warwick University Arts Centre in Coventry (1 February), the Solent Suite in Southampton (2), Donat's Arts Centre in Llantwit Major (4), the Arnolfini Gallery in Bristol (6) and the Strathallan Hall in Birmingham (7). As usual, there were tensions. Zorn's antics offended many (improvisor Martin Hackett, adherent to a Scratch Orchestra/Cage ethic, reported disgustedly that John Zorn blew game calls into a bowl of water with one trouser leg rolled up, more intent on drawing attention to himself than in contributing to the music). Backstage, Zorn would warm up by playing bebop licks (something he's more adept at than most).

Steve Lacy approached him and said, I hear you practising such wonderful jazz when you're warming up, why don't you play it at the gig? John was hating the tour so much and said, 'I don't need to hear that, especially from you.' The whole thing was really upsetting for him, the whole experience. [EC 28–ix–1998]

Such upsets are of course part and parcel of Company methodology, and Zorn was not deterred. Later in the year, Zorn played at a Company event at the Roulette in New York (16–18 December 1982) with Fred Frith on guitar, George Lewis on trombone, Bill Laswell and Joëlle Léandre on basses, Peter Brötzmann and Keshavan Maslak on tenor saxophones and Cyro Baptista on percussion (the line-up sounds like a Bill Laswell production, but no doubt the music was different). Zorn also played at Company Week 1984 in London (27 June–1 July). When I witnessed Zorn at Company Week in 1991, his contribution was terrific (see below).

COMPANY WEEK 1982

Company Week 1982 was held at the ICA between 29 June and 3 July, comprising Phil Wachsmann on violin, Fred Frith on guitar, George Lewis on trombone, Anne LeBaron on harp, Ursula Oppens and Keith Tippett on pianos, Motoharu Yoshizawa on bass, Akio Suzuki on glass harmonica, analapos, spring gong and kikkokikiriki (instruments he built himself) and Julie Tippetts on vocals and acoustic guitar. Ursula Oppens was a specialist in interpreting Beethoven and unused to improvising. Talking of Oppens's contribution – and that of instrument maker Akio Suzuki – Bailey says their naïvety and lack of ability (at improvising) had a 'salutary' effect on the other improvisors. In the 1984 sleeve note to the 2LP release of Company Week 1982 *Epiphany/Epiphanies* [Incus 46/47; re-released in 2001 as Incus CD42/43], Bailey said that the Company Week procedure 'had come to feel just a little cosy. Perhaps this was something we picked up from the stagnant condition of music generally where almost all areas, then as now, share an increasingly enthusiastic commitment to total predictability or maybe it had simply become so commonplace for any improvisor to play with absolutely any other improvisor that differences no longer made any difference.' Bailey thought enough of the music to release a double LP for the first time since the early seventies. Housed in an eye-watering plain yellow sleeve, the first disc was named *Epiphany*, consisting of an 47-minute improvisation by the entire cast of Company 1982 broken only by the limitations of vinyl; disc two was named *Epiphanies*, and consisted of six different groupuscules drawn from the assembly.

The first disc exemplifies some of the problems encountered when large ensembles attempt to improvise. Though a tentet may not seem particularly large, in Free Improvisation where musicians have not only developed extensive palettes of different sounds, but have complete freedom to follow their own lines, anything beyond five musicians presents huge problems. The solution hit on by Company 1982 was one that had been adopted by Cornelius Cardew's Scratch Orchestra, and surfaces in semi-improvised 'event' symphonies like Gavin Bryars's *Sinking of the Titanic*, Luciano Berio's *Laborintus II* and John Cage's *Roaratorio* (it also informs Butch Morris's series of *Conductions* and the music played by the London Improvisers Orchestra 1997–2001). In order to prevent an unalleviated racket, the musicians play continuous notes or repeated motifs while they tune their ears to the collective sound. This results in a drone. A drone has a very different emotional resonance to either the urgent chord sequences of jazz or the electricity-dependent feedback of rock: it tends towards folkish melancholy, regret and nostalgia for everything modernity has destroyed. In trained musicians (who are really, after all, superannuated craftspersons from a previous mode of musical reproduction), it brings out a latent conservatism. Moreover, the large space necessary for so many musicians recording together at a single place and time results in a 'classical' blurring of player individuality, an acoustic blend whose symphonic aura is the very opposite of the in-your-face immediacy of jazz and rock records. The tempo of the music becomes something ineluctable, unaffected by individual contributions, an unrolling canvas which reduces every sound to fantastic exotica. As you listen, you feel you're drifting downstream gazing at a series of grotesque wrecks. This surrender to time is the opposite of the heightened individuality and nervous tension that spike the best improvisations, and helps to explain Bailey's general distaste for large groupings.

Nevertheless, Bailey liked this particular tentet enough to issue it, and even proclaim it as a challenge to a 'cosy' scene. *Epiphany* begins with chiming atonal piano, and is at first dominated by Julie Tippetts's wordless vocal. Clear-ringing, capricious and favouring atonal swoops, this style began with Arnold Schoenberg's *Pierrot Lunaire*. It is the sound of the rationalism of the tempered scale gone moonstruck and crazy, though by injecting her own personality into the voice, Tippetts alleviates Twelve Tone anxiety with the glassy glamour of a Joni Mitchell and Meredith Monk. When trained musicians lacking the subaltern attitude of jazz and rock abandon their classical models, they are prey to minimalism's misinterpretation of the modernist crisis, recycling repetition and formal vacuity as a new sublime. Featuring two pianos, a harp and a zither, Company 1982 teeters on the edge of this minimalist aesthetic (the musicians cannot adopt it completely because minimalism's solipsistic seamlessness cannot be improvised, though the beginning of track five on *Epiphanies* gets close).

Orchestral improvisations often evoke the sea or the sky: just as reactionary economists refer to capitalist economic crises as 'natural' disasters, the failure to control the course of the music is interpreted as a porthole on natural sublimity. Lacking new structures of collectivity, the musicians regress to romantic naturalism: high notes represent the sky and low notes represent the earth. Flutes twiddle by like birds. As dissonance gradually develops, it's as if we're all tied to the mast of a ship whose sails swell with the hot breath of demons, lurid multiple sci-fi suns streaking the horizon with crimson gashes. When abstract artists regress to emphasising the 'values' of oil paint, they frequently improvise landscapes, the old romantic subject matter resurfacing like an unconscious: orchestral improvisations tend to regress likewise. The mere sound of harps and pianos and *bel canto* are honoured as values in themselves, and the collective process proper to improvisation is no longer the primary focus: you can't make a dada collage by relying on oil paint.

On *Epiphany*, Motoharu Yoshizawa's bowed-bass growls evince a completely different approach: rough, intensely personalised sonorities which can only be socialised by energy and work, by making them respond to their particular environment. George Lewis's vocalised trombone introduces something unexpectedly comic, and a section of improvised ping-pong emerges between plucked violin, harp and bass. Tippetts's long held notes introduce a ritualistic element: hippie campfire happenings, ear-in-finger bleating. Again, regression from the spirited modernity and here-and-now of Free Improvisation invites a kitsch evocation of pre-industrial integrity. Even Bailey's guitar – ever keen to abet a musical process, and only obstreperous when there's likelihood of a reply – begins to sound like church bells through interference caused by hot air rising off cornfields on a midsummer's day. Maybe Keith Tippett's ever-romantic chord choices are to blame. Improvisor speed and detail save the piece from utter bathos, but it seems clear that (a) asking classical musicians to 'improvise' ends up with automatic classical/folk noodling rather than freedom, (b) large ensembles determine a collectivity that is undialogic, and therefore false and sentimental. Without democratic structures immanent to the processes of industrialisation itself, the post-industrial mass is prey to reactionary fantasy.

Since it selects smaller groups, disc two – *Epiphanies* – is a better listen. It lacks the overall shaping which gave *Epiphany* a superficial resemblance to a symphony, but this is preferable since this classicising screen actually hid deeply irrational conjunctures and developments. In their duet, Oppens and Yoshizawa utterly fail to connect, providing just the kind of broken music Bailey delights in as 'unpredictable', but which can disappoint the record buyer. A quintet between Frith, Lewis, Suzuki,

Yoshizawa and Bailey is made exclusively of scraped and distorted sounds, a modernist junk sculpture with no straw men included. A trio between Tippetts, Wachsmann and Bailey restores the idea of music as the result of the energies of the individual players, while the closer – Yoshizawa, Suzuki and Bailey ('Sixth') – features some of the fiercest and wildest transitions Bailey has ever recorded. Here, instead of clothing irrational musical structures in evocative paraphernalia (the big piano chords and vocal incantation of *Epiphany*), the three players wield their irrational and aggressive impulses as scimitars of musical invention (Yoshizawa's bass screams must be heard to be believed). Bailey ups the tension by twanging a crude rhythm: he seems to have destroyed the piece, but the other players react and the sudden explosion of differentiated sonorities is mind-twirling.

Bailey's stress on process rather than product means that he frequently wishes to explore areas which seem unlikely to produce good music: what matters is the dialectic which can rebound with such unpredictable continuities as the devastating eighteen minutes of 'Sixth'.

COMPANY WEEK 1983

Company Week 1983 was held at the ICA between 24 and 28 May and included Hugh Davies on live electronics, John Corbett on trumpet, J. D. Parran on basset horn, Evan Parker and Peter Brötzmann on tenor saxophones, Ernst Reijseger on cello, Joëlle Léandre on bass, Vinko Globokar on trombone, and Jamie Muir on percussion. From the evidence of *Trios* [Incus 51], the music was sombre and low-register, somehow both suavely linear and agonised: the musicians were hearing harmony in a similar manner so that the freak-outs and protests come across with great clarity.

COMPANY WEEK 1984

Company Week 1984 was held between 27 June and 1 July at the ICA Theatre. Bailey's note in the programme was brief:

For Company in 1984 I have brought together a group of musicians who have not previously worked as an ensemble. They come from different parts of the musical universe and in some cases are completely unfamiliar with each other's work. We shall make music together on the basis of a shared interest in improvisation. Everybody appears each evening in groupings to be decided immediately before each performance. [programme note, Company Week 1984]

The cast comprised Phil Durrant on violin, Antony Pay on clarinet, Stuart Jones on cello, John Zorn on alto sax, Mick Beck on tenor sax, Phillip Eastop on French horn, Thebe Lipere on percussion and Will Evans on drums. This was a representative cross-section of people involved in avant-garde music, though none of them could be said to be committed to Free Improvisation with Bailey's exclusive zeal. Pay, Jones and Eastop all hailed from classical music.

In supplying biographical information, Pay detailed an illustrious career, and mentioned 'working closely with leading composers, notably Berio, Birtwistle, Boulez, Henze and Stockhausen'. Stuart Jones also mentioned working with Stockhausen, as well as improvising at the Drury Lane Arts Lab in the 1960s. Eastop talked about playing Britten and Messiaen with the London Sinfonietta and 'developing improvisational techniques with the French horn and experimenting with multi-tracking to produce improvised quartets'.

John Zorn pointed out that he was a rock musician and composer as well as an improvisor. Durrant noted his improvising trio with guitarist John Russell and soprano saxophonist John Butcher, but also his involvement with electronics and rock. The Soweto-born Thebe Lipere told of his original break with the cast of *Ipi Tombi*, and his subsequent involvements with Osibisa, Hugh Masekela, Dudu Pukwana and Chris McGregor. Will Evans did not submit a biography, so Bailey ghost-wrote one, calling him an 'archetypal free-improvisor' ignored by official promoting bodies like the Contemporary Music Network and inhabiting an East End squat (Bailey also mentioned his degree in archaeology). In this context, Free Improvisation appears as a social act rather than a musical style, a temporary rejection of the various roles thrust on the musician in class society. Asking people in orchestral music and rock to free-improvise seemed to be tantamount to asking them to misbehave.

In this author's experience, despite the best arguments stemming from the respectable end of Improv (for example, John Butcher and Michael Parsons demonstrating an improvisation and a composition respectively at the Moment of Music Conference at Middlesex University on 20 November 1999, and assuring their listeners that the 'gap' between is today being bridged by flautist Nancy Ruffer), improvisations by players who are not committed improvisors are usually tentative and shallow. You can tell the musicians think they're taking part in something trivial, something to be indulged between their prestigious interpretations of name composers ('we shall now "improvise" for ten minutes'). The classical hierarchy cannot be wished away by moonlighting at Company Week. This is why, however much it may superficially resemble the 'break all boundaries' pluralism of postmodernism, Free Improvisation implies the opposite: authentic musical expression as determinate statement stemming from the performer's actual social existence.

Charlie Parker's famous statement 'you've got to live it, or it won't come out of your horn' can be trivialised into justification of the 'rock' lifestyle (a myth seldom evidenced by the quality of the results, unless it's Johnny Thunders), but it's actually describing something else, closer to Marx's 'social being determines consciousness'. In making themselves the source of musical value, improvisors take on the heroic aspect of bluesmen and jazz players: musical truth as the unmediated voice of the people. Bailey can rail against the kitsch aspects of British emulation of black American models, but his attempts to involve moonlighting classical players rarely resulted in vital music, a judgement born out by his subsequent choices of releases and collaborators. Company Week 1984 never made it onto record, and the classical musicians who were invited did not become major players in the Bailey *oeuvre*.*

---

* Bailey strongly disagrees with this, pointing out that he played with Phillip Eastop from 1984 to 1987: 'he was great until he thought he could do it' [xi–2000] – i.e., the problem is not moonlighting classical players, it's improvisor professionalism.

BETHNAL GREEN LIBRARY

Ever on the look out for venues, Bailey discovered in 1984 that the music library in Bethnal Green was prepared to host concerts on Saturday afternoons. He played there with all the active improvisors of the time – finances dictated that these were all London-based players, apart from Han Bennink and Ernst Reijseger. Half of *Compatibles* [Incus LP50], a Parker/Bailey duet album, was recorded there on 27 July 1985, and part of *Han* [Incus CD02], a Bennink/Bailey album released in 1988, on 15 March 1986. Michael Gerzon, an active figure in the audiophile scene, made these recordings – bringing his equipment on public transport – and many others, which he deposited at the National Sound Archive.

Writing about these gigs three years later in *The Wire*, Gerzon explained how the uncommercial situation made for 'an intimate, concentrated, but totally relaxed seriousness'. Bailey sometimes remarks that really his music is about his own application to the guitar, the 'practising': gigs and recordings are glimpses of a continuous process. Attending these weekly gigs put Gerzon in a position to test this proposition.

No one hearing just the occasional concert, record or broadcast of an artist like Bailey can fully appreciate his playing. These only capture snapshots of isolated moments of time. Hearing his performances unfold week after week made me aware that his style is continuously developing, and one could hear the process of change as itself an important part of his artistic and musical statement. [Michael Gerzon, 'Do You Know What It Means to Miss Bethnal Green?' *The Wire*, February 1989, p. 45]

Gerzon particularly admired Bailey's duets with Lol Coxhill, Steve Noble, Phil Wachsmann and Phillip Eastop. The last performances there were in March 1986, trios with Bennink and Reijseger. Now no longer with us, Gerzon had some poignant advice to impart, reminding us that music is about the passage of a few people through time.

If at any time one comes across an exceptionally fine series of gigs (in any area of music), don't assume they will always be there and neglect to go. Rather, make the most of them. It will reward you endlessly, and prevent you from becoming one of the many who try to recapture a golden era of their music that they missed by going to the gigs of fading musicians whose time is now gone. [*The Wire*, February 1989, p. 46]

COMPANY 1985, A PERSONAL VIEW

It can be irritating when writers inflict their personal reminiscences on readers, but sometimes it's inevitable. As an Adornoite, I don't share Derek Bailey's scepticism about the possibility of developing a broad historical view of the development of music. Whether stated or not, significant music arises from worldviews, ways of understanding our place in the universe and history: the human ability to act stems from a conviction that what you are doing is correct, and that entails a relation to the totality of human endeavour. So I believe that scores and records and tape recordings do provide an opportunity for assessment, and that a musicology – provided it is based on historical-materialist investigation, rather than structuralist or postmodernist precepts – is possible.

However, it must be admitted that Bailey's scepticism about musicology is particularly well-served by Free Improvisation. Imbued with notions of Zen and anti-authoritarianism from its inception in the sixties, Free Improvisation has an engrained habit of shrugging off analysis. Since it's about playing in the now, recordings are travesties of its essence. What about the gigs you missed? What about the endless practising by musicians at home? What about the tunes Bailey whistled to himself driving home from gigs in the car? What about the sound of the wind in the leaves and the rain on the roof, and the lonely blast of a solitary car horn which would cause smiles among listeners at the Termite Club upstairs at the Adelphi Hotel, as we strained our ears to hear some long-dying note?

By way of anchoring things somewhere, here is a personal reminiscence. The first time I heard anything about Free Improvisation was in May 1977. An American colleague of my father had given our address to a student 'doing Europe', and she was staying in the family house. She was attending Company Week at the ICA. She showed me the LPs

Company 1 and *Company 2* with their pastel covers and Iain Patterson line drawing, and told me that Free Improvisation was the most important musical movement in the world. I remember being prepared to credit her, but – aged twenty-one and experiencing a delayed adolescence – the last thing I wanted to do was to sit quiet and listen to people play 'difficult' music. My music was rock – Elvis, Wishbone Ash, the Doors, Jimi Hendrix. The previous year I'd gone to see Patti Smith at the Roundhouse (though I was more impressed with her support band the Stranglers, whom I then went to see at the Nashville, Kensington, supported by the Vibrators, a free gig as I recall). As yet unconvinced by Charles Shaar Murray's line in the *New Musical Express* that the only way to go was punk, my big musical enthusiasm was Frank Zappa. And that particular May 1977, Little Feat were sounding particularly good: I had just borrowed *Feats Don't Fail Me Now* from Pete Reading, a fellow student.

I was playing records in my bedroom one night in May 1977 when the American student returned from the ICA, her ears ringing with Bailey, Braxton and Bennink. She knocked on my bedroom door, so I invited her in, gave her some of the wine I was drinking, and listened to her rave about this music she'd just heard. I was sympathetic, but at some point in the discussion I went over to the record player and put the needle on 'Rock and Roll Doctor' – *Feats Don't Fail Me Now*, side one, track one – and said '*This* is what I like!' and we both started dancing, and ended up toppling into bed together (it'd be cute to say something like, 'Improv is OK, but unlike rock'n'roll, it doesn't get you laid,' but although she was rampant, I was too drunk to do anything, and by the morning she'd vanished). However, the musical point is this: to me as a rock fan in the seventies, Company seemed intimidatingly cerebral and 'arty'. It was only after I had attended many gigs – both rock and improv, jazz and classical – that it became obvious to me that Free Improvisation was a surer guarantee of an intense musical experience than any other genre. No question.

However, just as Derek Bailey insists that his involvements with high-volume music and feedback have been continuous since he started playing, reflection on one's own listening reveals a far more dappled pattern than the date-bound CV one constructs in retrospect. I used to think I moved from punk and Rock Against Racism gigs to Free Improvisation because I objected to two efficient, well-rehearsed 'shows' staged by Killing Joke and Theatre of Hate at the Leeds Merrion Centre in November 1981, where nothing seemed in question, and there seemed to be room only for applause rather than participation. Actually, the extraordinary appearances of Lol Coxhill in my life – an aesthetic guardian angel whose interventions, far from being restricted to my personal case, seem to have been made in a million listening histories – were already under way before my encounter with the Company fanatic from over the Atlantic.

My first experience of Free Improvisation is still vivid. In August 1976, me and my girlfriend Caroline Arscott, both readers of *Undercurrents* magazine, attended the Bath Festival of Alternative Technology. We hitched down the west edge of England from North Wales, pitching our tent on hillsides that, as a result of a spell of good weather bordering on drought, smelt of hay. I can still recall the honeyed taste of the pints of Ruddles we drank in a pub down from the hillside where we'd pitched our tent. We were impressed by our final lift: the driver of the Bedford van was a guy who wore lipstick, a red silk dress and carried a handbag. He drove along with the slide doors open, his skimpy dress blowing in the wind. Intellectually, I was blown away by my first taste of full-on Marxist polemic, purchased from a stall (a volume named *The Incomplete Work of the Situationist International*, a collection put together by Christopher Gray, with graphics by Jamie Reid, soon to hit big with his visuals for the Sex Pistols). My musical introduction to live Free Improvisation was stepping into a dark, upstairs pub room dimly lit by candles in jam jars. By the door, on our right, was a quivering heap of rags from which strange squeaking noises emerged: this was Lol Coxhill, playing his soprano, hidden beneath a pile of sacking. We were then subjected to a 'performance' by artist *provocateur* Ian Hinchcliffe, who vomited at will, threatened the audience (until a woman at the front said 'don't be violent!' – he responded with a mad cackle and leaped back) and spilled strong-smelling paint from various tins. Everything happened around a stepladder in the centre (the pub was being redecorated). When it was over, a furious landlady appeared: who was this madman, and why had he made this terrible mess? In order to keep the venue open for subsequent nights, we all had to get down and scrub the paint off the floor. There was an extraordinary clash of interests when – after the telling-off and negotiation and scrubbing-up – someone said, 'Well, it might have been bad to spill the landlady's paint, but that was the *best piece of performance art I have seen for years*' and everyone clapped – and the landlady burst into tears and had to be comforted all over again.

Over the weekend people hung out and talked: my first taste of counter-cultural politics. The anarchists versus the Marxist emphasis on the organised working class: 'What am I meant to do, wait for the revolution while I work in a bank?' The Sonny Hayes magic show, which made subversive points alongside traditional conjury (the magician's assistant later became Mrs Xero Slingsby). The hippie-convoy flatbed lorry that played both sides of Frank Zappa's *Just Another Band from LA* over the PA system, at deafening volume. Watching the 'corporate long-hair' from Virgin Records talk to Lol Coxhill about releasing a reggae instrumental as a 7-inch single. Hearing a conspiracy theorist reveal that potatoes were originally given to the white man by the Red Indians as poison. A theatre group who walked around like robots for the entire weekend, told what to do by a 'leader' who whispered their next actions in each ear (a premonition of Devo). Back upstairs in the pub, Coxhill reasoned with Hinchcliffe, held up a wailing grandchild, told him he mustn't vomit on the landlady's lino today. Hinchcliffe opened up a Sunday broadsheet with a flourish, vomited into that, rolled it into a ball and threw it over his shoulder. I remember a drip of vomit escaping and marking the ceiling. Free Improvisation was indelibly associated with such experiences. Every note Lol played was fantastic (although even he wasn't above reproach: I remember us walking out when he was trying to play with some amusical hippies who moved on from rattling bells to tapping the window panes).

Impressed that Coxhill should tour with the Damned, Caroline and I went to see him in Leeds, where he was playing in St Michael's Church Hall by Hyde Park Corner in Woodhouse. Coxhill wore a daft wig and talked about a scab on his leg that was weeping. Even for rock listeners shy of the austerity of Free Improvisation, every one of his unaccompanied soprano sax solos was entrancing. Of course, Coxhill was acceptable to punks who were tuning into John Peel on Radio One every weekday night between 10 and 12. He fitted in next to Ivor Cutler and Robert Wyatt as one of Peelie's brilliant eccentrics. His records were available on Caroline, Virgin's budget subsidiary. Even if he was leftfield, Coxhill fitted into some cranny of hip rock culture. Derek Bailey, on the other hand, was different. An absolutist art rhetoric seemed to surround him, something cerebral and ought-ish, like Peter Maxwell Davies or Tom Phillips or Land Art. A frozen excellence that denied the easy democracy of proto-slackerdom.

This has been by way of a preamble to describing my first experience of Derek Bailey and Company, which was in 1985 (a year devoid of a Company Week). On Friday 22 March 1985, Bailey brought violinist Phil Wachsmann, cellist Ernst Reijseger, trombonist Connie Bauer and percussionist Gerry Hemingway to Leeds, a gig at the Clothworkers Centenary Concert Hall promoted jointly by the Termite Club and Leeds Jazz. Convinced it was going to be a high-art 'gruel sesh', I attended the gig on my own. Having discovered that the venue had no bar, I fortified myself with a 250cl bottle of Bell's Scotch whisky, humanising this antiseptic cathedral of High Modernist Art Intimidation with surreptitious slurps.

The music was sparse and kinky and continuous and collective. Reijseger played a 'solo' by wiggling in his squeaky chair. What was striking was the use of space: the five players occupied the centre of the hall and held their musical communion in collective equality. The gig went down in my memory as an extraordinary, unanswered proposition about how a band could co-operate, a creaking Heath Robinson sound sculpture, all bizarre connections and quaint supports. The sense of absurd teamwork – five musicians slaving away to produce something so insubstantial and rickety – militated against locating any instrumental hero. A powerful and lengthy outburst from Bauer received an exhilarating response from Bailey and Hemingway: electric pings and cymbal clatter combined into a metallic storm. What was undeniable was that this *wasn't* the 'meaningless rubbish' dissed by the music's enemies. Here suddenly was a controversial avant-garde that didn't leave you feeling frozen out and uninvolved (like art gallery experimentalism, where the non-purchasing 'appreciator' feels like a voyeur). The spikiness of the music and the realtime decision making of the musicians had a bravery and polemical correctness that reminded me of the heroic abstract art of the 1920s and 1930s: modernism without quotes or excuses. The music churned your insides, yet also gave you space to think – and to watch other people thinking. However, despite this excellent introduction, it took next year's gig with Han Bennink (at the Cardigan Arms on Kirkstall Road) to convince me that Derek Bailey was – as well as an instigator of this inspiringly perverse art movement – the ultimate guitarist.

We've already discussed what Bennink and Bailey played in Leeds on 21 March 1986 (selections appeared on *Han* [Incus CD02]), but of relevance here is the way the duo's brinkmanship could appeal to the sceptical punk rocker. Bailey's 'loud' guitar is particularly fascinating, because its aggression brings it into the orbit of players – Link Wray, Jeff Beck, Warren Cuccurullo – who cannot stoop to conceptual art postures. Jim Hall-derived commitment to staying in tune means that Bailey cannot exploit the whammy-bar growls and finger-slide slurps that characterise the sleaze-cheese merchants of the electric axe (Johnny 'Guitar' Watson, Frank Zappa, Jef Lee Johnson, Stefan Jaworzyn). Hearing Bailey play loud is like hearing the nerd from the science class suddenly down six inches of 90-degrees-proof alcohol from his test tube, rev up and detonate chat-up lines and clever paradoxes that devastate the opposition. The unbent nature of Bailey's notes is patently unrockist, yet the spleen of the clusters and atonal transgressions woofs like no mere power chord can. Bailey also used words to needle his opponent. Bennink played some of his 'fake free jazz' on the Cardigan Arms piano: 'while nothing's happening,' says Bailey, 'let me tell you about some new records available from Incus . . .', walking about and strumming his guitar like a salesman turned troubadour. A break in a torrential cascade of drum rolls, and instead of playing guitar notes, Bailey is muttering some verbal inconsequence. Ducking out of the welter of disbelieving gasps, giggles and shrieks, I went downstairs for a pint. When I returned, Bennink, sweating, was standing on the landing at the top of the stairs, out of breath, brandishing a huge football rattle and staring through the glass pane in the door at Bailey, who was strumming some arcane chords.

'Now behave yourself,' I said, 'after all, Derek is playing so sensitively . . .' Bennink responded by whirling his rattle in my face, like some Viking preparing to hurl himself into the *melée* in a baresark frenzy. I tiptoed past him into the packed room, carefully negotiating the door with my pint, and found my seat at the back. Shortly afterwards, Bennink burst through the doorway whirling his rattle, and the bout carried on. Although the CD *Han* is short on documenting the collective hysteria induced in audiences by this pair of lunatics, by presenting the music they played on that tour, it does tell us why. Bailey and Bennink tap the kind of energies unleashed by Hinchcliffe and Coxhill in that upstairs pub room performance in Bath in August 1976. They are why Free Improvisation is great.*

COMPANY WEEK 1987
(OR, WHY JASON STANYEK IS WRONG)

As Derek Bailey said in his sleeve note to *Once* [Incus CD04], after Company Week 1984 'although there were many Company events in many places' – or in other words, although Bailey had himself been actively gigging – 'there wasn't another full week until 1987'. For this week, held between 11 and 17 May, the line-up was Lee Konitz (alto and soprano saxophone, drums), Richard Teitelbaum (keyboards and electronics), Carlos Zingaro (violin), Tristan Honsinger (cello), Barre Phillips (bass) and Steve Noble (drums and percussion). They played at the Arts Theatre in London. *Once* gives an indication of where post-performance-art, post-classical Company music had got to.

The sextet with which producers Michael Gerzon and John Hadden chose to open the CD starts with Derek Bailey's electric guitar, a perfect illustration of Steve Lacy's observation that Bailey 'plays every note so that you can't pin it down'. Bailey's ambiguous, glancing, uncertain harmonic transitions (he needs to be perfectly in tune to achieve these determinate indeterminacies) set the stage for what follows. The bowed strings of Zingaro and Honsinger and Phillips dominate, almost a lament

---

* I'd like to go on about Bob Cobbing and Hugh Metcalfe and Lol Coxhill and Jennifer Pike in Birdyak . . . but I won't.

for the lost nursery of functioning tonality, summoning the mournful soundworld of *The Sinking of the Titanic*. Richard Teitelbaum's synthesizer delivers rich string sounds too, then follows Bailey's electric chimes with gleaming sonorities out of Olivier Messaien. It is hard to categorise this music, because it has the tension and abrasion of music improvised in the instant, yet is reliant on horizontal, flowing lines – an aspect of music mainly ignored in jazz (though see Miles Davis, *Blue Moods* (1955), 'Nem Um Talvez' from *Live–Evil* (1970), and Butch Morris, *Current Trends in Racism in Modern America* (1985)). This claustrophobic nostalgia resembles Luigi Nono's deployment of string textures out of Wagner and Mahler, but Bailey's deliberate plucked runs and Lee Konitz's sour, neighing alto also suggest something rugged and resistant. A final, restful section reconciles the contradiction with a passage of music that (ironically, considering that the only British musician here is Bailey, who says he 'wouldn't know Canterbury Rock from Blackpool rock') is reminiscent of the surrealist pastoral of the likes of Henry Cow and Robert Wyatt and Carla Bley: somehow simultaneously sentimental and sarcastic, wallowing and self-critical.*

Meditation on music like this caused Michael Gerzon to develop a highly original sketch of the dynamics of classical music. In 'Beethoven and Late 20th Century Music' [*Unfiled/ReR/Recommended Sourcebook 0402*, ISSN 0954–8807, pp. 32–42], Gerzon used Free Improvisation to reassess Beethoven. Refusing to allow classicists and academics the final word, Gerzon (in Walter Benjamin's famous phrase) 'wrests tradition from the conformism that threatens to overpower it'. He argues that Beethoven was the first European composer to emphasise *process* over *object*. Like Adorno, Gerzon points out that, rather than coining novel melodies, Beethoven's great virtue lay in his development of the musical materials. His late works, with their work-specific, intuitive forms which still bewilder musicologists (that is, resist reduction to general struc-

---

* After the performance – which had a strong emotional effect on the musicians – Lee Konitz surprised Bailey by asking him if it wasn't 'too Jewish' for him. He replied, No, but it did remind him of 'Focus' by Stan Getz. '*That* Jewish?' Konitz shot back. So the provenance of this particular minor-key, lamenting, yearning tone (which surfaces in Mahler, Berg, Carla Bley, Robert Wyatt and Butch Morris) may well be Jewish. Esther hasn't the Orthodox background required to inform me.

tures), need to be heard as improvisations, as ideas born in process. Gerzon sees fixed form – both the institution of the composed master-piece and the recorded commodity – as distracting listeners from true musicality, which is to experience musical motifs as they are born in specific circumstances: 'the project of the improvisation is to generate a process, unique to that moment in time and to that musical situation'. The free improvisors Gerzon considers are Derek Bailey, violinist Phil Wachsmann and viola player LaDonna Smith. Taking the long view of Western music, for Gerzon, means that the non-improvising, score-oriented methodology that has overcome Western orchestral music becomes an aberration, a betrayal of Beethoven's revolutionary promise (again, this corresponds to Adorno, who understands Beethoven as the Hegel of the musical sphere, a bourgeois torchbearer of freedom and revolution who was betrayed by his reactionary epigones). Far from needing to import improvisation from jazz, the creative dynamic of Western music has actually relied on improvisation all along: Beethoven's discovery of musical development as the core virtue 'opened up the West to process-based musics'.

The opening selection of *Once* fits Gerzon's thesis like a glove, presenting improvisation as a species of classical music that has regained its processual, speculative essence. However, track two – a dialogue between Steve Noble's drums and Barre Phillips's bass – explodes on the ear like a piece of free rock, suggesting another aspect of music entirely. Like Rip Rig & Panic (and like his inspiration Han Bennink), Noble has an affinity for the jagged verticalism of funk. The fresh energy brought in by this outburst of drum and bass makes the opening seem effete and decadent: a Mahlerian fantasy in an overripe, hothouse environment. Noble and Phillips are addressing the active body rather than the swooning soul.

Of course, the juxtaposition of these two pieces in itself shows that Company is broad enough to include both soundworlds (and many more). Barre Phillips's bowing provides a link to the previous track, and when Noble overlaps rolls on his different drums he creates something horizontal and orchestral. Bailey's own instrumental approach – with its harmonic negation and rhythmic determinacy – might be said to tilt towards an Afrocentric rather than a European concept, though his concept of 'non-idiomatic improvisation' actually refuses a place on such a scale. The point is the productive *process*, not a choice between readymade alternatives.

Gerzon's thesis is admirable for its understanding of the creative thrust of Beethoven, but like Adorno – with his preference for the exquisite agony of Alban Berg over the wake-up shocks of Edgard Varèse – there is the danger that the desire to turn Free Improvisation into classical music's 'true inheritor' will sap it of its destructive zest, its openness to distinctly unclassical energies. Bailey found orchestral playing and school music lessons utterly repellent: what turned him on was hearing Benny Goodman on the radio. Bailey's stylistic zigzags (chamber improvisation with Phil Wachsmann one minute, drum'n'bass or deathmetal blow-outs with the Ruins the next) evince resistance to any determinate options within music at all. However, such twists and turns are blows against commodity fetishism – the niching of music as social appearance – rather than anything basic to the way Bailey actually perceives playing. His attention to sonic specifics makes any choice (between rhythm and harmony, or vertical and horizontal, or space and time) palpably absurd. Indeed, it sometimes seems that it's only by avoiding the example of Company that music writers can carry on talking about music as sounding self-evidently 'black' or 'white'.

Unlike many righteous 'avant' boosters (including Michael Nyman in *Experimental Music*), Gerzon does not indulge Cage-like fantasies of importing unspoiled, exotic 'Eastern' or 'African' principles to alleviate a bad 'Western' or 'linear' rationality. Contrasting European 'objectivity' to African 'process' requires exclusive consideration of the classicising, commodifying, oppressive aspect of capitalist society – and refusal to recognise its creative, antagonistic, immanent opposition (namely, its creation, the working class). In contrast to such transcendent moralism – always in danger of essentialising the racial stereotypes it claims to criticise – Gerzon shows that European music is not monolithic, but riven with its own dilemmas and contradictions. This corresponds to the *Communist Manifesto*'s assertion that capitalism creates its *own* gravedigger – the working class. Stemming as it does from racial rather than historical-materialist categories, the African/European binary is woefully inadequate.

Seen from this perspective, Bailey's subversion of musical idiom via improvised process reveals the same revolutionary humanism that drove both Beethoven and Coltrane. Of course, to the postmodernists who condemn such universal humanism as an oppressive 'Western' ideology, Bailey's *oeuvre* must appear wilful and perverse, even less comprehensible than the late work of his two more lauded peers. Sadly, even the citadels of Free Improvisation are not immune from such blandishments. Writing about Evan Parker's 'Synergetics Project' in *Resonance*, the organ of the London Musicians Collective, Jason Stanyek used an epigraph from Theodore (*sic*) Adorno, but buried any trace of Frankfurt School historical-materialism beneath the whole-world moralism beloved of postmodern liberals.* The occasion for Stanyek's egregious manifesto was Evan Parker's Synergetics Project 2CD release [*Synergetics – Phonomanie III*, Leo LR239/240, 1996], a confused and sentimental summit meeting for improvisors where 'ethnic' sonorities seem to be deployed for reasons of political correctness rather than musical necessity. Demonstrating the profound connection between bad music and false theory, Stanyek found he needed to part company with Bailey on the 'non-idiomatic' nature of Free Improvisation.

Stanyek quotes Bailey's famous words from *Improvisation*: 'It has no prescribed idiomatic sound. The characteristics of freely improvised music are established only by the sonic–musical identity of the person or persons playing it' [*Improvisation*, p. 83]. Amusingly enough, Stanyek also quotes a Bailey remark that was partly a reaction to Evan Parker's regression to 'jazz' (namely, his late-eighties pastiche of sixties Archie Shepp):

There's a certain sound, for instance, which is produced by a saxophone player when his soul is being stirred, which to me freezes the balls, it

---

* Stanyek's quote is from *Aesthetic Theory* (1984 translation by C. Lenhardt, p. 212): 'The unity of art works cannot be what it must be, i.e. unity of a manifold. By synthesizing the many, unity inflicts damage on them, hence also on itself.' Adorno's line of reasoning was evidently too critical for comfort. The next sentence, which concludes a paragraph, is omitted by Stanyek, reducing Adorno's statement to a liberal plea for pluralism: 'Works of art then are deficient, regardless of whether they are immediate entities or mediated totalities.' This deficiency is what makes art a process rather than a product (Bailey's concept of Free Improvisation is Adornoite without knowing it), and only critical philosophy which relates art to the totality can understand it.

stops everything in its tracks. [quoted in John Corbett, *Extended Play*, p. 235]

Stanyek disagrees:

> I think it's difficult to apply this kind of thinking to the Synergetics project. There's something else going on there, a vital, not reified, connection with idioms and 'markings'. For instance, Sainkho Namtchylak, the Tuvan singer who performed with the group, is a free improvisor who also performs traditional Tuvan songs, which for her signify 'a kind of going home'. Her contribution to the Synergetics recording bears out her continuing relationship with her place of origin. [Jason Stanyek, *Resonance*, vol. 7 no. 2, p. 45]

Actually, Stanyek could have found a still more devastating critique of projects like Synergetics on page 102 of *Improvisation*:

> So, in performance, grunts, howls, screams, groans, Tibetan humming, Tunisian chanting, Maori chirping and Mozambique stuttering are combined with the African thumb piano, Chinese temple blocks, Ghanian soft trumpet, Trinidadian steel drum, Scottish soft bagpipe, Australian bull-roarer, Ukrainian stone flute and the Canton one-legged monster to provide an aural event about as far removed from the directness and dignity of ethnic music as a thermo-nuclear explosion is from a fart. [*Improvisation*, Moorland edition, p. 121; Da Capo edition, p. 102]

Stanyek quotes Mark Mattern, whose *Acting In Concert: Music, Community and Political Action* (for a critique see *Contemporary Politics* vol. 5 no. 2, June 1999) used John Dewey's categories to adumbrate a 'theory' whose grand conclusion is that music can either create communities or divide them, but that 'creating community' is the more desirable end. Unembarrassed that Mattern's liberal pragmatism (with its facile condemnation of Victor Jara's Nueva Canción for being 'confrontational'; Mattern reduces the struggle of labour versus capital in early-seventies Chile to a difference between – equally balanced – left and right 'communities') is diametrically opposed to the historical materialism of the author of his epigraph, Stanyek argues for Free Improvisation as a forum for the creation of a 'super community': 'Free improvisation is a particularly fertile "communicative arena" in which

Gavin Bryars graduates in philosophy, Sheffield, July 1964, mugging for the camera outside 329 Crookesmoor Road where the Joseph Holbrooke Trio recorded 'Miles' Mode'.

Encounters with the Dutch acrobats: Han Bennink (pregnant Masha behind) and Derek Bailey negotiate a swing bridge in Holland, 1969.

Further encounters: Han Bennink and Derek Bailey, 1972.

Derek Bailey and Anthony Braxton, Paris, 1974.

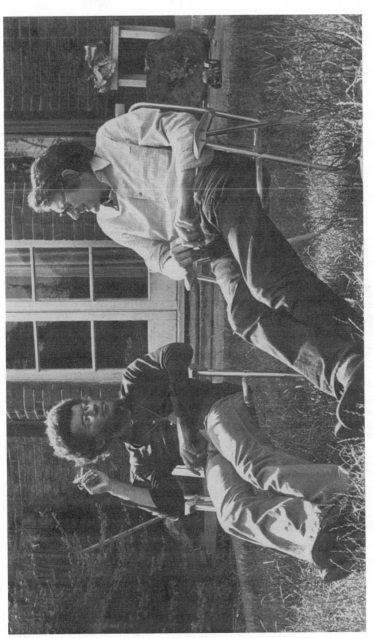

Anthony Braxton and Derek Bailey, London, 1974 © Val Wilmer.

Derek Bailey existential in a passport booth: 'No idea when that was taken ... early 70s?'

Pisa, 1975.

Observing street life in Downs Road, Clapton: a photograph by Aquirax Aida, 1977.

divergent individual and cultural narratives can be articulated' [Jason Stanyek, *Resonance*, vol. 7, no. 2, p. 47]. 'Communicative arena' is in quotation marks because it is Mattern's Deweyesque phrase to describe the social role of music. No doubt Stanyek's thesis went down well at the 'Across the Borders' symposium held at the University of California, San Diego, on 10 April 1999 (where it was delivered as a paper), but as a way of denoting the particular qualities of the avant-garde extremes plumbed by Free Improvisation, it's useless. Stanyek's blithe positivism fails to define Free Improvisation against its adversary – commodification – and so fails to acknowledge its critical spike. Far from encouraging any genuine assessment of the music, something that might help readers to distinguish between good and bad, to actively engage with it, Stanyek stockpiles the worthy-sounding phrases necessary to secure funding from grant-giving bodies. Portraying Free Improvisation as a multicultural, hands-across-the-oceans, United Nations-logoed 'communicative arena' (something to be staged in the ghastly Millennium Dome, perhaps?) gives no inkling of either the animosity it encounters or the enthusiasm it inspires. Stanyek's blandishments conceal the way Free Improvisation's dogged pursuit of authentic musical interaction shrieks protest at what capitalist business-as-usual does to music – and at what passes for musical communication in official channels, both commercial and 'art'.

Derek Bailey's words about non-idiomatic playing have also been contested by the critic and philosopher Andy Hamilton, who deployed both common sense (Free Improvisation is immediately recognisable to every listener, however ignorant, as a 'style') and analytical philosophy (Kant's critique of boundlessness) to question Bailey's use of the term [*British Journal of Aesthetics*, January 2000]. However, following Gerzon, one should interpret Bailey's 'non-idiomatic' not as a claim about a finished piece of music – a product – but as a practical programme for effective improvisation – a process. When John Tchicai and Tristan Honsinger played together in Cambridge in 1977, the collective improvisation suffered when they summoned the ghosts of Ayler and Bach. Deploying memories of their supposedly different backgrounds froze the dialogue, producing blur and congestion (the same sense of ill-assorted clutter, in fact, that vitiates Evan Parker's Synergetics Project). Bailey's approach – the guitar note that hovers like a question mark in front of

DEREK BAILEY AND THE STORY OF FREE IMPROVISATION

the other musicians – is an invitation to intercourse in the here and now, ditching the formality of unpacking the treasures from the bag, the self-regarding pomposity of mutual appreciation of cultural swag in an officially endorsed (and patronised) 'communicative arena'.

It is no accident that the best Company music has the bare-boned quality of Twelve Tone: it is equally eager to burn away the comfy 'stuff' of music in favour of wit and dialectic. At their best, Derek Bailey and Company put into effect the modernist manifesto proclaimed by the composer Adrian Leverkühn in *Dr Faustus* (a fictional portrait of Arnold Schoenberg which Thomas Mann derived from discussions with Adorno):

> Is it a sentimentality to say that music today – which after all stands for everything of any real value in contemporary society – burns to break from its dignified isolation, yearns to become accessible without becoming banal, and to speak a language which even the musically untaught could understand? . . . Besides, sentimentality could never be the right tool. What we need is *sarcasm* and *scorn* and *ridicule*, which – by clearing the air of romanticism, pathos and prophecy, sound-intoxication and literature – could enable us to experience the objective and elemental. I'm calling for recognition of music as it actually is: *organisation through time*. A difficult task! For close by lies the trap of false primitivism, and hence a return to the sloughs of romanticism by another route. We must keep our places at the vanguard of intellectual progress, taking off from the most refined aspects of European musical advance, so that the New is made available to everyone. We must put the musicians in charge, allow them freedom to use all these modernist inventions as building blocks, transform the tradition of innovation represented by Beethoven into something experienced from *inside*, rather than something picked-over and manipulated by academics and epigones! [Thomas Mann, *Dr Faustus*, Chapter 31, p. 310]*

---

* That Adorno/Leverkühn's argument is actually Musical Marxism may be established by comparing it to the following critique of bourgeois romanticism from *Grundrisse*: 'In earlier stages of development the single individual *seems* to be developed more fully, because he has not yet worked out his relationships in their fullness, or erected them as independent social powers and relations opposite himself. It is as ridiculous to yearn for a return to that "fullness" as it is to believe that with this complete emptiness history has come to a standstill. The bourgeois viewpoint has never advanced beyond this antithesis between itself and this romantic viewpoint, and therefore the latter will accompany it as legitimate antithesis up to its blessed end.' Karl Marx, *Grundrisse*, p. 162.

In Free Improvisation, modernist clarity and invention is not achieved by composerly diktat, but by activating the 'sonic-musical identity' of the musicians. Michael Gerzon eloquently explains how the academy has backwritten the exalted status of the composer today, an anachronistic projection onto European classical music's early history. In 1742, the *Frankfurter Allgemeine Zeitung* conducted an opinion poll as to the greatest living composers and performers: Bach came twelfth on the list of composers, but first on the list of performers. However, Gerzon's implication that classical composers were actually free improvisors is itself somewhat anachronistic. It underrates the significance of the emergence of the musician's personal sound onto the plane of musical history, something that needs to be credited to black American musicians and their close involvement with recording technology. The score allowed composers to give music a historical significance; now mechanical reproduction – recording – allows the *playing musician* to mould it.

With Free Improvisation, the composer genius has been brought down to earth, liberated from the alienation of his desk and redefined as a practical leader and fellow worker, open to questioning by the collective and subject to instant recall. In being open, yet spurred by the most progressive ideas available on the planet, Free Improvisation resembles the workers' council, the most radically democratic institution of the twentieth century: it is *that* heroic and utopian, and that hard to sustain in the face of the reactionary scourge known as 'capitalist business-as-usual' (or, 'having a musical career').

Stanyek finishes his apologia for the confusion that is Synergetics by quoting the Korean komungo player Jin Hi Kim, who first played with Derek Bailey at the Koncepts Cultural Gallery in Oakland, California, on 10 December 1989 (and made brilliant contributions to Company Week 1992). She talks about her 'identity' and its need to be recognised – the komungo, a traditional six-string zither, is a quiet instrument, and if other improvisors do not pay attention to what she is playing, her identity vanishes. Well, who would argue with that! As he did when quoting from Adorno, Stanyek examines intriguing materials only to extract banalities. In his hands, Kim's remarks are reduced to Mark Mattern's conclusion: community is a good thing, confrontation should be avoided, it's nice if people listen to each other. Music as a matter of polite manners and etiquette. This is to confuse a precondition with a result. It certainly fails to describe the drama and controversies experienced at a Company Week.

In other words, Stanyek's argument does not pass the first test of an aesthetic theory: does this help to explain why this art makes me feel as I do? In developing his theory of Free Improvisation as a social panacea, a strategy for global peace and the relative equality of all world customers, Stanyek forgets that liberal face-saving and feelgood ideology – that is, lies – are the enemies of artistic expression. Melting-pot positivism – the accumulation of world-music treasures in get-togethers sponsored by corporate America – results in aesthetic disaster, ear sores symptomatic of the hypocrisy of capitalist domination and exploitation.

Admittedly, the idea of music as articulate and revolutionary, rather than anodyne and conciliatory, may be unfashionable: but picking on Free Improvisation as the sound of conciliation shows an extraordinary reluctance to face musical facts. Grant-oriented humbug about 'multiculturalism' turns a blind eye to the searing, uncompromised character of Free Improvisation, its demand that you are absolutely *there*, or leave the room. It fails to discern Free Improvisation's true value, which is the baleful light it casts on a society dedicated to standardisation and commodification, Free Improvisation's insistence on vitality and dialogue. As well as destroying any terms of judgement, attempts to make Free Improvisation 'safe for society' occlude its message and meaning.

Bailey's 'non-idiomatic' absolutism can have no truck with Stanyek's one-world moralism. Far from creating 'community', authentic Modern Art speaks a moment of truth: controversial, nerve-wracking and critical. Stripping away the 'idiomatic' chaff is a necessity if improvisors are to do more than pile up postmodernist kitsch – musical materials uprooted from their various social functions and indulged vicariously by art-house audiences – and inform us of what we are and what we can hear, with no illusions that music is anything more than that. The attempt to play non-idiomatically is quite simply the attempt to face – in the words of the *Communist Manifesto* – 'with sober senses, our real conditions of life, and our relations with our kind'.

To return to *Once* and Company Week 1987. In his book *Extended Play*, John Corbett (not to be confused with the British trumpeter of the same name who played trumpet at Company Week 1983 and played on *Trios* [Incus 51]), warns his readers about the CD: 'all Company releases are full of interesting music,' he says, diplomatically, but 'some, like *Once*, also include some duller moments – such is the risk that improvised music takes to reach its peaks of unforeseen intensity'. There are indeed two weak passages in the CD: one where Carlos Zingaro plays folkish violin, and one where Lee Konitz falls back on quoting 'As Time Goes By'. Both illustrate Bailey's observation that 'idiomatic' playing is a barrier to Free Improvisation. Of course, musicians who improvise must come from somewhere, and it is not a matter of achieving some objective sound quality parallel to the 'legitimate' playing taught at conservatories. It's simply that the 'sonic-musical identity' of the individual's playing needs to be cognisant of the ensemble sound, and not off on some preconceived linear trip, some citation of positive musical culture. On 'Quartet', Konitz dumped citation and used his knowledge of harmony to take the music through a series of bizarre modulations, like successive trap doors swallowing the action in a dream. The joy of Free Improvisation – like that of revolutionary socialist politics – is hearing people talk of universals in unrepressed local dialects, and that aspect comes to the fore when Zingaro and Konitz really start to improvise. On 'Trio I', Konitz even takes to the drums, his flat-footed thwack evidently delighting Bailey, who responds with some of his most inspired playing on the disc.

Throughout *Once*, Steve Noble's aggressively transparent drumming seizes on musical ideas with glee, refusing to mystify with 'sounds-like-Oxley' prevarication (the curse of much would-be free percussion). It is the fizz that makes the punch. In 1992, Bailey told Corbett he deemed Noble 'a very significant figure in the music' [*Extended Play*, p. 242]. Already in 1987 Noble's avidity was heartening, like some earnest young student enlivening a seminar of greybeards by asking fundamental questions. The way Steve Noble's cartoon rhythms lay into the nostalgic strings – both synthetic and real – remains one of the delights of Company Week 1987.

COMPANY WEEK 1988

It was in 1988 that Derek Bailey announced that Free Improvisation was healthier outside the metropolis. Held at the ICA between 2 and 7 August, Company Week 1988 was the biggest yet ('at least twice as many players taking part as in any previous Company Week') as Bailey sought to expose the musicians he had encountered in 'places as different as Grantham and Chattanooga'. Returning to an old theme – the advantages of provincial life, away from the competition and hype of the capital city – he added, 'if you don't know how different these places are, then listen to the music'. Bailey's proposition voiced his scepticism about music biz values: established reputations and fame are an excuse to coast, and the music suffers.

> Improvised music is where you find it and whereas most of what passes for informed comment and virtually all publicity concentrates on a small number of well-known players doing the same things in the same places the reality is that improvised music in the great majority of its manifestations exists away from the usual centres. It is played, promoted and maintained by people who work in, and out of, all kinds of places scattered around the world. And perhaps as a direct benefit of operating outside the influence of the boss-eyed insularity which passes for a cultural climate in places such as New York, Amsterdam or London, these 'regional' people consistently produce some of the best, most independent and vigorous forms of improvised music. [programme note, Company Week 1988]

The Week was designed to introduce London audiences to these wildly 'different' musics. On the opening night, a Tuesday, viola player La-Donna Smith gave audiences a taste of the improvising scene in Birmingham, Alabama, which she and guitarist Davey Williams had been incubating since playing together in a blues band called Trains in Trouble in the early seventies – with workshops, festivals, a record label (Trans Museq) and a journal called *The Improvisor*. The Leeds Termite Club, active since 1983 (and which provided this author's own education in Free Improvisation), was represented by Alan Wilkinson (baritone, alto and soprano saxophones), John McMillan (live electronics), Paul Buckton (guitar and electronics) and Paul Hession (drums).

Wednesday introduced synthesizer player Dennis Palmer from Chattanooga, Tennessee – a representative from the Shaking Ray Levi Society, and himself a bizarre collision between contemporary electronic instruments and 'an Appalachian aboriginal heritage' – and bassist David Ellis from Hull, who'd been improvising since sitting in with the People Band in the late sixties and playing gigs with Eddie Prévost and Lol Coxhill. In 1987, Ellis founded Hull Time Based Arts. Hull was also represented by trumpeter Martin Jones, a trad jazz entertainer and big-band musician who was 'corrupted' into avantgarderie by bassist Simon Fell.

Thursday introduced percussionist Gregg Bendian from Teaneck, New Jersey, known for collaborations with top-bossa guitarist Pat Metheny and downtowners like Zorn, Frisell and David Moss (classical flautist Ashildur Haraldsdottir from Reykjavik, Iceland, was billed but did not show). Gavin Bryars also made an appearance on bass. His biog emphasised his status as composer rather than improvisor (he was planning operas based on Thomas De Quincey's *The Last Days of Immanuel Kant* and Gustave Flaubert's *Bouvard et Pecuchet*). At that time, Bryars held a lectureship at Leicester Polytechnic, so he was billed as 'from Leicester', along with Conrad Cork (alto and soprano sax), director of jazz studies at the same institution. Infant prodigy and clarinettist Alex Ward – a mere fourteen – was from Grantham, where he had been supplementing a classical-music education by improvising in groups led by the legendary vibes player Brian Parsons (Anthony Braxton, Frank Zappa and Olivier Messiaen were also listed as 'extracurricular influences').

Friday brought in Milo Fine, a devotee of Free Improvisation from Minnesota, adept at drums, piano and clarinet. He brandished a quotation from Robert Musil about the virtues of non-celebrity. There was also a delegation from Sheffield: Martin Archer (soprano sax, violin, metallophone), Charlie Collins (reeds), Mary Schwarz (viola), John Jasnoch (guitar) and Mick Beck (tenor). Jan den Boer on bass guitar and Luc Houtkamp on saxophones represented The Hague.

In Leeds, there was much excitement about being 'recognised' by this invitation to Company Week, but on return the musicians said they were disappointed. There had simply been too many musicians lining up to play, and the Americans were particularly pushy, offending what the Leeds musicians saw as the 'non-careerist' ethic of Improvisation. On the other hand, this was no place for blushing reticence: the idea was that musicians presented Bailey with ideas for groups. Unannounced in the programme, tenor saxophonist Tony Bevan (who'd met Bailey after his friend guitarist Greg Kingston invited him up to play at their improvising club in Oxford) had played on the Wednesday. On the last night he suggested he play a trio with Bailey and Bryars, which he did (a tape exists which is weirdly predictive of the helter-skelter of 2003's *Limescale* [Incus CD56]). Steve Beresford, another unannounced musician, played a trio with Bevan and Hession, supplying wonderfully absurd electronic keyboards.

Still, as far as the Leeds contingent were concerned, Bailey was right: the bright lights of the capital city had less to offer musically than regular promotions in upstairs pub rooms in a provincial city. No recordings from Company Week 1988 were issued, though five years later Bailey did issue Michael Gerzon's recordings of Bevan playing in Oxford in 1988, *Original Gravity* [Incus CD03], a brilliant trio with Kingston and *non-pareil* percussionist Matt Lewis.

COMPANY WEEK 1989

Late in the day, I know, but finally here is a Company Week – or rather a Company long weekend – this writer did actually attend. The only problem for the biographer being that Derek Bailey did not – or at least, he did not play (he was in the audience for most of it). The programme note read:

> Since its inception twelve years ago, Derek Bailey's Company has brought together varying groups of musicians whose common interest is in free improvisation as a way of making music. This year is different in that Derek will not be taking part and has asked Peter Cusack, Phil Durrant and Steve Noble to organise and programme the series.

The organisers explained that they wanted to maintain the tradition of putting on unfamiliar combinations of musicians and tapping that 'energy', but also wanting to choose a representative set of international players on both acoustic and electronic instruments. Company Week 1989 opened at the Old Bull Arts Centre in High Barnet on Thursday 21 September, then carried on for another three days at the Purcell Room on the South Bank. The initial participants were Co Streiff on sax, Phil Durrant on violin, Peter Cusack on guitar, Peter Kowald on bass, Connie Bauer on trombone and Steve Noble on drums. Zeena Parkins on harp and Andreas Bosshard on electronics joined in on the Friday, singer Shelley Hirsch on the Saturday. On the Sunday afternoon, everyone played, and pianist Alex Maguire – longtime sparring partner of Noble – joined in too.

Despite Bailey's lack of input, it's worth considering the music. Though Bailey likes to talk casually about Free Improvisation as 'this stuff' he stumbled on at the Little Theatre in the late sixties, an informal activity engaged in by musicians all over the world at all times – with or without audiences – Company, even one where he didn't play, still very much reflected his aesthetic.

The opening moments of Company Week 1989 are still vivid in my memory. Even if Bailey wasn't playing, I was finally present at the legendary metropolitan event. Company at the Clothworkers Hall in 1985, Bailey versus Bennink in 1986, 'Northern' Company in the absurdly jampacked Prince of Wales opposite Leeds rail station in February 1988 – these had all been local, Leeds-based experiences. Though I was in an arts centre in High Barnet on a wet Thursday night in September with just nineteen other people in the audience (four of whom left before the end), in my mind's eye I was sitting at the pinnacle of global music consciousness. I would still argue – using the tapes I made from my seat as evidence – that I wasn't far wrong. The musicians were lined across the shallow stage. They cracked open the boundless, chilly space of modern music at once. Steve Noble made a dramatic innovatory *éclat* using both skin and metal, Co Streiff made a harrowing cry on her soprano, and then Peter Kowald struck one of those reverberant notes on upright bass that sounds like a city collapsing and a tidal wave crashing all at once. Rather than the wheezing contraption that was Company 1985, this was Varèse-like (colder, mobile): extreme sounds hanging in space with gleaming precision. A slow, unstated tempo enveloped the players, giving the sounds a Joseph Holbrooke drama. Framed in this way, Co Streiff's sax was almost unbearably lush. The musicians played like lovers stunned by each other's presence.

The evening permutated the musicians and pushed and pulled at the central musical agreement that there should only be abstract sound and no lumber of association. Electronic texturing from Phil Durrant and Peter Cusack helped to foster an alien vibe. When Connie Bauer hinted at some jazz with his trombone, Noble buried his pastiche in an avalanche of drums. Bailey's contention that Company Weeks were about 'building something' proved correct.

On the second night – in the new venue at the South Bank – Andreas Bosshard was introduced on electronics. The opening improvisation was all electronic, with Bosshard, Durrant and Cusack. As the different musicians snapped cassettes of various sounds into their machines, the tension of the preceding night seemed to evaporate. The inevitable use of the sound of trickling water to trigger nostalgia for lost pastoral joys seemed more like a reference to the contemporary pop of Enya than anything made for the moment. When harpist Zeena Parkins and bassist Peter Kowald came on for a duet, it seemed like their music was a reply to what had gone before, an intensely physical workout. My companion Suzi Matthews wrote in my notebook: 'Isn't it funny how the last piece was so unsexy – but this, particularly when he fingers below the bridge on his double bass, becomes positively rude' [SM 22–ix–89]. Parkins and Kowald tangled up their strings in a bout of tremulously suggestive music making which had the audience gasping and left the musicians wreathed in grins.

And then there was Peter Cusack. The critic of Free Improvisation never has an easy time: the form was born out of an extreme suspicion of the written page. There is no hiding behind the anonymity of the arena venue or concert hall. The music is only to be experienced in intimate venues, where the critics must defend their printed words. The musicians are clannish, resenting anyone from outside their ranks who expresses an opinion. However, what is one to say when a particular musician's approach seems inept and rhythmically awkward, spoiling one's own idea of the piece's possible development? In the wake of Derek Bailey, free-improvised electric guitar seems peculiarly difficult to manage. There have been several spirited attempts – Peter Cusack, John Jasnoch, John Bisset – but to these ears they fall short, producing a bad imitation, exploiting the free brief without emptying the notes of associative content, failing to achieve the *negation* that makes room for genuine dialogue. A maniac like Hugh Metcalfe actually sounds better, because his barbaric riffing and highly developed sense of event are all of a piece. He isn't stranded between two musics. John Russell has almost uniquely been able to find his own voice, though by abandoning the piercing interrogations of Bailey for a more rhythmically supportive role. Eugene Chadbourne and Noël Akchoté have both emerged as free-improvising guitarists with things to say, but by pursuing very different soundworlds from Bailey's, and by developing aesthetics – Chadbourne's muddle and humour and protest songs, Akchoté's spectral horizontalism – very different from Bailey's purist anti-stylism.

Technique really is a bastard: it can pull musicians into the orbit of fascinating models, but doesn't necessarily allow them thoroughly to integrate it with their sense of the ensemble, their listening – which means that you always feel their timing is a little off (this is also true of nearly every pianist who attempts Free Improvisation, Alex Maguire being a notable exception). During the weekend, Peter Cusack alternately amazed me with the sound of his amplified and processed bouzouki and guitar, and dismayed me with the way his playing seemed to trip up the music. Bosshard's continual recourse to a tape of traditional African song, and the general way the electronica drifted towards drones and atmospheres, led me to conclude that improvisors had not yet mastered these tools enough to bring them into the collective interplay that is Company (that would have to await the arrival of Pat Thomas, Furt, Polwechsel and Phillip Marks's Bark! in the 1990s and 2000s). Zeena Parkins played traditional harp and also an electro model, benefiting both from the example of the electric guitar and punk's DIY ethic to deliver notes in which technique was married to character. Peering through the strings with a sadistic grin on her face, she looked like a cyberpunk villain about to lob a software bomb. Singer Shelley Hirsch arrived from New York on Saturday night and proved to be the cherry on the cake, topping the crash/scream/dada-cabaret process the others had developed under Noble's guidance with a vast voice like a cross between a Thérémin and a Human Beatbox, evincing a terrific understanding of the ensemble thrust. On the Sunday all-aboard finale, Co Streiff stepped forward and delivered a fluent, lengthy and persuasive alto saxophone solo which bravely made itself the centre of the music. Her playing was responsive and reflective and soulful enough to justify such hubris.

After witnessing Company Week 1989, if I'd had the economic clout of a promoter or manager, I would have formed a killer jazz quartet with Noble, Kowald and Maguire starring Co Streiff, who was stunning on sax throughout (a gift to the mainly male world of Free Improvisation from pianist Irene Schweizer and her longstanding women-only workshops in Zürich). Of course, that shows precisely the 'manipulative' or composerly mentality Bailey opposes (taking 'chunks' of improvisation and marketing them), but one of the frustrations of Free Improvisation is discovering musicians who are evidently superior to acknowledged stars, but who appear to be nowhere on the official map. The sad realisation is, of course, that we do not live in an instant meritocracy, but under a system of exchanges, where how individual musicians thank a promoter after the show – and how available and dependable they are – is as important as the quality of what they've played. After working on the Leeds Jazz Committee for nearly a decade, I became aware that a critic's conscience is just one aspect of the jazz scene. From an artistic point of view, Free Improvisation's distinct advantage is that it has much less capital and fewer careers riding on it.*

COMPANY WEEK 1990

Company Week 1990 was held at the Place Theatre, on Duke's Road, just behind the St Pancras Church erected on Euston Road in around

---

* After ten years of regular attendance at both Leeds Jazz and the Termite Club, I'll have to say that – in contrast to a good third of the Leeds Jazz gigs – I was rarely bored at the Termite, which is one hell of a recommendation for Free Improvisation as a way of doing things.

1820, with its distinctive pillars carved in the shape of betoga-ed women (after an Acropolis temple). Bailey has always liked theatrical spaces. The acoustics favour the softest sounds, while the setting makes the musicians appear larger than life. In plays, actors entertain the conceit of talking to each other rather than addressing the audience point-blank, providing a workable model for public Free Improvisation. The Place Theatre was then a modern, unfussy venue with a homespun bar selling bottles of beer and, in the auditorium, raked seats on scaffolding (somewhat creaky when latecomers arrive, but improvisors are usually able to take unforeseen sonic extras in their stride). The Place provided a venue for Company Weeks for the rest of their existence.

In a programme note, Bailey revelled in the way that what he called 'freely improvised music' hadn't been branded with an official name.

'Free music', 'total music', 'improv', 'improvised music' and, when all else fails, 'free jazz', are all labels which have never really stuck. This is logical: freely improvised music is an activity which encompasses too many different kinds of players, too many attitudes to music, too many different concepts of what improvisation is, even, for it all to be subsumed under one name. [programme note, Company Week 1990]

Of course, the title 'Company Week' printed at the top of the page wasn't included in Bailey's list of disparaged terms. Bailey went on to excoriate the timidity of promoters and arts bureaucrats, forever committed to either old warhorses or the latest novelties. 'So we do it ourselves. And however modest the financial resources, however strenuous the effort necessary to raise them, it is – just – still possible. And maybe better.' [programme note, Company Week 1990]

On the opening Tuesday night, guitarist Henry Kaiser introduced himself with a solo performance, Bailey and violinist Phil Wachsmann played a duet, pianist Chris Burn played with flautist Jim Denley, and Mats Gustafsson played sax with percussionist Kjell Nordeson – both representatives of what the programme called 'a new wave of young musicians working with free improvised music in Sweden'.

Wednesday started with drummer Steve Noble and Alex Ward, then only sixteen, though he'd been playing with Bailey for three years. He was playing confident clarinet and alto sax in a skipping atonal vein that was astonishingly congruent with Bailey's aesthetic: lithe, witty, anti-sentimental, fluent and crystalline. Bassist Marcio Mattos and keyboardist Pat Thomas played a duet. Eugene Chadbourne introduced himself with a solo performance. Drummer Eddie Prévost from AMM played a duet with guitarist Jim O'Rourke (an installation artist and member of 'well-known industrial group' Illusion of Safety, from Chicago) and saxophonist Peter van Bergen (member of the anti-ornamental abstract-funk band LOOS, from Amsterdam). On Thursday, singer Vanessa Mackness and saxophonist John Butcher played duets. The solo guitar slot was taken by Keith Rowe from AMM. Thebe Lipere and Louis Moholo played a percussion duet, and there was a trio between Max Eastley playing his resonant hand-built instruments, trombonist Alan Tomlinson and Hugh Davies with his live electronics. The Friday and Saturday evenings were taken up with permutations of all these performers.

An account of Company Week 1990 would be inadequate without reprinting Derek's contribution to the musician biographies, a description of a character named Charlie Appleyard.

Son of a Cricklewood glazier, Charlie Appleyard (57–73, estimates vary) made it clear from the start that he had no intention – citing 'destiny' – to do anything other than play music. His early career, still under investigation, suggests a weakness for the seedier environs of the entertainment industry and a tendency to make dubious musical associations.

Subsequently, although justly famous for the invention of improvisation (October 12, 1953) it was only through the sheer imagination and virtuosity of his Arts Council grant applications, his self-control in the face of promoters and an uncanny ability, even in the most difficult of situations, to find work for his wife and children which in the end led to the splendour of the career so widely admired today. High points are too numerous and well-known to need any mention here but, for the statistically minded, he has played in every known combination of musicians put together in the past 25 years in addition to appearing on 817 LPs and 274 CDs. Cassettes, he says, don't count.

In his musical maturity, Mr Appleyard has taken refuge in the academic bunker where, through the assiduous re-writing of history, he seeks to bolster his reputation and enhance his esteem. Furthermore, as the Founder, Chancellor, Secretary, Co-ordinator and Official Historian of the Appleyard Institute, a body dedicated to the Propagation, Promotion and Dissemination of Appleyard Improvised Music, he is presently preparing a book of rules, 'Appleyard Improvised Music: What it is and how to do it'. As he says, 'Let's get this stuff sorted out once and for all.' [programme note, Company Week 1990]

Appleyard Improvised Music: AIM. It was impossible to miss the acronym. Six years earlier, on Saturday 31 March 1984, the Association of Improvising Musicians – financially assisted by the Calouste Gulbenkian Foundation – presented a forum entitled: 'Improvisation: History, Directions, Practice'. It included papers delivered by Christopher Small, senior lecturer in music at Ealing College of Higher Education, and Alan Durant, bassist and lecturer in English at Strathclyde University. There was a lengthy discussion, with contributions from Evan Parker, George Weigand, John Tilbury and Christian Wolff. In quasi-Maoist fashion, though he wasn't at the conference, Eddie Prévost was designated 'current Chairman', and wrote a summing-up.

Derek Bailey's satire of AIM was meant humorously (Prévost was playing Company Week; there's some Derek in Charlie) but it was a thrust within a real debate. Prévost had distanced himself – and the other improvisors at the AIM conference – from Bailey's assertion about 'non-idiomatic' playing. In discussing form versus content, Prévost said:

> Much of the enduring confusion of this issue, as it relates to contemporary improvisation, is as Durant rightly notes due to lack of rigour in the debate. And we as a community of musicians have taken a long time to counter, for example, the erroneous idea of a 'non-idiomatic' form of improvisation. Maybe Derek Bailey's book, which is the main source of this idea, acquired so much uncritical credibility because publication gave it the status of an 'agreed objective'. As Christopher Small noted, habits and thereby conventions attend each and every performance – even of 'free' improvisation – and habit becomes idiom, perhaps as a consequence of the insatiable pattern-making propensity of the human mind. ['Commentary on the Proceedings of AIM', 1984, p. 11]

Prévost, like Jason Stanyek and Andy Hamilton, is confusing a proposal about the improvising process with a claim about the finished product.

Bailey recognises that improvisors get stuck in their ways, but he doesn't sentimentalise this as a natural human 'propensity', but as a failure of nerve, a decay in the musician's ability to play inventively in the here and now. Prévost's use of the jargon of 'community' – as we've seen, a term stemming from John Dewey's pragmatist sociology – is also sentimental, projecting a rural innocence on musicians who are actually operating in a highly competitive and mediated firstworld metropolis. The talk of music prefiguring a new society (Small's 'models for ideal social relationship', the plural of 'models' immediately cancelling the meaning of 'ideal') is moralistic, and fails to define the approach necessary for Free Improvisation to work (an approach perfectly summarised by Bailey's 'non-idiomatic').

Bailey's use of humour to argue with Prévost is characteristic (probably superior to this book's bitter intellectual polemic, but we're not all native wits). Looked at with hindsight, satire was an effective way of avoiding intellectual fads: improvisors' use of cybernetics, structuralism or postmodernism to justify themselves looks in later years like special pleading to academic and funding bodies, a cap-in-hand posture inappropriate to the independent-minded, confrontational spirit of the music. Rolling on John Tilbury to diss Pierre Boulez (as a recital pianist he'd found playing *Structures* 'no more significant than a complicated way of laying the dinner table, except . . . there was no dinner at the end of it') was a low move for a musical movement that is also an extension of Second Viennese School modernism. For AIM, pie-in-the-sky promises about the social 'good' replace aesthetic facts. The liberal relativism of claiming to be a 'community' rather than a high point of critical consciousness saps precisely the 'rigour' Prévost demands.

In his contribution, Evan Parker 'referred to theoretical differences between himself and Derek Bailey', but said this 'made little or no difference to performing compatability'. If so, why talk at all? Such an admission effectively demolishes the rationale of a conference on improvisation, reducing the event to a promotional device – an Appleyard Improvising Association for the promotion of Appleyards! A true theory of Free Improvisation would need to take into account its antagonistic relationship to both conventional listening and traditional modes of musical production: in which case the music of Boulez would no longer be cast as the 'hated establishment', but as a parallel modernism that raises similar issues.

Having reviewed the programme, this critic is too exhausted to write about the music. Company Week 1990 brought in a set of names who've all been highly visible in new music since: 'avant' was set to become a career, with many of the sad musical results one might expect.

A MOMENT OF AUTO-CRITIQUE

Company Week 1991 was held in July. It was preceded by a broadcast by BBC Radio 3 on 13 June 1991, one that Bailey considers exemplary: Company methodology at its best. Recorded on 7 March 1991 by the legendary Derek Drescher, Bailey played with Louis Moholo (drums), Thebe Lipere (percussion), Phil Wachsmann (violin and electronics), Vanessa Mackness (voice) and John Butcher (soprano saxophone). The BBC brought me into the studio to introduce the music, and I've just listened back to the tape, a pretty horrible experience. Drescher was training me in the soft cadences required of Radio 3 announcers, and the entry of that poised, confident tone of explanation – reassurance to the educated listener that all is in order – is precisely what you do *not* want in Free Improvisation. Also, there was a problem in that some passages – where Phil Wachsmann created a scudding ostinato with his bow, or where Mackness's nostalgic minor-key singing created her own echo chamber – went against the non-auratic immediacy of Free Improvisation. At the time, I explained these moments by comparing them to music by various composers – Gustav Mahler, Meredith Monk and Gavin Bryars – but in the cold light of a relisten, I'll have to admit that these patches of evocation sound modish and maudlin. Throughout, the legit production values at Broadcasting House create a weird feel. The introductory duet by Moholo and Thebe Lipere benefits from well-designed stereo spatiousness, but when at the climax Moholo starts shouting Xhosa war cries, he's off-mic and far too faint. In the next duet, though, a similar focus on the instrument as opposed to the musician made Wachsmann and Bailey sound extraordinarily clean and graphic, suiting their dense, concertinaed-Webern playing.

John Butcher and Vanessa Mackness were well-matched. Soprano saxophonists can easily drown a vocalist, but Butcher plays more quietly than most, concentrating on effects and textures that often begin below the threshold of audibility. The pair were also congruent in their textural leanings – extremities of spit and gargle, almost making a science of the vocal experiments children grow out of – and their timing. Joined by Wachsmann, they became wistful, producing harmonies that resemble the Wagnerian glimmerings that preceded Twelve Tone (on the broadcast, Vanessa Mackness's vocalese made me mention *Pierrot Lunaire*, but the real comparison should have been Schoenberg's *Tristan*-drenched *Verklärte Nacht*). Contrary to Derek's memory of an exemplary performance, to my ears the collective improvisation never quite produced the promised supersession of African and European musical approaches. The three percussive players – Moholo, Lipere and Bailey – do not seem to do much more than add exotic coloration to the melancholic sinfonietta performed by the other three.

One can speculate about the reasons for Bailey's overvaluation of the session. Perhaps, for someone who was unimpressed by the sensual thrust and political glamour of sixties Free Jazz, this form of Euro-African mix feels cooler and less hectoring. Certainly, the playing of the sextet is selfless, and maybe if you judge music by how much it supersedes competitive individualism SME-style (rather than how it makes you feel towards the world), it should be rated a success. However, as with much music issued by AMM, this collectivity appears to me to have been achieved by reticence and suppression rather than a genuine working through of differences. The spark of a really inspiring Free Improvisation – the sparks that flew at the three-night booking at the Vortex in Stoke Newington which preceded this studio effort (3–6 March 1991) – is absent. The music has been edited down, but the results are tamer rather than more concentrated.

Bailey, Moholo and Lipere played a kind of coda to the BBC broadcast on 29 November 1991 at the Huddersfield Contemporary Music Festival, where the featured composer was Harrison Birtwistle. Showing total ignorance of – or perhaps even hostility towards – Free Improvisation's egalitarian internationalism, the Festival billed Bailey as 'the king of British Free Improvised Music'. On the flyer, selective

quotation from Michael Marx's informative note in the festival programme promised a late-night knees-up. 'Round off the evening with a
session from the master of improvised music and witness his flutter-
picking, string scrubbing and behind-the-bridge bending. A great way to
start the weekend!' In their efforts to secure an audience, the festival
organisers had replaced Marx's second sentence – 'the improvisational
process, of course, involves great concentration' – with their own
customised fatuity.

The gig was held at the Venn Street Arts Centre, a tiny theatre-like
space with raked seating of the kind Bailey considers ideal for improvisors. Lipere began by blowing imbunbu (a kind of African didjeridoo),
and the whole sixty-five-minute performance that followed was highly
theatrical. Rather than getting down to the job in hand – the speedy
interplay Bailey uses for snappy percussionists like Cyro Baptista or
Robyn Schulkowsky – Lipere was given space to paint a universe with
his multicoloured percussion. Louis Moholo added polyrhythmic thunder, but Bailey's disinclination to 'get down' meant you heard it as
percussive colour rather than rhythm. The gig began at 10pm (after an
uncharacteristically lacklustre performance by Sheffield's Hornweb,
spoiled at the time by the ineptitude of a new member), and the audience
of sixty had dwindled to thirty by the end. (This was not snobbery or
timidity on the part of the audience. They had shown their willingness
to try Free Improvisation by purchasing tickets in the first place – there
were no all-concert passes at the festival. Heard after a long day of
concert attendance, the ear tuned to the fierce concision of contemporary
composition, Bailey's performance was hard to relate to. Besides, many
of the audience had buses or trains to catch, and no one likes being
stuck in Huddersfield town centre full of puking and fighting adolescents
on a freezing Friday night in November.) Thirty minutes in, there was
some magical Bailey guitar as he moved into the astral spaces created by
the percussionists, showing his longstanding interest in pointillism. The
evening ended in laughter, as Bailey stood up and walked about while
playing. Theatre, organically improvised process, site-specific spatial
experiment and humour: all the elements that distinguish Free Improvisation from conventional composition. Disappointment that the improvisors had not replied to the patronism of the festival's publicity with

unanswerably great music may have been misplaced: perhaps these modes of music-making simply are, as Bailey contends, incompatible. But since this is actually an even more depressing thought, I'll stick to the idea that this was just not a particularly wonderful gig.

COMPANY WEEK 1991

Company Week 1991 took place between 24 and 17 July at the Place Theatre. It was indelibly marked by the presence of altoist John Zorn and his protégé Buckethead: the metal guitarist played throughout in a Japanese white ceramic baby-mask, an inverted, sprayed-silver popcorn bucket on his head and a long robe draped over his body.* He moved his joints stiffly accompanied by whirring noises, like a robot assembling a car in a Honda factory. Since the Company tour in January 1981, Zorn had become a well-known figure. In 1986 *The Big Gundown: John Zorn plays the music of Ennio Morricone* [Elektra/Asylum/Nonesuch] had been a critical and commercial success. Although he'd parted company with Warner Bros, complaining that the corporate had no inkling of his artistic intentions, recognition had diminished Zorn's exhibitionist impulses. It had certainly not diminished his commitment to Bailey's concept. Every note Zorn played was decisive and poised, showing an astonishing capacity for instant structure. When he wasn't playing, he sat in the audience, showing a fascination for the whole process all too rare among Company participants (in turn, Bailey credits Zorn with being the only composer in Free Improvisation whose approach – based on instructions as to how to proceed rather than on attempts to dictate the end result – doesn't put a brake on improvisors).

The one moment when Zorn was nonplussed was when violinist Alexander Balanescu and singer Vanessa Mackness veered towards melancholic, folkish evocations: he prowled around at the back of the stage, scowling. Zorn's itchy, hard-edge sensibility obviously experienced this lachrymose indulgence as a barrier to genuine, active musical

---

* Harry Gilonis recalls Buckethead wearing a Greek tragedian's mask after someone stole his popcorn bucket . . . anyhow, you get the picture.

interaction. Which it is. Buckethead's super-precise, post-Van Halen hammering-on sounded like a cybernetic mating of digital-code output and arcade-game effects. He was evidently thrust together with Mackness to make him control his volume, and their duet also worked brilliantly. Wednesday night opened with a duet between keyboardist Pat Thomas and Bailey. Son of immigrants from the Caribbean island of Antigua to Cowley in Oxford, Thomas was classically trained on piano, and had honed his improvising skills in a family band (imitating Aswad's dub effects in real time). He was exposed to advanced Free Improvisation by regular workshops and concerts in Oxford featuring Tony Oxley. By 1991, Thomas was exploring electronics, creating sonic collages of birdsong, passing aeroplanes and decaying beatboxes. His opening duet with Bailey on the Wednesday night provided a piece of music where openness to anything and everything becomes the motivating force. Bailey likes percussive accompanists, thrives on speed and sudden change, and Thomas was just the ticket.

The Thomas/Bailey duet was followed by a duet between Buckethead and Zorn. Then the four musicians played in a quartet. The bravura spaces and surprises and instability of what Bailey and Thomas had improvised was a challenge; Zorn and Buckethead responded with spleen and vehemence. At the time Zorn was comparing the 'hardcore' rock onslaughts of Napalm Death, the Nottingham-based virtuosi of punk/metal attack, with the sixties Free Jazz of Shepp and Ayler. Zorn's Marshall Allen-like screech on alto approximated to a hardcore vocal in the midst of Buckethead's excited rockism. Since the advent of Rudolph Gray, Thurston Moore and Stefan Jaworzyn, these manoeuvres have become standard; at the time, Buckethead's rockist volume breaking into the Holy Temple of Free Improvisation was transgressive and exciting. However, it wasn't simply bluster. Being steeped in classico-math metal supplied a velocity that made the Buckethead's note choices incredibly pressured and vital. As anyone who reads William Empson on 'pastoral' in Shakespeare will be aware, high/low transgressions (the courtier meets the country clown) are not so much 'postmodern' as intrinsic to bourgeois cultural logic: the manoeuvres of an inbetween class. Nevertheless, as genres find class niches to service, they have a

tendency to degrade into cliché: Zorn and Buckethead were waking
Company up to new developments in youth-rebel pop, and so brought
a novel fervency to the Week.

The Bailey/Zorn/Buckethead/Thomas quartet was, if anything, still
better than the duets, as the musicians fused the speculative spaciness of
the English and the headlong vehemence of the American approaches.
Thomas and Buckethead were wielding novelty packs of cyberpunk
sonics, which with musicians as alert as Bailey and Zorn is like feeding
fish to seals. Anger, impatience, destruction all figure, but with no
slacker *épater-les-bourgeois* smugness: the blows and screams and
crunches were absorbed in response and dialogue. Compared to the
calculating tantrums of fine-art nihilism, such Free Improvisation is
extreme S&M sex rather than harassment by the boss. When the music's
this fierce, it's tempting to concur with Bailey's assertion that improvisations are invariably superior to the more organised – stage-managed –
musics that might be made using the same components.

Thursday night provided some striking contrasts, a grapple between
different principles of music making. Violinist Alex Balanescu – leader
of the well-known string quartet – was dragging himself into postmod-
ernity by appearing at Company, a parallel move to playing on a Pet
Shop Boys album. Watching him stand his ground like a puzzled, baited
bear, anxiously ascertaining the right moment to start (something no
orchestral musician ever need worry about), provided a striking illustration of the way classical training suppresses substantive utterance.
Teaming him with Vanessa Mackness was unfortunate, because his
training meant he could only follow her pitch changes rather than lead,
so she was reduced to presenting a phantasmagoria of gothic minor-key
intonings strafed with throat singing and dada vocalese. Free Improvisation abhors the horizontal, sustained note, especially when articulated
in purity: it can be used as a goad, but it's essentially an obstacle to the
real matter, which is interplay between the musicians (Polwechsel, Noël
Akchoté and Don Preston's Akashic Ensemble have shown that simultaneously voiced textures can work, but here the impurities in the tone
provide an abrasiveness that catches, creating in effect a rhythmic
dialogue). Drummer Paul Lovens exploded occasionally, producing
hilarious shocks, but unable really to shift the music.

The next improvisation – a trio between Zorn, Bailey and Thomas – opened another dimension. Knowing exactly how many notes you can poke in between everyone else's sums up what makes for great Free Improvisation: though the decorum-trashing devices may derive from Dada and Fluxus and Cage, this advanced take on rhythm brands Free Improvisation as jazz-based and Afro-centric rather than harmony-based and European. The point is an understanding of the other musician's personal rhythmic grid (a sensitivity beaten out of musicians in music school) and inventing a pattern to fit it, talk to it, challenge it. Zorn's sax, electrically sensitive to the exalted musicianship surrounding it – unmellowed by the *bonhomie* required to direct his downtown compadres – became lush and explosive, a richer sound than usual, but with more violent crises. This trio pretty much predicted what would emerge as 'Japanese Noise' over the next decade. But Bailey isn't looking for a new groove, so he took the second improvisation into delayed, static, sound-event, Joseph Holbrooke territory. The younger players responded by surrounding his existential assertions with a clutter of elements that quickly brought the music back to something more driving.

Singing in a trio with Buckethead and French trombonist Yves Robert, Vanessa Mackness was no longer tempted by nostalgic longueurs. Mackness – technically gifted, adept at notes and equipped with an immense vocabulary of vocalese developed by lessons with singer Phil Minton – pushes the poignancy of Free Improvisation to its limit. Unprotected by the machinery of an instrument, she has only her sense of humour and aggression to save her from the worst depths of performance-art pathos. The guitar/voice pairing has been well established by blues and rock, and she rode Buckethead's excesses, all the while responding to Yves Robert's cabaret humour and timing. A second trio, this time with Zorn and Thomas, was all birdsong twittering and strange intervals, provoking an extraordinary flurry from Zorn towards the end.

The Thursday night finale was a sextet comprising Zorn, Buckethead, Lovens, Robert, bassist Paul Rogers and Balanescu (in descending order of presence and audibility). Given music like this, it is understandable that Bailey should celebrate the fact that his favourite way of working has not been branded with a name. The ensemble writhed between the gifts of different genres – the utterness of power rock, the delicacy of Twelve Tone, even (a section led by Zorn and a quickly responding Robert, suddenly tailgate and gutbucket for the occasion) the collective ebullience of New Orleans jazz: demotic affirmation rather than high-modernist denial. Indicative of Bailey's desire to stretch his musicians (weirdly reminiscent of Frank Zappa) was asking Yves Robert to name the musicians at the end: his suave Gallic tongue twisted itself in knots to pronounce the names.

Friday night opened with music that seemed to have edited the exaggerations and mismatches of the previous days into a manifesto. A quartet of Pat Thomas, Yves Robert, Paul Rogers and Paul Lovens found a streaming atonal groove process that allowed individuals to stretch – Thomas went for a serialist voyage, Robert mimicked his electronics, turning flying-saucer whirrs into brass tube and breath – yet kept up a collective pressure: deal with what's been sounded, acknowledge the total sound, surprise us with what's next. The way in which music as objectively superb as this can be marginalised, condemned to a sordid vacant lot between the shining skyscrapers of Art and Commerce, is enough to make one a political revolutionary.

Bailey's duet with Balanescu was an object lesson in how his playing is exclusively focused on improvisation as a method of making music. Whereas Balanescu's duet with Mackness had mired itself in melancholy, a review of Victorian concepts of folk exoticism, Bailey brought out Balanescu's considerable knowledge of the modern string repertoire. Remembered lines from Bartók and Janáček met some of the most polemical discords and clusters I've heard Bailey play, the violin's swooning horizontalism the perfect foil. Aware that he needn't maintain a mood, Balanescu started scrubbing and scything at his strings, as if Bailey were tempting him into forbidden pleasures. The only thing in Bailey's released *oeuvre* that corresponds to the delicacy and detail and variety of his playing here – almost a rebuke to the whizzbang of Buckethead, but borrowing some of his avidity too – is *Viper* [Avant, 1997] and *Flying Dragons* [Incus CD50] (duets with Min Xiao-Fen, player of the traditional Chinese 'moon lute', the pipa).

Buckethead joined Zorn and Thomas for a trio, Thomas played in a quartet with Balanescu and Mackness and the ever-explosive Lovens. In the quartet, deprived of Bailey's mastery of listening, Balanescu again became a cipher, but – backed atmospherically by Thomas's effects and provoked by Lovens – Mackness was able to unleash all her powers, splicing gothic turgidity with cartoon cackles and trills. A terrific duet between Robert and Zorn proved that the success of the Zorn/Buckethead encounter was due not to some previous woodshedding, but to a common understanding of the sensuality and crisis required for an authentic improvisation.

On the final Saturday, Balanescu found a congenial situation with Buckethead and Paul Rogers on bass. Perhaps being placed in the midst of other strings – rather than having to front a drum/keyboard combo – made him feel at home. Rogers, one of the most gorgeous-sounding bassists in British jazz, bowed his instrument, immediately co-ordinating physically with Balanescu as the players do in a classical string quartet. Buckethead twirled his metal baroque lines about their modernist angles. For stretches Balanescu rhapsodised folkishly while Buckethead whizzed rockistically, providing the type of overlay – an invitation to multilinear thinking – familiar from Charles Ives and Ornette Coleman. Though one still missed the unedited invention that drives a full-on improvisor, Balanescu seemed to be finding his feet. The sound of skilled musicians dropping subservience to an overall concept in order to skip and dive and drone like kids playing aeroplanes is exhilarating outside the measure of music-as-normal. Indeed, it drives one to suspect that those who condemn Free Improvisation as 'mere noise' aren't simply ignorant, they're locked in a reactionary psychic armature that denies infantile play.

> The principle of the demonic in Beethoven is subjectivity in its randomness. [Adorno, *Beethoven: The Philosophy of Music*, section 120]

Bailey opened a trio with an astral abstract improvisation, Lovens on metallic clatter and Thomas on piano. Without his electronics, Thomas showed a passion for the wide-gapped disharmonies that characterise Xenakis's writing for piano. With Balanescu, Bailey had been extraordinarily notey: now he let his electric chimes and sustain burst like shells in a moonless sky. The difficulties and tensions of the previous days seemed resolved in four quintets by Mackness, Bailey, Balanescu, Zorn and Robert – developing towards a spacious Schoenbergian cabaret, though with a palette of timbres far wider than any pre-Second World War classical music, and driven by a jazzoid rhythmic agitation. It's here, traditionally, that Bailey starts getting itchy feet, distrustful as he is of any music where the musicians know precisely what they're delivering. However, a brief resurgence of 'gloomy piffle' (to borrow Auberon Waugh's memorable description of Arvo Pärt) favoured by the Balanescu/Mackness duo – artless doominess – had John Zorn pacing about at the back with frustration, knowing that any contribution he could make in this context could only be destructive.

Before Buckethead's appearance with Rogers and Thomas, there was some heckling. 'Too loud!'

'Turn it up!'

'Hardcore!'

The 'volume problem' was dealt with by a resort to theatre. The penultimate improvisation – before an all-cast finale – was to be a duet between Bailey and Buckethead. Karen Brookman had made Derek his own costume, with an old-man mask and his own super-hero cape in the form of a kimono. The duet began promisingly, a welcome reassertion of musical intensity after a Mackness/Balanescu/Robert trio that had plumbed the depths of emotion-sopped medievalism. However, after a few minutes, Bailey suddenly wacked up his volume to a painful height, producing an ear-piercing feedback whine. At first Buckethead tried to play to it, but finally accepted defeat, and allowed his feedback to merge with Bailey's, producing a superloud but uneventful sonic. The pair held each other's hands up in the air like triumphant gladiators, then exited, leaving their howling instruments to torture us. Then someone mercifully cut the power, and the audience – or some of it – exploded in rapturous applause. Personally, I was disappointed that Bailey didn't seem to think Buckethead's playing worth a real duet, reducing all his musical efforts – which included some fascinatingly agile negotiations of harmony – to I-can-take-it-louder-than-thou art-rock psychosis.

The debate about volume in Free Improvisation reruns the seventies argument about the use of electric instruments in jazz: a pseudo-debate where a superficial choice prevents any genuine assessment. The point is that Ascension's Stefan Jaworzyn plays fantastic – intoxicating, surprising, investigative, unsmug – electric guitar which must be wraparound loud to work, while Thurston Moore is okay as a texturalist, but hardly special, while Keiji Haino is an all-thumbs, corny thespian who only impresses style victims who think wearing shades, carrying a staff and dressing in black is some kind of existential statement. All play 'loud', but so what? The differences are completely evident to anyone who listens to the actual notes these guitarists play. Commitment to 'high volume' or 'low volume' guarantees a pointless discussion. These are the same imbeciles who worried that Howlin' Wolf's hair wasn't long enough to be 'cool' in 1966! At the penultimate improvisation of Company Week 1991, Bailey was responding to moves being introduced into Free Improvisation by players who appreciated the impact of punk and metal (just as he'd appreciated American dance music back in the fifties). Unfortunately, it was horrible to listen to.

Then the rest of the cast came back and attempted to regain an idea of uncynical musical communication, but unfortunately the churchy minimalisms of Balanescu and Macknesss prevailed. Company Weeks brim with arguments about the state of music. For me, the concluding two performances of Company Week 1991 were disasters: watertight consumer alternatives – Zorn's enthusiasm for hardcore ('Jazz Snob Eat Shit' etcetera); postmodernist rediscovery of the 'power of simplicity', or Holy Minimalism – remained unchallenged by an esemplastic improvising process more powerful than 'style'. On the other hand, for anyone concerned with the situation of music at the time, Company Week 1991 provided endless food for thought.

COMPANY WEEK 1992

Company Week 1992 was held at the Place Theatre between 21 and 25 July. Besides Bailey, there were seven participants: Jin Hi Kim on komungo; Tony Oxley on drums; Reggie Workman on bass; John Butcher on soprano and tenor sax; Oren Marshall on tuba and electronics; Matt Wand on 'tape switchboard'; David Shea on turntables. Paul Haines showed videos, but the audience was so unprepared to persevere with North American 'underground film' aesthetics, that they were used as excuses to retreat to the bar. Even Cambridge poets Denise Riley and Andrew Duncan couldn't stick them. 'Roswell Rudd larking about in some Thai temple,' I noted, before exiting for a beer myself. As in 1991, musicians were introduced gradually, often given the chance to perform an initial solo, so that the other musicians could assess their potential. Although this was satisfying for anyone who was attending the entire week, it meant that the first few evenings tended to be rather slight affairs, quiet and short. Visiting from Leeds, where both Termite and Leeds Jazz audiences usually received two hour-long sets, I found it quaint to attend performances that were over by 9.30pm. The Company idea was to focus on the key elements of the music – the musicians – and then observe them interact. Any other consideration would no doubt smack of showbiz, though it was noticeable that over the 1990s cannier ticket-buyers started preferring the last few nights, by which time the music had hotted up and you could hear more for your pennies.

Company Week 1992 at least opened with a bang: a Bailey/Oxley duet on the Tuesday evening. Their common interest in extreme timbral contrast was graphic. Oxley was using a lot of metal add-ons to his kit, making his drumskins sound peculiarly warm and mellow in contrast. Piercing feedback highs and scumbled thumbings produced a similar sense of contrast from Bailey's electric guitar. One can listen to the records and discuss them until you are blue in the face, but nothing ever quite prepares you for the impact of Oxley's drums live. 'Not playing the beat' is about making you feel each beat as a separate cataclysm. The electrified sustain on his metalware creates a special relationship to Bailey's guitar, which becomes a matter of amplified metal wires rather than 'guitar', though the resources of pitch aren't wasted, but used to facture myriad figurettes in the interstices of Oxley's metalzoic forest. Long before I'd worked out that Free Improvisation depends on a novel sense of time extrapolated by Oxley out of Elvin Jones, I was registering the special musicianship – raw, denuded, de-auratic – of this stroppy pair of modernists from Sheffield. Unembarrassed by the history of Improv struggles, faction fights and alliances in London, guided only by an ear trained by witnessing Alan Wilkinson and Paul Hession and Paul

Buckton and guests at the Leeds Termite Club, I made this entry in the notebook I kept during the Week:

> DB is using two levels of volume – seems to occasionally jack in to superloud. These two haven't finished (in the way that Lou Gare/Eddie Prévost seem utterly washed up). TO ups the stakes with a regular hit (not really a rhythm), DB locks in, & when TO frees it up, gets really *ugly*. Great.

After two improvisations – the second a compressed and elegant version of the first – Bailey and Oxley left the stage to Jin Hi Kim. After hearing the in-the-fingers serialism of Bailey and Oxley, Hi Kim's solo performance was completely apt. Boulez and Cage used so many of these sounds as part of their assault on romanticism – stubbed notes and untempered scratchings – that they now sound futurist rather than traditional. No one who has ever thrilled to the oriental twang in Hendrix's blues could fail to prick up their ears. Watching Hi Kim at work, seeing how the string is struck by the pick in the right hand and vibrated or stopped by the left, made the physical action of music making exceptionally clear: ripe for entry into Company's procedures.

Bailey and Oxley then played a trio with Jin Hi Kim, tentatively initiating a music in which she could not rely on traditional komungo patterns, but would have to improvise according to specific sonics. It was like watching two C. L. R. Jameses lead on a virgin! Although beginning with note values supplied by Hi Kim, the trio gradually became an abstract noise theatre of squeaks, scrunches and luminous gong reverb. Hi Kim's notes became questions, a rising tone the universal sonic raised-eyebrow. An enriched Bailey/Oxley dialogue surrounded her like some glistening castle curtain–wall in a Max Ernst fantasy landscape. Though I regretted the brevity of the concert (sixty minutes for £7 was *not* good value in 1992), there was no doubting the effect of the music, shattering and lurid and mysterious by turns.

Wednesday night brought in two musicians who'd been woodshedding on their instruments in the classic improv manner, exploring extrarange sonorities and taboo effects. Oren Marshall used a mic, amp and effects pedals to change the sound of his tuba, occasionally producing to-the-floor bass sonorities reminiscent of funk and dub. John Butcher stuck resolutely to his gurgling, spit-flecked saxophone textures, refusing to be drawn into the Wagnerian overblow invited by full-on tuba. It started as one of those feinting duets where Company musicians appear to be more listening to each other than playing. It's a necessary part of the process, but nevertheless frustrating: Marshall seemed to have been working on high-volume effects and could not really relate to Butcher's soft fizzes and in-the-tube gurgles. Indeed, Butcher was rather overshadowed throughout the week, attempting as he put it to 'draw the other musicians' onto his own quiet ground, and not really succeeding (it was a revelation for me when I saw him in his trio with violinist Phil Durrant and guitarist John Russell, where everyone is focusing on the subtlest creaks and whispers). There's a species of classicising atonal improvisation (aka Braxtonesque soprano-wittering), melancholic and theatrical, that surfaces when improvisors emphasise notes and forget rhythm and timbre. This appeared a couple of times in Butcher's playing, but there were also more rugged parts that looked like they could be returned to with justice later. By the conclusion – Butcher tongue-slapping and wheezing on tenor, Marshall scribbling complex vapour trails of tuba – they'd reached that plane of improv communication where the two instruments seem to be addressing (caressing? cajoling?) each other. However, Marshall and Butcher had needed to work through four duets to get to this point. Company Weeks are rarely without such periods of strain – indeed, they'd hardly seem authentic without them.

Ever on the look out for new players, Bailey included turntablist David Shea and tapeswitchboardist Matt Wand in this Company Week. Unfortunately, Shea appeared to be there because of his musical tastes – a stack of ethnomusicology, avant-garde classical and solo improvising albums – rather than any particular skill at manipulation. His citations introduced a deadening positivism to the music, a concentration on the affect of sound rather than on musical development. Because of his rhythmic spleen and edgy sense of attack, Matt Ward proved a far better demonstrator of the uses of technology. Wand was originally a DIY filmmaker turned on to sonic art by electrical equipment, and a member of Manchester's notorious Stock, Hausen & Walkman (a joke on composer Karlheinz Stockhausen, the Sony Walkman and the eighties pop production team Stock, Aitken and Waterman, one that threatens to outlive its trash-cultural reference points). Perhaps fearing that a Company Week audience would not credit Wand's musicianship, Bailey played a duet with him first.* The Wand/Bailey duet was not as fiery as what they had played at the Vortex (or on WDR Cologne) in April – perhaps this was simply the effect of the larger space – but the detail was ear-rinsing, Bailey was evidently well pleased to be dealing with Wand's torrents of unexpected bric-à-brac, shaking out the fresh, slippery novelties that occur when he is challenged. He played melodies of surpassing finesse to accompany Wand's industrial groans, and stopped playing to register any verbal soundbytes. Like hearing a grandfather question a grandchild about computer games, you could hear quandary as part of Bailey's playing, the intellectual excitement of listening to somebody work out their thoughts in public. It is this ability that makes Bailey such a formidable artist: everything, even puzzlement or failure, becomes grist to the mill. In the same way that people who heard Frank Zappa's *Hot Rats* in 1969 found it hard to credit the claims made about seventies jazz rock, those who had heard Bailey/Wand in 1992 found mid-nineties Japanese *Bruit Éclectique* somewhat underwhelming.

David Shea's solo set included an endless scratch version of what sounded like a komungo, which seemed superfluous with the non-virtual Jin Hi Kim on hand. Presumably it was the product of some post-Baudrillardian simulacrum syndrome. Indeed, the idea of playing a Company audience things that sounded *like* what they'd just heard seemed to rehearse a certain positivism. If you mentioned that it sounded like an inert heap of sonic material, you'd be asked, 'But hey, I thought you liked this stuff?' 'No, man,' runs the anti-reifying reply, 'I like what happens when people manage to make "this stuff" work for us in the here and now, which usually means smashing it to smithereens.'

The presence of Reggie Workman – born in Philadelphia in 1937, R&B bass player before graduating to work with Red Garland, Coltrane, Art Blakey's Jazz Messengers and Monk – was an event in itself (at least for those who do not use Bailey's *Aufhebung* of jazz as an

---

* The definitive encounter of Free Improvisation with post-eighties rave technology was made on 8 April 1992, when Oxley and Bailey recorded a broadcast on WDR Cologne with Matt Wand and Pat Thomas, though this astonishing music was not released until 1993: *The Tony Oxley Quartet* [Incus CD15].

opportunity for evasion of black music's history and struggle). Workman began with a solo improvisation that at first deserved the word 'showcase': a flashy display of his skills without the self-critical crises that make for authentic Free Improvisation, though his vocalised, pushy low notes carried a welcome visceral impact after Shea's tasteful downtown display. As Workman worked into his piece, it became evident that the flash was there in order to give himself materials to work on, which he then did with conscientiousness and poignancy. His talking high notes augured well for future dialogue with Bailey's ragtail circus. 'I'm not convinced, & his rhapsodic facial play-acting doesn't help,' I wrote in my notebook, registering the weirdness of witnessing this seasoned performer amidst the laconic arts crew. Now, when I listen back to my tape recording, his playing simply staggers me – musicality on such a high level I feel humbled. To twist so much skill and such a variety of techniques into a lyrical line of emotional conviction is amazing. As Workman's fireworks faded into the night air, he began playing the 'straight' plucked notes a jazz bassist would use for comping, and the humming resonance of the tone was hair-raisingly beautiful, so sure and solid it made everything outside the genre seem pale and shaky. If this is just one component of a jazz group, no wonder the music's so lauded!* To finish, Workman returned to his bow, bookending his piece with classical formality. As he said about the idea of improvisation in an interview for *The Wire*:

> It's part of the language we speak, it's a natural phenomenon as far as people I grew up with are concerned. That doesn't discount discipline on your instrument. Improvising is just something you do – we do it in our everyday lifestyle, we do it in our way of being and we do it when we pick up our instrument, it's no different. [*RW* 23–vii–1992]

For Workman, there's no contradiction in a jazz player contributing to Company. Workman sees Bailey as a fellow spirit, resisting the way capitalism degrades musical meaning into the search for profit. The idea that Free Jazz cuts itself off from the black community by going 'too far' is simply a libel applied by commercial interests.

* Musical judgement requires so many levels of understanding, it's surprising most critics don't just shoot themselves and get it over with.

OTL: You were involved in a very experimental era – with Dolphy, Coltrane and Monk – did you ever feel that the community might have problems relating to what you were doing?

RW: Never, never. As I said before, the community was very hip at the time, the community knew what was happening. They knew when something was real, they knew when it had a solid base, and they knew it was technically great. There was no problem with the community back then. In those days you had jobs in clubs that would last for a month – every night, six nights a week for a month. There were audiences to support that. This ran along with the whole strain of the country, it ran along with the natural evolution of a people. You give people something they can relate to, they will listen, they will develop with it, they will grow with it – particularly when you're dealing with the science of sound, this is a nurturing kind of force that deals with mentality on all levels. People listen to music because they *need* to hear music, it's a human phenomenon, human nature.

OTL: If you're playing that regularly, word of mouth serves to advertise – you don't need to be a name?

RW: That all came along with this whole marketing idea. When you take a society and you move them from thinking people, and you move them to people who are dealing with spectaculars, then you are setting yourself up for being able to manipulate the minds of the people with a marketing campaign and then the onslaught of more television, more striking advertising, more ability to manipulate the minds of people, you know how that is, how many colleges and universities there are that deal with advertising and graphics and all that, business etcetera. You are not allowing the people to be where their minds will naturally take them to. You're giving them an OD of [*sings*] 'We like doublemint gum, doublemint doublemint doublemint gum', or bubblegum, or whatever the case might be, and that's what they'll buy. Believe me, if your campaign is strong enough, you're going to pull the majority of the people, and by the time those people realise that they've been had, it's going to be many generations later and they're going to have spent their resources in the desired area. That's what has happened in this society in every walk of life, every kind of music has been like that, so you have the star syndrome, you have the spectacular, you have the sensationalism, and you put it in a frame and you market it and you make big business of that. And just like you see all the little oil companies closing down and going by the wayside, nothing left but Amcom and Exxon etcetera, the same thing happened in the world of art, there's nothing different. If you can understand that kind of marketing and that kind of business, you can understand what has happened to our people as far as the music and the art are concerned. It's a social situation as well as a business situation. [*RW* 23–vii–1992]

On Wednesday night, a concluding quintet – with Workman joined by Bailey, Shea, Marshall and Butcher – put everything together in a collective delirium. The musicians' keen listening helped keep every detail present and sparkling. Workman set the frame, and squirts and zips from Shea and Marshall decorated his girders, Bailey's notes hanging like twinkling questions. Shea's orchestral colouring made sense in a *Sinking of the Titanic* way, providing a kind of dreamy trip. The five players never quite reached the determinacy that makes for a truly inspiring improvisation – where forthright decisions are made, and real musical utterances are risked – instead providing a kind of collective compromise. One looked forward to hearing these people really work out their music on the following nights.

Thursday evening began with two trios from Matt Wand, David Shea and Oren Marshall. Because of his distaste for the way saxophonists tend to play for the audience rather than for the other musicians, Bailey says he'd rather hear a saxophone played on a sampler than experience the real thing. However, this is not enthusiasm for cyber virtuality over musical directness. Bailey's playing – his stabbing notes, his verve, his enthusiasm for sonic novelty – gives much-needed direction and crunch to improv electronica. Everything becomes so pressured there's no time to be cute. Without him – as here – one misses the emotional risk and personal exposure that happen when musicians have mastered their instruments sufficiently – in however idiosyncratic a manner – to make them into prosthetic extensions of their bodies, and hence tending towards what Valentin Voloshinov called *determinate social utterance*. Though Marshall attempted to set the stage with some ambitiously reverberant bass lines ('Funk & Wagner', as Don 'Sugarcane' Harris once put it), Shea and Wand took the music towards that locale of sniggering postmodernism where every reference is ironic, every bit of crude and heavyhanded scene-painting a 'clever' satire; where playing some scratchy old record of a Red Army Choir is deemed the height of wit – presumably because political commitment is the polar opposite of our shared 'avant' sophistication. Deprived of improv honesty and starkness, the music became snob decor, trivial and boring (yes, it was Communist Party fellow travellers – ironic socialists all – who hatched postmodernism).

A trio between Jin Hi Kim, Bailey and Workman brought back a sense of immediacy and tension, though created through pleasure in string reverberation rather than battle and antagonism. Initially Workman used a loose string sound to complement the komungo, while Bailey kept his harmonies supportive and lush; then bow scythings and astral twinkles took Hi Kim's instrument – now electrified, and sounding weirdly like one of Shea's records – into kitsch futurama. However, though the critic David Toop has made a persuasive case for the lounge music of Martin Denny and the jingles of Raymond Scott as essential sources for Sun Ra, he forgets that the mere presence of sonic material is not music (as his own releases demonstrate). As Adorno and Gerzon argue when talking about Beethoven, it is not the starting materials that matter (Beethoven's are actually rather unexceptional), but the *process*. Confusion is created when improvisors use pretty sounds, because there's the danger that listeners will pay attention to sound rather than process. That's why 'ugliness' is so often the hallmark of improvisations that really transmute their materials. They cannot be listened to with anything less than utter concentration. Here the sabotage was subtle, but frayed edges and weak endings from Bailey seemed to indicate that the musical interaction was the point, not the pretty exoticism.

Two quartets between Workman, Marshall, Butcher and Bailey pursued a similar agenda. Workman's electric bass and Marshall's unprocessed tuba provided a roiling sea in which Bailey's twangs sounded happy to be afloat. Butcher again seemed to be uncomfortable and constipated, his low dynamics failing to attract the others. In the second quartet, Workman essayed a funky ostinato, sensitively leaving spaces for the others to poke through, but providing a harmonic idea that allowed Bailey to play some outrageous, mad-sounding counterpoint, a sudden eruption of notey intellect amidst emotive textures. The piece dwindled into a twilight realm of squeaks and groans, Workman's throbbing bow complemented by assiduous Bailey feedback, Butcher's wrecked soprano notes suddenly entwined and relevant. Matt Wand and Tony Oxley played two duets. Once, reeling from a sharp exchange with Oxley about the quality of Denardo Coleman's drumming, Jan Kopinski rubbished Oxley's playing as 'old grandma Oxley rattling her pots and pans'. Kopinski was being rude, but there's many a truth in jest, and his comment reveals a social depth to Oxley's music. The way Yorkshire women dominate the domestic space (a result of textile mill and call centre income) is famous, a prol/matriarchal reproach to bourgeois patriarchy. The 'teapot' silhouette of camp posture ultimately derives its hand-on-hip stance from fired-up Yorkshire mothers as they stand their ground in the alley, and insist their beloved Dylan never did what the little horror obviously did do. Such resort to maternal power as style is not exclusively the preserve of northern drag comedians and gay stands-ups – it's also manifest in Henry Moore's sculpture. So it's not all Sheffield steelworks with Oxley, there's cosiness and domesticity and 'ta, love' too. It's a brilliant irony that what *aficionados* of the avant-garde find so 'alien' in Oxley's playing could actually be a transcription of household bustle and maternal care: a public vaunting of values screened off from bourgeois high art. On that particular Thursday night, Matt Wand fired off his confusionist array (including taped jazzy basses, news talkovers and the 'Match of the Day' theme) to Oxley's evident delight, a sonic Merz of mediated detritus for his super-extended beats to loop around and nail.

John Butcher flowered in a duet with Jin Hi Kim, amplification bringing her komungo into the sonic orbit of Workman's bass. The concluding improvisations were two quartets by Shea, Oxley, Workman and Butcher. Shea's gambit was to play a record of drumming. With Oxley there in person, this was the equivalent of glueing a sachet of L'Oréal shampoo on a Mondrian, but with Workman and Butcher on hand, it was just the gesture required to up the ante and provoke an event. Get the music out of 'good music' and into the realm of terror and surprise. Oxley's drums became positively erotic. His repeated thuds remind me of the time I watched Andrew Cyrille turn his snare drum over and spank her underside ('a drum is a woman', Duke Ellington), gestures that click below the level of art and plug into the nursery erotics of sadomasochism. When Free Improvisation this fantastic is dissed, you have to conclude that what outrages the guardians of high-minded blandness is the overload of truth about physique and desire. Here irrelevance and madness become the laughing bravado of high spirits, joy as infantile and necessary as eggs on toast.

Friday night opened with a trio of Bailey, Marshall and Butcher. Jane Williams – at the time promoting the 'new complexity' composers published by United Music Publishers – had criticised the Marshall/ Butcher duet that opened Wednesday night as 'too well-behaved'. It's interesting to ask what Bailey demands of his musicians: one answer is *a paranoid recklessness*. Evidently influenced by the scythings and crunches of the previous evening, Marshall and Butcher went beyond their atonal fugues ('I can play' demos) into Iskra-like improv. The three instruments merged into a single monstrous sonic, like listening to a contact-mic'd giant grunt and snore. As often when things are going well, a second outing was a portmanteau version of the preceding improvisation, encapsulating the virtues of the longer piece with greater punch and precision.

Matt Wand then engaged Jin Hi Kim in two improvisations. After some recordings of steam trains – all industrial puff and pant – he revealed a sensitive streak, twisting some of his tape stretches into approximations to her komungo twangs. Wand's adjustment of a tape of choral singing to Hi Kim's pitch was a graphic illustration that 'correct pitch' is simply a name for congruent speeds of vibrating air waves.

The big event of Company Week 1992 was an octet with everyone aboard. The music lurched between felicities learned during the past few days and total chaos. Oren Marshall's tuba provided the basic girder-work, coming on crude and blockish like Bill Laswell on a good day, a funk-meets-New-Age atmosphere abetted by Shea's drones. Bailey showed why he is so at home when lost in improvising chaos by plucking notes that hung above the tenebrous abyss like trembling stars. Playing unplugged enabled Marshall to walk behind the audience – recalling the tuba's deployment in marching bands – his authoritative riffing picked up and amplified by Workman.

A trio with Jin Hi Kim on acoustic komungo, John Butcher on

soprano behind a curtain at the side of the stage, and Workman on a raised portion of the stage, was a post-groove delight, the musicians concentrating on the bizarre fit between their exotic sonorities and their mutual comprehension of pitch. The final two improvisations saw Bailey playing in a quartet with Oxley, Workman and Wand, creating an eventful sonic collage teetering between the swing of jazz and the pure stasis of Joseph Holbrooke. The musicians both inhabited this environment and created it as different members stepped forward to increase the tension. Workman and Wand were respectful of the Bailey/Oxley duo, comping and amplifying the central paradox of their special art. At points it seemed that the great achievement of Bailey and Oxley is simply being able to let sounds sustain and decay in cadences that are both anti-romantic and highly charged. Company Week 1992 was heating up: Friday evening's concert lasted over one and a half hours, each minute packed with more musical ideas than you could credit.

Bailey was probably thinking of events like Company Week 1992 when he told music writer Linton Chiswick:

I like the early stages of relationships in free playing, before the music solidifies into any style. The early stages might last five days – the length of Company – but I find that after five or six days, they seem to find a limit to their fertile common ground. [*Time Out*, 25–30–vii–1994]

The last concert – Saturday night, 25 July – began with two quartets comprising Marshall, Shea, Butcher and Hi Kim. Marshall's instrument requires such a physical effort to achieve a note, it almost forces him to be determinate, and his strong notes moulded the shape of the proceedings. Shea, however, introduced shuffles and drones which submerged the pin-drop tension of true improv rhythm (the 18 quavers to the bar pioneered by Oxley) in a minimalist burble, introducing the kind of soundscaping that can sound surreal (the KLF's *Chill Out*) but can also constitute the babyfood fodder of Ambient flatulence. It is the sound of waiting – the impressionist overture – rather than the sound of attention, the promise of event rather than the event itself. It can be almost unbearably intense and erotic in affect, but finally leaves one feeling shortchanged: striptease rather than the sex act. Every one of Bailey's notes – interrogative, materialist, shrugging off association and reverie – breaks such spells.

Two duets between Bailey and Shea were bizarre affairs. Bailey seemed to induce a melancholic atmosphere as an invitation to Shea to do his worst, and, as expected, a cacophonic eruption soon occurred from the turntablist, with bursts of manic vocalese and laughter. After the outbreak, Bailey returned to his meditative melancholy as if the noise had been an intercity express train roaring through a provincial station: the guy with the guitar in the waiting room just kept on pondering his intractable clusters whether or not he could hear himself. Shea then resorted to more active scratching, a hands-on commitment that made Bailey resort to harsher and louder notes. The more active and percussive Shea became, the more Bailey engaged with him. Spindled skronks and desperate sonic smears procured a closing power cluster, almost a benediction, indicating that if anyone really tries, Bailey will give them the time of day. The second duet had Bailey adopting a more shrill and spiky sound, with Shea unleashing things that sounded like tuned percussion, drums and saxophones. Bailey seemed to be gradually paring away Shea's reliance on reference, making him pay attention to concrete sonority (that is, rhythm).

A trio between Matt Wand, Tony Oxley and Reggie Workman worked so well the musicians played three pieces. Oxley's idea of rhythm as continual interruption allowed both Wand's sonic bric-à-brac and Workman's questing lines room to manoeuvre. The musicians seemed to be taking greater pleasure in the process of their own thoughts and interactions than in any idea of 'performing'. In that sense, it was an exemplary Company performance, precisely the kind of music Derek Bailey says he enjoys. It flies in the face of every tenet of classical music, yet has none of the rhetoric of non-intentionality or chance one finds in John Cage. The paradox is that though it's all deliberate, there is no pre-set target. This provides an insoluble dilemma to the Kantian commonsense which sets duty and freedom in permanent opposition. However if, like Hegel, one defines humanity as beings whose duty is to be free, then this music – unlike all the classical and pop musics which shriek their 'humanity' from every cardboard speaker – actually enacts such a supersession of contraries.

The last hour of Company Week 1992 became the Matt Wand Show. His guests were Oren Marshall and Jin Hi Kim, who engaged in similar playing – unpressured and unshowy, kaleidoscopically speculative – to that of the preceding trio. Although there are many musical acts today that claim to use Free Improvisation – pure, or fused with composition, rock, jazz or electronica – very few have the opportunity to stretch out in this way, where the musical focus is tight, but the brief wide open. Though Bailey wasn't playing, the music was a vindication of his approach and philosophy. Wand then entertained David Shea for three short pieces – swooshing confrontations of sonic rejectamenta that kept a push and rhythm lively enough to digest their riches instead of being smothered by them. John Cage's point that any noise can become musical – because noise can be subjected to the parameter of duration – was borne out as Wand and Shea used dramatic cut-offs to illustrate their control over their source materials. The closing sextet – all the other Company participants – was dominated by Oxley's big beats and Hi Kim's twanging, bringing it into the orbit of Bill Laswell's contemporary productions, though by then celebration had taken over musical considerations.

The *Guardian* nodded to Company Week 1992 by publishing one of John Fordham's concise and informative reviews. He summarised the events of Thursday night, noting a citation from the Surfaris' 'Wipe Out' in David Shea's turntablism and Bailey smiling during a quiet passage as he heard a police siren go by on the Euston Road. Fordham defended Free Improvisation from its detractors by making qualitative distinctions:

> Company represents the most skilled and experienced end of what can be a frustratingly aimless process in some hands, its temporary members nowadays including off-duty classical musicians, sometimes plastic artists and dancers. At its best it is an object lesson in the most basic and un-partisan virtues of music. [John Fordham, *Guardian*, 28 July 1992]

COMPANY WEEK 1993

The innovation at Company Week 1993 – held at the Place between 20 and 24 July – was the inclusion of three 'groups' on the bill: Conspiracy from London, Hession/Wilkinson/Fell from Leeds and the Honkies from Manchester. Bailey's singleminded pursuit of spontaneous invention makes him sceptical about the value of fixed-personnel groups, but they did at least serve to kick off some of 1993's nights with a bang: more bounce to the ounce than presenting a string of solos and duos to introduce the various musicians.

Conspiracy, which kicked off the week on the Tuesday, was essentially the brainchild of keyboardist Nick Couldry: a quartet, with Adam Bohman on DIY electronics, John Telfer on sax and Andy Hammond on electric-guitar textures. Today a lecturer in sociology at Goldsmiths College, Couldry was very active in the London scene of the early nineties. Responsible for a series of concerts in London's 'secret places', Couldry brought in situationist concepts concerning power and the media that had not been invoked in Free Improvisation since the 1960s. In retrospect, the project of turning unpropitious urban spaces into sites for experimental art was a means of urban regeneration/yuppiefication, but the new attention to *mise-en-scène* also had musical repercussions.

Free Improvisation is by its nature site-specific, but promotions in defunct swimming pools and vacant railway arches drew particular attention to echo and post-industrial clangour (it was in this period that the London Musicians Collective named its journal *Resonance*). Conspiracy's music was appropriately doom-laden and gothic, fitting into a nineties style wave that included Steam Punk (William Gibson and Bruce Sterling's *The Difference Engine*, K. W. Jeter's *Morlock Night*, 2000AD's 'Nemesis & Torquemada in the Land of the Goths' strip), the Institution of Rot curated in Finsbury Park by artist Richard Crow, and the psychogeographic mock horror of Iain Sinclair.

Like illusion in painting, reverberance and echo are sticky topics. Standing at the unrepentant hard-modernist end of things, Derek Bailey favours speed and surface over illusion and depth. Echo, whether provided by churchy interiors or electronic processing, is avoided as a brake on musical wit. Like the use of abraded surfaces in art – the Pompeii fresco or cracked-icon 'look' so popular in late-eighties graphic design and decor – echo, especially when shaped by digital software, quickly degenerates into kitsch: spray-on sublime, pebble-dash gravitas.

Echo can be used to hide determinate utterance in dust motes and cobwebs, can be a sentimental prefiguration of the way the music 'should' be heard rather than an attempt at communication that risks penetrating unknown space. On the other hand, music *is* a matter of vibrating airwaves; to deny its ambient nature would be to replace its materiality with abstract or visual parameters (harmony, rhythm, melody: the score).

When New Zealand's Dead C – musicians relying on primitive, 'punk' musicianship, intuitive and unformalised – made reverberation the focus of their (realtime, improvised) performances, they produced an authentic and absolutist music. The take-up of their 'lo-fi' aesthetic (a misnomer, since the Dead C were actually concerned to record their – albeit scrapy and illegitimate – sonorities with maximum fidelity) by musically schooled improvisors has not always been successful. To hear Thomas Lehn and Tim Hodgkinson evoke crackle and fluff-on-needle textures in Konk Pack is rather like hearing an electric guitarist switch on the 'Hendrix pedal' at low volume; a stylistic reference point rather than a raw musical process. In contrast, Furt – the sampling duo of Paul Obermayer and Richard Barrett – take on board the echoic illusion of their samples: rather than remaining entranced, they overlay contradictory virtual spaces, producing an intricate sonic cubism that refuses to frame a stable illusion.

In 1993, Conspiracy lacked either the musical forebears or the digital equipment to make echo an exercise in stylism. As on their album *Intravenous* [Matchless MR21, 1992], what they played at Company Week was highly emotional, both brutal and affecting. Starting from squeezed, high-pitched textures and scrapes – a horizontalism derived more from AMM than the jagged ruptures of Tony Oxley or Iskra 1903 – the quartet used a sophisticated grasp of harmony to trigger turbulence and crisis. The main echoic device was Adam Bohman's 'prepared strings', where amplification is used to project an intense, private and obsessional dealing with table-top materials into public space. In keeping with Couldry's meditations about the division between private and public spheres in the modern metropolis, Conspiracy used Bohman's home-based logic as a foil for their more public skills. At Company 1993, Hammond and Telfer successfully translated his boinging provocations into powerful swathes of metal rhetoric.

Next, Alan Wilkinson, saxophonist from Hession/Wilkinson/Fell, was pitched against the synthesised trumpet of Andy Diagram from the Honkies. Still reverberating from Conspiracy's concerted blast, the duet seemed impatient to get straight to the point, reinforcing the impression that contemporary music is less the wide-open array of choices portrayed by postmodernism than a singleton genre driven by greed and necessity. Some lyrical handshakes were followed by a complex and involving climax, Wilkinson's stuck-donkey cries hacking notches out of Diagram's mad-scientist spectrographs and infusions. Diagram resorted to synth loops against which Wilkinson's histrionics and vocalese broke like surf on rocks.

Derek Bailey then appeared for a duet with percussionist Robyn Schulkowsky. Her programme entry ran:

> As a performer, she has concentrated on the contemporary classical repertoire and has worked closely with Feldman, Stockhausen, Kagel, Cage, Kevin Volans and many other composers. She has combined this with improvised performance and toured internationally both as a soloist, in duo with trumpeter Markus Stockhausen, and in other settings. [programme note, Company Week 1993]

Smart percussionists tend to make Bailey play brilliantly ('Derek Bailey semble particulièrement affectionner les rencontres avec les percussionistes' as Jacques Oger put it in *Jazz Magazine*, June 1996), and Schulkowsky is no exception (she has played with him twice since, at the Vortex in Stoke Newington, on 8 November 1998 and 23 March 2000). Their duets are arresting. Schulkowsky has no trace of the condescension that can prevent a score reader from improvising convincingly: each blow is delivered with ritualistic violence. Though her metrical sense is strong and there's nothing random about her playing, it's utterly different from watching Bailey with Milford Graves or Han Bennink, or even Tony Oxley. Schulkowsky takes seriously the sense of singular event instilled by John Cage into modern music, so each blow seems to be delivered as if for the first time. It is the opposite of the rolling continuity that characterises percussionists who hail from jazz. Although it is true that Oxley breaks that umbilical link, his beats are so awesomely environmental he never exposes his fellow musicians quite in Schulkowsky's manner. The most memorable image of her at Company Week 1993 was the slaps that issued forth as she beat the steps of her portable step-ladder with a pair of rubber flipflops, jarring assertions of now-time versus linear development. Bailey's notes crept into the raw pockets created by her non-rhythmic blows like an invading termite army. Contrasts of timbre are a hallmark of modernism: Shulkowsky used them to set up clockwork mechanisms, hinting at the astral objectivity of percussion pieces by Varèse and Cage. The sudden and arbitrary entry of her high-pitched wooden logs – a trilling set of full stops – suggested the Noh Theatre existentialism of Black Mountain School happenings. Though the interplay lacked the hefty, all-encompassing dynamism of an Oxley/Bailey encounter, Schulkowsky's starkness provoked a unique Bailey, splintered and rowdy. Crises would manifest themselves with high-volume, high-pitched notes, after which the dialogue would retreat into busy ratiocination, before reaching another exhilarating crescendo.

The final quartet of Bailey, Schulkowsky, Diagram amd Wilkinson wound its way from staccato dada constructivism to elegaic high pingings via an extraordinary section of aching texturation (Bailey rubbing his strings, Wilkinson squeaking). It sounded like a reply to Conspiracy's opening set. As so often in Free Improvisation, one's listening veered from total scepticism – 'nothing is happening, it's complete chaos' – to rapt admiration as the musicians made invention palpable in the instant. Starting from degree zero, shorn of the capital investments and power-broking that have locked Modern Art in the gallery, Free Improvisation delivers its promise: a universal language that requires nothing but your attention. Idiomless Nowness Volapük! Exploring the deepest registers of his baritone in a visceral manner reminiscent of Braxton on contrabass clarinet, Wilkinson sounded like Gargantua groaning to Pantagruel during an after-dinner siesta. The others flapped and piqued like gnats. Far from being the cerebral headtrip of journalistic lore, Free Improvisation became direct mimicry of the body, musical ideas arriving like thoughts during waking moments.

Because it was opened by Hession/Wilkinson/Fell, Wednesday night at Company Week 1993 was a special moment for this writer. This trio had formed as a result of activities at the Leeds Termite Club. Its power and expressiveness suggest something beyond Free Improvisation's *ad hoc* encounters. The fleetest and most sensitive drummer in Britain, Paul Hession had no problems at all about the concept of total – 'non-idiomatic' – improvisation, seeing his musical life as one long aspiration towards musical freedom (from rock bands in working men's clubs to jazz to Improvisation). Alan Wilkinson was deeply affected by alto saxophonist Xero Slingsby, Leeds's own funky, busking, post-Ornette populist (Xero died of brain cancer in 1990; Xero's widow gave Alan his alto) and plays with an unguarded emotionalism rare in any music, but especially rare in a scene often blighted by reticence and intellectualism. Bassist Simon Fell combines a highly informed overview of twentieth-century music – composed and improvised – with a recklessness that never fails to excite. Although it may well have transgressed the egalitarian, non-commercial ethos of Free Improvisation, Hession/ Wilkinson/Fell were (still are) a unit that deserved the kind of attention and commitment given to rock bands (this writer's term 'punk jazz' to characterise their full-on approach still earns him disapproval). As Graeme Murrell said after their performance at Bogey's in Huddersfield on 11 June 1991 (a quote omitted from the Bruce's Fingers re-release on CD):

> I thought this would be jazz, but ... you know, I used to be into Napalm Death and Bolt Thrower, and that's what it was like.

As often in the stale and stagnant waters of British musical life, this particular fish finger proved to be critical fantasy rather than commercial reality, and it was left to John Zorn's Naked City to garner the international tours and kudos for such a 'cross-over' concept.

However, at Company Week 1993, sitting at the back of the Place Theatre, I must admit I was bitterly disappointed in how the assault of Hession/Wilkinson/Fell was absorbed by the larger-than-usual space, providing an 'interesting' rather than cathartic experience for the Lon-

DEREK BAILEY AND THE STORY OF FREE IMPROVISATION

don audience. Like seeing the Clash on the open-air stage at the April 1979 Anti-Nazi League Carnival, it was a shock to realise how dependent on small venues a musical juggernaut can be. However, listening back to the tape I made that night, it's evident that the negotiation between power and freedom in their music is more convincing than that of Zorn's amusing – but somewhat arch – Naked City. Taking off from the Peter Brötzmann and Archie Shepp octets of the late-sixties, the fact that all the racket is produced by just three players means that there is less rhetoric and more interaction: even if it packs the confrontational punch of Iggy Pop with the Stooges, this *is* Free Improvisation.

Alan Wilkinson's understanding of late Coltrane is entirely without the aura of pastiche that vitiates many saxophonists. He locks with Fell onto the central task, which is the gradual accumulation of harmonic movements that speak for wider and wider freedoms. The music feels like a bomb going off that never stops going off, a blinding surge: one of the most powerful psychic and emotional experiences available in this time period.*

Hession/Wilkinson/Fell are different from *ad hoc* improvised encounters where musicians assert a dialogic individuality before inventing ways in which to reach a collective swell. The trio's sense of phrasing is not dominated by a conscious stylistic concept, yet their phrases are nevertheless stunningly compatible. Their phrases fit, not because the musicians have been drilled militaristically like formation dancers in pop videos, but because the labour is collective and free. The bullish power of Wilkinson's baritone and the parabolic perfection of Hessions' cymbal washes suggest natural forces like wind and waves, though this compatibility has been reached by persistent realtime playing: it's rooted in physical exertion, not surrender to external nature. Hession/Wilkinson/ Fell's phrases fit because they're measured by the stresses and strains of the active body. Of course, for the Marxist, who understands labour power as a natural force (a concept incomprehensible to the dualism of Kantian commonsense), it is no surprise to discover the infinitude of nature – the 'sublime' – *within* human effort. Commercial eclipse

---

* If you think I'm exaggerating, send off for *Bogey's* [BF31] from Bruce's Fingers, PO Box 57, Haverhill, CB9 8RD, or visit www.brucesfingers.com – and prove me wrong.

notwithstanding, Hession/Wilkinson/Fell's proof that free-improvised flexibility and openness do not automatically entail gentility and cerebralism is of pressing anthropological interest. Like all great music, that of Hession/Wilkinson/Fell provides a model for progressive thought about body and mind, desire and thought, necessity and freedom: these conceptual binaries are *not* forever at war!

Paul Hession brought the set to a climactic finish with snare-rolls-cum-rim-shots that sounded like machine-gun fire: triggered mechanical violence reimagined as the fleshly destruction and outrage it really is. Unfortunately, one twenty-minute set – when Hession/Wilkinson/Fell usually played two sets of nearly an hour each – only gave a taste of what they can do to your inner ear (Hession and Fell did not join in the rest of the Company Week). Hession/Wilkinson/Fell did not start from the ground zero that is Bailey's concept of Company, but as an introduction to the filth and fury of Alan Wilkinson's baritone and alto saxophonism, it was perfect. As with Conspiracy's set the previous night, the twenty-minute fusillade raised the intensity of the improvising that followed.

The next duet pitched Nick Couldry's keyboards against Ikue Mori's drum machines. Mori is a heroine of the New York post-punk scene, and it's hard to disentangle the musical point of her contributions from the cyberpunk need to see a Japanese woman using technology to 'play drums'. Couldry and Mori finally wrestled their random electronic bleeps and blats into something resembling music – some singing arpeggios – but it was more impressive to watch Phil Minton and Bailey attempt to throw their considerable musical knowledge to the winds, wrestling infantile mimicry and anthropological realism out of voice and guitar. In a duet with Minton, Couldry unleashed demonic church-organ to accompany the singer's vocal dementia, producing an instant Walpurgis Night, gothic and humorous.

A quartet of Bailey, Couldry, Minton and Mori – in three movements – presented an elegant microcosm of the improvising process. Sounds that could stand alone as evocations – Minton's whistling, Couldry's birdsong effects, Mori's stutters and clatters – were gradually forced into rhythmic relation by Bailey's persistent, edgy comping. Scene painting was converted into music as individual musicians asserted themselves versus the ensemble and demanded interaction. Eventually, after Couldry had whipped up a delirious storm and put the dynamics through the roof, the music made the stomach walls tighten. The audience felt they were being *worked on* (a sensation that occurs when the musicians actually work on their own responses to the sounds rather than second-guessing a putative audience response). Finally, all the extraneous sounds appeared to be integrated into a four-part groove, with decisive swerves towards climaxes and troughs of tension. Reaching an ensemble method appeared to mark the end of the process, and the musicians desisted. Perhaps sensing too triumphant a finality, Bailey frustrated applause by twanging on a little more. He could rest assured that any *group* complacency on the part of the players was going to be upset by his fielding of fresh musicians the next evening.

Thursday evening (22 July) introduced trombonist Thierry Madiot from France, clarinetist Don Byron from New York and Martin Klapper from Prague. In the programme, Madiot explained that he had dis-covered Free Improvisation at two Continental festivals – Chantenay Villedieu and Europa Jazz at Le Mans. He had been studying modern trombone techniques with Benny Sluchin. It will be remembered that Sluchin, a member of Pierre Boulez's Ensemble Intercontemporain, recorded Berio's *Sequenza V* (see 'Improvisation versus Composition, Round #23', pp. 167–71), and was taught by Vinko Globokar, who contributed alongside Bailey to Deutsche Grammophon's *Free Improvi-sation* 3-LP box set (and played twice with Bailey: in a trio with Tristan Honsinger in October 1978, and at Company Week 1983). Bassists and trombonists appear able to mix orchestral work with improvisation more successfully than violinists and trumpeters, as if dealing with the lower notes – the basis of the sound rather than its superstructure – gives them a firmer grasp of musical totality. Thierry Madiot's presence at Company Week 1993 – his lowering sounds shaping many pieces, his humour and rhythmic spirit always in play – testified to a tradition of trombone instrumentalism that transcends musical genres (perhaps that explains why Bailey, whose approach is instrumental rather than generic, is so fond of trombones).

Don Byron had just released *Tuskegee Experiments* on Elektra Nonesuch. Showing a grasp of politics unusual in both avant-garde and neo-conservative circles, Byron used his album to talk about experiments made at the Tuskegee Institute in 1932, when over two hundred black American men with syphilis were left untreated so that their suffering could be 'documented' (these events were also a source for Frank Zappa's scrofulous treatment of American race relations, *Thing-Fish*). For Byron, the atrocity wasn't a simple case of racism, but included a class component: the US Public Health Service 'experiment' was carried out by *black* medical professionals. Byron's 'Tuskegee Strutters Ball' was written to highlight 'the class scorn middle-class black folks feel for the people below them'. Such comments are unlikely to be rewarded with commissions from the Lincoln Center!

Like Matt Wand and Adam Bohman, Martin Klapper is a 'non-musician' who has been embraced by free improvisors for his ability to perpetrate sonic events and widen the musical vocabulary. Born in Prague in the late sixties, he was active in the visual arts from the early eighties, 'producing collages and multimedia environments' and 'junkyard' performances. He played with the hardcore punk band A/64 and founded the Alfred Startka group, before emigrating to Copenhagen where he made contact with John Butcher, Radu Malfatti, Erhard Hirt amd Jeffrey Morgan.

Thursday evening started with two trios by Bailey, Madiot and Wilkinson. Musicality was so in abundance that the players seemed to keep pinching themselves to avoid it. Bailey found a place between the long notes of the horns that made him sound super-crunchy; he was making all kinds of spiky connections between their notes, evoking both the struts in an atomic model of mica and crispy bacon inside an avocado sandwich. Consonance and toe-tapping rhythms kept arising, but as objects of discussion rather than environmental givens. As often on his alto, Wilkinson entered realms of undefended lyricism, Bailey's spangled notes the perfect foil. Madiot used his mute to play vocal rhythms on his trombone; Wilkinson responded with such abrupt phuts, it was as if he'd become the drummer. The trio fused into a single entity, the three musicians accelerating as if towards some bizarre object of desire that had suddenly and unexpectedly arisen.

On the second trio, Wilkinson played baritone. Bailey began with his patented harmonic ambiguity, indeterminate chords that refuse to set up a stable tonal horizon, yet suggest myriad rhythms and colours. The larger horn gives Wilkinson a wider spectrum of timbres; a police-car siren imitation suddenly bursts into a cornucopia of brightcoloured exotica. The contrast between Wilkinson's writhing saxophone – all muscle and flayed gut – and Bailey's amplified strings – all metal and shine – is surgical, an operation on sound almost obscene in its intimacy. When music is this good and people say they don't like it, you can only conclude they're repressed. Don Byron came prepared for Company antics with his own set of toys. He also disassembled his instrument a few times. Setting him against Martin Klapper was nevertheless a typical Baileyite interpenetration of contraries: the well-trained American reed player versus a Slovak junkyard dadaist. Suddenly deprived of the whoosh of the preceding trio, the music sounded intelligent, but one-dimensional: the musicians had to feel their way tentatively, rather than simply step out into mutually assured spaces. Byron's slippery 'anxiety' high notes sounded like something played by the right hand in a piano piece by Michael Finnissy. Klapper's tabletop of toys provide him with instruments that retain their silliness – ray guns and penny whistles – but he throws them into the music with such rhythmic punch that the net effect is expressive rather than whimsical. In a trio with Wilkinson and Couldry, Byron's bass clarinet produced film noir spook notes, resulting in a *Pink-Panther-meets-Soldier's-Tale* humoresque, with Wilkinson stabbing the rhythm and Couldry providing funky Monkisms.

Free Improvisation uses a dialectic of contingency that has not manifested itself in fine art so undimmed by auteur transcendence since the *Merz* of Kurt Schwitters. In terms of art status, Wilkinson's extraordinary ability to mimic the sounds around him is a liability. Despite the evidence about Charlie Parker supplied by Carl Woideck in his *Charlie Parker: His Music and Life*, which makes clear how mimicry is actually the essence of Parker's genius, mimicry is still considered rather childish (Adorno's epigones feel they need to dignify it with the word 'mimesis'). Actually, when Wilkinson puts the sound of a braying ass, a crying child or a police car into an improvisation, it is like a dadaist including a cigarette stub or a postage stamp in an artwork: it frees the music from the oppressive idea that art descends on us from a special realm, and begins to tap the magic complexities of reality itself. It matters that Wilkinson's using a sax. Sampler and tape-looping provide mechanical copies rather than mimicry, tending to result in a melancholic surrender to the power of technology and the unrepeatability of past experience. Wilkinson's ability to mimic some monstrously assymetrical sonic outburst is, in contrast, a genuine transformation of contingency into music: what was previously *in itself* is now *for us* (to paraphrase Friedrich Engels on the significance of the chemical synthesis of alizarin). Enoesque nostalgia and consumerist decadence have been chased from the room: suddenly, some monstrous expression of suffering, singleton and nominalist, can become part of the environment negotiated by the other musicians (a lick!) because of the *labour* put in by the player. The knob twiddlers of middle management (*aka* Ambient), pushing around their inert samples like morticians in a funeral parlour, will never know anything about such alchemical transmogrification.

By the end of Thursday night, Klapper, Madiot and Byron were playing a music bred on memory of how all previous music has proceeded, but with every contribution driven by risk: grotesques and drunken fanfares and baby wind and infarct agony all part of the hellscape. In a closing quartet (Schulkowsky, Bailey, Wilkinson and Couldry), the musical thinking suddenly became utterly uncluttered, even though Schulkowsky's percussive clangour remained refreshingly rowdy. Wilkinson and Bailey had another exchange – less surgical than before; what was impressive was Bailey's way of playing 'rhythm chords' as separate, ever-unexpected blows. Although the concept of serialised rhythm is a product of academic thought (Messiaen, Boulez, Stockhausen, Babbitt), Bailey uses it to keep his 'accompaniment' a dialogue, each strike at the strings suddenly present and obstreporous. As Couldry and Schulkowsky raised the volume, Bailey reached for that churning 'loud guitar' – all irascible process and flailing metal – that in the nineties made him the toast of enlightened rockists everywhere.

As usual, Friday night brought in a larger and noisier audience. Having had three nights' open rehearsal, the musicians were equipped to please the crowd yet still please and intrigue themselves. The novel ingredient was singer Phil Minton, longtime trumpeter in the Mike Westbrook Orchestra who has developed a completely different career as a vocal improvisor, using zones of the mouth, nose and throat usually only sounded in public by asthmatics, lunatics, vomiting invalids and drunks in the throes of the most abject self-pity. Ikue Mori's drum machines were still proving difficult to integrate, belonging more to the realm of theory than the processual dialectic of Free Improvisation (in other words, she did not seem capable of *controlling* her sonic emissions). Hence an opening quartet of Mori, Klapper, Couldry and Wilkinson proved puzzling and chaotic: too many typewriters, not enough calligraphy. In a trio with Bailey and Schulkowsky, Minton avoided the facile way a human voice can dominate any ensemble, and melted his sounds – high weazlings, low grunts, phlegmy snuffles – into the ongoing sonic, presenting an extraordinarily sharply defined phantasmagoria. Minton retains a stoical sense of the social meaning of his vocal excesses, which makes his vocalese both disciplined amd moving. A notebook entry I made at the time includes visual clues:

> The late-night terrace bistro music of your nightmares. A clapped-out destitute opera singer who wants to let you know it backed by a demented and vengeful flamenco virtuoso and a cigar-chewing voodoo mama from the main beach of Rio de Janeiro. [OTL 23–vii–1993]

A quartet between Wilkinson, Diagram, Madiot and Mori showed that the flexibility of brilliant horn players could make magic of mechanical toy beats. It would be hard to cite any other music so adept at splicing contradictory moods: here, nocturnal nostalgia and petulant violence seemed to be spun together in finer and finer strands. Madiot used a Camembert box as a mute – the old tradition of French mime and self-mockery dies hard – but was magnificently supportive, Wilkinson resorting to the superlative 'chuffa chuffa' of his vintage-locomotive imitation on baritone.

A quartet between Klapper, Minton, Diagram and Byron perpetuated the week's absurdity with a rigour one could almost call logical. Klapper's use of fluorescent whirli-pipes-that-hum and a green plastic slide-stick that gave off Dalek noises evinced the enthusiasm for consumer trash of an anti-communist rebel. Suddenly, with Byron's jazz clarinet in tow, Klapper's insane, squeaky-plastic aesthetic seemed to connect to the radical unseriousness and provocation of bebop, allowing

Byron and Wilkinson and Minton to whistle off into a crazed strato-sphere of helium-fuelled extremes. Indeed, Minton was suddenly whis-tling the bird house at the Regent's Park zoo (where Lol Coxhill recorded a memorable track of *Ear of Beholder*), and suddenly *everyone* was in the bird house at Regent's Park zoo. Mimicry becomes a song anyone can join in on, and 'cerebral' Free Improvisation became infantile delight.

Diagram and Couldry played over-exhibitionist free jazz with plunk moments; a duet between Klapper and Minton was superlatively mad (no surprise that since Company Week 1993, Klapper has recorded a dada classic with percussionist Roger Turner, Minton's longterm spar-ring partner: *Recent Croaks*, Acta 11, 1997). My notes ran:

> Little wind-up tin Sooty that rides a tricycle and tinkles a drum. MK now on contact-mic'd table football. He's good, even on scraping chair and scratching Dansette. With all this clutter about, PM suddenly sounds like the ring you get in a cracker which you blow into and a plastic wheel whizzes round, a 'wolf whistle' ringlet in green and pink plastic. [*OTL* 23–vii–1993]

A Minton/Schulkowsky/Byron/Wilkinson quartet erupted into a terrify-ingly wilful regressive racket. The audience adored it. The evening concluded with all the musicians on stage, and even though free impro-visations comprising more than five players are very rarely successful, this nonet sounds great even on the replay. This must be because the musicians had just played four nights of open rehearsal (though that term is not really sufficient to describe the tension and ambition of Company nights). As the horns of Byron and Wilkinson howled in intimate embrace, and Couldry and Madiot shook the bowels with their gothic sardonic, and Minton and Diagram locked on a kettle-whistle scream, it was obvious that the week had been a time of observation and waiting for opportunities. The pace of mutual listening turned into an acknowledged flow, a rhythm without a beat. Friday night was triumphant.

Free improvisors dislike discussion of less-than-brilliant nights. Stra-tegic career considerations mean that it's safer simply to avoid playing with another musician again than voicing criticism. For audiences, things are different. Though it is almost a heresy to express the needs of the audience in Free Improvisation – after all, it is meant to express the autonomy of the musician as fount of integrity and self-critique – only analysis and comprehension prevents a disappointed auditor from abandoning the entire racket. Hence, the closing Saturday night – probably the least satisfactory in terms of music – is hard to write about, but also extremely interesting.

Saturday night kicked off with Andy Diagram and the Honkies. Their LP *How Do We Prevent the Advance of the Desert?* – which I purchased on 8 November 1990, price £4.99 – was a cunning and strident blast of muso-punk protest, sounding like a drunken dinner party playing backwards James Brown riffs (in other words, they were in the vein of Rip Rig & Panic): winning in its gleeful trashing of tired commercial standards. The Honkies' combination of dole-queue punk and Free Jazz (surely the 'unique' Day-Glo orange spiral silkscreened on the LP cover was a reference to Pharoah Sanders's ESP-Disk 1003?) predicted much post-rock of the nineties – without the dreary and derivative industrial/terrorist chic that cursed the London scene. However, strategies designed to take BBC TV's *Top of the Pops* by storm look rather different on a stage that has just hosted four Company nights. My notes at the time ran:

> Costumes, bells, plastic trombone and a telephone wire. Tintops sewn to sackcloth dresses, cloth flowers (where's the mouldering fish heads à la *Captain Beefheart vs the Grunt People?*). A bass player with bare knees. Oh dear, improvised street theatre. Andy Diagram now really too too actorish, we come to Company for *reality*. I'd love to see 'em invade Ronnie Scott's, but after four nights of soberly presented dementia, they do look silly. Organised bits – brass and shouted slogans – sound pretty majestic, though. Kindergarten Rip Rig. Get back to the rock clubs, Honkies, and elevate the masses . . . Caroline Kraabel's got a baritone as well as an alto. There's a whiff of self-consciousness here I don't like. They've added John Edwards on bass to the original line-up. Punk rock for grannies and toddlers; Shuffle Demons meet the Au Pairs at a clown convention. R. E. Harrison, the drummer – an unappealing slob in flowery shirt and Hawaiian shorts – looks uncomfortable with his dangly black-glass earrings, I doubt he wears those to the day job. Arrangements are cute – clarity, contrast – unison

of trumpet and alto (written section) is poignant, it works after the enthusiastic chaos. Whoever's done it has listened to Gil Evans and Carla Bley; nice to have that abutted to shouting matches. Improvisation as a game of tag, yes. Infantile & why not? [*OTL* 24–vii–1993]

At the end of the set, Kraabel informed us they were playing the Samuel Pepys in Hackney in early August, which may have been a more conducive habitat. The fact that the Honkies' anti-showbiz *shtik* came across as artificial demonstrates how utterly alien – despite the frequent silliness – considerations of audience are to Company presentations. Derek Bailey's challenge to conventional 'musical discussion' – the comparison of competing acts and their releases – is so radical that, even examples of the retro-virus like the Honkies can appear stilted and contrived.

The arrival of the Honkies seemed to disperse concentration. My scribbled notes became hostile, something listening back to the tapes doesn't make me want to revise. Next on was a Couldry/Schulkowsky duet:

Couldry is a crap percussionist & shouldn't try to dramatically drum-stick the insides of his piano. Schulkowsky uses a long gold chain scraped over a pendent steel hoop, and now her cymbal. Couldry on beer bottle (Becks) isn't much better. [*OTL* 24–vii–1993]

After that, a Bailey/Byron/Mori trio:

Mori on automatic tinkles. Byron on half a bass clarinet. One silly noise deserves another. Being 'interested' in public – can this constitute art, or even Derek's 'building site'? Bailey finds his guitar amp had been switched off at the wall: 'this is what happens when you get regular groups to play'. Straight Byron clarinet *vs*. Bailey starts to sound okay. But Byron takes his clarinet apart again. Is this what Zorn does, is this wackiness the US concept of Improv? Bailey manfully negotiates Mori's windchimes, but truly nothing can be done against this *Tomita Plays Debussy* in a Temple Garden gift shop. The beats have no direction in them, no pressure, they're always flat and unengaged. The opposite of the get-up-and-use-me urgency of Schulkowsky's Noh violence or Matt Wand's aggressively triggered electro-storms. It's arch and cool and Flying Lizards ... *boring* ... I'm staring into the aisle on my left, on the linoleum-covered floor there's an inverted bottle-cap with some haberdasher's thread running through it, a dropping from a departed Honkie. Byron's reduced to playing half-hearted repetitions, as if – without the propulsion of proper music – real playing's beneath him. [*OTL* 24–vii–1993]

A Diagram/Madiot/Byron/Couldry quartet followed: 'Useless! Byron beats time on a tea-chest with his bass clarinet' [*OTL* 24–vii–1993].

However, despite successive line-ups, no one managed to unfreeze Mori's drum machine, to prevent it delivering preset prettiness, to let it get up and wail. A brief Mori-less episode – Klapper/Minton/Wilkinson – revived my flagging interest:

Yo! Sinuous aesthete screams in torc motion across inadvertent electronic interference. These three have a firm idea of where the music *is*, and this Newtonian confidence makes the chance squibs and dippy squalls something more than tiresome scrap and clutter. Minton and Wilkinson the straight men for Klapper's comic timing. Wilkinson switches to bamboo-plus-reed-ophone, maybe not such a good idea. A nice funky bass drum wells up – you look round, and it's Klapper tapping his finger on a mic'd-up white-plastic aspirin canister. He plays Jaco Pastorius on a cheese-wire fed through a clock spring. Eventually all eyes are on Klapper – despite/because of his paltry instrumentation. [*OTL* 24–vii–1993]

A final quartet – Minton, Schulkowsky, Byron, Madiot – had Madiot and Schulkowsky playing furiously, but by now Byron was sulking, as if disappointed with the company he'd been keeping.

In the coming decade, David Toop would applaud a marketable 'art' version of Avant/Improv that depended on technology viewed as novel commodities ('buy the laptop') rather than a grappling with the facts and possibilities of sound (Oxley's 'build an electro-drumkit and learn how to play it'; Klapper's table of toys). The evidence of Company Week 1993 was that mere resort to novel sonic gizmos like drum machines stunts the dialectic of improvisation. Like people whose conversation consists of 'outrageous' opinions they've picked up from *Independent* think columns, musicians sporting readymade equipment and readymade and unresponsive sonics would be the bane of Free Improvisation in the coming decade. Reduced to a free market of CD sales and celebrity, deprived of the form's realtime dialectic of mimicry and dialogue, all promises of 'freedom' and 'breaking boundaries' are hollow: weasel words for press releases and grant applications. It becomes the perfect static, inoffensive accompaniment to business, media and digital art networking – 'music has died/and no-one cried' [Frank Zappa, 'Yo Cats', *Meets the Mothers of Prevention*, 1985]. Bailey's critique stems from different considerations, but it pinpoints the flatness of the results.

> Lounge electronica . . . it's well attended, but the audience is not required to pay too much attention particularly, and they can in fact – and do – talk over it. It's quite unobtrusive. It's not 'accessible', because they're not bothered about that, but it's so unaggressive. It's like lounge jazz, it's background. Another thing in common with lounge jazz, they have lamps on the tables. If it was lounge jazz they'd have champagne, but they have bottles of water – several each. It must be great for the bottled water industry. I mentioned that to Karen: she said, that's because of the E. [27–vi–2000]

COMPANY WEEK 1994

Derek Bailey's last ever Company Week was held at the Place between 25 and 30 July 1994, and was a celebration of the sheer wackiness – all the fun of the post-fluxus circus – that Bailey cultivates to stave off the boredom of having played every music under the sun and being one of the few musicians to have done so. Fred Frith (guitar), the Shaking Ray Levis (keyboardists Dennis Palmer and Bob Stagner), Steve Beresford (keyboards) and percussionist Roger Turner played on the opening Wednesday night. Then it was international dance night, with butoh dancer Min Tanaka from Japan and tap dancer Will Gaines from the States. On Friday 27 July, cellist Tristan Honsinger and singer Koichi Makigami performed trios with Bailey. Over the weekend (28 to 29 July), Bailey played with Frith, Palmer, Gaines, Tanaka, Makigami and Honsinger. The last set of the week was a duet between Tanaka and Gaines ('*i.e.* no music at all, though there was some sound coming from Gaines', as Bailey put it). It was all too wacky for this gloomy Adornoite, who stayed away ('no fun after Auschwitz, at least, not at Company

Week' etcetera). Luckily, there were to be many post-Company appearances by the guitarist to make up for missing the Last Company Week of All. And even a new Company . . .

A COMPANY PS: TONIC, NEW YORK, APRIL 2001

In 2001, Derek Bailey re-released two Company albums: *Company 5* [Incus CD41] and *Epiphany* [Incus CD42/43]. He also released *Company in Marseille* [Incus CD44/45], an early recording (13 and 14 January 1999) of a group that formed the core of a Company Week he staged in New York between 17 and 20 April 2001. This review of Company at Tonic appeared in *The Wire*:

> Derek Bailey's concept of Company isn't easy to explain, even to denizens of New York's hippest club. A number of musicians freely improvise with each other on successive nights – in various combinations – finding out what each can do, using their powers of mimicry and invention to stretch their usual playing. For musicians with reputations, the prospect can be terrifying: there are no guarantees they won't be left high and dry, sounding awkward, stupid or embarrassingly unresponsive. Although Bailey is sceptical about reputations and commercial 'pull' – pointing out that most famous musicians have been hawking the same wares for the last twenty or thirty years – a Company event lets him exploit his own formidable reputation: improvised fluency and cliché-busting become the order of the day.
>
> Company nights have a tension, a pin-drop drama, that comes from musicianship stripped bare, deprived of the usual smoke and mirrors. This tension is addictive. Other musical events seem flaccid and stage-managed in comparison. Fluid as it is, Company recalls an anti-capitalist mobilisation: you don't know what the mood will be, what will happen, where you'll end up. Unpredictability is the holy grail of modern art: here it's pursued with an informed intelligence that's almost vicious.
>
> On Tuesday, Bailey preceded three nights of Company proper by showcasing five of the ten musicians. He performed a lengthy duet with tap-dancer Will Gaines, and there was a set by Ist, the spectral string trio comprising Simon H. Fell (bass), Mark Wastell (cello) and Rhodri Davies (harp). Coming from a family of dancers, 71 years old, Gaines

tap-danced with Duke Ellington and Count Basie and so had no problems at all with the immanent logic of Bebop. Bop is his rhythmic home, giving his taps an amazingly elastic and tricky attack. Gaines moved to London in 1963 and has worked in entertainment ever since. Bailey announced this was his first visit to the States in 38 years. Bailey likes working with dancers. His association with Min Tanaka, the Butoh dancer, is legendary. There's a characteristic moment in Bailey's playing, where he feels he's been trapped in a predictable rhythm and he scrabbles the beat, like a painter suddenly mixing his colours. Gaines has a neat set of hip rhythms, but nothing 'outside' can faze him either. It was fascinating to watch him respond to a Bailey 'scrabble' by suddenly jutting out his elbows and jabbing his fingers in cross directions. Quite apart from his beats – which have the speed and intricacy Bailey requires from his interlocutors – this physical, whole-body enacting of the music had a wonderful effect on the ensemble. Gestural actions result in responses which catch hold beneath the threshold of conscious thought. Throughout the next three nights, Gaines kept bringing this aspect to the surface.

Ist played one of the most intense and balanced sets they've delivered in their four-year existence. The players pushed beyond decency into assaults on their instruments, causing the attentive observer to wince. Mark Wastell digs into his cello body with the end of his bow and leaves a white scar: his playing sears the memory likewise. Rhodri Davies' harp is Bailey's guitar writ large, the soundworld of Pierre Boulez shot through with the funk and low-humour repartee of the improvisor. The simultaneous crisis and hilarity of Simon Fell's two-bow assault on his instrument is audio-science and Dada in one.

Company proper began on the Wednesday night before a packed, mostly standing audience – young, intense, agog. Min Xiao-Fen plays the *pipa*, a traditional Chinese 'moon lute'. She was immediately so conversant with Ist's Bailey-derived aesthetic – all tenebrous twangs, cruel clicks and tortuous scrapes – that the intimacy was shocking. Xiao-Fen's posture and gestures are utterly traditional, imposing and dignified, but she's capable of licks which sound like 12-bar blues. Her duet with Bailey was a high point. She ended one memorable tangle by scratching the body of her *pipa* just where Wastell had scratched his cello. Contrary to received wisdom, Improvisation's process of gestural reaction is less 'cerebral' than evocative of the surreal inventions and correspondences of sexual congress.

The four other New York musicians were Jennifer Choi (violin),

Annie Gosfield (sampler), Joey Baron (drums) and John Zorn (alto). Classically trained, Choi threw herself into heroic cadenzas, caught by the others like skilled trapezists. When her violin mewed at Wastell seductively, she was talking a language as universal as the baby's understanding of a smooth or wrinkled brow. Again, a duet with Bailey was a highlight, and her strings meshed productively with Ist. After Zorn got over a slightly patronising and jocular start – digging his pal Joey in the ribs every ten seconds – he looked challenged and developed some extraordinary cries that expertly answered Wastell and Fell's bowed upper-strings (unfortunately Zorn had ear-ache on the last night and Bailey sent him home, so the Ist/Zorn encounter wasn't quite consummated). After she'd dumped the atmospheric loops – strategies which freeze the dialogic process and bore the improv listener – samplist Gosfield became a powerful and canny Hammond organist. Her duet with Gaines turned him into Max Roach.

Watching Baron try effects – rolling a bundle of drumsticks to answer the torture-rack creaking produced when Wastell bows the body of his instrument – provided a good example of the Company process. By abandoning a repressive sense of dignity, by really *playing* (in both musical and infantile senses), new sonic orders are glimpsed. It's axiomatic in the visual arts that challenges to 'proper' technique – Dubuffet's infantilism, Asger Jorn's wilful brush stabs, Basquiat's paranoid speed – usher in fresh pictorial expression. Maybe because of the army of talentless clots in rock – who access the anthropomorphic bedrock of 'intuition' and merely produce oppressive bombast – skilled musicians are usually wary of such developments. Perhaps it's the laboratory-like focus of Company which encourages such risk-taking: an ensemble finds itself, drops the charade and plays with impassioned eloquence. Late on Friday night, soundman Ben Bailes handed Bailey the DATs of Company 2001. Here are the tablets of the New Music: a *Well-Tempered Clavier* for cross-cultural interaction. [BW, *The Wire*, June 2001]

6 IMPROV INTERNATIONAL

JAPAN

Japan has played a special role in American and European avant-garde music, both as historical agent and as myth. John Cage – enthused by lectures on Zen Buddhism by Nancy Wilson Ross in the late 1930s and by Daisetz Suzuki in the late 1940s – prepared the ground by developing a fantasy of Japan as a fount of nonlinear thinking, uncorrupted by bad 'Western' rationality. In the event, though, it was Japan's economic comeback after defeat in the Second World War – as linear and rational as any capitalist enterprise – that made sure its aesthetic concepts (and gig opportunities) would attract musicians in the West.

As defeated nations, both Japan and Germany were prevented by the victors from spending grotesque amounts of gross national product on standing armies and nuclear missiles. Nevertheless, both benefited from the long boom (1945–73) created by international Cold War arms spending. The net result was two postwar economic 'miracles' (commentators ignorant of Mike Kidron's permanent arms economy theory resorted to myths about 'national character'). In the late 1980s, Japan's influence – on cuisine, mass culture and hip music – peaked in Europe and America (later slackening off as it encountered slumps and crises of stock market confidence in the mid-1990s). As a form that draws from both avant-garde idealism and mass-mediated materials, Free Improvisation encountered Japan twice over: two shots from the same gun.

Japan's economic boom financed a consumerist binge; Japanese teenagers became fixtures at rock concerts in Western capitals, and Japanese Noise art became *de rigueur* at art festivals. However, this

efflorescence had its roots in less glamorous, more contested times.
When interviewed, current heroes Otomo Yoshihide and Masami Akita
(Merzbow*) cite the names of lesser-known forerunners: Masayuki
Takayanagi (guitar), Kaoru Abe (saxophonist), Motoharu Yoshizawa
(bass) and Aquirax Aida (critic, importer of Incus and ICP records,
promoter). In the 1950s and early 1960s, Takayanagi established a
reputation as a disciple of Lennie Tristano, but later took off into
dizzying realms of freedom, feedback and turbulence: music that speaks
the same high-flown language as Coltrane, Cecil Taylor and Hendrix. In
his obituary of Motoharu Yoshizawa, Bailey wrote:

> I don't know if it's widely known but Yoshizawa, before his adventures
> in the wonderful world of art music, was a working musician – in clubs,
> cabarets etc. – part of whatever passed for the band business in Japan
> in the 1950s and 1960s. That means he worked in and saw the music
> business from the BACK. And a pretty unpleasant sight it can be. So
> musicians/players are usually cynical – about music and often, in fact,
> about everything. To talk about any musical activity and not be cynical
> is usually to open the door to bullshit. Which is why they never talk
> about playing.
>
> But in itself, playing is a life and Yoshizawa lived it to the full and
> his lifetime musical experience was, I would guess, as wide as he could
> make it. And I don't think it's possible to do better than that.

Takayanagi and friends hated the Japanese establishment's infatuation
with jazz: with US bombs raining on Vietnam, the musicians' post-war
enthusiasm for all things American also looked naïve. In June 1970,
Takayanagi and Abe organised a concert named 'Projection for the
Annihilation of Jazz' (issued in an edition of 100 LPs at the time, now
available as *Deconstructive Exchange* [DIW 414]). Unlike most of the
Noise generation who followed, Takayanagi and Yoshizawa had a
grounding in music – in the Western key system, in jazz's rhythmic
syncopation and repartee – plus a commitment to the physical mastery
of their instruments. They had experienced the musical and social
limitations of show business. This allowed them to provide a genuine

---

* It seems extraordinary that anyone so distant from Kurt Schwitters's homely humour
should name himself after his *Merzbau* (Masami should have called himself 'Artaud-in-
the-Hole').

dialectical retort to the establishment's recuperation of jazz. One of the positive results of the fad for Japanese Noise has been the re-release of their extraordinary music. Like Coltrane, they broke open old forms armed with knowledge rather than ignorance. These were the species of rebel Bailey and Bennink could relate to. Aquirax Aida came to London in 1977. He suggested Bailey tour Japan. Although initially reluctant, Bailey finally agreed, and flew to Japan in April 1978. The tour lasted six weeks, with gigs nearly every night. As well as with Abe and Yoshizawa, Bailey played with trumpeter Toshinori Kondo, saxophonist Mototeru Takagi and percussionist Toshiyuki Tsuchitori (known as 'Torhi') – in every combination.

Aida was a kind of Svengali figure – everybody on the Japanese free music scene seemed to work through him. He created the work, I think he even housed some of the musicians, he supplied them with whatever they found necessary. The guys I played with I thought of as Aida's group – they had a name, like CNA or CMM, one of those 60s or 70s things where everyone had a group name made up of letters. Aida had the idea that at each concert I'd play solo, do a duo with each of them and then we'd all play together – I had to put him right about that! Even then I was somewhat decrepit. [Derek Bailey to Stefan Jaworzyn, *Resonance*, vol. 4 no. 2, 1995, pp. 42–3]

Aida put Bailey up in his own personal hotel room, the rest of the band sharing a single suite ('bodies everywhere'). No one knew any English, and Bailey couldn't speak a word of Japanese. He found he was a foot taller than all of them. Audiences were 'anything up to 600 or 700 people'. Bailey loved the trip, and earned enough to buy a car when he returned to England.

In 1999, the Starlight Furniture Company, a record label based in San Francisco, released a recording made during the tour, at Michada-Kavalinka on 3 May 1978. It was named *Aida's Call* [SFC9]. The musicians were Bailey, Yoshizawa, Abe and Kondo. When played a record featuring Takayanagi and Yoshizawa during his Invisible Juke-box for *The Wire*, Bailey noticed something that also characterises the music of *Aida's Call*.*

* A release that shouldn't be confused with *Aida*, a varied and busy solo album recorded

DEREK BAILEY AND THE STORY OF FREE IMPROVISATION

With this there is no reason to stop listening to it. You know what I was saying about the first one [a composed piece], you kind of know what's going on and what's going to go on, here you don't – the story's unfolding, right? But of course it's improvised. I can listen to this and enjoy it. I would guess they're American because they don't have any imperative to put in a bit of urgency just to prove that they're something or other. Europeans don't like playing as relaxed as this, it's like they've got to have their balls on show within the first few seconds of time, particularly in recent years I have to say . . . We could listen to this all afternoon. [10–xi–1998]

'Unfolding' is also a perfect way to describe how Bailey, Yoshizawa, Abe and Kondo played. There are none of the histrionics of nineties 'Noise', where the music appears to be some contribution to a debate about what it's possible to endure – or purchase – as music, gestures that only make sense given the catalogue of commodities known to the listeners. Here, in contrast, the music is self-explanatory. A warm, horizontal flow envelopes the playing. Squarks, pings and skronks are absorbed into a persuasive and beguiling narrative. The musicians are supplying traditional pleasures – harmonious chimes, chugging rhythms, vocalised solos, rich comping (especially Bailey) – as much as they're subverting or deconstructing. Yet they are not conforming to any predefined concept of form. There is sarcasm – reference to 'bad' melody-playing *à la* Albert Ayler – but these *gaucheries* are absorbed into the ensemble process, they do not break the collective spell. No one leaves the table.

The unpretentious lightness and grace of this music provide a contrast to the Free Improvisation being played in Europe at the time. When Bailey was interviewed by Elaine Barkin and John Rahn for *Perspectives of New Music* (a journal published by the University of Washington, Seattle) he expressed a certain alienation from the English scene.

I don't know whether I'm the best person to ask about this because I don't actually spend a lot of time here now, and when I am here I don't

---

in Paris in 1980, and dedicated by Bailey to the memory of the promoter, issued by Incus on vinyl as LP40, and by Dexter's Cigar on CD as dex5.

really look at the scene. A couple of years ago you couldn't walk down Oxford Street without bumping into at least 30 or 40 free improvisors – it was rife, not to say plagued. It seems to have quietened down a bit. But that's just a general impression.
How about Europe?
I think it's quietened down a lot there. The two places where it seems to be very active at the moment are Japan and New York. [*Perspectives of New Music*, Fall/Winter 1982 – Spring/Summer 1983, pp. 50–51]

To anyone but a few lucky globetrotters, Bailey's contentions remain unverifiable, but *Aida's Call* does constitute evidence of a different approach. In Britain, collective sensitivity tends to result in pointillism or reticence: either what Americans call 'ping pong', or a kind of grey and nostalgic emulation of classical modernism. With Yoshizawa, Abe and Kondo, Bailey had found players who maintained collective warmth without either sentimentality or stylistic regression. They could use long notes and harmony without locking themselves into choral sluggishness, maintaining the listening alertness without which Free Improvisation withers. Sadly, both Abe and Aida died in 1978 – aged twenty-nine and thirty-two respectively – depriving the Japanese scene of two crucial figures.

TOSHINORI KONDO

After his experiences with Bailey, trumpeter Toshinori Kondo threw himself into Free Improvisation in Europe, recording a great album named *Artless Sky* with guitarist John Russell and drummer Roger Turner in Luton, England, in 1979, for CAW Records, and playing in a magnificent trio with Han Bennink and Eugene Chadbourne in Rotterdam in 1980 (currently available as *Jazz Bunker* [Leo GY7/8], a two-CD release in Leo Records's Golden Years series). In 1981 he recorded an LP with drummer Paul Lovens, *The Last Supper*, on the Po Tovan label. In the later 1980s, Kondo pursued a career in hi-tech funk, releasing *Kondon* in 1986, an album produced by Bill Laswell – a Japanese trumpeter's version of Miles Davis's synthetic masterpiece *Tutu*. Kondo also pursued a career as a male model.

You could be on the street with him and people would come up and ask for his autograph – not because of his trumpet playing, but because they recognised him from TV adverts. I've bought two cameras in Japan and both times I went with Kondo because he's fantastic at bargaining. One time they gave us a whole bag of accessories just because he was Kondo! This was about 1987/1988. I think he's gone back more to playing now, but he's always had an eye to more mainstream activities. [Derek Bailey to Stefan Jaworzyn, *Resonance*, vol. 4 no. 2, 1995, p. 46]

MIN TANAKA

Dancer Min Tanaka was introduced to Bailey on the 1978 Japanese tour in Sapporo, Hokkaido, by his manager, Kazue Kabata, noted translator and literary interviewer (Tanaka spoke little English, but Kabata was fluent). Bailey and Tanaka first performed together at the Kitchen on West Broadway in New York that year, and in July 1980 in a disused forge in Paris. In 1981, Bailey toured Japan, America and England with Tanaka and drummer Milford Graves, a project that took 'fifteen to eighteen months'. A voluble personality and superbly dramatic performer (a kind of black American John Stevens), Milford Graves added 'dancing and ranting' to the mix, often roaming about the stage with Tanaka. In 1998, Incus released a video – *Mountain Stage* – of Tanaka dancing while Bailey played acoustic guitar. In his patented 'ribald toe-tickler' mode, Bailey described the Hakashu Art Camp organised annually by Tanaka and Kabata in these terms:

> It goes on for about eight weeks every year, and people come from all over the world to study with Min: studying with Min is like some strange religion – he gets them all to walk backwards for seven hours, and then go digging potatoes, then he talks to them about dance. You get these winsome Californians all covered in shit, and they do it just to work with Min – it's beautiful. [*Resonance*, vol. 4 no. 2, 1995, p. 45]

The Japanese use a word for Free Improvisation – *sokkyo* – meaning 'let rise here and now'. Following John Cage, many American avantists interpret such aestheticising abolition of past and future as equivalent to

Zen Buddhism.* In contrast, a historical materialist would point out that Free Improvisation – ritual without preset aim, dedicated to the pursuit of untrammelled musical freedom – actually springs from the Enlightenment, a project inconceivable outside an economy geared towards the limitless expansion of capital. Rather than reflecting the quietism of the traditional Zen poet – an upper-class dropout in rags, begging for rice, writing haiku about drinking saké while sheltering from the endless drizzle – Tanaka embodies the testing of existential limits that Antonin Artaud and Jackson Pollock contributed to the postwar practice of the avant-garde.

In June 1979, art critic John Roberts watched Tanaka and Bailey perform at the ACME Gallery in London. His review showed that writers honed on conceptual and performance art could catch the nuances of Bailey gigs better than critics whose purview is purely musical.

Min Tanaka, prodigious member of the Tokyo-based Body Weather Laboratory (a dance group devoted to the search for 'nature and freedom on both sides of the skin') was briefly in town in June to perform two extemporizations with guitarist Derek Bailey at the ACME. Bailey, whose percussive, rhythmic and harmonic versatility was a delight throughout the whole of the performance, moved around like some peripatetic minstrel, taking the sound to one end of the gallery then the other, forcing Tanaka to adapt his delicate movements to the relocation of sound and preventing his own playing from turning into a recital with dance ... The dance was not only taking place through limb and torso, but through the vibrations of the muscles themselves, bearing out his pronouncement that his dance is predominantly a dance of the skin. The essentialism of the piece – the pared-down movements, the compression and brevity of the style, or non-style – was insistently Japanese, an expression of refinement and understatement like the kabuki of T'ai Chi Ch'uan. The piece also reminded me of those conceptual body events that Fluxus got up to in the 60s and neo-

---

* John Cage's anti-dialectical, anti-social mysticism is actually common to T. S. Eliot's (Anglo-Catholic) *Four Quartets* and Ezra Pound's (Fascist) *Cantos*, a transcendental individualism which permeates all North American high-literary culture, from William James through to Robert Creeley.

Fluxians such as Acconci and Fox got up to in the early-70s, although neither had the guile and poetry of Tanaka.

Naked Japanese men crouching and twitching in corners invariably throws up ritualistic and Buddhist interpretations, but in fact it was remarkably non-religious. The expression was more animistic than anything, with its surface/body struggles, and although unworldly and at times verging on the static, the piece was never meditative, there was a lot going on, only it was articulated in subtle gradations.

Derek Bailey's dissonant, or 'non-tonal' improvisations as he has called them, were more a springboard for Tanaka's improvisations; Tanaka was as much dancing for himself as Bailey was playing for himself; there was counterpoint *and* contradiction. This exacting tension was the strength of the piece. Bailey wasn't simply accompanying Tanaka or vice versa. The music, the wall and the floor were boundaries to be struggled with (in the past Tanaka has 'danced' in a fast running stream) rather than acceded to. [John Roberts, 'Min Tanaka at ACME', *Artscribe*, no. 19, September 1979, p. 57]

'Counterpoint *and* contradiction': Roberts's account sets up the right way to view many free-improvised encounters, where it's more productive to ponder anthropological issues such as competition, co-operation and physical limits than 'musical' or stylistic niceties. In this sense, Free Improvisation is one of the few areas where the 1920s project of abstraction – a direct, natural language transcending divisive semiotic systems of musical genre and language – still prospers. Idiomless Nowness Volapük!

Bailey recalls Tanaka performing at the ICA during Company Week in May 1981:

Min initiated an experiment in which people simply walked on and off the stage playing wherever, whenever and whatever they chose for as long as they liked. Some hours later (this was an all-day concert) the stage was deserted except for Min, centre stage, trembling with exhaustion. Everybody else, it seemed, was in the bar. [*Improvisation*, 1992, p. 135]

One may be sceptical about the value of such exertions, but from the aural evidence, there is no doubt about the effect Tanaka has on Bailey (or, indeed, about Bailey's personal preference for rather more compact performance). *Music and Dance*, a recording of two duo concerts in Paris in 1980, was first put out on cassette, an indication of Bailey's conviction that Tanaka's dancing was important musically. It was only re-released on CD, by John Fahey's Revenant label, in 1996. The recording demonstrates that the movements of Min Tanaka's body bring a distinctive, robust sense of spatial architecture to Bailey's music.

MORE WORK IN JAPAN

Despite the deaths of Abe and Aida, long-term relations between Bailey and Japan were maintained after 1978. On 24 November 1981, he participated in a 'Japanese Company' at Tokyo's Zoujiouji Hall, with Tanaka, Yoshizawa and Kondo, plus saxophonist Mototeru Takagi, trombonist M. Kono, pianist Katsuo Habashi, percussionist Toshi Tsuchitori, and Akio Suzuki on 'tool' (a home-made instrument).

In 1993, Bailey held a full-blown Company Week (25–29 August) at the annual Hakushu Art Camp. The musicians were Motoharu Yoshizawa (bass), Shonosuki Okura (tuzumi, voice), Koichi Makigami (trumpet, voice), Sachiko Nagata (percussion), Kenichi Takeda (electric koto), Wataru Okuma (clarinets, melodica, accordion, voice), Kazue Sawai (koto), Yukihiro Isso (Noh flutes) and Keizo Inoue (alto and soprano sax) – players drawn from traditional Japanese music, jazz, academic ethnology, cabaret, 'anti-pop music' (Takeda), theatre, film music and dance. The oldest participants were Yoshizawa and Inoue (this was only the second time Bailey had played in a Company Week with someone older than himself: the first time had been with Lee Konitz in 1987). Born in 1922, Inoue was a jazz veteran. Previous collaborators he chose to mention for the programme were Steve Lacy, Butch Morris and Peter Brötzmann.

The programme for the first evening's music showed Bailey's habitual technique of 'introducing' the musicians to each other before going on to a full ensemble:

1. Trio: Yoshizawa/Takeda/Okura
2. Duo: Inoue/Okuma

3. Trio: Sawai/Makigami/Bailey
4. Duo: Inoue/Nagata
5. All ten together

Tokyo FM Radio recorded the concerts for a broadcast. It also included snippets from an interview with Bailey. Art Camp attendees were dotting the surrounding landscape and villages with improvised sculptures, and Tanaka led a troupe of nineteen naked acolytes on the Saturday night. Incus later issued a video of Mitsuo Tamura's film of the final two concerts, *Company in Japan* (the musicians remained clothed). Bailey was particularly keen to mention this new format when he spoke to *Resonance* magazine:

> We're putting out a video of one of the Company concerts – shot and edited by a Japanese guy. The editing's quite intriguing – it just cuts from the middle of one group to another – it's only about 30 minutes long, and it was a two-and-a-half-hour concert. It just goes bang bang bang through it.
> SJ: *That sounds kind of bizarre.*
> I like it, I think it works – I don't mind the bizarre. It will be available from 14 Downs Road, London E5 8DS, and worth every penny. [*Resonance* vol. 4 no. 2, 1995, p. 45]

AMERICA

Derek Bailey's relationship with American music has been complex, voracious, twisted and strained. For anyone growing up in the 1930s and 1940s, America was the fount of everything glamorous and swinging. Bailey idolised Charlie Parker and Charlie Christian (it's surely no accident that Derek's embittered alter ego is named *Charlie* Appleyard – or that the Yorkshire surname contains nicknames for both NYC and Bird). As possible musical colleagues, though, the beboppers may as well have been on a different planet from a jobbing guitarist in Sheffield (Bailey has jammed with members of the Count Basie Band and Lionel Hampton, but that was hotel lobby fun, not an entrée to the jazz pantheon). Early in the 1960s, Bailey, Oxley and Bryars realised that if they were ever to achieve anything authentic and innovative, they had to shake off the 'American' influence. The trio toured with Lee Konitz in 1966, but felt disappointed that Konitz had returned from his 'out' experiments to something approaching bebop (albeit an extremely personalised and dry version). In the late 1960s and 1970s, contact with Bennink and the Dutch and Brötzmann and the Germans allowed the British improvisors to feel that they were forging less a national music than a European one, but the break with America was crucial.

As had been the case for Japanese radicals, the background of the Vietnam War meant that any relationship with American culture was bound to be problematic (hell, it was problematic for *Americans*). At the battle of Grosvenor Square, British police charged demonstrators on horseback in order to 'protect the American embassy'. As Frank Zappa noted, what made the Mothers of Invention popular among hairies and students in the sixties was their perceived anti-Americanism. Sociological interpretations of pop emphasise how British youth used American culture to free themselves of a class-ridden and stuffy national culture; the more adult theme of opposing American imperialism – a pressing theme for anyone involved in radical culture – tends thereby to be obscured.

Given the dim view Bailey takes of showbiz and commercialism, the idea of American music as a liberating force had to be fraught with irony. Writing in *Time Out* about Free Improvisation in 1972, using a polemical tone he has since abandoned, critic John Fordham put it like this:

> The din, if you're unprepared, can verge on the traumatic. Not because it's that unpleasant, or that deafening, or even inexpert (it's far from being *that*) but because it continually reinforces this awesome, discomfiting *strangeness* . . . You've woken up on the other side of the world and someone's broken into your head and made a guinea pig out of your brain. The strangeness is not an accident. For some, it is a necessary adjunct to a real relaxation of outlook, not only toward music, but toward everything else. The politicising of music doesn't end with writing desperate lyrics about Vietnam from a swimming pool in Beverly Hills. Its sameness is its politics, its predictability is its politics. When [R. D.] Laing took his life in his hands and prefaced a book with

the warning 'few books today are forgiveable' he might have done the same for records too. Music can't afford to be surprising because if it sounded genuinely different you might not recognise it as music. And if *that* happened, you're faced with a decision that you can't draw on experience to resolve. Whether to risk listening in a new way, or to lock it out and go back to the game according to the rules. [John Fordham, *Time Out*, 6–12 October 1972, p. 22]

Derek Bailey's reluctance to call what he does 'jazz' is a product of these special circumstances. Musicians in mainland Europe benefited from transatlantic contacts forged in the immediate postwar years, contacts denied British musicians by an idiotic ban on 'foreign musicians taking our jobs' – instigated by the Musicians' Union and enforced by the state. Misha Mengelberg and Han Bennink could hardly feel the same need as Bailey and other British musicians for a complete 'break' with the likes of Eric Dolphy – they had played on one of his best records. Jean Georgakarakos's extraordinary Actuel series on the BYG label forged a lasting link between the ideals of May 1968 Paris and the militant free jazz of Braxton, Shepp and Sun Ra. Free-jazz bassist Alan Silva found conditions so much better in Paris that he moved to France.

Nevertheless, Bailey's demand for an utterly new music was not just a product of parochialism, as evidenced by the fact that Tony Oxley – celebrated as London's top jazz drummer – was also committed to the cause. Although Oxley's position at Ronnie Scott's meant he played with such legends of jazz as Sonny Rollins and Johnny Griffin, the music they were playing was already formed. He was there to supply a good approximation to Max Roach or Elvin Jones, not to introduce his own innovations. To this day, Peter Brötzmann is convinced that what he plays is 'jazz' (a claim supported by the fact that, in William Parker and Hamid Drake, his Die Like A Dog Quartet nabbed the strongest rhythm section in American jazz) and so has more to express than the anti-jazz posse 'fumbling around playing this artificial shit' [*The Wire* 188].* Yet, despite this retention of the 'umbilical link' to jazz, Brötzmann appreciates 'Mr Bailey, *le grand señor*, responsible for a lot of kicks in our

* Keith Rowe insists Brötzmann meant AMM [*The Wire*, 190/191, p. 8], which may or may not be the case.

asses' [7–iii–2000, sleeve note to the reissue of *Nipples*]. The endless debate notwithstanding, the high status Derek Bailey enjoys in America today – curating concert series at Tonic, New York's hippest venue, lauded by stars like John Zorn and Pat Metheny and Diamanda Galas – could not have come about without his aesthetic brinkmanship, his scorn for the museumification of a once-great music, his 'break with jazz'.

Looking back from the vantage point of the year 2000, Bailey had this to say to an interviewer who observed, 'I'd say the situation for Free Improvisation is much better than it was two decades ago. Free-er.'

As regards Company, when I started it in the mid-70s, there were all kinds of inhibitions between players regarding who they would play with and who they wouldn't play with. At that time, Company was necessary. Now, it's different. Apart from one or two monuments, everybody seems to be prepared to play with anybody. There's no need for me to put Company together now. There are Companys everywhere. [fax interview with Hannes Schweizer, vii–2000]

Given that Bailey has now recorded with American jazz stars like drummer Tony Williams, guitarist Pat Metheny and pianist Cecil Taylor, it is chastening to look down the list and see how slow and tentative the *rapprochement* between America and Bailey actually was. After Lee Konitz in 1966, Bailey's international contacts were from Holland and Germany. Anthony Braxton and Steve Lacy were the first Americans to show any enthusiasm for his playing, avant-gardists who had predicated their careers on leaps into the unknown. Bassist Kent Carter involved himself with Free Improvisation from the mid-1960s onwards and played with Bailey in combinations that included Lacy and Stevens in the early 1970s. Nevertheless, American jazz in general remained deaf to Free Improvisation until it became 'post-modernised' in the 1980s, vindicating Bailey's contention that by the late 1960s it was dying, a retrospective and sentimental genre.

This provides the opportunity for a fantastic debate about the relationship between music and society, aesthetics and politics. After all, the late 1960s saw incredible things: an upsurge in black militancy, riots in the ghettos, the Tet Offensive, near revolution in Paris. Situationist texts sprayed on walls in May 1968 provided 1970s punk and 1990s anti-capitalism with their sharpest slogans. How come jazz was going into reverse? A proper understanding of the role of art means disagreeing with a phrase of Trotsky's much quoted by left politicos who'd rather not be pestered by the claims of art: contra Trotsky, art is *not* always 'consigned to the baggage train of history' – it can be something dreamed by the train driver, a prophetic testing-out of possibilities.

In other words, the lack of interest shown by jazz musicians in what the European Free Improvisors were playing was an index of future compromise and defeat. Individually, this failure of nerve was evidenced by the flight of music radicals into academia (a flight well described by Frank Kofsky in *John Coltrane and the 60s Jazz Revolution* – Kofsky knew what he was talking about, he did the same thing himself). Jazz's immanent critique of commodified music bottled out by retreating to social zones which, while supposedly above the exigencies of popular-entertainment dumbness, actually confirm class society – though from a different perspective. Music is objective, subject to scientific scrutiny: however irrelevant-seeming to the new black middle class intent on preserving their retrospective 'heritage', Derek Bailey's pursuit of freedom is actual and concrete. Just like Coltrane's. The reaction of the 1980s – the rollback of progressive gains, the widening gap between rich and poor, the Pyrrhic victory of black culture as a museum piece policed by a middle-class elite – was not just experienced as economic and political misery by masses of people, it also shattered the truth and integrity and vitality of a counter-culture.

Of course, fusing intellect, body and soul – smashing the alienation of self (art) and society (politics) – cannot be achieved by any single individual, however determined. It's a result of the great, uplifting moments of history (Beethoven and 1789; Jimi Hendrix and 1968); nevertheless the seeds of such fusions are sown by people who are clear and uncompromising about pursuing whatever thread connects them to historical truth – whether that's Little Richard insisting on the most explosive, colourful shirt and electric guitarism possible (and thus producing Jimi Hendrix), or Guy Debord denouncing Parisian intellectuals for surrendering aesthetic truth to mass-market lies (and thus providing key slogans for May 1968). Put bluntly, in the 1970s, Derek Bailey and

Free Improvisation took the next step for the evolution of world music; the paucity of 'amens' from the leaders of American jazz was indication that a hard, reactionary rain was going to fall – which it did: an infamous period called 'the 1980s', dominated by Ronnie Reagan and Maggie Thatcher, the Human League and Haircut 100 . . . and Stanley Crouch.

In 1976, critic Steve Lake told of an exchange between Anthony Braxton and Stanley Crouch, one-time loft-scene drummer who became champion bully for corporate neo-conservative jazz in the 1980s. Crouch was telling Braxton that 'few white players have anything to say in improvised music, and European whites absolutely nothing at all'.

AB: There is nobody on the planet who plays like Derek Bailey.

SC: [*sighing deeply*] Well, maybe that's because nobody *wants* to sound like Derek Bailey. [Steve Lake, 'Bailey's Academy of Music', *Melody Maker*, 31 July 1976, p. 22]

These positions were prescient. Crouch's views won out in the 1980s, to the detriment of the development of both Free Improvisation and the black struggle for freedom.

The most progressive event in American music in the eighties was No Wave, a post-punk, Ornette-inspired explosion that occurred at the start of the decade in New York. Everyone played with everybody, and the music got pushed right out. Harmolodics grabbed aleatoric and improvised freedoms and aligned them to a funk that was populist and rowdy and unfinished, the opposite of the sleek, commodified cool of disco, jazz or fusion. However, it went off like a nuclear test underground, seismic in its implications, yet denied visibility by an increasingly conservative mass media. James Blood Ulmer was a new Hendrix, Shannon Jackson a new Muhammad Ali, but their radicalism was occluded by the racism, conformism and yuppie-flattering mores of the eighties.

Derek Bailey related to No Wave via two young Americans who wanted to rewire every known connection between pop and art, black and white, high and low, politics and entertainment: Eugene Chadbourne and John Zorn. On the way, the pair also happened to unearth – and relaunch – the project/object of Dada, Bebop and Freakdom:

everything can happen at once – pleasure, truth, songs, improv, fun, politics, education, sex, jokes, sensuality, intellect, electricity, abstraction, history, the future, my own weird proclivities – and anyone who says these things are incompatible and don't belong together and shouldn't be mixed, they are The Enemy. War!!!

In 1997, Incus issued a duet recording by Zorn and Chadbourne recorded in New York in 1980. It works as a summary of everything these two American Wunderkinder heard in the Free Improvisation of Derek Bailey, the result of three years' partnership in the pursuit of musical freedom. *Hi-Fi News* hailed the long-delayed release in these terms:

EUGENE CHADBOURNE/JOHN ZORN
IN MEMORY OF NIKKI ARANE
INCUS CD23 61m 16s
Back in 1980, Chadbourne and Zorn proposed an aesthetic in which the contrary impulses of Dada and Constructivism were indistinguishable. Inspired by the way Derek Bailey had dumped harmony and regular beats as so much cossetting kitsch, the duo created a spindly, rhythmically-decisive music that recalls the mad machinery of a Max Ernst collage. Or maybe not mad, just structural clarity in a world awash with consumer fantasies: a sonic record of engineers at work, rather than entertainers trying to ingratiate. Crystalline, humorous and totally original: the purist blueprint for two astonishing project/objects. [A:1] [*Hi-Fi News*, April 1997]

EUGENE CHADBOURNE

Eugene Chadbourne's take on Derek Bailey and Free Improvisation is particularly intriguing. His concept of musical freedom is unsectarian and politically sophisticated enough to make links between Free Improvisation and protest folk, underground rock, punk and jazz. Chadbourne was born in 1954 and raised in Boulder, Colorado. He took up the guitar at age eleven, after seeing the Beatles on the Ed Sullivan Show. He and his high-school friends listened to Hendrix, Zappa and Beefheart. As the rock scene became more commercialised, he lost interest, trading his electric guitar for a Harmony six-string acoustic, and studying bottleneck blues styles. Unusually for a left-wing folkie capable of hilarious topical songs (Phil Ochs was an early inspiration), Chadbourne has a huge appetite for music, the 'weirder' the better. For some years he wrote about jazz, interviewing musicians from the Duke Ellington Orchestra, the Sun Ra Arkestra and the Association for the Advancement of Creative Musicians. However, it was hearing Derek Bailey that made him decide to make a record. How did he find his first Incus releases?

> I remember getting them from a woman who sold records mail order, Mary-Lou Webb, she used to work for Cecil Taylor and for Arista when they were releasing all that stuff. I bought a Derek Bailey record with Evan Parker and Han Bennink, because I'd heard of Han Bennink, and I thought, this is a completely different kind of music – in blibs and blobs – very unique. Braxton also was praising Derek Bailey a lot in interviews, so I got interested. Here was a guy with a completely unique guitar style. I used to do this exercise where I would as quickly as possible try to do imitations of Charlie Christian, Chuck Berry and Derek Bailey, back-to-back as fast as possible – just because they're such different playing styles. The guy created his own guitar style – you can imitate it and instantly people will know you're imitating Derek Bailey. With that guitar style you can really play endless variations of it, it's like a fantastic system. The bugaboo for so many guitarists is – do you want to get drawn into it and just do that, because there's plenty of room in that kind of music, or do you want to do something else? [EC 15–vi–1993]

Chadbourne was impressed with Bailey's way of handling people too:

> He's decided not to make himself aloof. That's what I like about him. Right from the very beginning, the first time I ever sent him a record and wrote to him, he wrote back, a very nice letter. The first time I came to England he helped organise some things, and he continues to be very approachable, it's wonderful. That's one of the most important things about him, he's a touchstone. [EC 28–ix–1998]

To Chadbourne's ears, Bailey's approach to the guitar had staked out a particular possibility. It led him to suspect that the Columbia label's 'fusion' genre was not the solution to the 'art versus commerce' quandary encountered by underground rock and free jazz.

EC: I liked the electric jazz when it first came in, but it got really corny really fast. There was a dividing line even between one Mahavishnu album and another one. Chick Corea degenerated really quickly. Even some of the Miles Davis stuff with all the electric guitars that people like so much now, at the time we didn't really like it, we thought it was cheesy. One of my friends got a copy of *Pangaea* and said, it just sounds like a Deep Purple album!
OTL: But not as good . . .
EC: We were critical of the guitar players and we thought it was nothing compared to Derek Bailey or Hendrix even. We just thought it was cheesy. [*EC* 28–ix–1998]

Chadbourne's *Volume One: Solo Acoustic Guitar* was released in 1975 on Parachute, a label he founded with Zorn. In retrospect, it's a typically brilliant Chadbourne production, replete with virtuosity, humour and invention. However, for anyone who'd grown up with albums like *Sergeant Pepper*, *We're Only In It for the Money* and *Electric Ladyland*, the visual imagery was extraordinarily dour. The black-and-white was no doubt born of economic necessity, but Chadbourne was also making a point. Photographs on the back showed Chadbourne earnestly 'preparing' his guitar with skewers and pipe cleaners. In one photo he's playing the back of his guitar with a brush drumstick. The photograph on the cover showed a crumbling brick wall with a tiny window from which trailed a power line. The album title was scribbled over the wall like graffiti. In 1976, Caroline Records (a subsidiary of Virgin) released an album with tracks by four different guitarists: Fred Frith, Gerry Fitzgerald, Hans Reichel and Derek Bailey, a project made possible by Frith's rock band Henry Cow having signed to Virgin (and made affordable by the success of Mike Oldfield's *Tubular Bells*). Its black-and-white cover and technical diagrams about pick-ups, footpedals and loudspeakers were likewise rebuffs to the commercial glamour and pretention of progressive rock, a refocus on the actual means of musical production (the album was recorded in part on Tom Newman's barge and mixed in Nick Mason's studio). For both Frith and Chadbourne, Free Improvisation represented a rebuke to the overblown claims of the rock spectacle. Living in New York – in 1977 Chadbourne and Zorn played on Frank Lowe's *Lowe & Behold* with Billy Bang, Joe Bowie, Butch Morris and Polly Bradfield – Chadbourne had a healthy respect for jazz, but both musically and strategically, the example of Bailey and Incus was crucial.

Chadbourne produced several more records in this vein (he considers the second much better, cut once he'd recognised the 'mistakes' of the first). However, his love of songs reasserted itself – and meanwhile punk rock exploded.

> I wasn't listening to any rock, and then I read an article about the Dead Kennedys and Black Flag. I was living in New York and it was by Robert Christgau and of course he was completely wrong about everything and he said these were Nazi groups playing Nazi music – I don't know if I'm quoting him exactly, but that was the basic drift of it. I was intrigued – why should any bands be playing Nazi music? It seemed such an insane thing to do and then checking it out I realised it was *anti*-Nazi music. Reading descriptions of the music – it had no melody, it was a bunch of noise – I thought, well finally they're getting back to playing something decent. [*EC* 15–vi–1993]

Chadbourne wanted the freedom to break into a song during a Free Improvisation.

> In the late seventies we were tripping about in America and coming to Europe and trying to figure out, what direction can we go in that's different. When I played with Toshinori Kondo and the Italian drummer Andrea Centazzo, we got into playing little bits of other music. Now with Zorn, we would throw in some jazz or bebop and walk or swing for twenty seconds, but with a trumpet player and a drummer I was quoting songs from when I started playing guitar – Paul Revere and the Raiders, all this kind of stuff. As it went on, sometimes I'd play the whole song – the excerpts got longer. Some of these other improvisors didn't like that – if you play a song it's 'no longer free'. Well, it's free – you can do what you like on top of a song. It's going to end in a few minutes and the rest of the night's going to be before us, what's the big deal? Finally I liked it enough that I thought of doing a combination – the country songs with this kind of stuff. [*EC* 15–vi–1993]

It's important to note that Chadbourne does not compromise Free Improvisation by organising it from above. The songs arrive out of the improvising process. Drummer Jimmy Carl Black says Chadbourne can think of a song to go with practically any beat he can come up with. A duet performance with Billy Jenkins in east London (29 September 1998: as Ed Baxter's publicity had it, 'a meeting made in Stratford') became a virtuosic display of pop memory as the pair kept transforming songs they were playing into different songs. Free Improvisation loses its edge if it gets locked into regular harmony or rhythm, the musical gestures lose their dramatic isolation from each other, their sense of physical abrasion; Chadbourne's songs do not enforce such parameters, but arise as vectors of excitement within the flux. If the song happens to drag everything into its orbit, it's because there is enough energy to carry everyone.

Although Eugene Chadbourne is a name in indie rock – his band Shockabilly signed to Rough Trade, his collaboration with Camper Van Beethoven is famous – he has behaved careerwise like a free improvisor. He has an interesting slant on what signing to a major entails, and claims that he emerges from a tour – selling his own CDs and tapes out of a suitcase, smoking pot with fans, staying at friends' houses – better able to feed his family than a star who requires top hotels, hired limousines and a salaried entourage. Word-of-mouth ensures Chadbourne's gigs are packed, and the improv scene supplies him with brilliant musicians. Socialists who believe that mass-mediated culture is the only terrain worth contesting may cheer the chart positions of a Bruce Springsteen or Rage Against The Machine, but such idealism is continually disappointed by the fact that spectacular apparitions like these are driven economically by the worst side of the system: the pressure to accumulate capital for record labels and promoters ('the industry') is enormous. Corporate-sponsored 'socialism' becomes an ideological fixture that prevents the bands commenting on the ironies (that is, economic actuality) of the situation (so we reach the paradox that Zappa, George Clinton, Devo and Negativland are better dialectical materialists than many overt flag-wavers for the left). As against such sad splits between politics and aesthetics, Eugene Chadbourne has invented a new category: the hobo improvisor.

Derek Bailey has little time for the campfire simplicities of a political songwriter like Woody Guthrie, believing that Popular Front singalongs were almost sinisterly patronising. However, Chadbourne shows that Guthrie's ethic – leavened via Phil Ochs with marijuana – can connect to Free Improvisation: refusing the deals and compromises that create impersonal and boring musical events can be allied to the highest aesthetic aims. In other words, Chadbourne is not supplying phoney folk as a solace for urban ills (a corruption of consciousness that bedevilled Communist Party promotions and music criticism, and lives on in liberal preference for 'world' over commercial or art music). Chadbourne fuses cutting-edge experimentation to anti-corporatism, revealing thereby the politics that underlies all Free Improvisation (whether or not the musicians are conceptually equipped to know it). People who order CD-Rs from Chadbourne [Dr Eugene Chadbourne, 707 Longview Drive, Greensboro, NC 27403–2018, USA] are frequently sent 'unique mixes', featuring excerpts from unreleased gigs and home recordings, or even the originals themselves: Chadbourne thus pursues the project of radical Modern Art, which is to make every mundane fragment gleam with the light of the Absolute (which, for the Marxist, is nothing other than the total process of human interaction with nature and other humans: the social process determining Hegel's Spirit). Chadbourne liberates Free Improvisation from the bourgeois aspiration that would make it 'art', insisting instead that it's a clutter collage of the actual life of the itinerant musician. Like Bailey, Chadbourne defetishises virtuosity, forcing the audience to replace stunned admiration with responsive thought. He repels philistines who want proofs of quality with 'murk', 'chaos' and 'rubbish', and thereby avoids the creative paralysis instigated by record industry and promotional concepts of dependable product. The 'accident' becomes a new way of organising sound. Just make sure the CD-R is crackle-free.

JOHN ZORN

An unlikely cross between Phil Woods and Berry Gordy, John Zorn is simultaneously altoist, composer, label mogul, socio-musical prophet and tangfastic panjandrum of the 'downtown' tag. He deserves comparison to the most radical manifestations of American music. Politically, he lacks the historical-materialist understanding of capitalism and fascism that undergirds the songs and statements of both Zappa and Chadbourne, and instead he takes refuge in a dodgy brand of cultural Zionism. Some of the contributors to *Arcana* (a Zorn-instigated collection of writings about music, which was published in 2000) used social Darwinist formulations a professed anti-racist editor should be ashamed of. However, his wishywashy attitude towards bourgeois ideology notwithstanding, Zorn's musical integrity and support for Derek Bailey and Free Improvisation cannot be doubted. In turn, Bailey is fiercely loyal to Zorn. As a free improvisor – the touchstone of Bailey's practical reason – Zorn is quite simply fantastic. Bailey+Zorn is one of the most exciting duos on the planet, both exhibiting the fierce precision and decisiveness that make music shocking and erotic (Zorn's contributions to Company Week 1991 were detailed above, pp. 270–7).

The first recorded document of them playing together was made at the Kitchen in New York on 18 September 1981. Some idea of the perceived difficulty of Derek Bailey's music in America – after twenty years of regular appearances in Britain, Europe and Japan – may be gained from journalist Steve Lake's remark that what Bill Laswell had done in 1981 was get the audience in, let Bailey begin, and lock the doors [*The Wire* no 12]. Bailey had played in America before (there was a solo gig at the Museum of Art in San Francisco on 23 March 1973, another solo at Soundscape New York on 3 November 1979, and a brief tour with Evan Parker in October 1980 culminating in a concert at the Great American Music Hall in San Francisco with Henry Kaiser (guitar), Toshinori Kondo (trumpet) and the ROVA saxophone quartet on 21st October), but he was neither well known nor accepted when Zorn embraced him.

With Prime Time, Ornette Coleman made discordant music populist by mobilising an excess of electric guitars. Although Miles Davis flooded his post-*Bitches Brew* bands with keyboard players, he employed just one electric guitarist. To Twelve Tone or free-jazz ears, restricting this fabulous font of untempered noise to a single source kept Miles's music fairly square (or 'cheesy' in Chadbourne's terminology). Ornette on the other hand used two guitar players, playing loud and simultaneously, creating a link between the untuned onslaught of punk and free jazz. Zorn and Laswell went one better than Ornette. At the Kitchen, they used three electric guitarists: Fred Frith, Sonny Sharrock and Bailey. What was played was subsequently issued on Robert Musso's Muworks label. Unfortunately, *Improvised Music New York 1981* [1991, Muworks MUW1007] is not that great.

There is much boomy rhetoric, and heavy usage of anxiety intervals. Snatches of voices from short-wave radios (Fred Frith?) exacerbate the desolate, impersonal atmosphere. A powerful ensemble is threatened, but never quite happens. Bill Laswell (bass) and Charles Noyes (drums) sound like they'd like to rock out, but in this company feel shy. The Bailey/Zorn duet (track 4) is brilliant: the music suddenly focuses and becomes real. Zorn is vocalising through his alto, producing hysterical cries like a victim of rape or torture. Bailey's comping – differently fingered realisations of the same pitch following each other in slow succession – is cruelly measured, as if he is pointing out the architecture of Zorn's hysterical expressionism. The two musicians introduce an intent and control missing from the surrounding gothickry: the music becomes pliant, argued. Rather than merely evoking radical textures, Bailey and Zorn bring the light of consciousness to bear on their notes; sonority is no longer rolled off as its own justification, it's processed and developed. However, none of the other musicians take off from what the pair play, and the music drifts back to doomy rhetoric. Bailey and Zorn think like each other, their wits matched as equally as Bailey/Oxley or Bailey/Braxton. The compatability is uncanny.

By the 1980s, Jean Karakos had shortened his name from the 'Georgakarakos' who had produced the free-jazz Actuel series. Relocating to New York, he hooked up with Bill Laswell and founded a label named Celluloid. In 1983, they issued *Yankees*, a studio improvisation between Zorn, Bailey and trombonist George Lewis. In contrast to the blow-out at the Kitchen, this was a properly focused date. The three began with chirrups and squeaks, almost a parody of modernist sound dispersal, then inch towards jazzy exchanges. A sense of satirical humour pervaded the session, aided by Zorn's reed-only quacks and game calls, Lewis's trombone adding puff and grandeur. The album title was in line with Zorn's use of various sports as models for directing improvisation, and well describes the flash and speed of the playing. When *Yankees* was re-released by Charly in 1998, annotator Simon Hopkins made the point that it has often been guitarists – he listed Henry Kaiser, Elliott Sharp, Bill Frisell and 'even' Buckethead – who 'get' Bailey before other listeners, pointing to his awesome technical command of harmonics. Nevertheless, among Celluloid's other releases – which included Whitney Houston duetting with Archie Shepp on Hugh Hopper's 'Memories', Bill Laswell's robot-funk outfit Material, John McLaughlin, the Last Poets, a Shannon Jackson solo drum'n'poetry record and Manu Dibango's Afro-disco – *Yankees* sat as a bizarre and isolated example of drumless, open-ended speculation.

John Zorn played a great deal with Bailey in the eighties, playing a Company tour in Britain and Company weekend in New York in 1982, and a Company Week in London in 1984. On 14 and 15 September 1993, Bailey played two nights with Zorn at the Knitting Factory in New York. On the first night, they played with Ikue Mori on drum machines; on the second night, bassist Mark Dresser joined them. Before he confused the issue by introducing atrocity photographs as political 'protests' (and providing homilies about humanity's 'darker side'), Zorn had a fine line in connoisseur S&M pornography for his record sleeves. His keen ear for rhythm and the precision of his reed control also suggest something scarily violent and sexual, nowhere better manifested than in his playing over these two nights. Although in their opening duo, Zorn and Dresser were over-reliant on jazz motifs, what they played with Bailey was explosive and fantastic. Long notes would be leant on until they splintered, delivering cloudbursts of sonic shrapnel. The ability to play slowly while thinking fast – preparing for the next crisis – created startling music. Once pushed by Bailey into the realm of non-referentiality – abstract noise collage rather than 'music' – Zorn made things so directly *physical* it escaped the Cagean conceptualism that can freeze his compositions. Zorn's dramatic use of dynamics – sudden, hair-raising bursts of volume which fuse the histrionics of Marshall Allen to the *tutti* of Edgard Varèse – caused Bailey to resort to his volume-control foot-pedal, showing that resourcefulness that makes Bailey-watchers smile. These improvisations became Noh plays of physical limit and relief orgasm: rather than his gigantic back catalogue, or his fame as the panjandrum of the 'downtown' scene, it's gigs like these that explain Bailey's respect for Zorn.

A SOLO PERFORMANCE

In the midst of his international entanglements, Derek Bailey was still liable to pop up in England playing solo. On 24 April 1994, he played a solo set at the Cambridge Conference of Contemporary Poetry. He was introduced by poet and mail-order bookseller Peter Riley, who declared that Free Improvisation and the modernist poetry associated with Cambridge pursue parallel paths – mainly because they've been left by public purchasers and funding bodies to 'fend for themselves'. Highly amplified and clangorous – in marked contrast to the dulcet tones of the preceding poets – Bailey's first set suggested a post-tonal Bach improvising on an mbira (the African 'thumb piano'): a speculative structure built of sonorities which resist the servitude of temperance. Remnants of highly affecting modulations littered the music, as incongruous as plastic-drainpipe T-connections in a shanty-town construction. As in late Beethoven, the sole guarantee of coherence is the pursuit of freedom, a yearning for spaces unconstrained by the parameters of what has preceded. This quest itself generates 'form', but it's not balanced like a baroque portico, it's poised like a big yellow arrow. Harmonic turbulence – a hectic dialectic of contrary arguments – works itself into definite peaks which stay behind in the mind as markers of progress.

Conscious that he was trespassing in a festival devoted to words, Bailey said he felt he should keep his mouth shut, so he replaced his traditional mid-solo-set chat with 'some pictures': two videos that Anthony Howell had made of him playing guitar for his video magazine *Grey Suit* (Cardiff, ix–1993; the soundtrack is now available as an Incus CD-R, *Filmed*). One camera had been trained on Bailey's right hand, the other on the left: Howell had been left wondering how to combine them. The sheer oddness of mechanical recording, its dislocation of reality and personality, was suddenly made manifest. After the video show, Bailey did a fleet, light improvisation: 'not as good as the video,' he quipped.

Poets Helen Macdonald, D. S. Marriott and Pierre Alferi had already upset any ontological assurance about language and its relationship to the world, and it was amusing to watch Bailey do the same with his own, non-literary materials of presentation and re-presentation. His final improvised solo consisted of loud, dissonant clusters, with attention paid to their decay and the notes that hung behind, like an impressionist painter noting the colour of residual shadows.

DEREK BAILEY PROVIDES ACE ALBUMS FOR
US MARKET SHOCK . . .

In September 1994, Zorn and Bailey recorded an album at the Knitting Factory named *Harras*, a trio with bassist William Parker. Having severed relations with Warner Brothers in the late 1980s, Zorn was starting to build a distribution network for his own and other 'downtown' releases. In the mid-1990s, he proposed a series of albums that would feature Bailey playing with conventional rhythm sections, recorded in state-of-the-art hi-fi. These albums – *Saisoro* [Tzadik TZ7205] by Derek and the Ruins, *The Last Wave* [DIW 903] with Laswell and drummer Tony Williams, *guitar, drums 'n' bass* [Avan 060] with DJ Ninj, and *Mirakle* [Tzadik 7603] with Jamaaladeen Tacuma and Calvin Weston – are such clear showcases for Bailey's talents that some of his supporters felt suspicious. The editor of *Rubberneck* magazine, Chris Blackford, for example, confided to Simon Fell that he found the music two-dimensional and compromised. I too had misgivings about *Harras* (a release that, despite its lavish presentation, Bailey maintains 'disappeared without trace'). Writing in *Hi-Fi News* (where the brief of recommending 'product' for use on top-end audiophile equipment continually grates against the live ethos of Free Improvisation, yet where – for ten years, anyway – the lack of a music policy (and record-label advertising) has allowed uncensored opinion*), I compared

---

* This era may be gone; alarmed at the arcane nature of my recommendations, editor Steve Harris has now begun cutting my copy and interpolating 'mainstream' reviews on my page.

Harras unfavourably to *One Time*, a trio record issued on Incus, with Bailey, drummer John Stevens and bassist Kent Carter, recorded in Leicester in November 1992. As my column appears under the heading 'Jazz', I had to begin with some shuffling of generic tags:

> Guitarist Derek Bailey has resisted the 'jazz' pigeon-hole so successfully, he is in danger of being categorised as 'postmodern classical', alongside Kronos Quartet, Michael Nyman and *Jacques Loussier Plays Bach*. Two new Bailey releases feature two of the best bassists in modern jazz, serving to remind us how rooted he is in jazz seriousness about improvisation. Not that *One Time* [Incus CD22] sounds like 'jazz', though the luscious presentness of the instruments does recall Weather Report's first album. Bassist Kent Carter (Booker Ervin, Sonny Stitt, Paul Bley, Steve Lacy) and drummer John Stevens take Bailey into a charged and magical world on this superbly-3D recording from the City Gallery in Leicester.
>
> *Harras* [Disk Union/Avant AVAN056] was recorded live at New York's Knitting Factory, with altoist John Zorn and bassist William Parker. It is two-dimensional compared to *One Time*, the players don't create space so much as a single three-twine thread that twirls itself up into glittering frenzies. Zorn's jazz licks contribute to the linear feel. Rockists will wig out to Bailey's juicy distortions and Parker's funky freedoms. [*Hi-Fi News*, May 1996]

'Two-dimensional' (the term was chosen before Fell transmitted Chris Blackford's remark to me) actually registers the old quarrel between pop, rock and soul production, designed to give records maximum oomf in your loudspeakers, and audiophile classical production, designed to reproduce the real-space actuality of the original playing. Actually, it does not diminish the stature of Bailey's *oeuvre* that he is opportunistic enough – casual enough about his recorded legacy, judging record dates by the fun to be had in the studio rather than the quality of the results – to let slip some punchy commercial albums (indeed, it was the prospect of this dialogue with the world of commercial sound inhabited by most people that first suggested the commercial potential of a Bailey biography). As newcomers like John Zorn and Alex Ward and Pat Thomas insist, we are born into a world of commercial mediations, and to refuse to act upon that world is to live in cloud-cuckoo-land.

None of these considerations affected Bailey. As usual, he concentrated on the playing experience rather than the recorded product. This is what he said about *Harras*:

> That was a group that had no predetermined model. I liked it quite a bit. Rough as fuck, mind you. Nice playing with William but without a drummer; it gives me lots of opportunity to play rhythm, which I enjoy. Whether people recognise it as rhythm, I don't know, but I think of it as rhythm. [DB to John Corbett, *Pulse!* March 1996, p. 59]

Bailey might concentrate on the playing, but for the fan writing record reviews, Zorn's concept for Bailey releases was manna from heaven. Manifesto time!

DEREK AND THE RUINS
SAISORO
TZADIK TZ7205 CD

Music to be stuffed in the ear of every reader of *Guitar Player* and *Kerrang!* At last, accompanists have been found who can amplify the rock and blues fundamentals of Derek Bailey's guitar. The echo of Derek and the Dominos in the band's title can be no accident; surely this is a bid for 'Layla' supremacy, comeuppance time for rock's blinkered heroes.* If they hadn't been tied to John McLaughlin's music-school harmonies (and his one-dimensional, 'apron-string' concept of solos), The Mahavishnu Orchestra might have sounded like this.

The Ruins (Masuda Ryuichi – bass, Yoshida Tatsuya – drums) have a reputation as a Tokyo punk band, worthy constituents of John Zorn's 'hardcore triangle'. However, the meaning of 'punk' has mutated since 1977. There is no homely amateurism here; the Ruins' chops are Bad Brains-like, fusion sharp. Tatsuya has the trenchant brutality of a Shannon Jackson. The punk element is not lumpen but advanced: they can hear right into Bailey's atonal intervals and abrasive clusters. Spindly eviscerations flower into spiky alien blooms: genuine metal music. There hasn't been more exciting guitar mayhem since the No Wave tide of Blood Ulmer and Last Exit.

As a player, Derek Bailey has turned over a new leaf; for someone of his stature, this is a major achievement. The composer Anton Webern

---

* Derek says this was a joke of Karen Brookman's, said in Zorn's hearing, and that nothing more was said or thought about it until the CD arrived under this name.

brought atonality and attention to negative (or silent) shapes into music. By applying these to rock/jazz practice, Bailey successfully kickstarted a new genre (it resists naming, but Free Improvisation will do). The difficulties of his 80s playing – interpreted by many as an aesthetically correct denial of guitar power, an openness to accident and non-ego – now stand revealed as the essential gropings towards a new method.

Shanachie Records has announced that *Wireforks* is the album to break him in the States, but there duettist Henry Kaiser swamps him in one-world sentimentality: *Saisoro* showcases Bailey's guitar as never before.

The electric guitar is the ultimate populist instrument. Impulses towards innovation can imply airy disdain, as if the avantgardiste wished to fly by the nets of regular pleasure. However, Bailey is actually as blues-ridden as Charlie Parker. He has the bluesman's ability to weigh the impact of a single chord, listen out for its unique timbral density. The Ruins, too, have an ear for particular sound rather than its official key/rhythm designation; this means they can pin his aching arcs and digital scrambles into accessible rockist structures. Instead of interpreting Bailey's pioneering spirit as high-minded refusal of grunge, they frame his split-spectrum tangents into big, responsive rock onslaught.

There are calms in the storm. 'Shivareyanco' features Tatsuya's absurdist falsetto, almost parodying the offensively arbitrary, effete freedoms of twelve-tone, but then silliness was always part of heavy rock's dynamic (the Cream's cockney singalong on *Disraeli Gears*; Frank Zappa's moustache; Captain Sensible's tutu). It's also a Japanese reply to the way that western composers (from Mahler through to Boulez and Cage) have borrowed Noh Theatre grunts and yelps. 'Manugan Melpp' sounds like a field-recording, Bailey's volume pedal pushed to the limit: a pregnant hiss gradually reveals a Zen garden of birdsong and acqueous trickles. 'Dhamzhai/Sytnniwa' is abstract funk recalling the bands Material and Massacre, the instrumental music The Gang Of Four never got round to. It's as if McLaughlin's piercing brilliance had been invaded by the black-pearl grit and soul of Buddy Guy.

By bringing Bailey together with the Ruins, Zorn and Laswell have achieved a wondrous feat. Now that more people are making the noise/ improv equation (Ascension at Disobey; Skullflower at the Termite; Martin Archer with Rancid Poultry), this album constitutes both benchmark and celebration. Encased in a beautiful sleeve by Ikue Mori, all gold-leaf and crackled-glaze prettiness (Zorn proving that he is one of the few label directors to have understood how to package CDs), *Saisoro* is quite simply commodity-lust provocation: a gem. [*The Wire*, no. 139, September 1995]

Hmm. Hype may not age well (Martin Archer with Rancid Poultry??), but it does convey the kind of relief Derek and the Ruins could supply for a Free Improvisation fan who'd started with rock and doesn't despise people for educating themselves about music by purchasing records. *Down Beat* was kinder to *Wireforks*, but did notice 'a lightness (California-influenced?) about the proceedings that is unusual in the Bailey *oeuvre*' [October 1995, p. 51], which may explain this punk rocker's reaction. It wasn't just me: *Spin* magazine's response to *Saisoro* was so punk-rock, the reviewer missed the band name's reference to Eric and Duane.

My favourite improvisation-with-electric-instruments record of the past few years, Derek Bailey & Ruins' *Saisoro*, which shows up all the 'jam' bands for the don't-worry-be-happy conservative windbags they are. Punk rock lives in the most unlikely places. [Sasha Frere-Jones, *Spin*, 1995]

This is how the jazz page in *Hi-Fi News* greeted the next Zorn-induced project, *Arcana*, recorded in April 1995.

ARCANA
THE LAST WAVE
DIW 903 (60m 26s)
You wouldn't recognise Tony Williams here. Chicago born, the drummer started with Miles Davis, went on to epochal recordings with Eric Dolphy and Andrew Hill for Blue Note, then formed a jazz-rock band named Lifetime featuring John McLaughlin. His drumming on *The Last Wave* is still wildly impressive, but the music has shifted round, giving his beats the abstract brutality of hardcore. There is none of the pattering spaciousness of his modal jazz days. Bill Laswell's bass defines the genre: stubbed, New Wave funk (on 'The Rattle of Bones' he reprises the riff from 'Rock Lobster' by The B52s). Laswell's skillful mix creates solid textures for the perverse cavorts of Derek Bailey's guitar. By the end, it is Bailey's show. His eccentric intervals splinter Laswell's harmonies with brain-bursting persistence. Perhaps at last the rockist *hoi-polloi* will deign to listen to someone who has single-

handedly transformed the way the guitar can be played. [*Hi-Fi News*, October 1996]

Characteristically, Bailey's deepest impression of the date was Tony Williams's method of setting up his kit – he smoked a cigar while someone from an 'endorsed' drum company assembled the huge drum set in the studio (in the event, DIW failed to mention which company it was).

In the summer of 1995, Bailey had been sending 'tape letters' of some absolutely splenetic guitar-playing to correspondents, cassette recordings of himself playing to Hackney pirate radio at home, then buzzing and crackling with the crazy sounds of jungle, soon to be renamed drum'n'bass (he was particularly impressed that his local DJ could manage to telephone for a pizza and coke as part of the performance). Bailey hadn't been playing this ferociously since the early duets with Bennink (well maybe he had, but not all of us had heard it). Bailey wanted to release these DIY overdubs, but copyright issues loomed. Zorn contacted Napalm Death's Mick Harris, who found him a drum'n'bass guy in Birmingham named DJ Ninj. Bailey had developed a habit of making home tapes with unpredictable lengths of silence. This was to give his own play-along-with-tape practise sessions some edge: he couldn't tell when the pre-recorded material would start up again. Finding some sections of unacceptable keyboard harmony on Ninj's tracks, Bailey simply recorded silence over them. Then he played over the top, silences and all. As an introduction to a guitarist whose name was more ubiquitous – plugged in the music press by John Zorn, Thurston Moore and Jim O'Rourke (not to mention Pat Metheny) – than either his records or performances, *guitar, drums'n'bass* was hard to beat.

DEREK BAILEY
GUITAR, DRUMS 'N' BASS
AVANT AVAN060 (39m 6s)
Sitting at home in Hackney, Derek Bailey found it stretching to play along with the Jungle DJs on the local pirate radio. The machine complexities enthralled his practised ear. Hearing of this, John Zorn put him in touch with DJ Ninj in Birmingham: a collaboration was born. Bailey wiped some parts of the tape he did not like, creating silences for

unaccompanied patches. The result is deeply strange, as Bailey's flash super-control is pushed up against streamlined computer rhythms. At first it seems airless, and you miss Bailey's ear for real space, but Ninj provides occasion for some of his most astonishing timings and leaps. Free Improvisation's answer to *Charlie Parker with Strings*: bewilderingly beautiful (likewise the gold-target artwork). [*Hi-Fi News*, January 1997]

All this activity took its toll. In September 1995, Bailey was diagnosed with 'exhaustion' and had to abruptly return from an American trip to England for a period of rest. 'Which I guess means old age,' he said to John Corbett; 'having some element of youth helps immensely – I mean, it's OK for Michael Jackson' [*Pulse!* March 1996]. However, this setback didn't stop the growing interest in his work. At the end of 1997, Bailey obsessionalism skyrocketed. It was after submitting this round-up of Derek Bailey releases to *Hi-Fi News* that I first approached a publisher with the idea of a Bailey biography.

DEREK BAILEY ROUND-UP

Widespread recognition for avantgarde artists is frequently heralded by two developments: renewed interest in their early work, and plaudits from their more commercially-acceptable peers. Both are happening to guitarist Derek Bailey. Long a byword for challenging – almost intimidating – music, his early recordings are now appearing on a slew of labels. On top of that, he has just released a 3-CD album with – of all people! – Pat Metheny: *The Sign of 4* [Knitting Factory Works KFW197 (3 CDs, 191m 21s) A:1]. Pat Metheny has already shown signs of impatience with his 'easy-listening/samba' pigeonhole. He recorded with Ornette Coleman, *Song X*, and released an album of deliberately bad-mannered solo skronk-guitar called *Zero Tolerance for Silence* (the first was terrific, the second was useless). *The Sign of 4* pitches the two guitarists at each other from opposite speakers, with percussion supplied by Gregg Bendian and Paul Wertico. The first disc is a single 62-minute onslaught of breathtaking ferocity recorded live at New York's Knitting Factory; the second disc is a selection of studio cuts, in a prettier vein; the third consists of five live tracks back at the Factory, again rockist and impactful, but with a greater variety of beats and textures. Metheny will hardly penetrate his core market with this release (his contract stipulates that it is not marketed using his name), but it is a brave encounter with someone who has reinvented the way both guitar and improvisation proceed. Death Metal and Free Jazz fans are likely to find the music deliriously exciting; listeners looking for calmer fare should check out some of the re-releases. *Drops* [New Tone rdc5037 (39m 15s) A:1**] presents duets between Bailey and the Italian percussionist Andrea Centazzo from 1977. Bailey always sounds impressive against smart beats, and this is jaw-dropping. The guitar sound is more etiolated and stringily sensitive than ears used to recent Bailey's clarity and hardness will expect. Bizarre though it sounds, this is actually 'Webern that Rocks': the avoidance of cliché is well-nigh absolute, yet everything is played with a physical relish too often absent in abstract and innovative musics. *Incus Taps* [organ of Corti 10 (50m 19s) A/B:1**] is a digital re-release of customised spools of tape Bailey sold from his suitcase in 1973. The straight-to-tape sound has its own lo-fi aura; the notes are so round and gleaming they resemble chrome-oxide thought-bubbles. Bailey plays counterpoint with himself as different melodic progressions proceed simultaneously; the grace and sheer invention of his motifs has the kind of unanswerable logic that has made people hail Conlon Nancarrow.

The Spontaneous Music Ensemble's *Quintessence 1* [Emanem 4015 (69m 11s) A:1/2] and *Quintessence 2* [Emanem 4016 (66m 48s) A:1/3] revive 1974 recordings originally released on vinyl in 1986. John Stevens (percussion, cornet), Evan Parker (soprano), Trevor Watts (soprano) and Kent Carter (cello, bass) join Bailey at the ICA (London's notorious highbrow arts venue) to play quintessential 'free improvisation'. Maybe the institutional space cast a pall on the proceedings: there are some gripping ensemble passages (for example, the start of 'Ten Minutes'), but also too much 'hit the highest note' mannerism from the horns. Extra duets by Stevens and Watts (tacked on to make use of the CD timing) are infantile and ramshackle – not so much Ayler's 'Ghosts' as musicians who should know better playing at kids imitating ghosts by going 'woo woo'. Ghastly. *Music and Dance* [Revenant 201 (53m 47s) A:1] is duets from 1980 between Bailey and the Japanese dancer Min Tanaka. In responding to both environmental sounds and Tanaka's movements, Bailey resorts to some characteristic figures, but is evidently alert and responsive. The 'dialogue' has an open-ended quality lacking in *Incus Taps*, for example. A more sonically evident dialogue can be heard on *Close to the Kitchen* [Rectangle Rec-F (47m 5s) A:1**], stunning duets with the French guitarist Noël Akchoté recorded in August 1996. More successful than the encounter with Metheny, this whirls up improv, drum'n'bass urgency and lo-fi aggro into a truly astonishing tirade. Its issue on prime-grade, heavy vinyl will ensure legendary status among Bailey *aficionados*. Another big name in guitars who has 'discovered' Derek Bailey is Sonic Youth's Thurston Moore. On XIII Ghosts' *Legend of the Blood Yeti* [Infinite Chug CHUG5 (74m) A:1/3], Moore joins Bailey in trying to make sense of the antics of Alex Ward (alto) and Switch (electronics). Unfortunately, they contribute to different tracks. Only Bailey seems able to engage Ward in meaningful dialogue; Moore supplies a much-needed emotional core, but is also quickly buried in postmodernist *bric-à-brac*. Still, the collaboration shows that, even at age 67, Bailey is willing to risk practically any liaison. There may be signs that he is breaking through to his rightful place as one of the legislators of twentieth-century music, but he is not going to surrender the devil-may-care wilfulness that spurs his unique integrity. [*Hi-Fi News*, November 1997]

After all the claims about Free Improvisation as an anti-commodity operation, this slavering response to Bailey's latest albums may seem like treachery. However, that depends on whether one's criticism of com-modified music is aesthetic or moral. The problem is not that commodi-ties are *immoral* – in capitalism, our very life essence is reduced to a commodity (labour) – but that commodification has a tendency to weaken and homogenise the music we hear.

Anyone who's been thrilled by Marvin Gaye's *I Want You*, Frank Zappa's *Apostrophe(')* or the Sex Pistols' *Never Mind the Bollocks* (that is, anyone who can take their head out of their arse and *listen*) cannot deny that the mass market can yield amazing fruits. The Marxist critique of commodity production – the observation that it exploits labour and leads to economic crisis and wars as ruling classes squabble over the resulting surplus – should lead to practical *criticism* of commodification rather than holy disdain. The drive to accumulate profits certainly creates a tendency for the use value of music (its 'quality') to fall. However, there is a countervailing tendency: resistance to capitalism, and its need to find expression. Distinguishing between these two forces, and determining their relative spin inside any particular release, is the task of the anti-capitalist critic. Romantic 'anti-commodity' culture ends up with basketweaving and William Morris wallpaper.

True, there are hosts of crypto-reactionary critics around ready to convert Marx's anti-capitalism into moral scorn for the mass market, resulting in a gloomy, high-minded elitism which actually serves to confirm the topdown perspective of class society. They are aided in this by 'Western Marxism', a strain of Marxism produced by academics who lack the politics to read *Capital* through to the end (they moan about 'commodity fetishism', but never get onto the extraction of surplus value from labour or the tendency of the rate of profit to fall, which together create *class struggle*). For these beautiful souls, criticising mass culture is easy: it's *all* wicked!

The fact is, in the 1990s Derek Bailey put some excellent music onto the mass market (he'll add, 'those records didn't sell *that* well', but to these ears, a Robert Musso production is aimed at the *record consumer* rather than the improv connoisseur, and so contains the mass market as an aural index or aesthetic super-ego). Of course, the guitar playing on *Saisoro*, *The Last Wave* and *guitar, drums 'n' bass* wouldn't be at the high level it is if optimum sales and maximum accessibility had been the starting philosophy of Bailey's development as an artist (he'd be stuck in fusion, probably going a little 'world music' round the edges as the cuddly nineties' proceeded). The emergence of Bailey's guitarism as a commercial option in the mass market is a by-product of the evolution of music and society, both outside his immediate control (increased rhythmic sophistication, the acceptance of filmic noise and coloration as musically legitimate, progressive guitarism, avant-as-chic, hip-hop, drum'n'bass, Zorn's will to power etcetera). The records sound good because commercialism has caught up with Bailey (not least through the efforts of Musso, Laswell and Zorn), not because he has suddenly gone for the money.

Bailey's *oeuvre* needs to be taken as a whole. The explosive guitarism of *Saisoro* and *The Last Wave* derives from his myriad experiments, improvisations and bizarre encounters. The restless, rebellious spirit it encodes is not the sound of dogma or purism, but of impatience with dogma and purism. If Bailey and Oxley had given Columbia Records what they wanted in the early 1970s – the pretty, set-metre instrumental pop that John McLaughlin delivered to Polydor, the academic jazz-rock that Nucleus delivered to Phonogram – Bailey's guitar would not be able to rave and rail to the new beats of the Ruins or drum'n'bass. Openness to the contingent, the refusal to settle on a 'genre', has meant that his guitar playing remains vital and fluid – and can seize new opportunities created by the increasingly sophisticated and micro-stitial rhythmic concepts of younger players. Even if the CDs haven't actually sold the bucketloads this author hoped when puffing them in *The Wire* and *Hi-Fi News*, they do serve a purpose: they show that Free Improvisation is not about insisting on worthy, badly recorded 'documents', but about seizing every opportunity for music, and pursuing it with maximum focus and ferocity – whether that's playing upstairs in a pub to the proverbial two people and a dog, or a major recording with Pat Metheny or Tony Williams.

Perhaps the most unlikely rhythm section Zorn has yet found for Bailey is Jamaaladeen Tacuma (who plays an electric bass so funky it hurts) and Calvin Weston (inheritor of Shannon Jackson's harmolodic drum mantle). Here was a cool guitarist who detested the 'let's get it on' ethos of sixties hard bop getting down with two of the funkiest soul brothers on the planet!

BAILEY/TACUMA/WESTON
MIRAKLE
TZADIK TZ7603 (70m 46s)
As style-counsellor John Zorn may be less than convincing (the Masonic iconography decorating this release tells you nothing about the music), but in his role as executive producer he has the *chutzpah* (not to mention financial clout) to forge some extraordinary liaisons. Guitarist Derek Bailey has improvised with many an oddball – from soundless Zen performance-artists to veteran-jazz tapdancers (sometimes simultaneously) – but this line-up is still a shock. Philadelphians Jamaaladeen Tacuma and Calvin Weston are the bass/drums dream team of Harmolodics, brilliant at boiling up contorted funk behind the likes of Ornette Coleman and James Blood Ulmer. Recorded with state-of-the-art clarity by Robert Musso, Bailey improvises with vehemence and raw passion, upsetting a funk that is designed to thrive on upset. Starting out with a riff derived from 'The Creator Has A Master Plan', Tacuma and Weston show that a vital idiom can devour any transgression. After a brief pause, the final track appears, replete with bizarre vocal effects that seem to be coming from Tacuma's bass. Who

says No Wave hasn't a future? Hey, Derek, let's funk! [*Hi-Fi News*, August 2000]

(The last phrase derived from Jamaaladeen's opening exclamation at the studio session.) Not to be ignored simply because it provides a complete contrast to these 'loud' releases is *Viper*, one of Bailey's most delicate and lovely records. Recorded by Jim Anderson at Clinton Studio in New York on 16 December 1996 (erroneously attributed to 1997), it was yet another project made possible by Zorn.

DEREK BAILEY/MIN XIAO-FEN

VIPER

AVANT AVANO50 (54m 36s)

Min Xiao-Fen plays the *pipa*, a traditional Chinese string instrument; Derek Bailey plays acoustic guitar. You might expect oriental exotica backed by familiar strums, but that underestimates Bailey's radical reconstruction of western guitarism. Having absorbed Webern, flamenco and the blues – and listened to oriental instruments like the *koto* and *komungo* – he is ready to complement Xiao-Fen note-for-note in terms of attack, timbre and ornament. The two instruments tangle, swap places and improvise instant cameos of surpassing prettiness – an impression encouraged by Ikue Mori's artfully conceived (and gilded) packaging. These duets present a detailed and challenging case for serious students of east/west musical divides and fusions. A:1* [*Hi-Fi News*, May 1999]

WILL GAINES

As a collaborator who helps Derek Bailey escape generic paralysis, tap dancer Will Gaines is exemplary. Gaines was born into a family of dancers in Baltimore, Maryland, in 1928. He grew up in Detroit, associate of such *maestri* of hard bop as tenor saxophonist Lucky Thompson, pianist Tommy Flanagan and guitarist Kenny Burrell. He was what *Variety* at the time would call a 'jazz hoofer' – a performer who stands out front of a big band and dances audibly with special, metal-tipped shoes, a striking exponent of the jazz dialectic between physical movement and sound. Gaines performed at the Apollo in

Harlem as early as 1954. In 1957, he joined Cab Calloway's Cotton Club Revue. He opened for acts as big as Eartha Kitt, Nat 'King' Cole and Sammy Davis Jr, earning fees of $500 a night. In the 1960s, he performed at the Pigalle in Paris and at the London Palladium. In the 1970s, he played with Humphrey Lyttelton at the Queen Elizabeth Hall. In 1983, he gave a masterclass in Bebop Tap at the Riverside Studios. On 19 March 2002 he and Bailey performed an 'Esemplastic Tuesday' in the drawing studio on the seventh floor of the Royal College of Art.

In short, Will Gaines is someone straight from the tradition – he has danced with *everybody* – but whose chosen 'instrument' denies him the gravitas conferred by post-Coltrane jazz criticism. Bailey wanted every freedom that sixties art-lab wayoutness could grant a performer, but he has never relinquished the insight (which can variously be understood as anti-hierarchical humanism or as 'cynicism') that any crowd has a craving to be entertained, and that the most 'arty' crowd can be enthralled by what is basically a music-hall turn. Gaines was therefore an ideal co-conspirator, both rhythmically educated in swing and bebop, yet destructive of the transcendental pretention Bailey finds irksome in Free Jazz.

Will Gaines tap-danced at Company Week 1994. Tap-dancers are natural soloists, launching into an activity that is self-propelling. But they can also be accompanists and interlocutors. The way Will Gaines dealt with Company improvisors was to dance ahead, allowing the other musicians to ignore or complement him. Occasionally he would pause and readjust his metre if he felt that was appropriate ('counterpoint *and* contradiction'). The rattling speed of his taps – their bop velocity – is just what Bailey thrives on. When they are playing together, he'll drop into Gaines's metre at any moment, or wait and allow it to bloom on its own. In 1995, Gaines and Bailey made a video (*Will*, Incus VD01) at the Montage Gallery in Derby, a composite of performances on 10 and 11 May 1995.

Bailey has persistently been attracted to impossible-sounding projects, but by combining Ist – the string trio in which Simon H. Fell (bass), Mark Wastell (cello) and Rhodri Davies (harp) make an intense, cobweblike music of barely audible scrapes and squeaks and harmonics – with Will Gaines, he surpassed himself. A movement variously described as 'the new silence', 'new Berlin reductionism' or 'ambient improv' – all horizontal whisps and carefully judged pauses – is suddenly invaded with speedy beats that are all about verticality, physical movement and vaudeville (albeit updated to encompass bebop tricksiness). From a musical point of view, Bailey certainly needed some extra beats to deal with Ist; the extraordinary thing is that he should call on someone from such a popular (and hence, in avant circles, 'uncool') genre as tap dancing.

The bizarro quintet of Bailey+Ist+Gaines performed at the Théâtre des Bernardines in Marseille on 13 and 14 January 1999, to the great delight of both audience and musicians (the music was released as *Company in Marseille*, Incus 44/45). Bailey was so pleased with the results, he reconvened the group at the Klinker Club on 24 August 2000 (though harpist Rhodri Davies was unable to attend). The choice of venue, a cabaret run in a pub backroom by the indefatigable Birdyak guitarist (and Oxley associate) Hugh Metcalfe, was also typical: 'After a gig at the Barbican,' said Bailey, referring to a prestigious gig on 3 July, supporting John Zorn's quartet with Fred Frith, Bill Laswell and Dave Lombardo from Slayer, 'it had to be . . . the Klinker!' He also took the entire group to New York in April 2001, where they played a week at Tonic, billed as Company (see pages 308–10).

The fascination of watching Gaines with Company underlines the fact that Free Improvisation refuses the 'single sense' definitions of music deriving from Kantian aesthetics: a reminder of the fact that musical sound is a product of physical gesture. However, when heard on CD, Gaines's taps are equally arresting. The sonority is so bizarre – such a narrow range of timbres, yet so eloquent and rhythmically detailed – that it's not like anything in the history of Free Improvisation. It bears comparison to some of the new sounds brought in by Electronica and Glitch, especially those that reference electronic interference (the way Gert-Jan Prins makes a crackle start to resemble a techno rhythm). The taps can also sound like someone clucking their tongue and smacking their lips, giving the music a bizarre mouthnoise humour and intensity. At the Klinker, Mark Wastell picked up on Gaines's bop rhythms and the pair improvised a rousing duet. Ist have invented a music of thin lines and sparseness: when they play with Bailey and Gaines, the sense is of following a thread of time. Compared to the Pollock-like density and simultaneity of a CD by Hession/Wilkinson/Fell, *Company in Marseille* is like viewing the lengths of the Bayeux Tapestry, though the medieval charm of its embroidered motifs has been replaced by variegated abstractions and visual gags worthy of Paul Klee.

The presence of Gaines in Company returns the discussion to the old jazz versus improv chestnut. Gaines himself has no desire to be confined to jazz. According to Bailey, he told Alex Ward that he admired his facility on sax, but he didn't want to hear any of those old jazz licks again. However, a review in *Hi-Fi News* showed that one could feel uncomfortable with some of Ward's harmonic ideas without it really being a 'jazz' issue.

DEREK BAILEY & ALEX WARD
LOcatioNAL
INCUS CD37 48m 44s
Alex Ward has been playing clarinet with guitarist Derek Bailey since 1988, though this is the first time they've released a duo album: high-level banter between two quick musical minds. Ward runs the gamut from Braxtonish melancholy to Zornite violence and Wilkinsonesque animal-cries. His harmonic arguments ('Studio 3') do not get the best from Bailey, who is better at answering Ward's skronk and stab. There's a great moment in 'Domestic 1', where Ward unleashes an astonishing circular scrape-fest and Bailey is momentarily nonplussed, then pings along an inspired accompaniment. The CD ends with a 10m live track, and though the sound is raw, the bigger space and sense of onslaught confer a new coherence on the playing. This is the sound of two musicians trying to get beyond themselves: 'Studio 2' has tantalizing glimpses of complex machinic fold-in, with Bailey piling in an impossible-sounding assortment of guitar sounds. A:1 [*Hi-Fi News* November 2000]

Will Gaines doesn't like to hear young players using jazz because to him it sounds like a quote rather than live: the same thing applies to any residues of tonal functionality in Free Improvisation. In 2003, Incus released Will Gaines's *Rappin & Tappin* [Incus CD55], with a Bailey/Gaines duet from 1994 and generous samples of Gaines's habit of reminiscing to his audience about old times.

A DEMUR

If the story of Derek Bailey has been somewhat skimped for the eighties and nineties, that is because he had set the pattern by then, and was principally concerned to continue finding new people to improvise with, to maintain old liaisons and to take care of Incus. As his range of contacts increased, his music broadened, but there were no fundamental changes of direction. It was a matter of waiting for the rest of the world to catch up. Shrewd Bailey-watchers did notice that his playing got more flexible.

> If there is one aspect that seems to have developed over the years, it is that his playing now displays greater rhythmic freedom. It is not 'swing' in the old sense, but there is increased fluency in his playing. [Barry McRae reviewing *Solo Guitar Volume 2*, Incus CD11, *Jazz Journal*, December 1992, p. 20]

As Michael Gerzon observed in his article on the Bethnal Green Library concerts, Bailey's playing alters daily, so even the most assiduous CD- and tape-collector has only a partial view. Certainly, to take one example, the solo playing at the Koncepts Cultural Gallery in Oakland California on 10 December 1989 – you can hear from the laughter and applause that Bailey was in a jovial mood – has a rhythmic attack and coherence far removed from some of the arid and puzzled-sounding (pissed off?) performances I heard him perform at the Vortex in the mid-1980s. In the 1990s, exciting, headlong performances became more frequent – though anyone promising anything in particular to friends who'd never seen him before was likely to be embarrassed: 'dependability' is not a term in Bailey's lexicon.

At the end of the 1980s, press coverage of the Bailey phenomenon increased – in December 1987, the German music magazine *Spex* listed Bailey's name on the cover flanked by those of Janet Jackson and Salt'n'Pepa – but few articles had the charge of the *Melody Maker* coverage of the late sixties and early seventies, when jazz journalism wrestled with this new and unforeseen beast called Free Improvisation (which is why the scissors-and-paste method used in the first half of this book gradually gives way to direct descriptions of the music). Free Improvisation was now a known quantity, and the journalistic approach became a recitation of achievements rather than an inquisition by sympathetic or outraged gig-goers. Bailey cordially hated this 'elder statesman' status, and relished working with new players. He continued to play his sunburst Gibson ES-175 acoustic/electric, which he'd played since his jazz days, and his 1936 Epiphone Triumph archtop ('one of the loudest acoustic guitars ever built, designed to compete with the wailing saxes of the swingband era' – Sid Langley, *Sheffield Evening Telegraph*, 6–ii–1982). In 1987, Bailey acquired a new Martin D18 (premièred on *Domestic & Public Pieces*, Emanem 4001), and in 1997 a brand-new acoustic custom-built by a German cello-maker.

As regards Bailey's playing, the aural evidence (covered in non-technical terms by such phrases as 'zinging freshness', 'vitality' or simply 'good') is that Bailey was still developing – as the astonishing variety of his involvements attests. In 1987, he said:

> I like the nature of the guitar – that you can play middle C five different ways, and it will sound different in each position. You can play virtually any note, allowing for octave transpositions, in three basic ways, as a harmonic, open string, or stopped note. You can play the same notes and do a completely different set of fingerings. That's something I started to exploit – a mix of harmonics, open strings, stopped notes in different places.

That explains how notes can sail out of stunted clusters like slo-mo bullets. It is also an indication of the deliberation that precedes his improvisations: all these marvels are results not of intoxication by a higher power, but of thought and practice. Bailey takes written notes on what he discovers. He has a drawer bursting with jottings, and has made tantalising mention of collecting these together as a technical manual on guitar harmonics and fingering. Although he could easily establish some kind of pre-eminence in this field, one senses a certain reluctance to 'prove' the worth of Free Improvisation by such means. He rarely mentions guitar technicalities except in response to direct questions. Bailey has an avant-gardiste's relish for the way true art vexes a false world, and this means leaving the music to speak for itself.

THE AESTHETICS OF FREE IMPROVISATION
(A BRIEF RETURN)

Interviewed by Julian Cowley for *The Wire*, bassist and composer Simon H. Fell provided some useful observations on Bailey's aesthetic and his distinctive approach to running a record label.

Since 1983, Fell has run a label, Bruce's Fingers, issuing music simply on the basis that he liked it at the time of its release. He respects the different methodology that informs Derek Bailey's independent label Incus: 'Derek will put together things which no "sane" person would put together, going on past record.' Fell received firsthand experience of Bailey's approach in 1996 when he recorded *Registered Firm* for Incus with American jazz guitarist Joe Morris. 'Derek was intrigued by the perversity of putting someone like Morris with the Hession/Wilkinson/Fell trio,' Fell recalls. 'He made a commitment to put that record out before we'd even played together. Whether or not it proved awkward musically is not the point. The point is not to have music that everybody will like, but to follow the process through. It's not classic Hession/Wilkinson/Fell, and it's not classic Joe Morris. It's an interesting third thing.' [Simon H. Fell to Julian Cowley, *The Wire*, no. 198, August 2000]

This fits with Fell's caustic – and distinctly Bailey-like – criticism of the current scene:

There are certain records of improvised music you pick up, see who's on them and you know exactly what it's going to sound like, within certain parameters. My type of listener would be someone who would pick up one of my records and say, 'What the hell is he doing now? I'm intrigued – I'll find out.'

However, although committed to Bailey's hardcore modernism, Fell believes that composition – in other words, the resource of *im*practical or *premeditated* reason – can also help prevent the music from becoming predictable.

The point of composition is to create something that's different to the last piece. I often look at musicians and it's very clear what they are doing and they're completely on top of it, and sometimes I envy them. But then I think, well, in ten years' time they might still be doing that, and I'll have all these *strange things* which nobody else has done ... [Simon H. Fell to Julian Cowley, *The Wire*, no. 198, August 2000]

In a fax interview in 2000, Bailey admitted the presence of improv clichés, but nevertheless expressed his conviction that Free Improvisation provided the best opportunities for innovation: 'Clichés? Sure. There are whole groups out there that are clichés. But that doesn't matter. There's plenty of scope in this activity. Most of the potential of Free Improvisation has yet to be explored' [fax to Hannes Schweizer, summer 2000].

More interesting than the 'improvisation versus composition' debate is the idea that Free Improvisation is not simply one genre among others – requiring its own set of labels, promoters and boosters – but a principle of surprise and transgression that requires vigilance if it's to survive. Sure, Fell and Bailey disagree about *how* to prevent the music from congealing, but the fundamental stress on libidinal gratification for the producer (rather than dependable product for the consumer) is similarly militant, critical and uncompromising. As regards genuine musical communication and event, Bailey and Fell are at one.

Bailey's interest in Hession/Wilkinson/Fell+Morris did not stop at releasing their 'interesting third thing' on Incus: he attended their gig at the Adelphi, Leeds, in June 1996, and himself played with Hession/Wilkinson/Fell at the Three Legs on the Headrow in November of that year (part of the Termite Festival). That gig was like Bailey's encounters with Cecil Taylor, giving off music that seemed to lift the room itself into the air (a foretaste of what guitarist Stefan Jaworzyn would later achieve with the trio).

The sole contemporary composer Bailey respects appears to be John Zorn, presumably because works like *Parachute Years* achieve an ensemble texture hitherto unprecedented. He also loves a band he calls Cavanoconner, which puts together all the improvising DJs and samplists at his disposal ('it's so good, maybe I'll put it out one minute at a time'). Bailey declares Cavanoconner is in advance of all contemporary composition, though he has found it hard to find anyone among either the musicians or audience who shares his enthusiasm. Both Cavanoconner and *Parachute Years* are static, multiple-threaded musics without any teleological thrust (it is impossible to tell where the numerous performances and rehearsals of the pieces on Zorn's *Parachute Years* CD set stop and start). Bailey has an almost philosophical distrust of macro-organisation, and so parts company with Fell's attempt to include improvisation in grandiose compositional schemes. However, from the point of view of the listener who is committed less to method than to results, it's intriguing that Fell's artistic credo could serve Bailey just as well:

> Once I've explored something and realised the best examples of what that process can achieve, I don't feel any desire to keep repeating it. But that repetition is what most marketplaces want, even the experimental and improvised music marketplaces. I find it very irritating when people want to hear something which stopped developing a long time ago, but which they remember fondly. It becomes repertoire music, which I've always found difficult. Maybe I should change the classification to 'perverse music'. Perversity is a convenient word to use. [Simon H. Fell to Julian Cowley, *The Wire*, no. 198, August 2000]

If one can raise the discussion above quarrels over method (maybe even credit Bailey's increasing ability to draw on improvisors from different genres – which requires a rare mix of musical judgment and hard economics – as a species of 'composition'), then Bailey's recent work with such unlikely forces as Laswell/Williams, Tacuma/Weston, DJ Ninj and Ist/Will Gaines are surely consummate examples of *perversity*. In the late capitalist era, the ability to supply 'quality product' has become the assumed aim of everyone, from manufacturers of chicken tikka to suppliers of industry-friendly graduate students. The ideology of commodity production means everything must serve the needs of the accumulation of capital, or be decried as useless, self-indulgent and anti-social. In such circumstances, it's no surprise that 'perversity' has become a word for what the bourgeoisie promised us in its early, heroic, revolutionary epoch: freedom.

TWO SNAPSHOTS: CECIL AND BLOOD

During May 2000, Derek Bailey played a season at Tonic in New York, a Manhattan club on Norfolk Street. At the time, it was enjoying a similar buzz to that of the Knitting Factory a decade before. This was an opportunity for listeners to assess him in the light of New York's jazz and downtown scenes. This was not a Company Week, where a set of musicians play night after night, gradually building an ensemble music from scratch. Indeed, the spare, oblong, candlelit space and relaxed atmosphere suggested rather a series of seances with the master. Nor did Bailey play every night (though he was billed as the club's 'curator' for May, many of the acts seemed to belong more to Tonic than to the Bailey orbit: composition and jazz, two areas that have long ceased to interest him, were notably present). However, his own first two appearances were pure improvisations, duets with two of the best musicians New York has to offer: Cecil Taylor and James Blood Ulmer.

Derek and Cecil played together on the evening of 5 May, a Friday. Cecil insisted on a 7-foot grand piano, so the instrument that had been originally installed needed to be swapped. An excited queue formed down Norfolk Street in the early-summer dusk as the new, monster instrument was unloaded. Once allowed in, sheer numbers forced the audience into unusually intimate relations, as they waited patiently for over an hour: drinking, sweating, smoking cigarettes and chatting to strangers rammed right into you (hello Jack and Emily). However, the music – played at a pitch of avidity that was chilling – banished any discomfort. There was something transfixing in the way everyone hung on each note. Although the pair have played together before (in Berlin and Manchester in 1988) and released a CD [*Pleistozaen mit Wasser*, FMP16], the concert was historic, a joust between two continents' most uncompromising players.

Cecil began softly with a blues, Derek answering his runs with harsh strokes across the strings of his unamplified electric guitar. Their rhythmic interplay recalled the supercharged feints and double bluffs of fencers, teetering with hesitation, then delivered with total conviction and punch. While Derek comped with violent, jagged scrubs, Cecil toyed with a sweet mode worthy of Alice Coltrane. When Cecil picked up some of Derek's farflung intervals, one's impression was of bizarre, irregular cogs meshing. Derek says that Cecil is one of the few pianists to really inhabit the piano, to bust through its drawing-room formality to create fluidity.

> One of the many remarkable things about Cecil is his pedalwork. He does get a lot of different sounds out of the piano. I've played with a lot of Cecil imitators, and the one thing that's constant all the time – usually – even with a good one like Freddie [van Hove] – is the sound of the piano. Cecil does some amazing shit, just shifting the sound, and I think it's his pedalling. Occasionally he refuses to accept that it's a piano, he goes down to one finger. Sometimes he's the ultimate piano player, a nineteenth-century kind of piano player, at other times he's pointing out everything that's wrong with the piano. [27–vi–2000]

Cecil's scary, machinegun-like attack supersedes conventional ugly/ pretty violent/peaceful oppositions. Derek showed a heady appreciation of Cecil's lightning and avalanches, producing a music both detailed and majestic, not a note that wasn't meant, and not one too many: a mutual revelling in freedom and space.

One thing is immediately apparent with Cecil: 'style' for him is no arbitrary choice, but an inevitable outcome of exceptional musicality and virtuosity. He'll play lulling chords, but then introduce a contrary tension that tightens the gut. Cecil's attack is so precise and hard it seems vicious, while his sense of architecture redeems the violence of the individual notes. Derek's stunted strums (bizarre clusters that prevented the instrument from singing) seemed deliberately to degrade Cecil's flights – questions and perversity and intense privacy versus the high drama – whilst simultaneously stoking the rhythm. The duel peaked, each musician attempting to unleash the harmonic run that would unseat his opponent. The beauty of the resultant music was a by-product: rainbow-coloured vapour trails ignored by the hard-pressed pilots.

Derek's lowering tones began gleaming with the alien light that arrives when guitarists play for the joy of the instrument's material components, his foot-pedal volume control allowing him to punch out asymetrical rhythms. By rapt attention to detail – each dissonance purposeful and willed – the two musicians arrived at free open spaces. This is music beyond genre. Derek and Cecil have checked out and absorbed Charlie Parker, Anton Webern, Marvin Gaye: now they're pondering about where they can go, and their dialectic throws out those absolute sparks that signify an art that cannot be other than what it is.

The first improvisation over with, the pair visibly relaxed: these duets could let them stretch, flex their imaginative muscles. A particularly rude and violent note from Bailey had Cecil grinning ear to ear, like an old friend appreciating the humour of a well-aimed curse word. In the second set, Bailey's return to acoustic was stunning, as if he had absorbed all the magical tremor of the electric into his unamplified strings. He walked around the stage with his guitar, his ear listening for the specific resonances of the club space. Cecil threw in some lines of poetry: 'having no other choice . . .', he began, every touch at the keyboard an illustration of the dialectical definition of freedom: recognition of necessity.

Musicians and writers from Thurston Moore's Noise axis tend to misconstrue Bailey's 'skronk': it's not about deploying effects, it's the generation of new sonics via attention to note order (compare John Coltrane's 'sheets of sound'). What Cecil and Derek played was totally rich, yet all edge. Cecil was by now off into pure lyricism, drunk on the joy of playing. Derek strolled down the aisle into the audience, again strumming his acoustic: 'Cecil never wants to stop . . .' he quipped. Cecil quit right away. Despite having had to line the block outside the club and the hour's hot and thirsty wait inside, the packed audience clapped them to the echo. Huge reputations encourage players to coast: here not a note was played without determination or care, without a sense of its relation to the other player, to the club space and to the whole history of music.

The duet with James Blood Ulmer occurred on a Saturday matinée. It illustrated Derek's refined ear and his courteous interest in different styles and approaches. Ulmer soloed first, playing his trademark Delta blues drone, so attractive and deceptively simple it leads people to miss how wild and speculative he's being in the upper register. He uses his wah-wah pedal to create the effect of two voices at once: a persistent conversational witter chopped by decisive chords. In his own solo piece,

Bailey emulated this by using his foot pedal to cut out the amplifier at intervals, weaving unamplified chords through piercing electric tones.

This lunchtime show lacked the pressured atmosphere (and high admission price) of the night with Cecil, but what was played had a similar fine-etched quality. Bailey's acoustic comping highlighted the bebop resources of Blood Ulmer's vocabulary (Ulmer's achievement in successfully fusing Delta blues and bebop is too rarely celebrated). When Bailey turned to electric, Ulmer's high tones began sounding uncannily like Bailey's: the two wove a glittering counterpoint around Ulmer's perpetual pentatonic-blues motion. The intricacy, seriousness and charm of what they played was moving. The idea of Bailey's free-improvising concept as post-fluxus annihilation of sense and order may apply to some Company antics: this, in contrast, was simply fantastic music, improvised in the instant by two flexible, open-minded musicians. Two guitarists jamming together has an intimate, on-the-porch feel; like Eugene Chadbourne's encounter with Billy Jenkins in Stratford in 1998, Bailey and Ulmer grasped that intimacy and made something historic out of it.

Andy Hamilton has argued in the *British Journal of Aesthetics* [January 2000] that Free Improvisation and jazz draw on 'an aesthetics of imperfection'. He should have been at Tonic. Derek's duos with Cecil and Blood in May 2000 saw the musicians tying up loose ends and answering hanging questions with a logic that was searing in its care and precision – and perfection.

IN NORWAY TOO

Ingar Zach is a percussionist based in Oslo. He leads a trio that play a highly propulsive form of improvisation, comparable in jazzoid intensity (if not excess) to Hession/Wilkinson/Fell, or Phillip Marks' Bark! In what has become an increasingly familiar move for improvisors seeking to make a mark on the international scene, he played a set with Bailey in Oslo (on 20 October 2000) and released it on his own Sofa label: *llaer* [NOR-CD 2001]. However, what is business-as-usual in Free Improvisation can be a staggering event in an increasingly stagnant music scene. In 2001 drummer Michael Welch released *Untitled Impro-visations* [Illegal Radio unnumbered], duets with Bailey recorded in Florida in March 1999. 'No noise reduction, compression, equalisation, limiting, filtering or effects' meant the document gives the impression that percussionist and guitarist never really connected (Welch subse-quently relented, increasing the level by 6 decibels). In contrast, on Zach's disc, an unambient, 'mixing desk' feel (when the musicians speak, their voices are artificially distant) gives a full account of the sonority of the instruments, and the duo's musical logic is graphic. Improvisation has become an international language where local hosts can give Bailey the kind of inspiration he used to need Stevens or Oxley to supply. Bailey's peripatetic and unsettled methodology keeps his music voracious.

The disc attracts the ear at once. Frank Zappa once said that what electric guitarists needed to find was their 'tone'. Once you've established the right sound with your equipment, then the instrument seems to play itself. You can feel Bailey hit that 'tone' with his opening notes, long, unhurried, feedback-sustained assertions that could be an excerpt from some ancient, slowed-down melody, though the subject matter is actu-ally electricity and amplification. It's a good illustration of why his guitar needs to be perfectly in tune: he uses very deliberate pilings-up of simultaneous tones that alternate between sweet consonance and strain-ing dissonance. Zach's spiky accompaniment allows Bailey's magisterial, dreamlike pacing to set the tempo, his beats a rich panoply of the pings and pops with which Bailey offsets his own horizontalism. Bailey admires the way Johnny 'Guitar' Watson is so decisive about whether he plays two notes or three: likewise, you can hear Bailey explore his left-hand fingerings by arpeggiated strums across certain strings or by simultaneous soundings. It would be interesting (though perhaps not for Bailey) to set this opening next to Frank Zappa's 'Zoot Allures' as a study in the erotics of feedback and sustain, the heady rush that comes from realising that the mechanics of sound production and psychic expression are in perfect sync, the wide-eyed joy that wishes and actuality may at certain moments flow together. The vertical offsets to this charged flow – so charged the sound flickers with interference crackle – accumulate to the point where there is a genuine guitar/

percussion tangle, though this consummation is glimpsed rather than adopted. This seven-minute opener – named 'Shiny Crimp' by Zach in retrospect – is followed by another seven-minute piece, 'Jerky Heads' ('Hepp' and 'Warts 'n' All' are seven minutes long too, implying a natural arc for Bailey/Zach attention spans). 'Jerky Heads' is more obviously a dialogue: the measure and mystery of 'Shiny Crimp' is left behind as finished and complete.

Though Bailey regards his own playing as a permanent practical activity – one on which audiences and CD listeners eavesdrop when they hear him 'play solo' – when he plays with other musicians, he is scrupulous about respecting the internal logic of a piece and its distinctness from other pieces of playing. He may be combative and dialogic, but that's when it's expected of him: his ideal of personal freedom only signifies in relation to the objectivity of the music. On 'Jerky Heads', the pace is hectic and there's more strenuously packed-in variety. Towards the end, Bailey adds in flourishes which sound like woodshedded considerations of harmonic runs. They are pasted into the improvised design like pretty butterfly prints or sweet wrappers onto a Schwitters *Merz*: their beauties are ironised and tilted by their relation to the whole.

'Horizontal Rain' is still speedier, with both players lightening their sounds to allow for more action. Bailey refuses the clock-oriented definitions of time which make much minimalism and electronica a time-filling chore (35 seconds of buzz, followed by . . .). The superstructural logic of the music comes from focus on the strings under his hands, a ceaseless ripple'n'roll over the same spot, like G. W. F. Hegel continually underlining the insufficiency of stand-alone, unmediated concepts. A long feedback sustain turns a note into texturation, and Zach responds by introducing metal chimes (on the cover, one of Zach's bells hangs in front of Bailey's head, making him look as if he's sporting a conical elf's cap). You suddenly realise you're in the midst of an extraordinarily original and powerful piece of music, though these effects are all a product of the players' fascination with the instruments in their hands. Just when you think Bailey has found a pretty area of play – strings of notes hanging in the Nordic air like bejewelled cobwebs – he trips up his own time and tears an ugly electric-noise gash in the surface. This 'mistake' – though only a mistake according to closed and formal definitions of music – breaks the previous frame of excellence and widens the scope. It's like an artist deciding to scorch the paper he's drawing on: putting the very foundations of the music into play forces a crisis which exacts increased efforts of design and imagination.

'Hepp' is a seven-minute drum solo. Roger Turner-like fascination with scraped cymbals and echoic thuds allows Zach to extend the full sound palette of what has gone before. Zach's jazzoid heat and flow is more evident without Bailey's stop-time focus on the instant, but this track is dramatic and compositional too, not simply a rhythmic shuffle, evincing the musical *clarity* that belies popular impatience with drum solos. In other words, 'Hepp' is a piece of music, Zach's thinking completely immersed in the timbral levels and chronic tensions of his soundings (from the applause, the audience in Oslo's Bla Club was also delighted).

The Bailey solo 'Warts'n'All' returns to the measured pace of 'Shiny Crimp': 'The Inch Worm' pegged out on a dissection slab, all quivering pink viscera and shiny metal pins. In his 'Invisible Jukebox' for *The Wire* (see Appendix 3), Bailey responded facetiously to Zoot Horn Rollo's rendition of Captain Beefheart's 'One Red Rose that I Mean', but hearing a track like this makes it clear why younger musicians such as Henry Kaiser play Captain Beefheart to Derek. The bizarre manner whereby antique sentimental pre-rock'n'roll motifs are cut up and recombined – according to a logic simultaneously savage, comic and wistful – is strikingly similar to Beefheart. On 'Warts'n'All', Bailey's *largamente* musings gradually worm themselves into the musky knots he finds exciting: pitch and volume rise as he follows up his ideas.

'Real Flying', with its enthusiastic echo of Lionel Hampton's crowd-pleaser 'Flying Home', is not a title you can imagine an English improvisor choosing, but it's apt. The audience applauds as Zach picks up his sticks, but Bailey keeps playing, keen to develop the ideas of his preceding solo. Zach sounds still more confident and forthright than before, and the music is getting better and better. Bailey's notes acquire the wild, almost reckless quality that Andrew Shone noticed about his playing with Joseph Holbrooke. Everything about Free Improvisation is directed at ridding musicians of self-consciousness and status anxiety: pushing back the super-ego's petty concept of correctness and letting the ego play with the id's daftest desires, bouncing the regressive sex doll on daddy's greasy knee. Bailey gets very loud, but this isn't rock music's spectacular sacrifice of the superego (aka parents), submerging the ego in a simulacrum of the id (the warm collusion of tribal-rock volume). The sense of analytic attention here ('let us study this phenomenon!') is keen and chill, but so avid and fierce it would be wrong to call it cerebral. Thus Free Improvisation overturns the lame heart/head polarity of a degraded commercialised romanticism, where to be authentic you must be stupid (Oasis). Maybe the reason Free Improvisation inspires partisanship is because it proposes a new model for the balance of our psychic forces – where we can face the most anti-social, embarrassing and downright silly drives of the unconscious without surrendering the prospect of consciousness and control.

Eleven minutes in, and it's 'Real Flying' indeed: great assertions that risk becoming coarse and overblown. Zach relents, and Bailey goes into a long, piercing, feedback-sustained note, a kind of testing of the drama that's gone before, pops of electric sound disappearing off to the horizon like exponentially diminishing telegraph poles. A final two-minute 'Buckle Up!' salutes the audience by providing an intuitive, gestural summary of the preceding piece. Ingar Zach's release is determinate proof that Derek Bailey's disdain for manufactured image and corporate sales strategies is the true way to create masterpieces of recorded guitar.

Although llaer was a terrific reassertion of the actualities of Free Improvisation – in an 'avant' market where technology is confused with progress and novel texturation with musical event – it paled beside Seven (Incus CD54), a second duet album recorded in London on 15 February 2002. Here Bailey played acoustic rather than electric guitar, yet the sonic is far more spiky and aggressive. Toby Hrycek-Robinson's recordings at the Moat Studio had been getting better and better, and this one is astonishingly present: Bailey's guitar notes have never sounded so detailed and jagged. Bailey now seems to trust Zach enough to unleash everything he can do with time, almost as if he was pulling punches on llaer. Seemingly titled after the 'natural' length of a Bailey/ Zach duet, only the opener, 'Shuffle', is actually seven minutes long, though the lengths (from 9:37 to 5:38) do hover around a seven-minute mean. You have to know the high esteem Bailey has for percussionist

Jamie Muir to realise what a great compliment he was paying when he said, 'I like *Seven*, Ingar plays great on it, he reminds me of Jamie Muir' [14–vi–2003].

BALLADS

Great interest was aroused when John Zorn suggested to Bailey that he record an album of ballads. The nonpareil production team of Toby Hrycek-Robinson (recording) and Scott Hull (mastering) meant that sound was state-of-the-art. Bailey's selection was bizarre from the point of view of jazz – especially given the dozen or so tunes deemed 'standards' at Berklee School – but it allowed him to play songs he found evocative of a long-gone era: 'Laura', 'My Melancholy Baby', 'Gone with the Wind' (twice!), 'You Go to My Head'. The closing track (rather pointed coming from a 73-year-old) was 'Please Don't Talk about Me when I'm Gone'. The ballad titles are printed in tiny pink twirly script on grey on the CD tray-insert, making them hard to read (Derek and I got round to talking about *Ballads* – TZ7607 – by discussing old age and failing eyesight, an advantage of which – according to Bailey – is that you cannot read music magazines any more).

DB: If I'd had my way they wouldn't have printed the titles at all because *Ballads* is nothing to do with the tunes. That record is about improvisation. I got a phone call from a musician in Germany, he said, Listen, I think that record's great because it's so non-PC – which it is, isn't it? It's like the opposite of whatever fashions are going on now, it's the complete opposite – but it's actually about improvisation. I'm trying to make sense out of playing ballads and free improvisation together. I only do it once.

OTL: It'll become your *Hot Rats*, the one 'listenable' Derek Bailey album.

DB: It's already become like that. There was an electric guitar festival in Amsterdam I would have played at last Monday, but for injuring my finger. In the beginning this woman rang me up and said, Would you come and play for twenty minutes at the Concertgebouw? I said, Yes, I'd love to. She said, We'd like you to play some ballads. I said, I won't be playing any ballads! She said, I'll have to go back to my committee.

I thought that was the end of that, but she came back – or another guy – and said, Listen, you can play what you like. I said, In that case I can do it. There's been a few things like that . . . no, that's exaggerating . . . just a couple of occasions people have shouted out, 'play "Laura"'. [*laughs*]

Bailey's stingingly precise, pure and simple renditions of these emotive, almost cheesy tunes do have a special charge – especially when set against the abstract, white-cube 'tastefulness' that floods the avant-garde once it becomes product. Nevertheless, his response to the Concertgebouw promoters shows that he wasn't going to let the success of *Ballads* become a straitjacket. On 'Rockin' Chair' (that is, at 1:58 on track 11) there's a fantastic illustration of the way Bailey's improvising focuses on crisis and emergence ('Aufhebung') as its life principle.

THE LATEST NEWS

Derek has found a second home at Tonic on New York's Lower East Side, playing there frequently. In April 2003 he was proud to be invited to a Passover meal in the club. A gig with Brazilian percussionist Cyro Baptista – with whom he hadn't played for fifteen years – was a 'revelation': '. . . completely different from how we used to play, much heavier, we had a very good night, all that's recorded so it might creep out' [14–vi–2003]. Bailey was especially gratified by the unpredictable nature of the events at a Company Week at Tonic held in November 2002.

The usual suspects, people who all know each other, but I put the word round that anyone who turned up might get to play, and all kinds of people turned up. It accumulated. The type of music changed. When it started there were a lot of electronic people – Voice Crack, a Swiss couple, Casey Rice. Jim O'Rourke was in it, Ikue. Then it turned into being very stringy, a classical string player came from uptown, Fred Sherry. Some of them sheered off, some of them came for one or two nights, and some of them absurdly just wanted to play with me, so we did all that. There was this Jewish guy, a friend of Zorn's, who played percussion, sat at the front with his bits and pieces, so we had three percussionists. Young guy from Chicago, black guy, Chad Taylor, very good player. Then a guy who looks like Jim O'Rourke and is a friend of Jim O'Rourke's. So it got very percussive. Electronic – stringy – percussive. I was playing electric most of the time. On the last night this Polish klezmer band from Kraków turned up, six of them. I thought, I'm not sure about this. But only two of them wanted to play, a violin player and an accordion player. The violin player was very good, mainly concerned with showing you he's a very good player, but the accordion player – Jarek Bestier – was amazing. Firstly, he was the best free accordion player I have ever heard, and he's also the most impressive new guy I've heard. It could be Cecil Taylor on accordion, except he does all kinds of feedback, brilliant player. We were about sixteen pieces – I got sick of asking people for groups, so I said, 'Why don't we all play?' Which we did. It was great, I know you think that's a recipe for disaster, but it was fucking great. It worked out beautiful. It was one of the most interesting Company Weeks I've done, with all the changes. [14–vi–2003]

An innovation at Incus is the production of CD-Rs. With conventional print runs, by the time review copies have been mailed out and distributors have taken their cut (or failed to pay at all), releases are making increasingly less money. The Incus Sideline series – 'releases from the store' – was heralded by a leaflet which reproduced a photograph of a nineteenth-century New York department store above this caption:

NO REVIEWS, NO DISTRIBUTORS. STRICTLY COTTAGE INDUSTRY: YOU
SEND £10 OR $15 AND WE BURN YOUR CD-R AND SEND IT TO YOU.

Like releasing reel-to-reel tapes in 1973, this is an attempt to make Incus music available faster and bypass the usual channels. Singer David Sylvian, who had a brush with corporate pop in the band Japan in the 1980s, called on Bailey to find out how Incus operated, and resolved to release his new album by website and mail order alone, cutting out the percentages due to distributors and record shops. His *Blemish* [Samadhi Sound, 2003] has some Bailey guitar on it.

He came here to see what we were doing, how we did this. He does it more strict than us because he claims he's not going to give them to distributors – he's only going to do it through mail order, that's what he says. I'm on three tracks and I think he works it quite well against what I do. He doesn't sing the same as what I play. I'm quite low in the mix. My impression is that his voice is so distinctive all the pieces sound the same – a very special voice and special words, but my impression is that they're all the same. If you like his voice you'll like it, otherwise, forget it. Why he asked me to play on it, fuck knows – but he came to that gig with Milo Fine at Flim Flam, he seems to show some interest. He's a strange cat. He's English, lives in America but he's English. [14–vi–2003]

CD-Rs enabled Bailey to respond quickly to current affairs. The attack by Bush and Blair on Iraq in March 2003 resulted in *Watch Out*, a three-and-a-half-minute speaking-improv where Bailey's anger – 'if you see the Axis of Idiots waddling towards you, watch out!' – put a new, sinister rasp into his voice. This wasn't listed in the catalogue, but mailed to colleagues, friends and loyal customers. It became a staple on my Resonance 104.4FM Wednesday broadcast: out art and left politics in uproariously eloquent disharmony.

Returning from Barcelona in early June 2003, Bailey had an accident when fetching his luggage from the airport carousel. His finger got caught, and he heard a disturbing 'crack' noise. After the swelling had subsided, he went for an X-ray: the finger was not broken, but several gigs – including the Amsterdam Concertgebouw and a solo appearance at Flim Flam, Alan Wilkinson's club at Ryan's Bar on Stoke Newington Church Street – were cancelled.

What else has Bailey been up to since we last talked?

Other than the Tonic gigs, what I've been doing is playing with a lot of women. Min Xiao-Fen in Berlin in October [2002], we had a great time, a Chinese event, some Chinese–German society. I was the only occidental on stage. Min was booked to play solo and she said she wanted to play solo and play with me. She played solo – I'd never heard her live play solo, brilliant – and then we had a very good duo. There was an orchestra there, fourteen guys, all farmers. They cooked their own food and never went out except to play. They played this Chinese orchestral music. I might play with Cyro Baptista at the Barbican because Zorn asked me to play with this Electric Masada, I'm not sure about that, but Cyro's in it, so I said to Zorn, Why don't you let me and Cyro do a duet, and then all of you can pile in at some point? He said, Yes, yes, great! So we'll see what happens. I don't know whether my critical faculties are fading in old age, but the recent concerts have been excellent, I think – even the ones I've played in England, which is not always the case. I enjoyed the one with Milo [Fine] and the one in Leeds, I enjoyed that, with Paul [Hession]. [14–vi–2003]

Multi-instrumentalist Milo Fine (drums, piano, clarinet) played with Bailey at Flim Flam (26–iii–2003); drummer Paul Hession played with him at the Adelphi in Leeds, courtesy the Termite Club (21–iii–2003). Although music journalists are doubtless doing Bailey a favour by emphasising projects that will sell CDs (*Ballads*, *Blemish* etcetera), it's gigs like these which produce the important music.

Not every encounter was as good. Even in the 'avant-garde', record labels seem to prefer names with a buzz to pertinent music. Franz Hautzinger's quarter-tone trumpet is an amazing thing. His solo trumpet release on Grob [211, 2001] resembled some new kind of super-vocalised, serial electronic music. However, it appears to have been arrived at through compositional strategies: teamed with Derek Bailey [Grob 425, 2002], Hautzinger was far less impressive. At the end of the fifteen-minute 'Talk', Hautzinger finally erupts in response to Bailey, but it's been a long wait (not helped by a remix of track 1 which destroyed the realtime logic of the duo's playing). Fashion weighs heavily on contemporary improvisors: according to Roger Turner, interaction and response are currently dismissed as 'old-fashioned' by the New Berlin Reductionists. I was shocked to hear even drummer Paul Lovens suc-cumb to contemporary devitalised 'sound art' with a dry and tedious release (*Achtung*, Grob 537, a duo record with Thomas Lehn). However, all such vogues – based upon assessments of CD marketability and art-money possibilities – can be ignored if the live experience is taken as primary (even it's at 'non-prestige', musician-run clubs like Flim Flam or the Termite).

A glance at Appendix 1 will show that Derek Bailey reissues continue unabated. However, these haven't always been brilliant, and there is a danger that digging out every last scrap means that Bailey's particular aesthetic may be obscured. *Hi-Fi News* published this unusually lukewarm review, in July 2000, of Iskra 1903's *Buzz Sound-track* [Emanem 4066]:

In 1971 film-maker Michael Grigsby asked his friend, the trombonist Paul Rutherford, if Iskra 1903 (Rutherford with Derek Bailey on guitar and Barry Guy on bass) would play the soundtrack for a film named *Buzz*. The trio made him a mono recording on three reels of tape. The film is lost, but the tapes survive. Iskra 1903 played some of the most explosive, obstreporous and exilarating music of the twentieth century (check out *Chapter One 1970–1972* [Emanem 4301], and *Cohesion*, a concert at Goldsmiths College on 9 March 1972, deposited at the National Sound Archive – C776/19–21 – but so far unreleased). This achievement may explain why this curiosity has been unearthed. Unfortunately, 'soundtrack' consciousness weighs on the date. The trio know they are not the main event, and hold themselves back. Reliance on long, slow notes dampens their interactions, as if the regular Iskra had been drugged or lobotomised. Suppressing his astonishing vocabulary of vocalisations and outsqueaks, Rutherford resorts to mournful arpeggios and tired jazz licks (it all sounds disturbingly like AMM). Thirty years later, the trio Ist (Simon Fell, Mark Wastell, Rhodri Davies) would show these 60s barnstormers how to summon the quiet storm (though film-makers brave enough to use Ist's cutting-edge sounds have yet to appear). A:2

On the other hand, John Corbett's Unheard Music Series, whose choice of old improv 'classics' for re-release appears to be entirely random, hit lucky when it issued unreleased takes from Peter Brötzmann's 1969 *Nipples: More Nipples* [Atavistic/UMS, 2003]. There's a fine tradition in jazz where an extended in-chorus on electric guitar drives a saxophonist nuts ('how can this electrified *twanger* compete with my ambrosial breath?'), so when the saxophonist comes in, he appears to explode (the relevant examples are 'Marchin' Along' from Coleman Hawkins's *Blues Groove* recorded in 1958 [Prestige, 1970], where the goad was Tiny Grimes in R&B mode, and 'David-Mingus' from David Murray's *Children* [Black Saint, 1985], where the goad was James 'Blood' Ulmer in 'harmolodic' – (that is, R&B) – mode). In 1969 there were no less than two saxophonists for Bailey to drive into apoplectic fury (Peter Brötzmann and Evan Parker), which simply doubles Bailey's splenetic wickedness: his playing on the seventeen-minute 'More Nipples' is fantastic, anti-social evil heat to the max. It makes you want to eat broadsheet newspapers and cause pile-ups on continental motorways!

Derek and his partner Karen Brookman have been enthusiastic about the city of Barcelona for many years. In July 2003 they decided to move there for a year, renting a flat on Via Roca in the Barri Gòtic from September 2003 onwards. Their Incus operation remains in Hackney for the time being, but if it all works out, they may move it to Spain. When I last visited them, they were buzzing about two new Incus releases: Will Gaines's *Rappin & Tappin* [Incus CD55] – which mixes the veteran tap dancer's volatile conversation and taps, and includes a duet he performed with Bailey in Holland in 1994 – and *Limescale*.

LIMESCALE

Limescale is the most recent Incus release [Incus CD56], a title suggested by T. H. F. Drenching, one of its five participants. Like Ingar Zach, Drenching is a new arrival on the scene whose approach is commensurate with the major motivational force acting on Free Improvisation from the start: a player's polemical outburst against repetition, sterility, snobbery and 'style'. Drenching emerged in the late nineties in an indie-pop duo named Pence Eleven, with the CD release *How the Nimrods Stopped Me Sinning* (Middle Class Records, 1998), when he was still using the name Stu Calton. Obsessed with Varèse, Messiaen, Zappa, Hip Hop and 80s-pop like Prince and Erasure, he and a circle of friends – which included Pence Eleven's Nathan Blunt ('Nes.Co'), Neil Monks ('Dogbiz'), Marie-Angélique Bueler ('Sonic Pleasure') and Patrick Atkinson ('Dallas Boner') – worked out ways and means to satirise the culture industry using utterly unironic commitment to formal musical values. This set them apart from those 'subversive' groups who imagine slacker carelessness (and narcotic indulgence) will bring the system tumbling down. Pence Eleven rejected the florid immediacy of rock, turning their gigs into bizarre collisons of tightly programmed minidisc backing tapes, all pop sparkle and auto-pump, and onstage frenzy, petulance and awkwardness. Blunt's strict-tempo bass playing complemented Calton's perverse guitar. Through the provocative pop gloss, unconscious echoes of Egg and Jan Steele – in truth refreshingly untrendy recognition of the English traditions of

Henry Purcell and plainsong – proved they were accessing deeply sedimented musical forms.

Pence Eleven's Devoesque assault on rock authenticity didn't suggest any particular connection to Free Improvisation (Blunt still claims he can't make 'head or tail' of Bailey's playing). However, Drenching and Pleasure began manufacturing home-made albums by playing Dictaphone and bricks hit with various implements. One notable release, *Llançà & Elsewhere* [Fenland Hi-Brow, 2001], had tracks recorded in the car park of Les Palmiers in Lançà, Spain, and in a disabled toilet at Liverpool airport. Aware that the way they were making music for their releases was actually 'improvisation', they sent Bailey a nine-minute track (the Liverpool toilet recording, in fact). Bailey shot back an encouraging postcard saying he 'didn't think anyone did that anymore', and suggested they ring him. They phoned. Bailey said he was busy for six months, but would they ring again in November? They did, and that's how they ended up playing with him.

Drenching carries his Dictaphone with him wherever he goes. He records external sounds and bursts of his own mouth noise, and then plays back the results with his finger jogging the fast-forward button, shaping the sounds by muting the speaker with his palm: a piece of antiquated office equipment has become a kind of recording-tape harmonica. Like punk 'incompetents' breaking down rock into the skiffle which gave it birth, Drenching breaks through the arch formalism of 'avant' DJ-ing and sampling ('plunderphonics'), making the Dictaphone as much a personal prosthesis as a bluesman's guitar or a hip-hop DJ's turntable. Bueler is a composer, but one whose first concern is with concrete sonority rather than rulebook playability: as Sonic Pleasure she attacks her bricks with hammers, chisels and wallpaper scrapers, producing a variety of unpredictable percussive events any serialist would die for. Spiked by the vocalised, expressive quality of Drenching's Dictaphone, the chance and specificity of Pleasure's bricks reassert Free Improvisation's shock to the ear: revolutionary classicism. In the late 1920s, Theodor Adorno was panned by his composition teachers for reviving the 'old hat' of 1910s free atonality – Stravinsky's neo-classicism was by then all the rage – but his polemics nevertheless went on to lay the foundations for the post-war avant-garde. As with Ingar Zach, the intransigence of Drenching and Pleasure will doubtless annoy those postmodern critics (like *Signal To Noise*'s Dan Warburton) who deem the jagged, crunchy, *unmusical* sound of Free Improvisation a 'dead dog'. Drenching's Middle Class Records subsidiary Fenland Hi-Brow Recordings has so far released nine Dictaphone/brick duets, all ashake with the couple's fervidly irregular rhythmical impulse. This pair *know* that they are solving problems which have reduced practitioners of bourgeois genres to an impasse (the rhythmic banality of 'cross-over', from Steve Martland through to Jaga Jazzist): each release has a polemical, manifesto-like quality. They call their duo 'Pleasure-Drenching Improvers'.

Pleasure-Drenching Improvers were based in York and now live in Manchester, far from the London scene. They didn't make contact with Bailey by promoting him at a local improv club (the time-honoured method by which provincial musicians get in touch), but by sending him a CD, a method that rarely works (for Bailey's dread of CD listening, see Appendix 3). Bailey was especially impressed with the exterior of the packet, plastered with Drenching's witty, updated-Schwitters detritus. The couple visited him twice at Downs Road in Hackney for a play. On the second occasion, Alex Ward was on hand with his clarinet, making a quartet possible: Bailey recorded what they played on DAT, and eleven minutes were used as the last track on the Incus compilation *Visitors Book* [Incus CD-R] – rightfully last, as there's a rhythmic vim to the playing after which anything else would sound insipid. Just before Christmas 2002, on 21 December (the birthday of a present-day composer important for both Drenching and Pleasure), Bailey went into the Moat studio with Drenching and Pleasure, Ward and Tony Bevan, the latter now devoting himself to the bass sax.

As with Joseph Holbrooke and the Spontaneous Music Ensemble – or hooking up with Matt Wand and Pat Thomas in 1992, or Ist and Will Gaines in 1999 – Bailey had alighted upon a collective *esprit* which doubles the power and significance of his playing. Drenching's sensibility – his hip-hop impatience and cartoon nervousness – riddles the quintet. The horns sound better than usual: the last vestige of conscious saxophone 'statement' has been eradicated in favour of high-speed dementia; the ritualistic, hippie aura of the SME has been invaded by post-

Simpsons clutter, chatter and velocity. In less pressured circumstances, Ward's alternations between superintelligent harmonic argument (a kind of bebop) and mewing vocalese (a kind of post-Ayler expressionism) can sound desperate; here he sounds rich and fantastic. Tony Bevan's *Three Oranges* [Foghorn, 1998] – a mini-CD of unaccompanied bass saxophone – was an incredible demonstration of chops on his new axe, but on *Limescale* the guttural eloquence of his playing has found something to talk about (together, Drenching and Pleasure add up to Matt Lewis, Bevan's best percussive foil). Although achieved more via a conceptual leap than by jazz dues-paying, Pleasure's bricks rediscover the weird collision of ornamental commentary and unexpected eruption in Oxley's drumming. It's always fascinating when Bailey improvises with a single musician, but there is something individualist and stark and rather depressing (existential? anti-social?) about the prospect of music as a series of duets, however high-powered. Here, the collective fully absorbes him, giving him a pivotal role, conductive yet insider ('a-rhythm guitar'?). One doesn't think of *Limescale* as a 'Bailey record' so much as another dazzling contemporary ensemble to put beside Bark! (drummer Phillip Marks's trio with Rex Casswell on guitar and Paul Obermayer on sampler) or Hiss (Ingar Zach's new quartet with guitarist Ivar Grydeland, bassist Tonny Kluften and keyboardist Pat Thomas). Despite all the groans coming from the postmoderns (and Adornoite epigones) about the impossibility of originality and invention in contemporary culture, here it is – and it's Bailey's latest Hot Five. Amazing.

CONCLUSION:
ON IMPROVISATION

It's not a question of why be a free improvisor. It's a question of what else? It offers more playing per cubic second than any other type of music making. [DB to Tony Mostrom, *Guitar Player*, January 1997]

For listeners, Free Improvisation is taxing music.

Listening to Free Improvisation – at a gig, or to live tapes, or to authentic CDs, where the improvisors are not rendering a predefined style – requires complete concentration. It's like listening to people converse. If you don't pay attention, the extreme dynamics and the breaks and changes are incredibly annoying. In a period when music is mass-marketed to confirm sociological identities – a kind of lifestyle wallpaper – the focused listening required by Free Improvisation is unlikely to attract large audiences. Nevertheless, the music is profoundly egalitarian. No prior listening – only the concept of listening – can prepare you for what lies ahead.

Free Improvisation also leaps over a chasm that divides today's philosophies of advanced music. Theodor Adorno's critical campaign was waged to protect subjectivist lyricism and truth from the profit-oriented functionalism of the culture industry. John Zorn, on the other hand, maintains that the era of lyrical subjectivism is past, and all that remains is the postmodern project of managing external elements. As proposed by Derek Bailey and Tony Oxley, Free Improvisation transcends this opposition. All sounds are indeed made alien, treated as flotsam from the shipwreck of bourgeois civilisation, but instead of being treated with cool postmodernist objectivity, these fragments are worked upon by the musicians in real time, an intensely subjectivist baring of soul, full of risk and opportunities for embarrassment. Ironic manoeuvres are subsumed by processual sincerity – or the process wilts, and everyone recognises the results are trivial and boring. The wager is that any roomful of humans can find community, whatever their linguistic or musical systems, simply by the act of listening and playing: and, unlike the 'communities' created by folk and world music, this is done without surrendering one jot of musical awareness achieved by historic technical advance.

The many stages of American music have brought the use of melody under the gun (the very word); melody, is staring down the gun barrel. Any person in today's music scene knows that rock, classical, folk and jazz are all yesterday's titles. I feel that the music world is getting closer to being a singular expression, one with endless musical stories of mankind.

Is there a mood everyone wishes at the same time and space? By listening and dancing one finds those wishes to come true in whoever might be playing or singing. [Ornette Coleman, 15–iii–1977, sleeve note to the LP release of *Dancing in Your Head* (omitted from A&M's CD reissue)]

Ornette Coleman's words were carefully weighed. *Dancing in Your Head* combined the recorded debut of Prime Time, his twin-guitar electric band with Shannon Jackson on drums, plus Ornette's own saxophonic 'listening and dancing' to the Master Musicians of Joujouka, Morocco. His responses to this wild, untempered music were an example of how anyone should understand and hear a music, however 'alien'. If Ornette were not – as an American – deprived of any knowledge of Karl Marx, he'd have quoted Marx's favourite Latin tag: 'nihil humanum me alienum puto' (nothing human is foreign to me).

Bailey occupies a special place in the development of Free Improvisation. No other musician has been so single-minded in developing an instrumental approach specifically designed to pursue it. For rock-generation listeners (including this author), Bailey's tone isn't what attracted you to the electric guitar in the first place. Like that of Jim Hall, it's designed to hit a note dead on and stay there. If it's tweaked after that, the move is made with deliberation. There are none of the wows and twangs that characterise post-war amplified blues: Bailey does not stressify.* His note shapes are not vocalised, they do not imitate the tone and cadences of his personal speaking voice (a blues device which marks every authentic rock guitarist, from Frank Zappa to Johnny Thunders and Steve Albini, and which marks the playing of T. H. F. Drenching and Alex Ward). Bailey eschews personal expression for surrender to the objectivity of the language. Like the deadpan prose of Samuel Beckett, Bailey's cool and precise – yet piercing and aggressive – tone denies the generic associations and pleasures previously associated with the electric guitar. Just as, to emerge as a distinctive writer, Samuel Beckett needed to shake off the Irish prolixity of James Joyce, Bailey needed to shake off the waggle and quake of blues and jazz. Though the music he plunges it into is often hot and messy and human, his instrument is as cold as a surgeon's scalpel.

Sheffield guitarist John Jasnoch makes for an interesting contrast. His playing is replete with the whirrs and buzzes that make blues and bluegrass so rich. In fact, Jasnoch's notes are more attractive in terms of sonority than Bailey's, and if one were selecting musicians for some particular purpose – for a rock band, or a film soundtrack, or a collage symphony – one might well prefer Jasnoch to Bailey. However, considered as a contribution to Free Improvisation, Jasnoch's style reveals deficiencies. One night (5–ii–1988) in a tiny upstairs pub room in Leeds, the Termite Club hosted what was named 'Northern Company': Linda Lee Welsh (voice), Mary Schwartz (viola), Martin Jones (trumpet), Alan Wilkinson (alto, baritone), Charlie Collins (reeds), Peter Minns (tenor), Paul Buckton (guitar), Dave Ellis (bass), Martin Howard (acoustic guitar), Paul Hession (drums), with John Jasnoch and Derek Bailey on electric guitars. This was an extraordinary lesson in the value of Bailey's thinner, less gorgeous notes: acupuncture needles rather than vibrational massage, they pierced to the heart of the complex, multi-threaded music, redirecting it, suggesting new harmonic avenues. Though Jasnoch's notes always sounded lovely, they were too coarse to negotiate what the ensemble was playing, and seemed to cover up more than they revealed.

* The word *stressify* was invented by Johnny 'Guitar' Watson to describe his own finger-on-string technique, characteristically (and like his own soul music) fusing the idea of rib-digging innuendo – 'stress' – with the confessional, gospel-truth implications of 'testify'.

Artistic innovations are frequently perceived as sabotage of existing pleasures. The guitar playing of Bailey sabotages merely sonic pleasures, redirecting attention to the totality and direction of the music. With Bailey, a guitar note is not an end in itself, but a purposeful contribution to musical development – a question. Bailey's playing is therefore progressive in the true sense. It articulates the values of socialism as against those of capitalism: life lived as a dialectical contribution to human history, rather than cowering in positive and defended comfort. Free Improvisation tears away the comfort blanket and drops the temperature, making each musician's motifs gleam against a backdrop of black nothing. It's as exhilarating and cold-to-breathe as the revolutionary idea itself – but if you won't learn to breathe this ether, a nonlife of conformity and repetition beckons.

DEREK BAILEY'S POSTCARD, AN ANTI-IMPROV COMMUNIQUÉ

Before me on my desk I have a postcard from Derek Bailey. In the 'Invisible Jukebox' published in *The Wire* in December 1998 (see Appendix 3), I'd got his birth date wrong. My excuse is that his date of birth was not that easy to find. It's not printed on the flyleaf of his book *Improvisation*, and it's not included on any of the innumerable Company Week flyers and programmes that have piled up on my trestle table creaking with Derekobilia. A magazine deadline was looming, but I did not wish to telephone him and distract him from practising his guitar with a silly question. So I computed the year of his birth by subtracting his age when serving in the navy from the year of his trip to board HMS *Arthur*, and my maths went awry.

Derek's riposte was to paste a photocopy of his entry as held at the International Biographical Centre, Cambridge, England – a piece of semi-transparent, grey-veined, heat-sensitive paper from the Incus fax machine – onto the message portion of a postcard, along with a rebuke to my weak scholarship: 'I didn't know that you didn't know how old I am' (a quote from his 1994 solo CD *Drop Me Off at 96th*).

On the picture side of the postcard there is an old man's hand, palm outwards, photographed against a white plaster wall. His stubby fingers are parted between the middle fingers, like the sign for scissors in the schoolyard game. Although the fax cutting is stuck down over the caption, Derek has left a corner unglued so I can squint beneath. It's actually a publicity device for John Lee Hooker's *Chill Out* album, issued in 1998 (three years before the great bluesman's death in 2001). The photograph is by Anton Corbijn (I recognise the documentary/sepia style Corbijn used for his famous photographs of a haggard Captain Beefheart standing in the Mojave Desert).

Upside down, scribbled across Hooker's palm, is this slogan, a bizarre *détournement* that connects Bailey to art subversives as various and obscure as Kurt Schwitters, J. H. Prynne, Michael Thompson, Jamie Muir, Paul Minotto and Dogbiz:

IMPROV IS STILL RUBBISH

Derek Bailey. What a card.

Min Tanaka and Derek Bailey, Tokyo, 1981.

Min Tanaka, Derek Bailey and Unk., Tokyo, 1981.

At the Egg Farm, Japan: Kazuko Saito, Derek Bailey and Karen Brookman – 'where there's woman ...', 1987.

Tony Oxley, Viersen, Germany, June 1999 © Ben Watson.

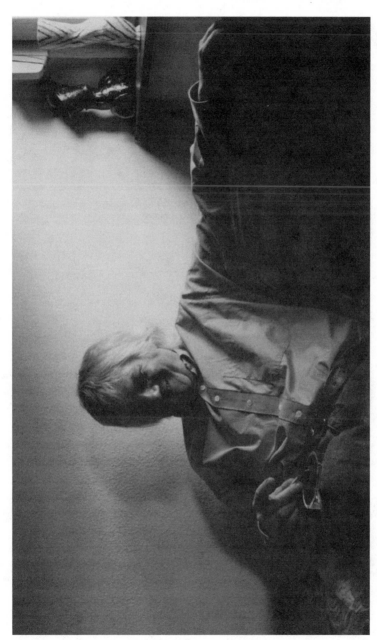

Tony Oxley, Viersen, Germany, June 1999 © Ben Watson.

Plaça Reial, Barcelona, 2003 © Carmen LLussà Fernández: 'I'm trying to start a club, I'm playing there on Friday, a photographer's studio. I've got him to get out his bass clarinet, people say he's good. They don't want more than thirty people there. That's no problem …' [18-i-2004].

Plaça Reial, Barcelona, 2003 © Carmen LLussà Fernández.

La Rambla, Barcelona, 2003 © Carmen LLussà Fernández

APPENDIX 1

A DEREK BAILEY DISCOGRAPHY

Releases are in Derek Bailey's name, unless indicated otherwise between brackets [thus]. The title of the album, if there is one, appears in italics. The label and catalogue number appear between parantheses (thus). Abbreviations for instruments are as follows: as = alto saxophone; b = double bass; b-cl = bass clarinet; bs = baritone saxophone; b-tbn = bass trombone; cl = clarinet; d = drums; el = electronics; el-b = electric bass guitar; fl = flute; fl-h = fluegel-horn; fr-h = French horn; g = guitar; keyb = keyboards; p = piano; perc = percussion; ss = soprano saxophone; synth = synthesizer; t = trumpet; tbn = trombone; ts = tenor sax; v = voice. Formats: release is on CD unless otherwise stated (LP = vinyl 12-inch long-playing record; 10-inch = vinyl shorter-playing record; 7-inch = vinyl single; V = video). R = re-release. Recording dates are in European format – dd-mm-yyyy – with the month in Roman numerals. Hence 29 January 1930 would appear as 29–i–1930.

The best way to acquire both Incus releases and the burgeoning quantity of Bailey on independent labels is via the mail-order service run by Bailey's widow, Karen Brookman. A catalogue is available from: Incus Records, 14 Downs Road, London, E5 8DS, England; fax +44 (0) 20 8533 2851; e-mail <karenin-cus2001@yahoo.co.uk>; website <www.incusrecords.force9.co.uk>. Many thanks to Peter Stubley and Richard Shapiro, whose on-line sessionography provided a starting point for what follows, and to Harry Gilonis, who provided fact-checking beyond the call of duty. Stubley's European Free Improvisation website provides a wealth of data on Derek Bailey and other free improvisors: <http://www.shef.ac.uk/misc/rec/ps/efi>).

Albums are listed in order of release-date. Bailey expressed surprise about this. My reason is that releases delineate a different chronology from playing, to do with outreach, fame and capital investment. One can reconstruct a 'sessionography' from discs (the usual practice in jazz), but to do so without reference to the gigs – and the continual practising – seems particularly meaningless in Bailey's case. Listing releases by release date allows one to assess Bailey's presence in the public sphere. Bailey does not encourage interest in his early session work.

1968

Karyobin [Spontaneous Music Ensemble] (Island ILPS 9079) with Kenny Wheeler t, fl-h; Evan Parker ss; Dave Holland b; John Stevens d. 18–ii–1968 LP

Cybernetic Serendipity Music (ICA O1) with Evan Parker ss; Richard Howe fr-h; Gavin Bryars b; Bernard Rands cymbalom. 28–viii–1968 LP

1969

The Baptised Traveller [Tony Oxley Quintet] (CBS 52664) with Kenny Wheeler t, fl-h; Evan Parker ts; Jeff Clyne b; Tony Oxley d. 3–i– 1969 LP

[Spontaneous Music Ensemble] (Marmalade 608008) with Kenny Wheeler fl-h; Trevor Watts as; Peter Lemer p; Johnny Dyani b; John Stevens d; Maggie Nicols v; Carolann Nichols v; Pepi Lemer v. 6– ii–1969 LP

European Echoes [Manfred Schoof] (FMP 0010) with Manfred Schoof t; Enrico Rava t; Hugh Steinmetz t; Paul Rutherford tbn; Peter Brötzmann ts; Gerd Dudek ts; Evan Parker ss, ts; Fred van Hove p; Irene Schweizer p; Alex von Schlippenbach p; Arjen Gorter b; Buschi Niebergall b, b-tbn; Peter Kowald b; Han Bennink d; Pierre Favre d. vi–1969 LP

[Instant Composers Pool] (ICP004) with Han Bennink d. 30–vii–1969 LP

1970

4 Compositions for Sextet [Tony Oxley] (CBS 64071) with Kenny Wheeler t, fl-h; Evan Parker ss, ts; Paul Rutherford tbn; Jeff Clyne b; Tony Oxley d. 7–ii–1970 LP

Nipples [Peter Brötzmann Sextet/Quartet] (Calig-Verlag CAL30604) with Peter Brötzmann ts; Evan Parker ts; Fred van Hove p; Buschi Niebergall b; Han Bennink d. 18–iv–1969 LP

Fragments [John Tchicai] (ICP 005) with Misha Mengelberg p; John Tchicai reeds; Han Bennink d, perc. 3–iii–1970 LP

The German 12th Jazz Festival in Frankfurt Am Main [Various Artists] (Scout Records SC-S12/13/14) with Malcom Griffiths tbn; Paul Rutherford tbn; Willem van Manen tbn; Buschi Niebergall tbn; Peter Brötzmann reeds; Willem Breuker reeds; Evan Parker reeds; Fred van Hove p; Han Bennink d. 21–22–iii–1970 LP

Groupcomposing (ICP 006) with Paul Rutherford tbn; Peter Bennink as, bagpipes; Peter Brötzmann ts; Evan Parker ss, ts; Misha Mengelberg p; Han Bennink perc, oe-oe, gachi. 15–v–1970 LP

The Topography of the Lungs (Incus 1) with Evan Parker ss, ts; Han Bennink perc. 13–vii–1970 LP

[Music Improvisation Company] (ECM 1005) with Evan Parker ss; Hugh Davies live el; Jamie Muir perc; Christine Jeffrey v. 25–27–viii–1970 LP

1971

Improvisations for Cello and Guitar [David Holland, Derek Bailey] (ECM 1013) with David Holland cello. i–1971 LP

'So, What Do You Think?' [Spontaneous Music Ensemble] (Tangent TGS 118) with Kenny Wheeler t, fl-h; Trevor Watts ss; Dave Holland cello, b; John Stevens d. 27–i–1971 LP

Solo Guitar (Incus 2) ii–1971 LP

Ichnos [Tony Oxley] (RCA SF8215) LP with Evan Parker ss, ts; Paul

Rutherford tbn; Tony Oxley perc, amplified perc; Kenny Wheeler t, fl-h; Barry Guy b. 1971 LP

1972

[Iskra 1903] (Incus 3/4) with Paul Rutherford tbn, p; Barry Guy b. 2–ix–1970 and 3–v–1972 2LP

Ode [London Jazz Composers Orchestra] (Incus 6/7) with Harry Beckett t; Dave Holdsworth t, fl-h; Marc Charig t, fl-h; Paul Rutherford tbn; Mike Gibbs tbn; Paul Nieman tbn; Dick Hart tuba; Trevor Watts as, ss; Mike Osborne as; Bernhard Living as; Alan Wakeman ss, ts; Evan Parker ss, ts; Bob Downes ts, fl; Karl Jenkins bs, oboe; Howard Riley p; Jeff Clyne b; Chris Laurence b; Barry Guy b; Tony Oxley perc; Paul Lytton perc; Buxton Orr conductor. 22–iv–1972 2LP

Live at Verity's Place [Derek Bailey and Han Bennink] (Incus 9) with Han Bennink perc. 16–17–vi–1972 LP

1973

TAP 1 (Incus) iv–1973 reel-to-reel tape
TAP 2 (Incus) iv–1973 reel-to-reel tape
TAP 3 (Incus) vi–1973 reel-to-reel tape
TAP 4 (Incus) vi–1973 reel-to-reel tape

1974

Lot 74 Solo Improvisations (Incus 12) Spring 1974 LP
Free Improvisation [Iskra 1903/New Phonic Art/Wired] (Deutsche Grammophon 2740 105) with Paul Rutherford tbn; Barry Guy acoustic and amplified b. 21–24–vi–1973 3LP
First Duo Concert [Anthony Braxton and Derek Bailey] (Emanem 601) with Anthony Braxton reeds. 30–vi–1974 2LP

1975

[Tony Oxley Sextet] (Incus 8) with Evan Parker ss; Paul Rutherford tbn; Tony Oxley perc, amplified perc. 1971 LP

The Crust [Steve Lacy] (Emanem 304) with Steve Lacy ss; Steve Potts as, ss; Kent Carter amplified b; John Stevens d, perc. 30–vii–1973 LP

Hamburg '74 [Globe Unity Orchestra and the Choir of the NDR-Broadcast] (FMP 0650) with Manfred Schoof t; Kenny Wheeler t; Gunter Christmann tbn; Paul Rutherford tbn; Peter Brötzmann reeds; Rudiger Carl reeds; Gerd Dudek reeds; Evan Parker reeds; Michel Pilz reeds; Alex von Schlippenbach p; Peter Kowald b, tuba; Han Bennink d, perc, cl; Paul Lovens d, perc; Choir of the NDR-Broadcast conducted by Helmut Franz. 19–xi–1974 LP

The Sinking of the Titanic [Gavin Bryars] (Island/Polydor/Obscure No. 1) 'Jesus' Blood Never Failed Me Yet' with the Cockpit Ensemble: Michael Nyman organ; John Nash violin; John White tuba; Sandra Hill b; Gavin Bryars conductor. 1975 LP

Ensemble Pieces [Christopher Hobbs, John Adams, Gavin Bryars] (Island/Polydor/Obscure No. 2) '1, 2, 1–2–3–4' with Gavin Bryars double b; Christopher Hobbs p; Cornelius Cardew cello; Mike Nicolls d; Celia Gollin v; Brian Eno v; Andy Mackay oboe; Stuart Deeks violins; Paul Nieman tbn. 1975 LP

The London Concert [Derek Bailey, Evan Parker] (Incus 16) with Evan Parker ss, ts. 14–ii–1975 LP

Dreams [Steve Lacy] (Saravah SH 10058) with Steve Lacy ss; Steve Potts as, ss; Irène Aebi cello, v; Kent Carter b; Kenneth Tyler d; Jean-Jacques Avenel b; Jack Treese g; Boulou Ferre g. 12/15–v–1975 LP

improvisation (Diverso No 2) 16–ix–1975 LP

1976

1968-1971 [Music Improvisation Company] (Incus 17) with Evan Parker ss, amplified auto-harp; Hugh Davies live el, organ; Jamie Muir perc. 4–vii–1969 and 18–vi–1970 LP

First Duo Concert [Anthony Braxton and Derek Bailey] (Denon DJ7554AX) with Anthony Braxton reeds. 30–vi–1974 LP

First Duo Concert [Anthony Braxton and Derek Bailey] (Denon DJ7555AX) with Anthony Braxton reeds. 30–vi–1974 LP R

Saxophone Special [Steve Lacy] (Emanem 3310) with Steve Lacy ss, gramophone; Trevor Watts ss, as; Evan Parker ss, ts, bs; Steve Potts ss, as; Michel Waisvisz synth. 19–xii–1974 LP

Guitar Solos 2 [Fred Frith, Gerry Fitzgerald, Hans Reichel, Derek Bailey] (Virgin/Caroline C1518) xii–1975 or i–1976 LP

Duo [Derek Bailey, Tristan Honsinger] (Incus 20) with Tristan Honsinger cello, voice. 6–7–ii–1976 LP

Company 1 [Company] (Incus 21) with Evan Parker ss, ts; Tristan Honsinger cello; Maarten van Regteren Altena b. 9–v–1976 LP

1977

Song for Someone [Kenny Wheeler] (Incus 10) with Kenny Wheeler t, fl-h; Ian Hammer t; Greg Bowen t; Dave Hancock t; Keith Christie tbn; Bobby Lamb tbn; Chris Pyne tbn; David Horler tbn; Malcolm Griffiths b-tbn; Alfie Reece tuba; Duncan Lamont ts, fl; Mike Osborne as; Alan Branscombe p, electric p; John Taylor electric p; Ron Mathewson b; Tony Oxley perc; Norma Winstone v; Evan Parker ts. 10–11–i–1973 LP

The Crust [Steve Lacy] (Victor (Japan) VIP6635) with Steve Lacy ss; Steve Potts as, ss; Kent Carter b; John Stevens d, perc. 30–vii–1973 LP R

Company 2 [Company] (Incus 23) with Evan Parker ss, ts; Anthony Braxton ss, as, E-flat cl, B-flat cl, contrabass-cl. 22–viii–1976 LP

Company 3 [Company] (Incus 25) with Han Bennink d. ix–1976 LP

Company 4 [Company] (Incus 26) with Steve Lacy ss. 11–xi–1976 LP

Drops [Derek Bailey and Andrea Centazzo] (Ictus 003) with Andrea Centazzo perc, whistles. 3–4–iv–1977 LP

Fictions [Company] (Incus 38) with Misha Mengelberg p, celeste, v; Lol Coxhill ss, v; Steve Beresford p, toys, v; Ian Croall v. viii–1977 LP

1978

For Example: Workshop Freie Musik 1969–1978/Nr. 1 [Various Artists] (FMP R1/2/3) 27–iii–1976 3LP

Company 5 [Company] (Incus 28) with Leo Smith t, fl; Maarten van Regteren Altena b; Tristan Honsinger cello; Anthony Braxton cl, fl, as, ss; Steve Lacy ss; Evan Parker ss, ts. 26–v–1977 LP

Company 6 [Company] (Incus 29) with Leo Smith t; Maarten van Regteren Altena b; Tristan Honsinger cello; Anthony Braxton cl, fl, ss, as; Steve Lacy ss; Lol Coxhill ss; Evan Parker ss, ts; Han Bennink d, viola, banjo; Steve Beresford p, t. 25–27–v–1977 LP

Company 7 [Company] (Incus 30) with Leo Smith t; Maarten van Regteren Altena b; Tristan Honsinger cello; Anthony Braxton cl, ss, as; Steve Lacy ss; Lol Coxhill ss; Evan Parker ss, ts; Han Bennink d, viola, cl, banjo; Steve Beresford p, g. 25–27–v–1977 LP

Improvisations [Globe Unity Orchestra] (Japo 60 021) with Kenny Wheeler t; Manfred Schoof t; Günter Christmann tbn; Albert Mangelsdorff tbn; Paul Rutherford tbn; Gerd Dudek fl, ss, ts; Evan Parker ss, ts; Peter Brötzmann as, ts, b-cl; Michel Pilz b-cl; Tristan Honsinger cello; Alex von Schlippenbach p; Peter Kowald b, tuba; Buschi Niebergall b; Paul Lovens d. ix–1977 LP

K'Ploeng (Claxon 78.2) with Maarten van Regteren Altena b; Maurice Horsthuis viola; Tristan Honsinger cello; Terry Day perc; Michel Waisvisz synth. 14–17–xii–1977 LP

Machine Music [John White, Gavin Bryars] (Polydor/Obscure OBS8) with Fred Frith guitars; Gavin Bryars guitars; Brian Eno electric guitars. 1978 LP

Duo & Trio Improvisation (Kitty MKF1034) with Toshinori Kondo t, alto horn; Kaoru Abe as; Mototeru Tagaki as, ts; Motoharu Yoshizawa b; Toshi Tsuchitori d, perc. 19–iv–1978 LP

New Sights, Old Sounds (Morgue 03/04) 21–iv–1978, 3–v–1978, 5–v–1978 2LP

1979

Solo Guitar (Incus 2R) ii–1971 LP R
[Derek Bailey and One Music Ensemble] (Nondo 002) split records with Dave Panton various instruments on obverse. 3–iv–1973 LP
Time [Derek Bailey, Tony Coe] (Incus 34) with Tony Coe cl in C. 23–24–iv–1979 LP
Domestic & Public Pieces (Quark 9999) i–1976, 22–v–1975 LP

1980

Live at Wigmor [Anthony Braxton and Derek Bailey] (Inner City IC 1041) with Anthony Braxton reeds, flute. 30–vi–1974 2LP R
Idylle und Katastrophen [Johansson/Schlippenbach Improvisors] (Po Torch Records PTR/JWD6) with Alexander von Schlippenbach p, honky-tonk piano; celeste; Sven-Åke Johansson perc, accordion, v; Maarten van Regteren Altena b, cello; Günter Christmann tbn; Candace Natvig violin, v; Wolfgang Fuchs sopranino sax, b-cl; Paul Lovens perc, saw, zither. 26–xi–1979 LP
Fables [Company] (Incus 36) with Evan Parker ss, ts; George Lewis tbn; Dave Holland b. 17–18–v–1980 LP
The Science Set – Volume 2 Metalanguage Festival of Improvised Music 1980 (Metalanguage ML117/Beak Doctor BD6) duet with Jon Raskin bs and trio with Larry Ochs ts; Toshinori Kondo t. 21–x–1980 LP

1981

Views from 6 Windows (Metalanguage ML114) with Christine Jeffrey v. i–ii–1980 LP
Pisa 1980 [Improvisors' Symposium] (Incus 37) one track with Maarten van Regteren Altena b. 26–28–vi–1980 LP

1982

Aida (Incus 40) 4–vii–1980, 3–viii–1980 LP
Dart Drug [Derek Bailey and Jamie Muir] (Incus 41) with Jamie Muir
perc. viii–1981 LP

1983

Yankees [Derek Bailey, George Lewis and John Zorn] (Celluloid
CEL6706) with George Lewis tbn; John Zorn as, ss, cl, game calls.
1982 LP

1984

Royal Volume 1 [Anthony Braxton and Derek Bailey] (Incus 43) with
Anthony Braxton ss, as, B-flat cl, contrabass cl. 2–vii–1974 LP
Les Douze Sons [Joëlle Léandre] (Nato 82) with Joëlle Léandre b; Ernst
Reijseger viola. vi–1983 LP

1985

Epiphany/Epiphanies [Company] (Incus 46/47) with Phil Wachsmann
violin, el; George Lewis tbn; Julie Tippetts acoustic g, v, fl; Fred
Frith g; Ursula Oppens p; Keith Tippett p; Anne Le Baron harp;
Akio Suzuki glass harmonica, analapos, spring gong, kikkokikiriki;
Motoharu Yoshizawa b. 29–vi to 3–vii–1982 2LP
Notes (Incus 48) iv–1985, vii–1985 LP

1986

Eighty-Five Minutes Part 1 [Spontaneous Music Ensemble] (Emanem 3401) with John Stevens perc, cornet; Kent Carter cello, b; Evan Parker ss; Trevor Watts ss. 3–ii–1974 LP

Eighty-Five Minutes Part 2 [Spontaneous Music Ensemble] (Emanem 3402) with John Stevens perc, cornet; Kent Carter cello; Evan Parker ss; Trevor Watts ss. 3–ii–1974 LP

Dreams [Steve Lacy] (Saravah 2H10058) with Steve Lacy ss; Steve Potts as, ss; Irene Aebi cello, v; Kent Carter b; Kenneth Tyler d; Jean-Jacques Avenel b; Jack Treese g; Boulou Ferre g. 12/15–v–1975 LP

Compatibles [Derek Bailey, Evan Parker] (Incus 50) with Evan Parker ss, ts. 22–iv–1985, 27–vii–1985 LP

Trios [Company] (Incus 51) with Vinko Globokar tbn, v, fl; Joëlle Léandre b, v; Hugh Davies live el; J. D. Parran basset horn, piccolo; Peter Brötzmann ts, bs; Jamie Muir perc; Ernst Rejseger cello, electric cello; Evan Parker ts, ss; John Corbett t, fl-h. 24–28–v–1983 LP

Legends of Jazz Guitar [Various Artists] (Rhino R2 70717) iv–1985 ('Scaling' from *Notes* Incus 48)

1987

Moment Précieux [Anthony Braxton and Derek Bailey] (Victo 02) with Anthony Braxton as, sopranino sax. 4–x–1986 LP

1988

In Whose Tradition? (Emanem 3404) 26–vii–1971, 29–vi–1974, 22–v–1975, iii–1977, 2–v–1979, ii–1987, 12–vi–1987 LP

Cyro [Derek Bailey and Cyro Baptista] (Incus CD01) with Cyro Baptista perc. x–1982

Han [Derek Bailey and Han Bennink] (Incus CD02) with Han Bennink perc. 15–22–iii–1986

1989

Once [Company] (Incus CD04) with Lee Konitz as, ss, d; Richard Teitelbaum keyb; Barre Phillips b; Carlos Zingaro violin; Tristan Honsinger cello; Steve Noble perc, bugle, saw. 12–17–v–1987
Pleistozaen mit Wasser [Cecil Taylor and Derek Bailey] (FMP CD16) with Cecil Taylor p, v. 9–vii–1988

1990

Figuring [Derek Bailey and Barre Phillips] (Incus CD05) with Barre Phillips b. 12–v–1987, 4–ix–1988

1991

Company 6 & 7 [Company] (Incus CD07) with Leo Smith t, fl; Maarten van Regteren Altena b; Tristan Honsinger cello; Anthony Braxton cl, fl, as, ss; Steve Lacy ss; Lol Coxhill ss; Evan Parker ss, ts; Han Bennink d, viola, cl, banjo; Steve Beresford p, g. 25–27–v–1977 R
Improvised Music New York 1981 (Muworks Records MUW1007) with Fred Frith g; Sonny Sharrock g; John Zorn horns; Bill Laswell b; Charles K. Noyes perc. 18–ix–1981
Duos Europa – America – Japan [Peter Kowald] (FMP CD21) with Peter Kowald b. 10–vii–1987

1992

Duos Europa [Peter Kowald] (FMP 1260) with Peter Kowald b. 16–viii–1987 LP

Village Life (Incus CD09) with Louis Moholo d, perc, v; Thebe Lipere perc, v. 25–ix–1991

Solo Guitar Volume 1 (Incus CD10) ii–1971 R

Duo & Trio Improvisation (DIW 358) with Toshinori Kondo t, alto horn; Kaoru Abe as; Mototeru Tagaki as, ts; Motoharu Yoshizawa b; Toshi Tsuchitori d. 19–iv–1978 R

Yankees [Derek Bailey, George Lewis and John Zorn] (Celluloid CEL5006) with George Lewis tbn; John Zorn as, ss, cl, game calls. 1982 R

Solo Guitar Volume 2 (Incus CD11) 22–vi–1991

1993

Karyobin [Spontaneous Music Ensemble] (Chronoscope CPE2001) with Kenny Wheeler t, fl-h; Evan Parker ss; Dave Holland b; John Stevens d. 18–ii–1968 R

1968–1971 [Music Improvisation Company] (Incus CD12) with Evan Parker ss, amplified auto-harp; Hugh Davies live el, organ; Jamie Muir perc. 4–vii–1969 and 18–vi–1970 R

Darn It! [Paul Haines] (American Clave AMCL1014/18) viii–1986 2CD

The Aerial #5 [Various Artists] (Aerial AER1992/5) 1990 Derek's track, here amidst a grisly selection of avant dross, was reissued in 2001 as 'Henry' on *Chats* (Incus CD-R)

[Tony Oxley Quartet] (Incus CD15) with Tony Oxley perc; Pat Thomas keyb, el; Matt Wand drum machine, tape switchboard. 8–iv–1992

KomunGuitar [Jin Hi Kim] (What Next? WN12) with Jin Hi Kim komungo. Summer 1992

Playing (Incus CD14) with John Stevens d, mini-trumpet. 14–viii–1992

1994

Drop Me Off at 96th (Scatter 02) 12–v–1986, 3–vi–1987

Moment Précieux [Anthony Braxton and Derek Bailey] (Victo 02) with Anthony Braxton as, sopranino sax. 4–x–1986 R

Company91 Volume 1 [Company] (Incus CD16) with Alexander Balanescu violin; Vanessa Mackness v; Yves Robert tbn; Paul Lovens perc; Paul Rogers b; Pat Thomas keyb, el; Buckethead g; John Zorn as. 26–27–vii–1991

Company91 Volume 2 [Company] (Incus CD17) with Alexander Balanescu violin; Vanessa Mackness v; Yves Robert tbn; Paul Lovens perc; Paul Rogers b; Pat Thomas p, el; Buckethead g; John Zorn as. 27–29–vii–1991

Company91 Volume 3 [Company] (Incus CD18) with Alexander Balanescu violin; Vanessa Mackness v; Yves Robert tbn; Paul Lovens perc; Paul Rogers b; Pat Thomas keyb, el; Buckethead g; John Zorn as. 29–30–vii–1991

New Year Messages 1–4 (Table of the Elements Table11 Na) 1–i–1994 7-inch

1995

Verity's Place, London [Derek Bailey Han Bennink] (organ of Corti 9) with Han Bennink d. 16–17–vi–1972 R of Incus 9

Incus Taps (organ of Corti 10) iv–1974, vi–1974 R

Domestic & Public Pieces (Emanem 4001) 22–v–1975, i–1976, iii–1977 R of Quark 9999, Virgin/Caroline C1518 and Emanem 3404

Dart Drug [Derek Bailey and Jamie Muir] (Incus CD19) with Jamie Muir perc. viii–1981

One Time [John Stevens, Derek Bailey, Kent Carter] (Incus CD22) with John Stevens d, mini-trumpet; Kent Carter b. xi–1992

Wireforks [Derek Bailey and Henry Kaiser] (Shanachie 5011) with Henry Kaiser g, 8-string el-b. xi–1993

Banter [Derek Bailey and Gregg Bendian] (OO Discs 20) with Gregg Bendian perc. 12–ix–1994

Saisoro [Derek and The Ruins] (Tzadik TZ7205) with Masuda Ryuichi b; Yoshida Tatsuya d, v. ix–1994

Harras [Derek Bailey, John Zorn, William Parker] (Avant/Disk Union AVAN056) with John Zorn as; William Parker b. ix–1994

1996

Ode [London Jazz Composers Orchestra] (Intakt 041) with Harry
Beckett t; Dave Holdsworth t, fl-h; Marc Charig t, fl-h; Paul
Rutherford tbn; Mike Gibbs tbn; Paul Nieman tbn; Dick Hart tuba;
Trevor Watts as, ss; Mike Osborne as; Bernhard Living as; Alan
Wakeman ss, ts; Evan Parker ss, ts; Bob Downes fl, ts; Karl Jenkins
bs, oboe; Howard Riley p; Jeff Clyne b; Chris Laurence b; Barry
Guy b; Tony Oxley perc; Paul Lytton perc; Buxton Orr conductor.
22–iv–1972 R

First Duo Concert [Anthony Braxton and Derek Bailey] (Emanem 4006)
with Anthony Braxton reeds. 30–vi–1974 R

Drops [Derek Bailey and Andrea Centazzo] (New Tone/News/Robi
Droli rdc5037) with Andrea Centazzo perc, whistles. 3–4–iv–1977
(this CD reissue of the 1977 *Drops* LP erroneously gives the year of
the recording as 1967 on the back – and 1997 in the insert) R

Aida (Dexter's Cigar dex5) 4–vii–1980, 3–viii–1980 R

LACE (1989) (Emanem 4013) 15–xii–1989

Will [Derek Bailey, Will Gaines] (Incus VD01) with Will Gaines tapdance. 10–11–v–1995 V

Mountain Stage [Derek Bailey, Min Tanaka] (Incus VD02) with Min
Tanaka dance. Summer 1993 V

Company in Japan [Company] (Incus VD03) with Kazue Sawai koto;
Koichi Makigami v, t, shake-shake; Sachiko Nagata perc; Shonosuki
Okura tuzumi, v; Yukihiro Isso Noh flutes; Motoharu Yoshizawa b;
Wataru Okuma cl, melodica, accordian, v; Kenichi Takeda electric
koto; Keizo Inoue as, ss. viii–1993 V

Gig [Derek Bailey and John Stevens] (Incus VD04) with John Stevens d.
viii–1992 V

Boogie with the Hook [Eugene Chadbourne] (Leo LR242) with Eugene
Chadbourne v, g, banjo, rake. 1–ii–1995

The Last Wave [Arcana] (DIW 903) with Bill Laswell 8-string el-b; Tony
Williams d. iv–1995

guitar, drums 'n' bass (Avant AVAN060) with DJ Ninj drum-programmes.
ix–1995

Music & Dance [Derek Bailey and Min Tanaka] (Revenant 201) with Min Tanaka dance. 4–vii–1980, 6–vii–1980

1997

Sequences 72 & 73 [Paul Rutherford and Iskra 1912] (Emanem 4018) with Rutherford conductor; Maggie Nichols v; Norma Winstone v; Kenny Wheeler t, fl-h; Malcolm Griffiths tbn; Paul Nieman tbn; Geoff Perkins tbn; Dick Hart tuba; Evan Parker ss, ts; Dave White contrabass-cl, ss; Howard Riley p; Barry Guy b; Tony Oxley live el. 19–x–1973, 26–x–1973

Withdrawal [Spontaneous Music Ensemble] (Emanem 4020) with Kenny Wheeler t, fl-h, glockenspiel; Paul Rutherford tbn, perc; Trevor Watts fl, v, oboe, as, vibraphone, glockenspiel, perc; Evan Parker ss, ts, glockenspiel, perc; Barry Guy b, p; John Stevens d, glockenspiel, perc. 3–iii–1967

Quintessence 1 [Spontaneous Music Ensemble] (Emanem 4015) with John Stevens perc, cornet; Kent Carter cello; Evan Parker ss; Trevor Watts ss. 3–ii–1974 R (of *Eighty-Five Minutes Part 1*)

Quintessence 2 [Spontaneous Music Ensemble] (Emanem 4016) with John Stevens perc, cornet; Kent Carter cello, b; Evan Parker ss; Trevor Watts ss. 3–ii–1974 R (of *Eighty-Five Minutes Part 2*)

improvisation (Cramps CRSLP6202) 16–ix–1975 LP R

improvisation (Cramps CRSCD6202) 16–ix–1975 R

Soho Suites [Derek Bailey and Tony Oxley] (Incus CD29/30) with Tony Oxley el and acoustic perc, violin. ii–1977, 19–ix–1995

Music & Dance [Derek Bailey and Min Tanaka] (Table of the Elements Table40) with Min Tanaka dance. 4–vii–1980, 6–vii–1980 LP

Live from Soundscape Back on 52nd Street [Various Artists] (DIW 406) with George Lewis tbn. 25–ix–1981

Trio Playing [Bailey/Butcher/Marshall] (Incus CD28) with John Butcher ss, ts; Oren Marshall tuba. 30–xi–1994

Tout for Tea [Derek Bailey and Eugene Chadbourne] (Rectangle Rec-L) with Eugene Chadbourne v, g, banjo, rake. 13–i–1995 10-inch

Guitars on Mars [Various Artists] (Virgin AMBT24) Spring 1995 2CD

Legend of the Blood Yeti [XIII Ghosts with Derek Bailey, Andrew Clare and Thurston Moore] (Infinite Chug CHUG5CD) with Alex Ward cl, as; Switch el, Hammond organ. mid 1996

Close to the Kitchen [Derek Bailey and Noël Akchoté] (Rectangle Rec-F) with Noël Akchoté g. 29–viii–1996 LP

Drawing Close, Attuning – the Respective Signs of Order and Chaos (Tokuma Japan TKCF-77017) with Keiji Haino g. xi–1996

The Sign of 4 [Derek Bailey/Pat Metheny/Gregg Bendian/Paul Wertico] (Knitting Factory KFW197) with Pat Metheny g; or guitars Pikasso; Gregg Bendian perc; Paul Wertico perc. 12–15–xii–1996 3CD

1998

Saxophone Special + (1973–4) [Steve Lacy] (Emanem 4024) with Steve Lacy ss, gramophone; Trevor Watts ss, as; Evan Parker ss, ts, baritone sax; Steve Potts as, ss; Michel Waisvisz synth. 19–xii–1974 R (of *The Crust* and *Saxophone Special*, plus one unreleased alternate take)

Yankees [Derek Bailey, George Lewis and John Zorn] (Charly CDGR221) with George Lewis tbn; John Zorn as, ss, cl, game calls. 1982 R

Viper [Derek Bailey and Min Xiao-Fen] (Avant AVANO50) with Min Xiao-Fen pipa. 16–xii–1996 (not 16–xii–1997 as printed in insert)

TOHJINBO [Derek and The Ruins] (Paratactile PLE1101–2) with Sasaki Hisashi b; Yoshida Tatsuya d, v. 4–iv–1997

No Waiting [Derek Bailey and Joëlle Léandre] (Potlatch P-198) with Joëlle Léandre b. 9–v–1997

Takes Fakes & Dead She Dances (Incus CD31) v–1997, 24–ix–1997

Root [Thurston Moore] (Lo LCD11) May 1997

And [Derek Bailey, Pat Thomas, Steve Noble] (Rectangle Rec-S) with Steve Noble turntables; Pat Thomas keyb. viii–1997

Musikprotokoll im steirischen Herbst 97 [Various Artists] (MP7 ORF15) with Steve Noble turntables; Pat Thomas keyb. 4–x–1997

1999

Joseph Holbrooke '65 (Incus CD Single 01) with Gavin Bryars b; Tony Oxley d. 1965

The Baptised Traveller [Tony Oxley Quintet] (Sony/Columbia 4944382) with Kenny Wheeler t, fl-h; Evan Parker ts; Jeff Clyne b; Tony Oxley d. 3–i–1969 R

4 Compositions for Sextet [Tony Oxley Sextet] (Sony/Columbia 494437) with Kenny Wheeler t, fl-h; Evan Parker ss, ts; Paul Rutherford tbn; Jeff Clyne b; Tony Oxley d. 7–ii–1970 R

Dynamics of the Impromptu (Entropy Stereo ESR004) with Trevor Watts ss; John Stevens d, cornet. 12–xi–1973, 18–xi–1973, 17–i–1974

Fairly Early with Postscripts (Emanem 4027) 26–vii–1971, 30–vii–1973, 29–vi–1974, 2–v–1979, 28–v–1980, ii–1987, 12–vi–1987, 20–x–1998 R of various Emanem releases (plus four unreleased solo pieces: three from 28–v–1980, one from 20–x–1998) with Anthony Braxton sopranino sa, fl (two tracks, 29–vi–1974) and Kent Carter b; John Stevens perc 30–vii–1973

Aida's Call [Abe/Yoshizawa/Kondo/Bailey] (Starlight Furniture Company 9) with Kaoru Abe as; Motoharu Yoshizawa b; Toshinori Kondo t. 3–v–1978

Arch Duo [Derek Bailey and Evan Parker] (Rastascan BRD 045) with Evan Parker ss, ts. 17–x–1980 R

II (of) XXVIII Sliverfish Macronix [Derek Bailey/Ben Watson] (Rectangle Rec-BA) i–1993 7-inch

Playbacks (Bingo BIN004) with rhythm tracks by Darryl Moore, Henry Kaiser, Casey Rice, John Herndon, Tied + Tickled Trio, Bundy K. Brown, John French, Casey Rice, Ko Thein Htay, Sasha Frere-Jones, John Oswald, Jim O'Rourke and Loren MazzaCane Connors. 19–iii–1998

UNanswered Questions (BVHaast 9906) [Intermission with Derek Bailey, Chris Burn and Gilius van Bergeijk] with Klaas Hekman bass saxophone; Wilbert de Joode b; William Parker b; Hideji Taninaka b. 2–3–iv–1998

Daedal [Derek Bailey/Susie Ibarra] (Incus CD36) with Susie Ibarra perc.
   7–ii–1999

Post Improvisation 1 When We're Smilin [Han Bennink and Derek
   Bailey] (Incus CD34) Bailey plays g to tape supplied by Han Bennink
   d. Summer 1999

Post Improvisation 2 Air Mail Special [Derek Bailey+Han Bennink]
   (Incus CD35) Han Bennink plays d to tape supplied by Bailey g, v.
   Summer 1999

2000

Nipples [Peter Brötzmann Sextet/Quartet] (Atavistic/Unheard Music
   Series UMS/ALP205) with Peter Brötzmann ts; Evan Parker ts; Fred
   van Hove p; Buschi Niebergall b; Han Bennink d. 18–iv–1969 R

Chapter One [Iskra 1903] (Emanem 4301) 2–ix–1970, 1971, 3–v–1972,
   21–x–1972, 1–xi–1972, 23- or 24–x–1972 R (of Iskra 1903's Incus
   3/4, plus 107 minutes of unreleased material)

improvisation (Get Back GET6202) 16–ix–1975 LP R

improvisation (Ampersand ampere2) 16–ix–1975 R

Outcome [Derek Bailey, Steve Lacy] (Potlatch P299) with Steve Lacy ss.
   25–vi–1983

Live in Okayama 1987 [Bailey/Sabu/Brötzmann] (Improvised Company
   CD002) with Yoshisaburo Toyozumi perc; Peter Brötzmann ts, as,
   tarogato. 16–xi–1987

And [Derek Bailey, Pat Thomas, Steve Noble] (Rectangle Rec-S2) with
   Pat Thomas keyb; Steve Noble turntables. viii–1997 R

LOCationAL [Derek Bailey and Alex Ward] (Incus CD37) with Alex
   Ward cl. x–1998, i–1999

Mirakle [Derek Bailey/Jamaaladeen Tacuma/Calvin Weston] (Tzadik
   TZ 7603) with Jamaaladeen Tacuma b; Calvin Weston d. 29–xi–
   1999

String Theory (Paratactile PLE1109) with Vanessa Mackness v; Alex
   Ward v. 29–vii–1999 (track 14), 10–11–i–2000

Joseph Holbrooke '98 [Derek Bailey, Gavin Bryars and Tony Oxley]
   (Incus CD39) with Gavin Bryars b; Tony Oxley d. 2–xii–1998

Songs [Keiji Haino and Derek Bailey] (Incus CD40) with Keiji Haino v. xi–1996 R

Muckraker #9 (Muckraker grd-030) Incus advertisment on compilation including Sun City Girls and Ceramic Hobs

2001

departures [Vertrek Ensemble and Derek Bailey] (Volatile VCD002) with Ron de Jong d, perc; Vadim Budman g, cornet, reed cornet. 13–v–1998

llaer [Derek Bailey/Ingar Zach] (Sofa 503) with Ingar Zach d, perc. 20–x–2000

ORe [Derek Bailey/Eddie Prévost] (Arrival ARCD001) with Eddie Prévost d, perc. 13–14–iii–2000

Vortices & Angels [John Butcher with Derek Bailey and Rhodri Davies] (Emanem 4049) with John Butcher ss, ts. 23–iii–2000

Company 5 [Smith/Altena/Bailey/Honsinger/Braxton/Lacy/Parker] (Incus CD41) with Leo Smith t, fl; Maarten van Regteren Altena b; Tristan Honsinger cello; Anthony Braxton cl, flute, as, ss; Steve Lacy ss; Evan Parker ss, ts. 26–v–1977 R

Epiphany/Epiphanies [Company] (Incus CD42/43) with Ursula Oppens p; Fred Frith g, live el, perc; George Lewis tbn; Anne Le Baron harp; Akio Suzuki glass harmonica, analapos, spring gong, kikkokikiriki; Julie Tippetts acoustic g, v, fl; Motoharu Yoshizawa b; Keith Tippett p; Phil Wachsmann violin, el. 29–vi to 3–vii–1982 2CD R

Company in Marseille [Bailey/Davies/Fell/Gaines/Wastell] (Incus CD44/45) with Rhodri Davies harp; Mark Wastell cello; Simon H. Fell b; Will Gaines tapdance. 13–14–i–1999

Agro Jazz [Panicstepper] (Flo Records FLO013) with Nathan Moore g, programming; Michael Welch d.

Untitled Improvisations [Derek Bailey and Michael Welch] (Illegal Radio unnumbered) with Michael Welch perc. 14–iii–1999, 20–iii–1999

Close to the Kitchen [Derek Bailey and Noël Akchoté] (Blue Chopsticks BC6) with Noël Akchoté g. 29–viii–1996 R

Daybreak [Ian Smith] (Emanem 4059) with Ian Smith t; Gail Brand tbn; Oren Marshall tuba; Veryan Weston chamber organ. 21–22–viii–2000

Hello, Goodbye [Gjerstad/Stevens/Bailey] (Emanem 4065) with Frode Gjerstad as; John Stevens perc, mini-trumpet. x–1992

The Appleyard File (Incus CD-R No. 1) 2001

Chats (Incus CD-R No. 2) 1990–2001

2002

Buzz Soundtrack [Iskra 1903] (Emanem 4066) with Paul Rutherford tbn; Barry Guy b. 1970 or 1971

New Sights, Old Sounds (Incus CD48/49) 21–iv–1978, 3–v–1978, 5–v–1978 R

Flying Dragons [Derek Bailey and Min Xiao-Fen] (Incus CD50) with Min Xiao-Fen pipa. xi–1999

Fish [Shoji Hano/Derek Bailey] (PSF Records PSFD-8009) with Shoji Hano d. 10–vi–2000

Duos, London 2001 [Derek Bailey/Julian Kytasty/Roger Turner/Alan Wilkinson] (Incus CD51) duos with Julian Kytasty fl, bandura; Roger Turner perc; Alan Wilkinson bs, v. 2–iii–2001, 23–iii–2001, 5–x–2001

BIDS [Derek Bailey, Susie Ibarra] (Incus CD52) with Susie Ibarra perc. 6–vii–2001

[Franz Hautzinger, Derek Bailey] (Grob 425) with Franz Hautzinger quartertone t.

Ballads (Tzadik TZ7607)

Pieces for Guitar (Tzadik TZ7080) 1966, 1967

Visitors Book (Incus, unnumbered CD-R) with Antoine Berthiaume g; Ingar Zach perc; Tony Bevan bass saxophone; Will Gaines tapdance; Oren Marshall tuba; John Butcher ts; Sonic Pleasure bricks; T. H. F. Drenching Dictaphone; Alex Ward cl. 2000–2003

Right Off [Derek Bailey, Carlos Bechegas] (Numerica NUM1100) with Carlos Bechegas fl, piccolo, synth, live el. 16–vii–2001

Tristan (Duo) [Derek Bailey and Tristan Honsinger] (Incus CD53) with

Tristan Honsinger cello, v. 6–7–ii–1976 R of Incus LP20 plus 26–
x–1975

Barcelona [Derek Bailey, Agustí Fernández] (Hopscotch HOP10) with
Agustí Fernández p. 12–xi–2001

[Derek Bailey + Simon H. Fell] (Sound 323 (1)) with Simon H. Fell b.
15–viii–2001

Seven [Derek Bailey, Ingar Zach] (Incus CD54) with Ingar Zach perc.
15–ii–2002

Solo Guitar Series Number 1: In Church (Incus, unnumbered CD-R)
1994, 2001

Solo Guitar Series Number 2: South (Incus, unnumbered CD-R) 1999

Solo Guitar Series Number 3: Different Guitars (Incus, unnumbered
CD-R) with Min Tanaka dance. Early 1970s, 8–xii–1987, iv–1992.

Visions: Performances from the EMIT Series (Isospin Labs) one track
on compilation (including Evan Parker, Sam Rivers, Peter Kowald,
Eugene Chadbourne) with Jim Stewart d. 12–iii–1999

John Zorn *John Zorn's Game Pieces: Cobra Volume 2* (Tzadik TZ7335)
with Jennifer Choi, Mark Feldman violin; Erik Friedlabder cello;
Trevor Dun, Mark Dreser bas; Josh Roseman trombone; Marcus
Rojas tuba; Ikue Mori laptop; Jamie Safy keyb; Sylvie Courvoisier p;
Cyro Baptista perc; Susie Ibarra d; John Zorn cond

2003

Watch Out (Incus, unnumbered CD-R) iii–2003

Solo Guitar Series Number 4: Filmed (Incus CD-R) ix–1993

Live at Lamar's (Incus CD-R No. 4) with Dennis Palmer synth; Bob
Stagner perc. 25–iii–1999

Barbarian (Incus CD-R No. 5) with Pat Thomas el; Steve Noble turntables. 3–vii–2000

Nearly a D [Frode Gjerstad and Derek Bailey] (Emanem 4087) with
Frode Gjerstad cl, as. 7–viii–2002

Jiyu No Ishi/Free Will [Yuji Itsumi] (PSF B-1) CD + BOOK two minutes
unaccompanied guitar on compilation including a great eight minutes by Yoshizawa Motoharu and much nonsense by clowns of the
Onkyo scene

Soshin [Derek Bailey, Antoine Berthiaume, Fred Frith] with Antoine Berthiaume g. viii–2001

More Nipples [Peter Brötzmann Sextet/Quartet] (Atavistic/Unheard Music Series UMS/ALP236) with Peter Brötzmann ts; Evan Parker ts; Fred van Hove p; Buschi Niebergall b; Han Bennink d. 18–iv–1969

The Social/Science Set [Bailey/Goodman/Kaiser/Kondo/ROVA/Parker] (Beak Doctor 5/6) duet with Jon Raskin bs and trio with Larry Ochs ts; Toshinori Kondo t. 21–x–1980 R

Rappin & Tappin [Will Gaines] (Incus CD55) with Will Gaines tapdance. 1994

Limescale (Incus CD56) with Alex Ward cl; Tony Bevan bass saxophone; Derek Bailey g; T. H. F. Drenching Dictaphone; Sonic Pleasure bricks. 20–xii–2002

To Play: The blemish sessions (Sound S008).

blemish [David Sylvian] (P-Vine PVCP-8775) David Sylvian v, instruments; Christian Fenesz el

Scale Points on the Fever Curve [Derek Bailey and Milo Fine] (Emanem 4099) with Milo Fine cl, keyb, d 26–iii–2003

Derek [Derek Bailey and Cyro Baptista] (Amulet AMT023) with Cyro Baptista perc, v

Poetry & Playing (Paratactile PLE1116-2) Bailey reads poetry by Lyn Hejinian, Peter Riley, Steve Dalachinsky

Good Cop Bad Cop [Derek Bailey, Tony Bevan, Paul Hession, Otomo Yoshihide] (No-Fi NEU01) with Tony Bevan sax; Paul Hession d; Otomo Yoshihide g, el

2004

Meanwhile, Back in Sheffield … [Derek Bailey, Mick Beck, Paul Hession] (Discus 21CD) with Mick Beck tenor sax, bassoon, whistles; Paul Hession d viii–2004

Bruise with Derek Bailey [Tony Bevan] (Foghorn FOGCD006) with Tony Bevan tenor sax, bas sax; Orphy Robinson perc, el; John Edwards b; Ashley Wales sound collage; Mark Sanders drums 17–viii–2004

2005

Carpal Tunnel (Tzadik TZ7612)

APPENDIX 2

AN INCUS DISCOGRAPHY

Artists as listed on spine (if names are separated by spaces they've been separated here by commas to avoid confusion). Title of the album, if there is one, in italics. Catalogue number appears between parantheses (thus). Abbreviations for instruments are as follows: as = alto saxophone; b = double bass; b-cl = bass clarinet; bs = baritone saxophone; b-tbn = bass trombone; cl = clarinet; d = drums; el = electronics; el-b = electric bass guitar; fl = flute; fl-h = fluegel-horn; g = guitar; keyb = keyboards; p = piano; perc = percussion; ss = soprano saxophone; t = trumpet; tbn = trombone; ts = tenor sax; v = voice; vln = violin. R = rerelease. As in Appendix 1, recording dates are in European format, with the month in Roman numerals (ie dd-mm-yyyy).

The best way to acquire Incus releases is via Bailey's own mail-order service. A catalogue is available from: Incus Records, 14 Downs Road, London, E5 8DS, England; fax +44 (0) 20 8533 2851; e-mail <karenincus2001@yahoo.co.uk>; website <www.incusrecords.force9.co.uk>.

Long-Playing 12-inch 33RPM Vinyl records

Evan Parker, Derek Bailey, Han Bennink *The Topography of the Lungs* (Incus 1) Evan Parker ss, ts; Derek Bailey g; Han Bennink d, perc. 12–vii–1970
Derek Bailey *Solo Guitar* (Incus 2) Derek Bailey g. ii–1971
Derek Bailey *Solo Guitar* (Incus 2R) Derek Bailey g. ii–1971 R (with different selections)
Iskra 1903 (Incus 3/4) Paul Rutherford tbn; Derek Bailey acoustic/

amplified g; Barry Guy acoustic/amplified b. viii–1970, v–1972
2LP

Evan Parker, Paul Lytton *collective calls [urban] [two microphones]*
(Incus 5) Evan Parker ss, ts, home-made instruments, cassette
recorder; Paul Lytton perc, live el, sound effects and noise. 15–16–
v–1972

London Jazz Composers Orchestra *Ode* (Incus 6/7) Harry Beckett t;
Dave Holdsworth t, fl-h; Marc Charig t, fl-h; Paul Rutherford tbn;
Mike Gibbs tbn; Paul Nieman tbn; Dick Hart tuba; Trevor Watts
as, ss; Mike Osborne as; Bernhard Living as; Alan Wakeman ss, ts;
Evan Parker ss, ts; Bob Downes fl, ts; Karl Jenkins bs, oboe; Derek
Bailey g; Howard Riley p; Jeff Clyne b; Chris Laurence b; Barry
Guy b; Tony Oxley perc; Paul Lytton perc; Buxton Orr conductor.
22–iv–1972 2LP

Tony Oxley (Incus 8) Evan Parker ss, ts; Paul Rutherford tbn; Dave
Holdsworth g; Howard Riley p; Barry Guy b; Tony Oxley perc,
amplified perc. 1975

Derek Bailey and Han Bennink *Live at Verity's Place* (Incus 9) Derek
Bailey g; Han Bennink perc. 16–17–vi–1972

Kenny Wheeler *Song for Someone* (Incus 10) Kenny Wheeler t, fl-h; Ian
Hammer t; Greg Bowen t; Dave Hancock t; Keith Christie tbn;
Bobby Lamb tbn; Chris Pyne tbn; David Horler tbn; Malcolm
Griffiths b-tbn; Alfie Reece tuba; Duncan Lamont ts, fl; Mike
Osborne as; Derek Bailey g; Alan Branscombe p, electric p; John
Taylor electric p; Ron Mathewson b; Tony Oxley perc; Norma
Winstone vs; Evan Parker ts. 10–11–i–1973 LP

balance (Incus 11) Ian Brighton g; Colin Wood cello; Frank Perry perc;
Radu Malfatti tbn, khène, bass recorder; Philipp Wachsmann violin.
10–11–ix–1973

Derek Bailey *Lot 74 Solo Improvisations* (Incus 12) Derek Bailey g. 13–
v–1974

Howard Riley *Synopsis* (Incus 13) Howard Riley p; Barry Guy b; Tony
Oxley d. 19–x–1973

Evan Parker & Paul Lytton *At the Unity Theatre* (Incus 14) Evan Parker
ss, ts, lyttonophone, pole drum, bullrorarer, cassettes of prior performances; Paul Lytton perc, live el, v. 7–i–1975

'*Teatime*' (Incus 15) Garry Todd ts; Dave Solomon perc; John Russell g; Nigel Coombes violin, low-grade el; Steve Beresford p, toys. viii–1974 to iv–1975

Derek Bailey, Evan Parker *The London Concert* (Incus 16) Derek Bailey g; Evan Parker ts, ss. 14–ii–1975

The Music Improvisation Company *1968–1971* (Incus 17) Derek Bailey g; Evan Parker ss, amplified auto-harp; Hugh Davies live el, organ; Jamie Muir perc. 4–vii–1969, 18–vi–1970

Tony Oxley *February Papers* (Incus 18) Philipp Wachsmann violin; David Bourne violin; Barry Guy b, el-b; Ian Brighton g; Tony Oxley d, violin. ii–1977

Evan Parker *Saxophone Solos* (Incus 19) Evan Parker ss. 17–vi–1975, 9–ix–1975

Derek Bailey, Tristan Honsinger *Duo* (Incus 20) Derek Bailey g; Tristan Honsinger cello, v. 7–ii–1976

Company 1 (Incus 21) Maarten van Regteren Altena b; Tristan Honsinger cello; Evan Parker ss, ts; Derek Bailey g. 9–v–1976

Barry Guy *Statements V–XI for Double Bass and Violone* (Incus 22) Barry Guy b. 30–x–1976

Company 2 (Incus 23) Derek Bailey g; Evan Parker ss, ts; Anthony Braxton ss, as, E-flat cl, B-flat cl, contrabass cl. 22–viii–1976

Spontaneous Music Ensemble *Biosystem* (Incus 24) John Stevens perc, cornet; Nigel Coombes violin; Roger Smith g; Colin Wood cello. 28–vi–1977

Company 3 (Incus 25) Derek Bailey g; Han Bennink d. ix–1976

Company 4 (Incus 26) Steve Lacy ss; Derek Bailey g. 11–xi–1976

Evan Parker *Monoceros* (Incus 27) Evan Parker ss. 30–iv–1978.

Company 5 (Incus 28) Leo Smith t, fl; Maarten van Regteren Altena b; Derek Bailey g; Tristan Honsinger cello; Anthony Braxton cl, fl, as, ss, ts; Steve Lacy ss; Evan Parker ss, ts. p. 26–v–1977

Company 6 (Incus 29) Leo Smith t, fl; Maarten van Regteren Altena b; Derek Bailey g; Tristan Honsinger cello; Anthony Braxton cl, fl, as, ss; Steve Lacy ss; Lol Coxhill ss; Evan Parker ss, ts; Han Bennink, perc, viola, banjo; Steve Beresford p, t. 25–27–v–1977

Company 7 (Incus 30) Leo Smith t; Maarten van Regteren Altena b; Derek Bailey g; Tristan Honsinger cello; Anthony Braxton cl, fl, ss, as; Steve Lacy ss; Lol Coxhill ss; Evan Parker ss, ts; Han Bennink d, viola, cl, banjo; Steve Beresford p, g. 25–27–v–1977

John Russell/Richard Coldman *Guitar Solos* (Incus 31) split LP: John Russell g. 17–xii–1978/Richard Coldman g, preparations, v. 11–iv–1979

Garry Todd, Roger Turner *Sunday Best* (Incus 32) Roger Turner perc, tbn; Garry Todd ts. 25–ii–1979

Lytton/Toop/Eastley/Burwell/Nicolson/Parker/Davies/Lovens *Circadian Rhythm* (Incus 33) Paul Lytton perc, live el; David Toop fl, alto fl, bass recorder, piccolo, home-made and found instruments; Max Eastley self-designed automatic instruments and other small home-made instruments; Paul Burwell perc; Annabel Nicolson charcoal, sparks, branches, twigs, fire, pine needles, draughts, smoke; Evan Parker ss, ts; Hugh Davies live el; Paul Lovens perc, singing saw. 29–30–vii–1978

Derek Bailey, Tony Coe *Time* (Incus 34) Derek Bailey g; Tony Coe cl in C. 23–24–iv–1979

Evan Parker, George Lewis *From Saxophone and Trombone* (Incus 35) Evan Parker ss, ts; George Lewis tbn.

Company *Fables* (Incus 36) Derek Bailey g; Dave Holland b; George Lewis tbn; Evan Parker ss, ts. 17–18–v–1980

Improvisors' Symposium Pisa 1980 (Incus 37) Evan Parker ts, ss; George Lewis tbn; Derek Bailey g; Barry Guy b; Paul Lovens perc; Paul Lytton perc, live el; Phil Wachsmann violin, el; Paul Rutherford tbn; Ginacarlo Schiaffini tbn; Maarten van Regteren Altena b. 26–28–vi–1980

Company *Fictions* (Incus 38) Misha Mengelberg p, celeste, v; Lol Coxhill ss; Steve Beresford p; Derek Bailey g, v; Ian Croall v. viii–1977

Evan Parker *Six of One* (Incus 39) Evan Parker ss. 18–vi–1980

Derek Bailey *Aida* (Incus 40) Derek Bailey g. 4–vii–1980, 3–viii–1980

Bailey/Muir *Dart Drug* (Incus 41) Derek Bailey g; Jamie Muir perc. viii–1981

Evan Parker *Tracks* (Incus 42) Evan Parker ts, ss; Barry Guy b, live el; Paul Lytton perc, live el. 7–i–1983

Anthony Braxton, Derek Bailey *Royal Volume 1* (Incus 43) Derek Bailey g; Anthony Braxton ss, as, B-flat cl, contrabass cl. 2–vii–1974

[*Volume 2* was promised as Incus 44 on the sleeve of the above, but was never issued]

Evan Parker *Hook, Drift & Shuffle* (Incus 45) Evan Parker ts, ss; George Lewis tbn; Barry Guy b; Paul Lytton perc. 4–ii–1983

Company *Epiphany/Epiphanies* (Incus 46/47) Ursula Oppens p; Fred Frith g; George Lewis tbn; Anne Le Baron harp; Akio Suzuki glass harmonica, analapos, spring gong, kikkokikiriki; Derek Bailey g; Julie Tippetts acoustic g, v, fl; Motoharu Yoshizawa b; Phil Wachsmann violin, el. 29–vi–3–vii–1982 2LP

Derek Bailey *Notes* (Incus 48) Derek Bailey g. iv–1985, vii–1985

Evan Parker *The Snake Decides* (Incus 49) Evan Parker ss. 30–i–1986

Derek Bailey, Evan Parker *Compatibles* (Incus 50) Evan Parker ss, ts; Derek Bailey g. 22–iv–1985, 27–vii–1985

Company *Trios* (Incus 51) Evan Parker ss, ts; Peter Brötzmann ts, bs; Jon Corbett t, fl-h; J. D. Parran basset horn, piccolo; Vinko Globokar tbn, v, fl; Hugh Davies live el; Derek Bailey g; Ernst Reyseger cello, el-cello; Joëlle Léandre b, v; Jamie Muir perc. 24–28–v–1983

Extended-play 7-inch 45RPM Vinyl records

AMM *At The Roundhouse* (Incus EP 1) Lou Gare ts; Eddie Prévost d. viii–1971

CDs

Derek Bailey and Cyro Baptista *Cyro* (Incus CD01) Derek Bailey g; Cyro Baptista perc. x–1982

Derek Bailey and Han Bennink *Han* (Incus CD02) Derek Bailey g; Han Bennink perc. 15–22–iii–1986

Bevan/Kingston/Lewis *Original Gravity* (Incus CD03) Tony Bevan ts; Greg Kingston g, toys, recorder, tapes; Matt Lewis perc, cello drum, bird calls. 9–ix–1988, 11–ix–1988

Company *Once* (Incus CD04) Lee Konitz ss, as, d; Carlos Zingaro violin; Richard Teitelbaum keyb; Derek Bailey g; Tristan Honsinger cello; Barre Phillips b; Steve Noble perc, bugle. 12–17–v–1987

Barre Philips, Derek Bailey *Figuring* (Incus CD05) Derek Bailey g; Barre Phillips b. 12–v–1987, 4–ix–1988

Steve Noble/Alex Ward *Ya boo, reel & rumble* (Incus CD06) Alex Ward cl, as; Steve Noble perc. 11–iii–1989, 1–vii–1990

Company 6 & 7 (Incus CD07) Steve Lacy ss; Lol Coxhill ss; Evan Parker ss, ts; Anthony Braxton fl, cl, ss, as; Leo Smith t, fl; Derek Bailey g; Tristan Honsinger cello; Steve Beresford p, g; Maarten van Regteren Altena b; Han Bennink d, viola, cl, banjo. 25–27–v–1977 R of Incus LP29 and LP30

Tony Bevan/Steve Noble/Paul Rogers *Bigshots* (Incus CD08) Tony Bevan ts, ss; Paul Rogers b; Steve Noble d. 25–v–1991

Moholo/Lipere/Bailey *Village Life* (Incus CD09) Derek Bailey g; Thebi Lipere perc, v; Louis Maholo d. 25–ix–1991

Derek Bailey *Solo Guitar Volume 1* (Incus CD10) Derek Bailey g. ii–1971 R of Incus LP2 and LP2R

Derek Bailey *Solo Guitar Volume 2* (Incus CD11) Derek Bailey g. 22–vi–1991

Music Improvisation Company *1968–1971* (Incus CD12) Evan Parker ss, amplified auto-harp; Derek Bailey g; Hugh Davies live el, organ; Jamie Muir perc. 4–vii–1969, 18–vi–1970 R of Incus LP17

The Shaking Ray Levis *False Prophets or Dang Good Guessers* (Incus CD13) Dennis Palmer synths, 16-second delay; Bob Stagner d, perc, nail violin. i–iv–1992, vi–1992

Derek Bailey, John Stevens *Playing* (Incus CD14) Derek Bailey g; John Stevens d, mini-t. 14–viii–1992

Tony Oxley Quartet (Incus CD15) Pat Thomas el, keyb; Derek Bailey g; Matt Wand drum machines, tape switchboard; Tony Oxley perc. 8–iv–1992

Company91 *Volume 1* (Incus CD16) Vanessa Mackness v; John Zorn as; Alexander Balanescu violin; Yves Robert tbn; Derek Bailey g; Buckethead g; Pat Thomas keyb, el; Paul Rogers b; Paul Lovens perc. 26–27–vii–1991

Company91 *Volume 2* (Incus CD17) Vanessa Mackness v; John Zorn as; Alexander Balanescu violin; Yves Robert tbn; Derek Bailey g;

Buckethead g; Pat Thomas p, el; Paul Rogers b; Paul Lovens perc. 27-20-vii-1991

Company 91 *Volume 3* (Incus CD18) Vanessa Mackness v; John Zorn as; Alexander Balanescu violin; Yves Robert tbn; Derek Bailey g; Buckethead g; Pat Thomas keyb, el; Paul Rogers b; Paul Lovens perc. 29-30-vii-1991

Jamie Muir/Derek Bailey *Dart Drug* (Incus CD19) Derek Bailey g; Jamie Muir perc. viii-1981 R of Incus LP41

John Zorn, Fred Frith *The Art of Memory* (Incus CD20) John Zorn as; Fred Frith g.

Vanessa Mackness, John Butcher *Respiritus* (Incus CD21) Vanessa Mackness v; John Butcher ss, ts. 5-xii-1994, 14-iv-1994

John Stevens, Kent Carter, Derek Bailey *One Time* (Incus CD22) John Stevens d, mini-trumpet; Kent Carter b; Derek Bailey g. xi-1992

Chadbourne/Zorn *In Memory of Nikki Arane* (Incus CD23) Eugene Chadbourne g, dobro, contact-mics; John Zorn ss, as, B-flat cl, game calls, water bucket. 1980

Roger Smith and Neil Metcalfe *S&M* (Incus CD24) Roger Smith g; Neil Metcalfe fl. 26-vii-1994, 24-vii-1995, 22-x-1995, 28-xi-1995, 22-xii-1995

Stefan Jaworzyn/Alan Wilkinson *In a Sentimental Mood* (Incus CD25) Stefan Jaworzyn el g; Alan Wilkinson as, bs. 27-ii-1996

Kaiser/Oswald *Improvised (Vancouver)* (Incus CD26) John Oswald as; Henry Kaiser g. 7-ii-1978, 6-v-1996

Beresford.Palmer.Stagner.Turner *Short in the UK* Steve Beresford keyb, mini-trumpet; Dennis Palmer synth, v; Roger Turner d, perc; Bob Stagner d. vii-1994

Bailey/Butcher/Marshall *Trio Playing* (Incus CD28) John Butcher ss, ts; Derek Bailey g; Oren Marshall tuba. 30-xi-1994

Oxley/Bailey *Soho Suites* (Incus CD29/30) Derek Bailey g; Tony Oxley perc, amplified perc. ii-1977, 19-ix-1995

Derek Bailey *Takes Fakes & Dead She Dances* (Incus CD31) Derek Bailey g, v. v-1997, 24-ix-1997

George E. Lewis and Bertram Turetzky *Conversations* (Incus CD32) George E. Lewis tbn; Bertram Turetzky b. 26-xi-1997

Hession/Wilkinson/Fell+Morris *Registered Firm* (Incus CD33) Alan Wil-

kinson as, bs; Joe Morris g; Simon. H. Fell b; Paul Hession d. 14–
vi–1996

Han Bennink+Derek Bailey *Post Improvisation 1: When We're Smilin*
(Incus CD34) Han Bennink d (on tape); Derek Bailey g. 1999

Derek Bailey+Han Bennink *Post Improvisation 2: Air Mail Special* (Incus
CD35) Derek Bailey g, v (on tape); Han Bennink d. 1999

Derek Bailey and Susie Ibarra *Daedal* (Incus CD36) Derek Bailey g;
Susie Ibarra perc. 7–ii–1999

Derek Bailey and Alex Ward *LOCationAL* (Incus CD37) Alex Ward cl;
Derek Bailey g. x–1998, i–1999

Jim O'Rourke and Mats Gustafsson *Xylophonen Virtuosen* Mats Gustafsson ts, fluteophone, fl; Jim O'Rourke g, junk. 23–ix–1999

Bailey/Bryars/Oxley *Joseph Holbrooke '98* (Incus CD39) Derek Bailey
g; Gavin Bryars b; Tony Oxley d. 2–xii–1998

Keiji Haino and Derek Bailey *Songs* (Incus CD40) Keiji Haino v; Derek
Bailey g. xi–1996

Smith/Altena/Bailey/Honsinger/Braxton/Lacy/Parker *Company 5* (Incus
CD41) Steve Lacy ss; Anthony Braxton cl, fl, as, ss; Evan Parker ss,
ts; Leo Smith t, fl; Derek Bailey g; Tristan Honsinger cello; Maarten
van Regteren Altena b. 26–v–1977 R of Incus LP28

Company *Epiphany/Epiphanies* (Incus CD42/43) Phil Wachsmann violin, el; George Lewis tbn; Derek Bailey g; Julie Tippetts acoustic g,
v, fl; Fred Frith g; Ursula Oppens p; Keith Tippett p; Anne Le Baron
harp; Akio Suzuki glass harmonica, analapos, spring gong, kikkokikiriki; Motoharu Yoshizawa b. 29–vi–1982, 3–vii–1982 2CD R of
Incus LP46/47

Bailey/Davies/Fell/Gaines/Wastell *Company in Marseille* (Incus CD44/
45) Derek Bailey g; Rhodri Davies harp; Mark Wastell cello; Simon
H. Fell b; Will Gaines tapdance. 13–14–i–1999

Jim McAuley/Nels Cline/Red Poole *Acoustic Guitar Trio* (Incus CD46)
Jim McAuley g; Nels Cline g; Red Poole g, bowed g. 9–ix–2000

Noble, Edwards, Ward *False Face Society* (Incus CD47) Alex Ward el g;
John Edwards b; Steve Noble d, perc. 30–x–2000

Derek Bailey *New Sights, Old Sounds* (Incus CD48/49) Derek Bailey g.
v–1978 R of Morgue 3/4

Derek Bailey and Min Xiao-Fen *Flying Dragons* (Incus CD50) Min Xiao-Fen pipa; Derek Bailey g. xi–1999

Derek Bailey/Julian Kytasty/Roger Turner/Alan Wilkinson *Duos, London 2001* (Incus CD51) Julian Kytasty fl; Derek Bailey g; Alan Wilkinson bs, v; Roger Turner perc. 23–iii–2001, 2–iii–2001, 5–x–2001

Derek Bailey, Susie Ibarra *BIDS* (Incus CD52) Derek Bailey g; Susie Ibarra perc. 6–vii–2001

Tristan (Duo) [Derek Bailey and Tristan Honsinger] (Incus CD53) Derek Bailey g; Tristan Honsinger cello. 6–7–ii–1976 R of Incus LP20 plus 26–x–1975

Seven [Derek Bailey, Ingar Zach] (Incus CD54) Derek Bailey g; Ingar Zach perc. 15–ii–2002

Rappin & Tappin [Will Gaines] (Incus CD55) Derek Bailey g; Will Gaines tapdance. 1994

Limescale (Incus CD56) Alex Ward cl; Tony Bevan bass saxophone; Derek Bailey g; T. H. F. Drenching Dictaphone; Sonic Pleasure bricks. 20–xii–2002

CD-ROM

Joseph Holbrooke '65 (Incus CD Single 01) Derek Bailey g; Gavin Bryars b; Tony Oxley d. 1965

Videos

Will [Derek Bailey, Will Gaines] (Incus VD01) Derek Bailey g; Will Gaines tapdance. 10–11–v–1995

Mountain Stage [Derek Bailey, Min Tanaka] (Incus VD02) Derek Bailey g; Min Tanaka dance. Summer 1993

Company in Japan [Company] (Incus VD03) Keizo Inoue as, ss; Wataru Okuma cl, melodica, accordian, v; Shonosuki Okura tuzumi, v; Yukihiro Isso Noh flutes; Koichi Makigami v, t, shake-shake; Kazue

Sawai koto; Kenichi Takeda el koto; Derek Bailey g; Motoharu Yoshi-
zawa b; Sachiko Nagata perc. viii–1993
Gig [Derek Bailey and John Stevens] (Incus VD04) Derek Bailey g; John
Stevens d. viii–1992
Gutter Cleaners [Milo Fine, Susan J. Speri] (Incus VD05) Milo Fine el, cl,
p, d; Susan J. Speri dance

Incus 'From the Store' CD-Rs

Visitors Book (No. 1) Derek Bailey g; Antoine Berthiaume g; Inga Zach
perc; Tony Bevan bass saxophone; Will Gaines tapdance; Oren Mar-
shall tuba; John Butcher ts; Sonic Pleasure bricks; T.H.F. Drenching
Dictaphone; Alex Ward cl 2000–2001
Live at Lamar's (No. 2) with Dennis Palmer synth; Bob Stagner d 25–
iii–1999
Barbarian (No. 3) with Pat Thomas el; Steve Noble turntables 3–vii–2000
Robyn (No. 4) with Robyn Shulkovsky perc 9–xi–1998
Howdy (No. 5) with Christopher Williams b *v*–2004 CD-R
Songs (No. 6) Otto Fischer g, b, v

Incus 'Solo Guitar' CD-Rs

The Appleyard File (No. 1) v–2001
Chats (No. 2) 1990–2001
In Church (No. 3) 1994, 2001
South (No. 4) 1999
Different Guitars (No. 5) with Min Tanaka dance early 70s, iv–1992
Filmed (No. 6) for Anthony Howell's video magazine *Grey Suit* ix–1993
At the Sidecar: Live at G's Club, Barcelona (No. 7) 10–ii–2004
Then (No. 8) 1972, 1974, 1980

Posthumous Releases

Incus

guitar (Incus CD57) Spring 1974
A Silent Dance [Derek Bailey & Agusti Fernandez] (Incus CD58) with
Agusti Fernandez p v–2005
The Ducks Palace [Baker/Bailey/Baptista/Rudd/Zorn] (Incus CD59) with
Duck Baker g; Cyro Baptista perc; Roswell Rudd tbn; John Zorn
as16–iii–1993, 5–i–2002, 4–vii–2002, 28–iii–2004
More 74 (Incus CD60) 1974

Old Sights New Sounds [Lol Coxhill, Alex Ward] (Incus CD61) Lol
Coxhill ss; Alex Ward cl 14–x–2010
Concert in Milwaukee (Incus CD62) 31–*iii*–1983

Incus CD-Rs

Under Tracy's Bed (No. 7) with Tony Bevan bass saxophone 28–xi–2011
(re-release of Foghorn release from 2003)

Other

Standards (Tzadik, 2007) i–2002

DVDs

Playing for Friends on 5th Street (Straw2Gold Pictures, 2004)
Live at G's Club (Incus DVD01, 2009) 10–ii–2004
All Thumbs (Incus DVD02, 2009) *vii*–2004
MTT (Incus DVD03, 2011) Toshinori Kondo el-t; Toshi Tsuchitori d,v;
Min Tinaka dance 18–*viii*–2006

APPENDIX 3

DEREK BAILEY'S COMPLETE
INVISIBLE JUKEBOX

At home in Hackney on Tuesday, 10 November 1998, Derek Bailey was subjected to an 'Invisible Jukebox' for the music magazine *The Wire*. He was played various tracks blind – on the portable cassette player in his kitchen – and was asked to voice his responses. For reasons of space, his words needed to be trimmed for publication. Here is the unexpurgated version of an interview that caused much astonishment and hilarity when it was published in December 1998. Further thoughts on music and politics may be found on the website of Ben Watson and Esther Leslie, Militant Esthetix <www.militantesthetix.co.uk>.

MICHAEL FINNISSY
'Come Beat the Drums and Sound the Fifes'
from *English Country-Tunes* (Etcetera)

[*almost straightaway*] Does it carry on like this all the way through? So we've heard it, right? A bit louder, a bit faster . . .

It's only four minutes long.
Who is it? I think I ought to explain something about my relationship with recorded music. I think of this as 'highly performed'. It's fine for me, I like it, who am I to complain about anything like this? It's very performed, it's specific, they know exactly what they're doing and they knew what they were doing I think before they did it.

What instrument is it?
I thought there were two instruments, so I assume it's a piano, I thought

maybe two pianos, or a guy playing . . . anyway, I don't want to display my ignorance completely.

That's the idea! Speculate about what it is.
It's a piano. It's a guy playing a piano or maybe a woman playing the piano.

You reckon it's prepared?
Not the piano – in the Cageian sense – but in the performance I think they knew exactly what they were going to do before they did it. That's one of the differences, isn't it, between what I do and this. I would say it's a piece.

Not someone like Cecil Taylor, then?
I don't think it's Cecil [*laughs*] – I'm sure it's not Cecil! Why don't we establish a *modus operandi* for this, I'd like an opportunity to rework some of this, I mean our conversation. Do I get to see it before publication?

Well, I don't normally agree to that, but with you . . .
I feel fairly exposed. I never voluntarily listen to records. This reminds me of one of those flip definitions of the difference between improvisation and composition, which is – and this is where I'll need to rework, I might have forgotten it – 'With composition, you know what you do before you do it and with improvisation you don't know what you're doing until you've done it.' That's not quite right, that's why I asked for the facility of reworking, it's much better than that, when I first thought of using that it was much better. I always find the second time around – talking's like playing – the second time around, forget it – regurgitate it. I thought it was a fucking beautiful piece – what else is there?

He's using pedal-depressed resonance quite interestingly.
I like it, nice nice nice, wonderful. But . . . [*piece finishes*]

Michael Finnissy is the composer. I wish I'd brought the score to show you. It's extraordinary.
You should have brought the score instead of the thing. The score's the thing, the interesting bit.

Finnissy does improvise to get ideas, but then he writes down every note. Ian Pace who plays it spends hours studying each bar to get the irrational rhythms right.
I think the lad did very well, but it was pretty clear he wasn't going to change anything once it was off. That was maybe the main characteristic of the piece, like so many pieces.

It's the climax of a suite, the great explosion at the end.
Yes. But what you played me – you get what you've got, as it were. You start with it and if you like the taste of it you can carry on with it and if you don't you may as well stop. It's not going to get any different. Mind you, I suppose you can say that about pretty much most music, but it's specific to composed things. It reflects a definite intention and it's not open to negotiation.

But that's true as soon as anything is recorded. We can't affect an improvisation once we're listening to it back.
This is the problem for me about recordings. There's a lot of things about records I don't like. Virtually everything about recording I do like. I like doing it. I like the social side. I like studios – it makes an interesting contrast. The last two days, for example, I spent one day in concert and one day in the studio. The two situations provide a totally different ambience – if I can use that word – in which to improvise, even though it's with the same person. Completely different feeling, it's nice, the only problem is that it produces an end result, a record. Recording's fine if it wasn't for fucking records. Personally, the way I would like to work isn't possible because there's no appropriate technology.

You'd like to do broadcasts from the studio rather than make a record, in fact? I noticed when I brought some poets in to perform at the old Resonance FM they performed differently from in front of live audiences. They were really keyed up, but it wasn't a recording session.
It's not to do with that, that makes it interesting. The problem with records . . . I'm just speaking personally, I don't mean as a general problem. Nobody has problems with records, people love records! The whole of people's listening lives is built around records if I understand it right. But it's all endgame – it introduces the endgame to something that

is for me primarily not about endgames. It collects it and says that's the end of that. And there is no end as far as I'm concerned.

You might get the odd musical idea off a record, some rhythm . . .
I get more than the odd idea, I get my entire living from them. I'm being unreasonable about this wonderful thing, and let's face it, recording and records are wonderful pieces of technology. Imagine, we're listening to this piece of music. The ingenuity and the invention and the development that's gone into the material, into the technology so that we can listen to it – usually the music on the record is nothing compared to the actual vehicle. So I think recording and records are wonderful. But from my point of view, it introduces an element into what I do which I don't like. There's no technology to handle what I want to do.

It's a bit hard to get Michael Finnissy to come over to Hackney and play for you – it's a useful snapshot.
I don't listen to records voluntarily. I'd never have heard Michael Finnissy if it wasn't for you bringing this thing here. I might have heard it on the radio. Radio's better for me. Most of the recordings I hear in fact are on the radio. I don't buy records.

Imagine this is Radio Wire then . . .
This house is full of records, but they're all Incus records – [*plugging-his-label voice*] Incus, 14 Down Road, London, E5 8DS records. I can't remember the last time I bought a record.

I'm aware of all these facts, but that's not really helping me get you to talk about some music other than your own.
Ah, no.

You're like someone who keeps noticing the marks on a windowpane – when I'm trying to make you look through it.
I don't like that analogy.

What you're saying now you could say about every one of the tracks I'm going to play you – 'it's a record, I don't buy records' – but what I'm interested in is the differences between them. For example, how do you think this compares? I think it's a development of a tune that's pretty well known . . .

CONLON NANCARROW
'Study for Player Piano No. 42' from
Studies for Player Piano Vol. V (Wergo)

This gets more and more embarrassing. I don't know what the fucking tune is!

Don't you think it's like that Bach tune that goes [*sings*] 'dah-doo dah-dah-diddle-derr-derr-derr'?
Is it? I probably don't know the Bach tune.

It doesn't say it is in the sleeve note, it just reminds me of it.
It doesn't mean anything to me – except it's another fucking piano. What is this? A furniture demonstration?

So how do you think this is being produced?
This is nice. I think they're all nice. I thought the Michael Finnissy piece was absolutely wonderful. This also is absolutely wonderful. You're not going to get me to publicly criticise anybody, I'm not into that game. The whole culture of listening to records I don't understand. Where do you look? Do you stare at the wall when you listen to records? *How* do you listen to records? I know what you do as a critic – you start writing as soon as the bloody record's on, so you've got something to do, but what about us?

I've spent years playing records to people, talking about them . . .
So what do you do when you put the record on? I notice that you start talking as soon as the record's on. I'm listening to it and you're asking me questions [*untrue – Derek himself started talking over both records straightaway*]. Normally, what do record buyers do? Do they buy the record, take it home, put it on and for the next . . . I mean, they can last for 74 minutes! Do they sit there for 74 minutes, they don't do the dishes, just sit and look at something, or close their eyes . . .

Make cups of tea . . .
So you don't have to give it your complete, full, unadulterated attention?

Depends why you're listening.
That's one of the things that's wrong. If when you play the record, both as somebody involved in improvisation and as somebody who runs a record company, if you could only play a record *once*, imagine the intensity you'd have to bring into the listening. Like, if I play something I can only play it once. There might be a great similarity between each time I play, but I cannot repeat what I play. If you could only listen to it once, don't you think it might concentrate the eardrums?

That's what I do if I'm reviewing a record.
You're a professional listener.

I didn't used to do that. I used to bung things on and have them around for a long time. That's before I'd acquired lots of records.
The point of a record is that you can play it again. That's what the word means. It's a record, you've got the thing forever, you can play it a million times, what do you need to listen to it closely for? Stick it on again. It'll all eventually become mood music, right? Anyway, this is absolutely wonderful, and there's just one of them doing this, it's amazing isn't it.

Do you think it's improvised or composed?
I think there's some improvisation involved in it. Unless it's some taping, overdubbing – it sounds like some overdubbing to me, but as I say, if we could come to some agreement where I exposed my ignorance as little as possible I'd be very pleased about that. Anyway, I get the impression there's either two people or there's been some overdubbing.

It's player piano.
One of the reasons I'd like to do a revision of this is to ramble on about things – which you could always take out. When I was a kid my mother always had a piano. She'd often change them. At one time she bought this huge player piano, big iron frame, great sound. Coming with it were a bundle of rolls, I can remember for years behind one of the easy chairs in the front room there were these long boxes. I used to play these things and pedal them, but I got bored with it so I'd put holes in them, make things. A lot of things were programmatic – there'd be the Battle of Waterloo, Chinese classical music. All these things generally speaking

were incredibly active, but also martial in some ways. They were programmatic – realist music. I found that by just sticking little holes in the thing at random, it was amazing – it let a bit of air in. I did that with lots of them, my mother didn't care because she only played the piano anyway, nobody used these rolls except me. The rolls just came as a bonus, she just liked the sound of the piano because it had a big iron frame, it was a monster thing. Player pianos are intriguing things.

This is Conlon Nancarrow, recordings made possible by Henry Kaiser . . .
That's very nice that piece, when you consider how it's made. Listening to the opening, I wouldn't have thought it was a player piano, but subsequently it becomes fairly clear.

It's got a pretty tinny sound.
It's funny how they often have that. I wonder if it's because they don't use the whole set of strings or something. My mother's didn't used to sound the same when you actually played it. We've done two now haven't we . . .

Yes, I think we've got a few quotable things – do you know the format in *The Wire*?
Yes. The thing I'm mainly bothered about is the photograph. This guy came and photographed me, and he had this Cyclops thing, look down there and look up at me, it made me think of Robert Newton in *Treasure Island* [*shuts one eye*]: 'Aye, Jim Lad . . .'

NEW DIRECTION 1970
featuring the guitar of Masayuki Takayanagi
'Intermittent' from *Call In Question* (PSF)

[*Derek listens to more than thirty seconds of the track before speaking; finally* . . .] You see, with this there is no reason to stop listening to it. You know what I was saying about the first one, you kind of know what's going on and what's going to go on, here you don't – the story's unfolding, right? But of course it's improvised. I can listen to this and enjoy it. What else do you want me to say about it?

Things like what instruments you can hear, date, how it feels to you . . .
I've no idea about date, that doesn't mean anything to me.

What the background of the musicians sounds like to you perhaps, how they play.
I would guess they're American because they don't have any imperative to put in a bit of urgency just to prove that they're something or other. Europeans don't like playing as relaxed as this, it's like they've got to have their balls on show within the first few seconds of time, particularly in recent years I have to say. I like it very much of course, but I like it all. We could listen to this all afternoon. I don't understand why people don't find improvised music totally riveting to listen to. And I mean, good or bad, if it's *honest* improvised music and it's not programmed to prove some kind of point, because all kinds of shit goes on in improvised music as in any music. If there are guys playing together and reacting to the kind of stimuli which they're providing for each other in the way that you do when you play together – I don't understand why people have a problem listening to it. I've never understood that. I don't ever expect to know why, but I don't understand it. I suppose it doesn't supply them with what they're looking for in music. It doesn't make their arse shake and it doesn't make your eye wet – necessarily. It might do, but it's not about providing that kind of thing. I suppose it's the absence of those things normally looked for in music that makes it so unpopular. It seems to me eminently listenable. Eminently listenable music. I said to somebody recently that they should try this shit in elevators. He said, I'd be really interested to play a record of yours in an elevator and gradually introduce it in one of those elevators that goes from ground floor to the 88th floor – and you can't get out until the 88th floor – and I'd love to make a film of the people as they come out of the elevator! Which I took to be a veiled insult. I was saying, but imagine you've got to pass a bit of time, it'd be nice to play this in a railway station. It's just something to listen to instead of being reminded of something. Even at this point I don't know what's going to happen next with this music. There's obviously a kind of vein to it, a feel to it,

but the detail is not established by details that have gone before. It's truly developmental in that sense, these people are playing and they're not so bothered about what happened earlier on. I haven't the faintest idea who it is. I played recently with – with great pleasure, I have to say – with Susie Ibarra and the drumming here [Toyozumi Yoshisaburo] reminds me slightly of Susie.

I was thinking of playing you a David Ware track with her on it.
I've never heard David Ware. That kind of drumming is free playing out of early free jazz drumming it seems to me, lovely playing.

There's a new instrument that'll be coming in.
Will that be that sustain thing that was in earlier? The guitar? [*listens, then smiles at some of Takagi Mototeru's sax squeals*]

What's funny?
I was thinking to myself that you can always rely on saxophone players! [*laughs*]

Because he's showing us his balls?
Not necessarily that. There's a role for them.

They're the singer.
Sort of – at some point they have to step out front, don't they? Generally speaking and roughly – and you can overdo this I know, and it has been dreadfully overdone in the past – there is some generally adopted collective aesthetic or ethic in free improvisation, which saxophone players feel at liberty to discard whenever the urgency grabs them.

What did you think of Eugene Chadbourne's statement [*The Wire* 177] that he likes people 'stepping out and taking solos', that Free Improvisation sometimes downplays that?
Yes, well . . . Eugene . . . you can't rely on Eugene, can you? [*laughs*] I don't know, I think I'm attracted to that kind of music where when you're playing it – I don't know what people listen for – where you can hardly tell who's you and who's somebody else. It might have got rarer and it's probably got more unpopular. There is a tendency with most players as they get – let's say – 'more experienced', to feel that their qualities shouldn't be buried in all this jumble going on in

the backrground, and we all perhaps 'step out' more than we would have done at earlier stages. I have to say I like that incoherence – indecipherable rubbish that scrambles around – I love that shit. There have been very few saxophone players in my experience who've actually been able to accept that non-solo role. Let's face it, if you go out and buy a saxophone, you don't do it to be just one of the run-of-the-mill. I think nowadays – I'm hardly a young man – saxophonists think of themselves as soloists. Fifty years ago they would not necessarily think that.

They'd be playing in big-band reed sections.
Yes. No other instrument carries the baggage – I wish I hadn't got onto saxophones, I'm afraid – or at least such a *weighty* baggage as the saxophone. In jazz it's the solo instrument and that's it, you're stuck with it. People don't go out and buy saxophones in order to play brass band music.

A friend [Kitty Rees] who came to hear you play with Robyn Schulkowsky on Monday night, thought you were referring to heavy metal when you got loud on the guitar. I said, well Derek has played with this rock band called The Ruins, but I don't think he plays tongue-in-cheek stuff . . .
I've come to like certain electric treatments of the guitar, come to find things in it I didn't previously find. It's more resourceful than I might have thought – bit and pieces, harmonics, what's in it and what's not in it, what you can get out of it. It's not a stylistic adjustment. Some guy came here a couple of weeks ago and said, Do you think you play rock now because you didn't play it years ago?

It's a fair enough question.
But I don't play fucking rock. Then again, he was a free-music/jazz critic, so he didn't know anything about rock. Naturally he thought that if anybody played louder than the saxophone you're playing rock. Loud guitars play rock as far as he was concerned. [*track finishes*] So who was that then?

It was a band called New Direction 1970 with Masayuki Takayanagi on guitar, Takagi Mototeru on saxophone, Toyozumi Yoshisaburo on

drums and Motoharu Yoshizawa on bass. I'm not as relativist as you – I think really good improv records are rare, something to shout about. I didn't say all improv records are good – it's great to play, perhaps. I never heard this before. It's nice. Takagi, the saxophonist, I saw him recently. He became a very close follower of Steve Lacy's, he got a soprano saxophone, I don't think that was such a good idea. Korean guy.

It sounds like the free-jazz end of improv to me.
I think it's got a kind of relaxation about it that is to do with early free jazz, which somehow got lost, it's hard to find that now. That's what I liked about Susie Ibarra, she doesn't feel it's necessary to *keep something up*, more a participant, maybe an equal participant with the others. I don't know how she plays in Ware's quartet; in the duo I played with her she wasn't interested in accompaniment – you might accompany *her*! Working like that, the drums accept some kind of equal role, they don't have a preordained role, they come and play with the others in the same way that the others play. Whatever they contribute is not pre-scribed, that's the way I hear it. That seems to me what those early guys did. They were getting rid of the beat, weren't they?

Okay, this one's three minutes long and it's very quiet.
Is it playing now? [*it hasn't started yet; Derek is in an impish humour*] How about a cup of tea? It's tiring this.
[*While making the tea, Derek explains his demand for a new technology of musical distribution.*]
This is the ideal. Whatever you play goes out, whatever you play – so that the whole selection procedure which if you're doing what I do is fraught with question marks . . . – so you just put everything out. I play pretty much every day. Sometimes more, sometimes knock off, whatever. We'll not worry about the technological details, I've got enough to worry about – just say it goes out and it can be picked up by anybody who's sufficiently interested to want to pick it up, otherwise they can get on with something that's more appealing to them. But when they pick it up, it passes them, but once it's passed them, that's it – it doesn't come back. That is, their experience of it is the obverse of my experience of it. When they listen to it, they'd better get hold of it while it passes – it's

not recordable, it's not savable. But if you haven't heard it before you can hear it if you want to. At the moment I'm waiting for someone to show me how to do that.

An auto-destruct play mechanism?
No, it doesn't destruct, it's there forever for anyone who hasn't heard it. Your facility to hear it is on auto-destruct! The thing itself just goes on, if somebody else wants to hear it, they can hear it.

You'd need bio-engineering for that wouldn't you, a citizen-ident key that would match with the recording and mark the transaction as 'done' to make it unrepeatable?
This is old hat now isn't it.

OK, tell me what this is.

ANTON WEBERN
'Six Bagatelles for String Quartet' from
Werke für Streichquartett (Emerson String Quartet) (DG)

[*After three bars*] I think it's beautiful.

I should have put something on here that you'd really hate.
It's not possible. [*listens to another three bars*] I can't identify these fuckers. I once did a journey across Germany in a car with two classical musicians. We were going across Germany so it's pretty easy to pick up German music on the car radio. They were playing this stuff all the way through. As soon as any piece came up, they were right at it: 'What is it?' They didn't listen to it any more than I am to this – they had to identify it, they were not satisfied if they couldn't identify it, then they would have to wait for the announcement to find out what it was. If they didn't announce it afterwards, it drove them mad. That identification thing is worse in the classical listening world than it is in the jazz world – there also it's essential, identification is essential. Is that the end of it?

Pretty much, there's a bit more.
[*as it starts again*] Crafty.

It's Webern.
Yeah, it's beautiful. I've heard this many times. I didn't remember it at all.

It's been absorbed.
What, Webern?

It's everywhere now.
Yeah, yeah. Yes I suppose he must be one of the basic pillars of modern music, of course this is the cliché, we all know this, this is what the experts tell us. I told you I got all his works out of the library when I was living in Fulham donkey's years ago in the sixties. I got 'em out of the library, Robert Craft's recordings which I think were done in '59 or something. They were thought badly of apparently, but I didn't know that. They all fitted onto two reels of tape – less than two hours. I copied them. I used to play them over and over, listening to them. I was living in a bunch of bedsitters and the woman next to me –

This is the Rolling Stones fan, she couldn't stand it . . .
She couldn't stand it. She was a dressmaker and made clothes for groups, a complete one hundred per cent rock fan. She played stuff pretty loud, but she couldn't bear Webern. She'd come banging on the door – take it off! I thought it was great. Intolerable, she found it intolerable.

I did think of playing you some of Adorno's music. You know he wrote compositions? He studied with Alban Berg.
No, I didn't know. I spoke with someone recently. He said that the problem Adorno had with jazz was that he only ever heard Germans play it. [*laughs*] I wondered about that. Theodor Adorno Platz [*the name of a square in Frankfurt Derek was delighted to find full of winos*] – you never went there?

Esther did – took photographs – the winos are still there, appear to be pissing against the wall in her photograph actually. **So you knew that was composed?**
The Webern?

You didn't think it was improvised by Maarten Altena and Maurice Horsthuis?
Oh no. There's something about it. I suppose it's just the matter of quality. It really stands out. I was thinking the same about Albert Ayler recently. It's a stupid thing to think and even more stupid to allow yourself to say it, but nobody plays like that any more. I put the 'any more' in, but it's not necessary, just nobody plays like that. It's just quality or ability and the same with Webern. There are millions of people doing it now, but they had a sense of risk in the music.

Ayler did some pretty terrible things, but that one on ESP, did you ever hear that? It's called *Spiritual Unity* . . .
I might have, yeah, I think so.

With a screenprinted naked man cradling a saxophone on the cover – that's astonishing.
I probably only ever heard one or maybe two records of Albert Ayler. I'm aware of Albert Ayler by the people who play like him. At least, I assume they do, I'm being too loose – but I just thought once when I heard a record by Albert, how much it stood out. It's something about the risks taken, like with Webern's music, nobody would quite do that now. It takes it further than anybody else would, even if they're working in that vein.

Here's another track.

AMM
'Aria' from *Before driving to the chapel we took coffee with Rick and Jennifer Reed* (Matchless)

Do you recognise this?
No. I don't recognise any of 'em. All sound the bloody same to me.

How does this music make you feel?
Nervous. I wonder what to say. I don't normally talk when I listen to music. [*the track sounds like a whistling kettle*] One of the advantages I've found of increasing age – it might be the only one I've found, there aren't many around – is that some of the really high stuff, I don't hear it any more. It disappears! It's like volume. They ask me why I play so loud now. I say because I'm fucking deaf! [*coughs*] Who is this?

It's AMM. The review I did of this got me into trouble with Evan [Parker]. It's from 1996, recorded in the States.
I'm not familiar with AMM. I know Keith's playing. I think he's a remarkable artist. I think he's the kind of person we should all be in a way, but AMM . . . I don't know whether this was the last time I heard them, but the play that I have in memory of them, if I were to think of what AMM are, is going back a bit because [Cornelius] Cardew was playing with them. At that particular performance, Cardew seemed to provide . . . he was primarily there as a cello player, but he seemed to provide a number of other things that were performance-related, unless he accidentally did it – he fell over, for a start. Anyway, there was a disruptive element about what he did that seemed to me quite welcome, given the general placidity of the rest of what was going on. He provided something that I thought stood out and in a sense complemented the rest of what was going on. That was this particular performance, but I can't remember AMM after that. I might have heard them, I just can't remember it.

Track six, this is five minutes long.
Six? Hmmm . . .

SOFT MACHINE
'Virtually Part One' from *4* (CBS)

This reminds me – you know, I've spent over fifty years trying to get my guitar in tune. A large proportion of my playing has actually been tuning the guitar. I notice with other people it's quite a difficulty. What is it?

You've got no association?
Well, I think it's wonderful. [*laughs*] But who the fuck it is, I've no idea, it doesn't mean anything to me at all.

[Fishes cover out] There's no guitar on it.
Oh. It sounded like a slightly-out-of-tune guitar to me.

It's bass, drum, organ, sax . . .
There you go you see. I should've stayed out of this game. I can't even recognise the absence of a guitar.

This is Soft Machine from 1970, Tony Herrington wanted me to play you some progressive rock because of the Chris Blackford versus Evan Parker debate about Improv and Prog Rock . . .
Well I think it's lovely, Mr Herrington. I only heard them once, matter of fact.

You met them?
I don't think I knew them, except I met whatnot – the drummer [*snaps fingers*] . . .

Robert Wyatt?
. . . Robert – met him many times. But Robert was around in all kinds of ways.

He came to gigs?
Oh, he did for years, used to come to the Unity Theatre in the seventies . . .

Did he play?
No, I'm not aware of that. I've played in concerts, something Victor Schonfield put together, where Robert played piano and sang. And I think Evan and I played a duo.

Would that be his politics – that he'd be interested in the ethic of Free Improvisation?
No idea. I don't know what his interest is, or even if he's interested, though I keep bumping into him. One of the connections that might explain it is Paul Haines, we've both worked with Paul Haines in some way or other. I think I once heard this group at Ronnie's or something

like that when I was playing there with somebody. Anyway, I would never have recognised them.

The chords are so English pastoral, so Canterbury Rock . . .
I'm not any more familiar with Canterbury Rock than I am with Blackpool rock – ho ho! [*laughs*]

Strapline for the article!
Oh fuck, sorry about all this. This goes on for a heck of a long time. How long does this one last?

It's only five minutes.
[*Reading sleeve notes as if the names are totally new to him*] . . . Hugh Hopper, Mike Ratledge, Robert Wyatt on drums, and Elton Dean.

That's a trombone isn't it?
He's playing alto saxophone and saxetto [*he means saxello*] . . .

What's that? a sax with a trumpet mouthpiece or something?
Oh, Roy Babbington double bass, I know him . . . wait a minute – Marc Charig cornet, lots of them, lots of them, Nick Evans trombone – how did I miss all these people? – Jimmy Hastings alto flute and bass clarinet, Alan Skidmore tenor saxophone . . . blimey, it's a go out there, by fuck!

Funny you should say Paul Haines – all these extra horns make it sound like Carla Bley's *Escalator over the Hill* – which set Paul Haines's lyrics . . . It fades here . . .
It fades out.

I faded it out at the start of the next track – it's a continuous suite on the record.
Well it sounded like a masterpiece to me, not that I'd recognise a masterpiece if I drowned in one.

Are you sure? The next one *is* a masterpiece.
Is a masterpiece? Good. It's about time we had one, I think. OK I didn't say that.

JOHNNY 'GUITAR' WATSON
'Three Hours Past Midnight'
from *Three Hours past Midnight* (Flair/Virgin America)

[*After three guitar notes*] That's a masterpiece straightaway. Now *that's* a guitar! I can say with absolute confidence that this is a *guitar* – I'd go further, it's an electric guitar. Let's see, it's not Eugene! This is rather like the Webern [*laughs*] (these are the kind of things that are so beautiful to say aren't they, like, 'You can see the things this has in common with Elgar's *Pomp and Circumstance Number* . . .'). By fuck, where would we be without this shit?

What I like is he's singing and playing guitar, but the guitar notes are so unruly, almost like it's not him . . .
It's fantastic actually. Buddy Guy does a little bit of this sometimes. I can imagine him coming at the guitar, looks at it and then goes – 'right, take that!' – it's beautiful I think. Who is it?

Johnny 'Guitar' Watson.
Hmm. I've only read about this, but I can't imagine anyone updating this stuff, I mean a young blues player. I wonder what a young blues player can do – he can do the same thing or forget about it. I'm thinking of that as a good thing. I used to think that about jazz, if you're born in the right place at the right time and maybe the right race, you've got a chance – otherwise, forget it. I know it's not a fashionable point of view now. [*listens to the solo break*]

The guitar sound is very brittle.
That kind of sound has absolutely no ambiguity about what's being played.

He's not making it sing?
That's right. Also, it's so clear what he's doing – things like the chords or when he plays two or three notes.

The pauses with time too, the jokes where he holds back the phrase . . .
Should you be idiot enough to want to write it down, there would be no

problem writing it down, in a sense (yet you would still not have anywhere near the essence of it, of course, I'm not talking about that), but the actual physical part of the sound is so clear. He's got no doubt about whether he's playing what he should be playing.

He was a pianist originally.
Was he?

Turned to guitar because he wanted to show off at the front.
Didn't we all – well that's behind the saxophone player of course.

He invented the hundred-foot lead so he could jump into the audience still playing.
Did he? Oh beautiful. I saw old whatnot do that. You know when I did those programmes I wanted to use the blues guitar player Albert Collins, he's dead now – I went to see him at the Camden Palace in the eighties, fronting a six-piece, very rocklike this band. John Zorn used him on something once. Albert Collins did that, spun himself out into the audience with this long wire. He had a saxophone player who was the lewdest player I've ever seen, he was magnificent. If he'd have got his cock out, it would have been a gesture of modesty. What he was doing with the saxophone was extraordinary. The whole thing was a terrific performance I thought. We didn't use him because Jeremy [Marre] thought he was incoherent, I thought he was saying exactly what he wanted to say, it's just we didn't understand what it was. Marre wanted more of the 'I grew up in Mississippi and my mama sent me out on the road', the usual. I asked Collins where he lived and he said Las Vegas. I said, Why Las Vegas? And he said, B. B. King lives in Las Vegas. That was all the explanation needed! He was staying in a hotel in Holland Park, had these English girls with him, great guy.

You had Buddy Guy in those programmes didn't you?
Yes, Buddy was great, lovely.

CAPTAIN BEEFHEART
'One Red Rose That I Mean' from
Lick My Decals Off, Baby (Bizarre/Straight)

See what I mean about tuning? It's a problem with the guitar. It's a written piece isn't it? Who is it?

It's Bill Harkleroad – or Zoot Horn Rollo – playing a piece written for him by Captain Beefheart.
One of the problems I have listening to music – or not so much listening to music as discussing it – is the 1955/1956 break – where to you chaps there is no music before 1955 except classical music. So I think, wonder if he's heard so-and-so? There was a kind of jazz player, a guy called George Van Eps, played seven-string guitar. He made one or two jazz records, commercial ones – guitar, bass and vibes type shit – but he had that type of solo playing off to such a degree it was . . .

There's a flamenco thing in that?
Well, I suppose you could hunt all sorts of things out of it . . . but this self-accompaniment thing, with chords and bass, a bit of melody here and there, this guy was terrific at it. It's one of those things you get with musicians – musos as you call them – where you think, [*awed whisper*] what the fuck's going on? Like just in itself, the idea that there might be any aesthetic quality either there or sacrificed is totally beside the point, the fact that the guy can do this is like riding four horses at once.

Alan Tomlinson is like that when he's got all his hoses out and he's playing eighteen notes at once on his taken-apart trombone . . . or Fred Frith when he fills the room with his pentatonic psychedelic waves of sound.
It's a long tradition. Fred's one of my favourite guitar players, but in this case I'm not sure what we're talking about is the same thing. What I'm talking about is some kind of observable skill that's completely out of any human being's reach. You get examples of this – or attempts at it – in solo playing in improvised music, but it goes back to music halls. I shouldn't think anyone who's likely to read this would know what a

431

music hall is. When I was a kid I used to go to music hall regularly, there'd be eight or nine acts and one of them would be a novelty instrumentalist. Often they were female, a little bit overweight and virtually undressed, what little they were wearing would be star-spangled. There were two kinds of instruments. You either squeezed it – a concertina or an accordion – or you blew it – so it could be a trumpet or a saxophone, very often a saxophone actually. They'd be doing this at the same time as they'd be careering round this stage at a terrific lick on roller skates, but that was just the background to a musical performance that'd require tremendous physical dexterity. A ridiculously active piece of music, like something for pianola, a mountain of work going into this thing and meanwhile she's shooting around, this pink flesh is flashing backwards and forwards. And she'd be playing an accordion or a saxophone with circular breathing, all kinds of lines, and shooting backwards and forwards on roller skates, absolutely essential. You had to keep moving, look kind of good and be dressed in a certain way and play this multi-multi-multi . . .

Would you play with Evan again if he was on roller skates?
[*waves question aside*] At some point you think, well this is terrific, but what is the point of all this? Because I was kind of interested in music at that age. It was only when the thing finished, and from all quarters of the house you'd get this tremendous eruption of applause, that you understood what the point was – it was about audiences. They loved this high display of skill. That seems to be a thing that's always gone in music. Paganini used to imitate farmyard animals.

Heavy metal is where it happens with the guitar now.
In rock, but there's all kinds of things that happen with the guitar outside all that stuff as a matter of fact. Some of the flamenco players are astonishing technical players. The dancers are the thing in flamenco too. That idea of astonishing appearance combined with some unbelievable physical act reminds me of music hall . . .

Is there less bullshit with that kind of show?
I think it's all bullshit! Show business, it's pure bullshit. It's meaningless, it's about applause. Can you imagine someone doing that on their own

with nobody there? [*laughs*] They'd be locked away, confined immediately!

CHARLIE CHRISTIAN
'Breakfast Feud' from *Charlie Christian with the Benny Goodman Sextet* (CBS)

Nice, isn't it? You know one of the old things that used to happen with discussing jazz was to guess whether it was black or white. I'd guess this is . . . no, I'm going to change it, it's black . . .

It's a mixture.
That's one of the beautiful things about it, it was so difficult to tell in this period. What is it, 1930s? This is really sophisticated music – don't you think? – particularly the piece they're playing at the beginning. But, like, cosy at the same time, but maybe that's just distance.

Characteristic playing from the pianist here.
Here I'm tempted to have a go at the names. Teddy Wilson?

Count Basie.
[*hearing guitar break*] It's Charlie Christian, isn't it? That puts it as early forties.

1941.
I've got all these recordings. Tony Mostrum – who's a cartoonist in California and has a radio station and likes free music – sent me them on tape. [*looking at record cover*] These titles . . . one of the problems is nostalgia, things like 'Gone with *What* Wind?' and then 'Gone with the Draft', it's a wartime thing. That was very much the style of the forties, like [*reading sleeve*] 'Wholly Cats', these horrible puns. 'Gone with the Wind' was a tune and a novel as well as the film. 'Gone with the Draft' is about being called up into the army; 'Airmail Special' . . . 'Solo Flight', they're about the air force. This was recorded 13 January 1941, recorded before America came into the war, Pearl Harbor was December that year. 'Seven Come Eleven' . . . they were so hip these titles, if you were a kid growing up and you were taken with this music, a tune title like

'Seven Come Eleven' was fantastic, you didn't know what the fuck it meant.

It's like that now with those names for hip-hop bands which sound like codes for military hardware.
Yes, same thing.

PACO PEÑA
'Palmas y Guitarra' from *Flamenco Passion* (Decca)

Did you ever see that film, by Mike Figgis, who used to be a trumpeter, *Leaving Las Vegas*? He made a film about flamenco, good film, got a copy of it. In fact I use it as part of my percussion bank [*sets of tapes Derek uses for practising at home*]. He reversed the guitar and the feet, so the loudest thing in the music, especially when there's a vocal, is the dancing. The dancing is *much* louder! Percussion wise, it's great sounds, the sound of these feet.

What I like about this CD is that as it proceeds it gets wilder and wilder and you hear more and more clapping and stamping.
They do that, make it sound as if something's happening.

Does your very brittle sound on guitar derive from flamenco playing, that hard attack?
I like flamenco. Early this year I was in Barcelona and I know this flamenco aficionado – I said, what's the chance of going to one of these backstreet flamenco things? Does it happen? Is it pure romanticism? Not the festival or concert-hall stuff. I said I understood that there are one or two cafés here where you can get it. He says, yes it happens, but I can't take you. They just don't allow strangers in.

I joined a circle like that in Madrid once, in the basement of a café at three in the morning. We all sat in a circle and clapped, there was a guitar being played but no one paid it much attention, it was the singing. People took turns – it was really emotional singing, from the throat, Arab-style. I was really shattered by the experience.
The singing's terrific, that's supposed to be the ultimate thing in

flamenco, not the dancing or guitar playing. That was nice. Who was it?

Paco Peña, the guitarist you interviewed for your TV series. He's playing at the Kentish Town Forum next week – I noticed a poster on the way up your street just now.
I've got a couple of recordings of him with that singer who died, another genius figure . . . oh I'm sorry I thought it was Paco de Lucia because it was so conventional, but he used to be conventional, Paco de Lucia, many years ago. This is of no interest to anybody here is it, this shit? What's next?

It's fun to irritate the *Wire* readership with unhip things.
Did you say you could pull the plug after eight? I might be listened out.

No you're not.

FRANK ZAPPA
'While You Were Out' from *Shut Up 'n Play Yer Guitar* (Rykodisc)

Is this Sonny Sharrock?

No.
Why don't I keep my mouth shut about who it is? I don't know who it is. Who is it?

Zappa.
Oh, Zappa.

Did you think it was improvised?
Yes. As much to do with the sound as anything. At times he got a sound like that.

I've got a really nice tape of Sharrock in New York in August 1985 and he sounds quite Zappaesque there – kind of like Santana but with more complex harmonies . . . The drums are very fluid. I played a tape of you and John Stevens to Frank, so I thought I should reciprocate.
Well I'm not the kind of prick Frank was, so I'm not going to take the

opportunity to throw a few gratuitous insults about. *[referring to Zappa's response to being played Derek in duet with John Stevens: 'it sounds to me like the music I wrote for Lumpy Gravy . . . improvised by me with a guitar in one hand and playing drums with the other', see* my Frank Zappa: the Negative Dialectics of Poodle Play, p. 543] Yes, it's OK.

He only said he thought he could play like you.
Who knows, perhaps he could do it on roller skates. These fellows are very resourceful. That interview that you were kind enough to lend me to read [*Downbeat* 18 May 1978] which was such a boring fucking interview, he mentioned he likes to play in ice-hockey rinks, maybe he'd like the whole band skating around, imagine that, a rock band on roller skates – has anyone done that?

Rick Wakeman did *King Arthur on Ice* . . .
That's not quite the same thing. People have done all kinds of things on ice. *[listens a while, notices some suspect intonation]* As I say, I sometimes wonder if it's completely impossible to get the guitar in tune, although Jim Hall does a very good job of it.

It's very odd watching guitar players improvising – watching you recently I realised that they clamp their hand on some new chord with the left hand and then all they have to do is scrape across those strings with the plectrum in the right.
I know, it's a piece of piss. Thank fuck I came across it or I'd have been reading gas meters all my life, a demanding job like that. That's right – when I teach guitar I say, take a good firm grip with the left hand, don't drop it, a little bit of – what do they call it? – *pumping iron* with the right hand.

I think you might like the next one – shall we go forward to it?
I like 'em all! I don't know how you interpret it.

It's damn irritating actually.
I'm not here to slag off people who might give me a gig or something like that.

The form of this was set up by *Downbeat* and that was when the community of New York jazz musicians was so tight that they *knew* immediately when they heard the record who everybody was, so when they made comments they knew exactly who they were praising or dissing – now it's so broad a field you can't tell.
Yeah. That's true. I can't tell one from the other.

CLIFFORD BROWN AND MAX ROACH
'Gertrude's Bounce' from *At Basin Street* (EmArcy)

Is this the one I'll like? [*laughs*] Is this a period piece, early-fifties white jazz?

It's not white. In fact it was considered to be hard bop of a pretty uncompromising nature.
West Coast stuff isn't it?

No. You told me you liked this band. I was surprised because I think you like very strict time in music and this band always struck me as rather easy and loose.
Who is it then?

It's the Clifford Brown/Max Roach Quintet with Sonny Rollins on sax.
Well I fucked up there. I always liked this group. I have to say – I can wriggle out of this one – I always liked it for what it stood for. I wouldn't describe it as hard bop anyway – but I'm not sure that this kind of hair-splitting argument at this stage about fifties jazz is going to be either profitable or entertaining, but the move at this time was to hard bop which I thought was – as so often – edging downmarket in a sense, I mean aesthetically, I don't mean marketwise, but they carried on. It doesn't sound like bop for instance.

It hasn't got that bebop dada.
It's all sorted out, isn't it? This'll be '55 or '56.

Yes.
Sorted out, yes, beautiful.

This is more mature – original bebop is kind of crazy.
Looking over the precipice all the time, they don't know quite what's happening, or at least that's the impression you get.

Oh all right, since you're complaining, let's stop.
I think the coherence is probably slipping as well.

MARTIN KLAPPER – ROGER TURNER
'Twombly' from *Recent Croaks* (Acta)

Is it George Lewis on trombone?
No.
Our next Incus record is with him, a great record, I don't know if you'll like it.

This is Roger Turner and Martin Klapper.
[*surprised*] Is it? Resourceful, these fellows, aren't they?

Has that speed I like.
Yes, it's nice, Roger's very good at getting that liveliness into something that's going on.

That's over then.
Good.

Except we've got Tony Herrington's CD to play to you, but we'll need to find a CD player.
Well it's not terribly reliable. Let's go in the office. It'll be a bit chilly.

ALEC EMPIRE
'Stahl und Blausäure' from *The Geist Of Alec Empire* (Geist)

It's not a track off the *Wire* compilation is it?
No.
[*Derek starts dancing like an epileptic skeleton, a* danse macabre *around*

*the fetish character of the music we're hearing; the interviewer doesn't
know whether to join in or to call the men in white coats . . .]*
It's like the first piece, isn't it? Shortly after it's started you know what
the rest of it is going to be. There's a crowd gathering outside, gyrating
up and down the street. Who is this?

Alec Empire.
Oh yes. I nearly played with him once. I got a gig with a DJ in Berlin or
Vienna or somehow where this kind of stuff is quite big. I was supposed
to take a DJ, and I said to somebody, Listen can you suggest a DJ? I
spoke to Trevor [Manwaring at Harmonia Mundi] because I wanted a
DJ in Europe because the only ones I'd worked with live at that point
were in the States. As it actually happened they brought one from the
States because I'd worked with him before. Trevor gave me four pieces
and I thought the Alec Empire piece was quite nice. I said to the people
who were organising, Try to get hold of Alec Empire. He's well known.
This fucking agent rang up, so I said I've got to tell you I don't have
good relationships with *any* agents. I said, Don't deal with me, deal with
the people running this thing. He said, Alex is really busy. I said that's
all right, Tell the guy in Germany, but he had to go on about this. It
turned out that you couldn't book Alec Empire for like a *year and a half*
– it's like an opera singer! This was about two years ago – you'd be able
to get him about now. At that time I had no idea who he was, hadn't
the faintest idea, but these guys – particularly in Germany – they work
all the time. Soulslinger, this guy I did this thing with who I'd worked
with in New York, he came over and did this gig. We were in Berlin. I
said, Have you been in Berlin before? He said, Yeah, I come here all the
time. Terrific, huge club scene. It was all right, I could get a certain
amount out of it. It's not an endless thing, but last time I worked with
these pranksters I did enjoy it.

I found that a bit predictable compared to some drum'n'bass I've heard.
There's no drums in it are there?

You're saying it's safe whiteboy music that doesn't swing?
No. It's like a lot of music, it's kind of established – songs are like that.
Actually songs, one of the basic musical forms, do allow for one change

– they have a bit in the middle that goes somewhere else. But this kind of thing – and this dominates a lot of composition it seems to me – is about establishing something you're going to stick with.

I like dance music, but the dance music I like is tricky to dance to. I don't know exactly where I'm going to be putting my foot. That's swing to me.

This piece of Alec Empire that I heard before I thought was much more interesting than that, the reason I suggested working with him. I think the stuff I liked was earlier, crude drum'n'bass – maybe when it used to be jungle. Now the technological side has maybe swamped that. They pile so much stuff on it it's kind of become like music or something.

It's perceived as being very radical, I think because it's got a gritty sound to it, but actually the beat's pretty conventional in my opinion.
I like Casey Rice. He contributed to this thing I did for Bingo [*Playbacks*].

I haven't heard it.
That's because it's not out until January – we've had so many requests for it, inundated. It was a very enjoyable record to make. It's not a drum'n'bass record, I'd say merely half the tracks were drum'n'bass. One or two of them were really very nice, or three or four, but this guy Casey Rice, Chicago electronics guy or something, a very nice track. Fast as fuck and really shifting. Funnily enough, the old jazzers reckoned that the one thing you can't do with machines is make 'em swing, but these guys can make it swing and he does. A lot of it is just the impetus of it – things happening you couldn't have physically done, or things people wouldn't have attempted. It just skates them on in such a terrific rush, it's nice to play with, certainly. Casey Rice, he's interesting. I think some of these guys are doing something, it's very inventive – but that track didn't mean anything to me. Just the rhythm, the fact that it is a demanding or forceful rhythm doesn't mean anything to me. There is plenty of it like that, I believe. The money's good, ridiculous.

PHONECALL ADDENDA
11–xi–1998

(*replacement for the 'flip definition' of the difference between improvisation and composition on page 412*) Improvisation is not knowing what it is until you do it, composition is not doing it until you know what it is.

(*Derek's philosophical objection to the whole exercise:*) The reason I'm unqualified for this game is that I have very little interest in the end product. My preoccupation is with the nuts and bolts, how they fit together, what it is that makes this stuff work and how sometimes it doesn't work. In so far as I listen with interest to a record, it's usually to figure out how it was arrived at. The musical end product is where interest starts to flag. It's a bit like jigsaw puzzles. Emptied out of the box, there's a heap of pieces, all shapes, sizes and colours, in themselves attractive and could add up to anything – intriguing. Figuring out how to put them together can be interesting, but what you finish up with as often as not is a picture of unsurpassed banality. Music's like that.

BOOKS CITED

Theodor Adorno, *Aesthetic Theory*, 1969; translated C. Lenhardt, London: Routledge and Kegan Paul, 1984.

——, *Beethoven: The Philosophy of Music*, 1940; translated Edmund Jephcott, Cambridge: Polity, 1998.

——, *Philosophy of Modern Music*, 1948; translated Anne G. Mitchell and Wesley V. Blomster, London: Sheed & Ward, 1973.

Derek Bailey, *Improvisation: Its Nature and Practice in Music*, New York: Da Capo Press, 1993.

Stephanie Barron, ed., *Degenerate Art: The Fate of the Avant-Garde in Germany*, catalogue, Los Angeles County Museum, 1991.

Samuel Beckett, *Malone Dies*, 1951; translated by Samuel Beckett, London: John Calder, 1956.

Tony Cliff, *Lenin Volume 1: Building the Party*, London: Pluto Press, 1975.

Richard Cook and Brian Morton, *The Penguin Guide to Jazz on CD, LP and Cassette*, London: Penguin, 1992.

John Corbett, *Extended Play: Sounding Off from John Cage to Dr Funkenstein*, Durham, NC: Duke University Press, 1994.

Guy Debord, *Mémoires*, 1958; Paris: Jean-Jacques Pauvert aux Belles Lettres, 1993.

William Gibson and Bruce Sterling, *The Difference Engine*, London: Victor Gollancz, 1990.

Christopher Gray, ed., *The Incomplete Work of the Situationist International*, Croydon: Free Fall, 1974.

G. W. F. Hegel, *Science of Logic*, 1812; translated A. V. Miller, London: George Allen & Unwin, 1969.

K. W. Jeter, *Morlock Night*, 1979; London: Grafton, 1989.

Mike Kidron, *Western Capitalism since the War*, London: Weidenfeld and Nicolson, 1968.

David King, *The Commissar Vanishes: The Falsification of Photographs and Art in Stalin's Russia*, London: Canongate, 1997.

Frank Kofsky, *Black Nationalism and the Revolution in Music*, New York: Pathfinder Press, 1970; reissued as *John Coltrane and the Jazz Revolution of the 1960s*, New York: Pathfinder, 1998.

V. I. Lenin, *Collected Works*, Vol. 38, translated Clemens Dutt, London: Lawrence & Wishart, 1961.

Graham Lock, *Forces In Motion: Anthony Braxton and the Meta-Reality of Creative Music (Interviews and Tour Notes, England 1985)*, London: Quartet, 1988.

Thomas Mann, *Dr Faustus*, 1947; translated H. T. Lowe-Porter, London: Penguin, 1968.

Karl Marx, *Capital*, 1867; translated Samuel Moore and Edward Aveling, New York: Modern Library, 1906.

——, *Grundrisse*, 1858; first published in German, 1953; translated Martin Nicolaus, London: Penguin, 1973.

——, and Friedrich Engels, *Communist Manifesto*, 1848; Bristol: Western Printing Services (TU), 1939.

Mark Mattern, *Acting In Concert: Music, Community and Political Action*, New Brunswick: Rutgers University Press, 1998.

George Novack, *Origins of Materialism: The Evolution of a Scientific View of the World*, New York: Pathfinder, 1965.

Michael Nyman, *Experimental Music: Cage and Beyond*, London: Studio Vista, 1974.

J. H. Prynne, 'Not-You' (1993), in *Collected Poems*, Newcastle upon Tyne: Bloodaxe, 1999, pp. 381–408.

Ronald M. Radano, *New Musical Figurations: Anthony Braxton's Cultural Critique*, Chicago: University of Chicago Press, 1993.

Peter Riley, *Company Week*, London: Compatible Recording & Publishing, 1994.

Curt Sachs, *The Wellsprings of Music*, London: 1944.

Michael Thompson, *Rubbish Theory*, Oxford: Oxford University Press, 1979.

Valentin Voloshinov, *Marxism and the Philosophy of Language*, 1929; translated Ladislav Matejka and I. R. Titunik, Cambridge, MA: Harvard University Press, 1986.

Kevin Whitehead, *New Dutch Swing*, New York: Billboard Books, 1998.

——, *The Instant Composers Pool: 30 Years*, Amsterdam: Stichting Haast, 1997.

Carl Woideck, *Charlie Parker: His Music and Life*, Ann Arbor: University of Michigan Press, 1996.

INDEX

'The most renowned member of the British free-form jazz movement.' *Independent*

'A towering giant of the guitar. Singular, unique.' David Sylvian

'One of the most original and idiosyncratic musicians I have ever known.' Gavin Bryars

This outstanding biography of the cult guitar player will likely cause you to abandon everything you thought you knew about jazz improvisation, post-punk and the avant-garde. Derek Bailey was at the top of his profession as a dance band and record-session guitarist when, in the early 1960s, he began playing an uncompromisingly abstract form of music. Today his anti-idiom of 'Free Improvisation' has become the lingua franca of the 'avant' scene, with Pat Metheny, John Zorn, David Sylvian and Sonic Youth's Thurston Moore among his admirers.

'I am an enthusiast for the Watson method and I'm prepared to follow him, even to places where I wouldn't under other circumstances go.' Iain Sinclair

'The ideal biographer of Derek Bailey.' John Fordham, *Guardian*

BIOGRAPHY/MUSIC

www.versobooks.com
$26.95/£16.99/$31CAN

ISBN 978-1-78168-105-3

52695

9 781781 681053

Cover design: Dan Mogford